975

Sociology

The Study of Human Relationships

SECOND EDITION

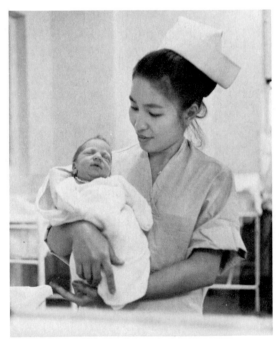

Sociology

The Study of Human Relationships

SECOND EDITION

W. LaVerne Thomas / Robert J. Anderson

HARCOURT BRACE JOVANOVICH

New York Chicago San Francisco Atlanta Dallas **and** *London*

THE AUTHORS

W. LaVerne Thomas has been teaching courses in the behavioral sciences at Wheat Ridge High School, Wheat Ridge, Colorado, since 1960. These include courses in sociology, psychology, and contemporary social problems.

Mr. Thomas received his B.A. in education at Nebraska Wesleyan University and earned his M.A. in sociology at the University of Denver. He has taken advanced courses in the behavioral sciences at Reed College and the University of Northern Colorado. He is active in several professional organizations, including the American Sociological Association and the National Education Association.

Mr. Thomas has written instructional materials for both high school and college students. He prepared the laboratory projects, bibliographies, and annotated teacher's edition of *Living in Social Groups* (1967 edition), a high school sociology textbook. He is also co-author of *Studying Human Society*, a workbook of adapted readings and research projects to accompany the college sociology textbook *Human Society*.

Robert J. Anderson is currently Assistant Professor of Sociology and department chairman at Trenton State College, Trenton, New Jersey. He is also the principal adviser for all sociology teaching majors at Trenton State College and supervisor of student teachers. He has had experience in teaching sociology at both the high school and college levels.

After receiving his B.A. in sociology at Rutgers University, Mr. Anderson earned an Ed.M. at Rutgers in the Sociology of Education. He has a M.A. in sociology from the New School for Social Research, where he has also completed course credits for a Ph.D. degree. He is a member of both the American Sociological Association and the Eastern Sociological Association.

Mr. Anderson has taught courses in contemporary social problems, American minority groups, and sociological theory as well as introductory sociology. Recently he has been involved in curriculum development. He is the author of the Teacher's Manual for Berelson and Steiner's *Human Behavior* (Shorter Edition).

Printed in the United States of America.

ISBN 0-15-371115-9

Contents

v

Tables, Charts, and Graphs

THE STUDY OF SOCIOLOGY

Sociology explores the ways people interact with one another. Sociologists study relationships within groups, such as your class. They examine relationships in social institutions, such as your family. And they study the organization of societies, such as your own. Sociologists also deal with vital issues and social problems. They use scientific procedures to try to improve our understanding of human relationships and the problems of society.

1 Sociology and Sociologists

▶ How can sociologists study human relationships scientifically?

▶ What methods do they use?

▶ How accurate are their results?

SECTION 1:
What Is Sociology?

The study of sociology provides a way of understanding human behavior. There are other ways. Poets use their imagination and creative ability to describe human behavior. Physiologists study people's organic processes and activities. Historians record and interpret the past expressions of human behavior. Sociologists also have their own approach to an understanding of human behavior. Sociologists use the scientific method to study people's relationships with others. For sociology is a science. To be specific, SOCIOLOGY *is the science that deals with the investigation and analysis of human relationships, and seeks explanations of their causes and consequences.* It makes use of the scientific method to study the ways in which people relate to one another.

Sociology Is a Science

Some people associate science with laboratories, precise equipment, and such fields as chemistry and physics. They are thinking only of the natural sciences. The natural sciences deal with explanations of the objects, events, and behaviors of the physical, chemical, and biological environment. These explanations, as in all sciences, are testable. But there is another major division of science—the social sciences. The social sciences deal with people and their social relationships.

Three of the social sciences—anthropology, sociology, and psychology—have become known as the behavioral sciences, because their primary concern is with human behavior. These three disciplines overlap each other in certain areas. In general, however, the anthropologist studies the ways of life among simple technological communities throughout the world. The sociologist focuses on social group relations in complex technological societies. The psychologist is

3

concerned with the individual behavior of organisms, both people and animals.

Each of the sciences has its own particular field of inquiry. Yet there is one unifying element. Every science uses the scientific method to acquire knowledge. Both the natural and the social scientists apply the scientific method to their particular field of study.

The scientific method. What is this method? *The* SCIENTIFIC METHOD *is an empirical way of collecting data and arriving at explanations of the objects, events, and behaviors investigated.* "Empirical" refers to evidence that comes from observation and sensory experience rather than from theory. It provides a method of study or analysis by which different researchers may reach the same conclusions, regardless of their differences in personal values. It permits different researchers to test in a detached and unbiased manner the conclusions of the social scientists whose studies they are repeating or advancing.

The scientist employs logic, once he or she has empirically derived facts. That is, the scientist practices the principles of valid reasoning and accurate inference. The use of logic and human reasoning is important because facts cannot speak for themselves— they must be interpreted. A fact by itself is meaningless unless it is related to some other fact or series of facts. For example, suppose you overhear someone say, "It is six feet high." The statement has meaning only if you know what "it" is and compare it to other objects. If "it" is a chest of drawers, you would know that it is rather tall in comparison with other chests. If "it" is a telephone pole, you would consider it to be rather short. Scientists must make logical conclusions from their data by relating them to other data through the use of human reason.

The objectives of science. Scientists have several goals or objectives in mind as they use the scientific method. One of these objectives is to describe and classify the data they gather so the data have meaning. The object under investigation is described and then placed in a category with other objects that have similar characteristics. For example, the chemist classifies substances according to their characteristics as acids, bases, or salts. The biologist classifies all living things into phylums, kingdoms, and species on the basis of similar characteristics. The sociologist classifies people, groups, organizations, or relationships into categories according to their similarities. In the process of describing and classifying knowledge, scientists hope to be able to better understand the phenomena related to their field of study.

Another objective of scientists is to be able to predict certain things about their data on the basis of the various classifications. For example, the chemist can predict that if a chemical that has been classified as a base is mixed in the proper proportions with another that has been classified as an acid, the two will neutralize each other and will react to form a salt. Because of the difficulty of controlling all the factors involved, the social scientist cannot predict with the accuracy of the natural scientist. However, the sociologist can predict the *probable* success in marriage of a man and a woman on the basis of their personality characteristics, past experiences, attitudes, values, religious beliefs, and other factors.

A third objective of scientists is to contribute to the total knowledge of their discipline. One of the ways in which they make this contribution is by reporting their findings in professional journals or at scientific meetings.

Scientists arrive at their findings through stating a hypothesis and then testing it. *A* HYPOTHESIS *is a tentative assumption, an untested generalization.* It is often a grand design for experimentation. It is an educated guess about a relationship between two or more events, situations, or factors. These relationships are then subjected to empirical tests.

After testing their hypothesis, scientists either accept or reject it. They then report their findings as generalizations or as theories. *A* GENERALIZATION *is a statement about the relationship between the events or situations under study, based on the particulars of that study.* Scientists do not observe the total number of events or situations. They make generalizations about the whole on the basis of observing a part. *A* THEORY *is a combination of generalizations to explain some phenomenon.* Theories are plans or explanations based on principles that are supported by experiment or observation. That is, they are testable. An example is the molecular theory. After scientists completed a great amount of research and made a number of generalizations about the various properties of matter, their findings were combined to produce the theory that all matter is composed of molecules. This theory then must stand the test of many other experiments, or empirical searches for evidence to support or defeat the theory.

Most of the generalizations and theories that scientists make are the result of research carried out by the scientific method. When scientists report the results of their research, their findings are then examined, analyzed, and eventually supported or proven incorrect by the research of other scientists.

Sociological Investigation and Analysis

We have stated that sociology is the science that deals with the investigation and analysis of human relationships, their causes and consequences. We've just seen that sociology is a science. It is a body of knowledge gathered through empirical and objective research, analyzed by human logic and reason, and supported by the research of many scientists. The next important parts of our defi-

Sociologists use the scientific method to study many different aspects of human behavior. For instance, they conduct research on the voting behavior and trends of the American people.

nition to consider are investigation and analysis. *An* INVESTIGATION *is a careful and thorough study carried out by the use of the scientific method.* In conducting an investigation, all scientists want to know four things about the object they are investigating. They want to know about its structure, its functions, its patterns, and its processes.

Structure. *The* STRUCTURE *of something is the organization of its parts and the relation-*

5

Some sociologists study patterns of employee behavior. As a result, they can predict how employees will react in various work situations.

ships of these parts to each other. For example, the biologist might study the structure of a leaf. The physicist might investigate the structure of the atom. And the sociologist might examine the structure of a group, organization, or institution. In each case the scientist asks the questions "How is it put together?" and "What are the relationships of the various parts?"

Function. *The* FUNCTION *of an object or structure is simply what it does.* The scientist wants to know what the structure or a part of the structure does. The biologist is interested in the functions of the various parts of a plant. The physicist studies the functions of the electron, neutron, or proton. The sociologist wants to know the function of the individuals in a group, the group itself, an

organization, or an institution. Function is very closely related to structure, because a change in the structure usually produces a change in function.

Pattern. PATTERN *is concerned with the repetition of behavior that makes prediction possible.* For example, the biologist can predict what kind of plant will result from cross-pollination. The physicist can predict what will result when an atom is split. And human beings tend to act in the same way consistently enough that the sociologist can predict with some accuracy how people will behave in certain situations. Sociologists study the patterns of behavior that develop among people living together in a society and that set them apart from people in other societies.

Process. PROCESS *is change taking place in a*

specific way or ways. For example, the biologist is concerned with the process by which some trees change the color of their leaves from green to red and yellow. The physicist is concerned with the process of nuclear fission. The sociologist is interested in the processes that bring changes in individuals, groups, societies, and institutions. Process is the concept that allows us to examine the object of study to determine what changes are taking place and how these changes occur.

In addition to investigation, our definition includes the word analysis. ANALYSIS *is a process by which the data are separated into parts and examined very carefully to determine the relationships of the various parts.* Scientists use analysis as they study the structures, functions, patterns, and processes related to their object of study. Some scientists apply statistical analysis to determine more accurately the meaning of statistical data. Later, after analysis of all the data, social scientists try to synthesize, or combine, what they have found into a pattern.

In using investigation and analysis to arrive at the meaning of their data, social scientists have an additional element that does not exist for the natural scientists. Since social scientists study social phenomena, they must deal with an object of study of which they are a part—human beings. Social scientists often face the problem of not being removed from their data, since they themselves are members of society. In striving for objectivity they must try especially hard not to be influenced by their own sentiments or by the sentiments of the people under study. When natural scientists study a phenomenon, on the other hand, they are separate from the object of study that they are investigating. For example, when geologists study a rock they can approach the rock as external observers. They know that the rock has no sentiments and no meaning to itself—only to the geologist.

Sociologists Study Human Relationships

Let's look now at the last part of our definition of sociology—the study of human relationships, their causes and consequences. Sociologists limit their investigation to human group behavior, or human relationships. HUMAN RELATIONSHIPS *are the ways in which people relate to one another in their interactions as members of groups.*

The sociologist's basic concern is to determine the causes and consequences of these human relationships. Why, for example, do people organize themselves into various kinds of groups, associations, and institutions? Why do some people discriminate against other people? Why do people sometimes cooperate with one another and at other times conflict with one another to the extent of killing each other? What causes people to place others in a social class level? Sociologists ask these and many other questions about the causes of human relationships.

Just as important as the causes are the consequences, or effects, of these various relationships. People do organize themselves into groups. But what are the consequences of membership in these groups? What are the consequences of discrimination? What are the consequences of people cooperating together or conflicting with one another? What are the consequences of social class status? Sociologists investigate the many consequences of human group behavior.

To summarize, then, sociology is the science that deals with the investigation and analysis of human relationships, their causes and consequences. The object of study is human relations. People are very interesting creatures. However, they are also very complex and changeable. Therefore it is difficult to make accurate predictions about their behavior or to acquire a body of knowledge about them that is scientifically accurate.

As a sociologist, you would investigate the ways in which people relate to one another. You might analyze the interactions of volleyball players, such as these.

Yet the difficulties involved contribute greatly to the fascination and challenge of sociology. Every investigation brings to light new and exciting facts about human beings and their patterns of relationships.

SECTION REVIEW

1. Define sociology as a science.
2. What is the scientific method?
3. What are the objectives of science?
4. What are the four things that all scientists want to know about the object they are investigating?

KEY TERMS

Explain the meaning of each term.

analysis

function

generalization

human relationships

hypothesis

investigation

pattern

process

scientific method

sociology

structure

theory

SECTION 2:
The Tools and Techniques of Sociology

How do sociologists carry out their investigations and analyses of human relationships? What tools and techniques do they use? First, *a* TOOL *is an instrument, apparatus, arrangement, or situation used by the sociologist to help in the collection of data. A* TECHNIQUE *is the method or manner by which research is carried out.* Often sociologists use a particular tool or tools with a particular technique. For example, the questionnaire is a tool they commonly employ in the survey technique. Some of the following tools and techniques are used mainly by sociologists, while others are shared with scientists in other disciplines.

The Case Study Method

A CASE STUDY *is an intensive study of a person, group, organization, institution, or problem.* To collect all possible information about the particular object under investigation, the sociologist turns to documents, interviews, and observation.

This method is often used by social workers—people who strive to improve social conditions in a community. A social worker may be working with a couple who want to adopt a child. The social worker will put together a case history of both the couple and the child. This information can help the social worker place the child in the most suitable family environment.

Sociologists who specialize in industrial problems might use the case study to provide information about a particular organization, such as a labor union. They might trace its development over the years to determine the changes in its structure, functions, or patterns. Their intensive study of a particular case can contribute to a better understanding of other labor unions.

The case study is very useful because it enables us to examine a situation in depth. However, the case study method has one major limitation. This is the difficulty of making correct generalizations on the basis of one case. And, as you know, generalizing is a necessary part of the scientific method.

The Survey Method

In a survey, sociologists gather data from *some* instead of *all* the people whose attitudes, opinions, values, or behavior they wish to study. The survey method involves using a sample. *A* SAMPLE *is selected from the population in such a way that all members of the population have an equal chance of being represented.* By surveying a sample, the sociologist hopes to obtain data that accurately reflect the whole population.

The sociologist uses two specific tools in conducting a survey—the schedule and the questionnaire.

The SCHEDULE *is a list of questions that the sociologist asks a person being surveyed in an interview situation.* The advantage of the schedule is that the sociologist can obtain more accurate answers to the questions during the interview. The sociologist has the added benefit of interpreting facial expressions, tone of voice, and the gestures of the individual. Also, if the sociologist does not understand the answer given, he or she can ask the individual to restate it, clarify, or explain it more fully. The disadvantage of the schedule is that interviews are very time-consuming and often expensive, making a large sample difficult to obtain.

The QUESTIONNAIRE *is a list of questions that is filled out by the person being surveyed.* It is relatively simple to get a large sample with a questionnaire. It is easy to distribute and can be filled in by many people at the same time. However, a questionnaire has the disadvantage that the sociologist cannot know if the individual has interpreted the questions correctly. All the sociologist has to go on is the individual's answers on the sheet of paper.

In some survey studies sociologists will use both tools. They will use the schedule to get more accurate and detailed answers from a small sample, and the questionnaire to get less accurate and less specific answers from a large sample.

The anthropologist Margaret Mead (left)
uses the technique of observation as she
studies the behavior of people on the island of Bali.

Observation

Observation is probably the most accurate of the techniques. It is the technique most frequently used by researchers in the natural sciences. It is also effective for many types of social research. There are three basic types of observation that sociologists use in their research.

The first type is NATURAL OBSERVATION, *in which scientists observe from afar so that they will in no way cause change in the natural phenomena taking place.* Suppose you wondered if the difference between the scores of two football teams had any influence on the conduct of the cheerleaders. You could satisfy your curiosity simply by observing and recording your observations of cheerleaders at a number of different football games. You would then relate your observations to the difference in scores. You would not tell the cheerleaders that you were making a study of their movements because you might then cause them to change their behavior. And you want to study their natural behavior. You would also try to be as objective and unbiased as possible so that your observations would be accurate.

A second type of observation is CONTROLLED OBSERVATION, *in which the scientist sets up a variable to determine how people will react to it. A* VARIABLE *is a situation, event, or factor that usually changes or varies.* For example, you might hang a "Wet Paint" sign in the hall of your school. You have introduced a variable that changes the natural situation. You want to observe how people will react to this variable. Will the students touch the wall to see if the paint really is wet?

When you control the variables in a situation, you are conducting an experiment. In an experiment all of the variables are controlled except one, which is called the independent variable. *The* INDEPENDENT VARIABLE *is the factor under study.* It is separated from the other variables and is manipulated, or varied. *The change that results from varying the independent variable is called the* DEPENDENT VARIABLE. It is dependent on and is caused by the independent variable.

Suppose you had conducted the experiment of hanging a "Wet Paint" sign in your school. The independent variable would be the "Wet Paint" sign. The dependent variable would be the different reactions of the people as they come down the hall and see the sign. Sociologists use many controlled situations, or experiments, of this type to study human behavior.

The third type of observation is PARTICIPANT OBSERVATION, *in which the observer is involved in the interaction under study.* This type of observation was used by Robert and Helen Lynd in their community study of "Middletown" (actually Muncie, Indiana). They lived in the community and participated in its activities with the other residents. At the same time they recorded their observations of group life in the community.

Later they published the results of their study. Also, anthropologists often use participant observation in studying tribal and other kinds of societies. When using this method, however, observers who are seen and identified must always be careful to account for the effect that they have on the situation being observed, since they always have some effect.

Content Analysis

Content analysis involves counting the number of times a given word, stereotype, attitude, or value appears in a given context. This method is most commonly used to analyze the content of the mass media. For example, you might want to make a study of how many advertisements for a particular kind of merchandise appear in a selected group of magazines. You might be seeking answers to such questions as what kind of

merchandise is most commonly advertised in science magazines, women's magazines, or farm journals.

Historical Analysis

Historical analysis is related to the past experiences of human beings. The social scientist attempts to determine what has taken place in the past. The materials of history fall into two categories—remains and records. Sociologists, historians, and anthropologists use remains left by the Mesa Verde Indians, for example, to reconstruct the culture of the Indians and determine many aspects of their daily life. From bodily or skeletal remains they can determine such things as the stature of the people, physical health, disease, average life span, and burial customs. From the remains of objects that people made, such as buildings, weapons, agricultural tools, and pottery, they can

After living in these cliff dwellings in southwestern Colorado for many centuries, the Mesa Verde Indians left them around 1300 A.D. Social scientists depend heavily on these remains to learn about the Mesa Verde culture through the technique of historical analysis.

generalize about some aspects of the social culture. Another type of remains are the institutions that have been inherited from the past. For example, social scientists can gain some knowledge of the Mesa Verde culture by studying the institutions of the family, religion, and government among the descendants of the Mesa Verde Indians living today in Arizona, Colorado, New Mexico, and Utah. They can also learn about an earlier culture from verbal remains, such as myths, ballads, legends, traditions, superstitions, and folklore handed down from generation to generation by word of mouth.

However, the chief materials of history are records and documents. Literate societies have left behind them masses of records and documents in the form of laws, newspapers, pictures, books, personal letters, and so forth. These records provide sociologists and historians with clues as they study such phenomena as social and cultural change. For instance, it is easy to compare changes in American culture through an analysis of the mass media over a period of time.

Some environmental studies also make good use of the historical method. For example, a study of the development of a city from a small town can be traced through various historical documents to determine the environmental factors that influenced the city's growth over the years. Comparisons of organizations, societies, or nations can be made by historical analysis. The historical method does, however, present social scientists with the problem of insuring the accuracy of the historical remains or documents that they use in their research.

Statistical Analysis

The last research technique for our consideration is statistical analysis. Actually it is not a technique in itself. Rather, it is used with many of the other techniques, such as observation, survey, or content analysis. The other techniques provide the mathematical data that the sociologist must have in order to apply statistical analysis. Through statistical means the sociologist can test the mathematical data to determine accuracy, consistency, the degree of relationship, and a number of other factors.

Statistical analysis serves two basic functions. It allows sociologists to describe empirical data. And it permits them to make inferences and generalizations about a population of which they have observed or investigated only a part.

We've seen that the sociologist who wishes to carry out research can choose from a number of techniques — the case study method, the survey method, observation, content analysis, historical analysis, and statistical analysis. Some of these techniques make use of specific tools, such as interviews, questionnaires, or historical documents. Next we will consider how to evaluate the data obtained through these techniques and tools.

SECTION REVIEW

1. What is the difference between a research tool and a research technique?
2. What factors should be considered in determining the best technique to be used in testing a hypothesis?
3. What problems can arise in collecting accurate data by the survey method?

KEY TERMS

Explain the meaning of each term.

case study method	questionnaire
content analysis	sample
controlled observation	schedule
dependent variable	statistical analysis
historical analysis	survey method
independent variable	technique
natural observation	tool
participant observation	variable

SECTION 3:
The Evaluation of Data

Once scientists have collected and analyzed their data through using specific tools and techniques, they are ready to interpret the data and make accurate conclusions. The sociologist works with two basic kinds of data—verbal and mathematical. Neither kind speaks for itself. Each must be interpreted. We will discuss guidelines for evaluating verbal data here. These guidelines are useful not just to sociologists but to every individual who needs to determine fact from fiction.

Each day we are bombarded with a mass of data presenting varying degrees of truth. We are exposed to information on a multitude of topics through newspapers, magazines, the radio, television, books, movies, and various kinds of pamphlets. Also, we pass information from person to person through casual conversation. How much of this information is fact, and how much is misleading, slanted, or completely false?

In attempting to separate fact from fiction, we must be careful not to develop a complete mistrust of all information and refuse to believe anything that we see or hear. On the other hand, the person who accepts every bit of information as fact is an easy target for others to exploit.

Perhaps the best approach is to begin by evaluating every statement of information to determine how important it is to us as individuals. If we decide that it does have meaning in our lives, then we need to analyze it carefully to determine its truth and accuracy. If we find that the particular information does not affect our lives very much, we should not waste our time trying to determine its accuracy.

Once we decide that the information is important to us, we can apply certain guidelines to find out how much of it is fact and how much is fiction. We can ask the following ten questions to evaluate any statements of information.

Guidelines for Evaluating Statements

1. *Who said it?* It is necessary to consider who made the statement. Is the person an "expert"? For example, what makes the barber, the grocer, or the mechanic an expert on world affairs?

2. *Who supports, sponsors, publishes, or distributes the information?* If the information is printed and comes from a reliable source, a statement telling who wrote it, published it, or distributed it is usually given. If none of these data are given, you might consider the information as questionable. In the United States libel and slander laws make it illegal to issue statements about others that are untrue and can hurt a person's reputation or status. Originators of such information may not identify themselves because they want to protect themselves from a possible lawsuit.

We might also be skeptical of statements about groups of people. For example, if you say, "John Doe the grocer is a crook," John Doe could sue you for slander. However, if you make statements about a group, no one is likely to sue you. For example, suppose you say, "All grocers are crooks." Who is going to sue you? For this reason we should be cautious of any accusations made against a group of persons.

3. *Is the information specific, or does it use weasel words or vague, sweeping generalities?* Weasel words are words that are used to avoid making a direct statement. The result is generally a statement that is misleading but not factually wrong.

For example, mouthwash promoters may wish to give the impression that the use of

13

One way of evaluating the accuracy of information presented to you is to examine the logic of the statements. Are they reasonable? Or are they misleading?

their mouthwash will stop bad breath. They would like to say directly that it stops bad breath, but they can't prove this statement. They might be challenged by the government for false advertising. (Doctors tell us that often bad breath starts in the stomach, which mouthwash does not affect.) Promoters, to protect themselves, say that their mouthwash will stop all bad breath caused by local mouth conditions. This statement implies that it stops all bad breath. But, if challenged, they can point out that they never claimed their mouthwash would stop bad breath completely.

Vague, sweeping generalities also can be very misleading. We should examine carefully the use of such words as "always," "the majority," or "most." The statement that "most college students use drugs" may

have little actual meaning, because "most" may turn out to be only 1 or 2 percent of the students.

4. *Does the information seem logical?* We might ask whether or not the information seems reasonable in light of our own experiences. Take, for example, the many reports of flying saucers in the last few decades. These reports do not seem to fit in logically with our present ideas about space. They do not seem reasonable in light of our own experiences. We may also wonder why one saucer-sighting almost always leads to many others. Is it simply the power of suggestion that brings about the many sightings, or do flying saucers really exist? We don't know. But until we have specific evidence, we should view the whole situation with an open and questioning attitude.

14

5. *Can the information be verified?* When people make statements that can be verified, or proven, easily, they are much more likely to be telling the truth. For example, a statement such as "the cost of public school education has doubled in the last five years" is apt to be accurate since it can be checked very easily. The data are kept by school districts, states, and the federal government. In fact, the more easily a particular statement can be verified, the more likely it is to be factual and correct.

6. *Are the conclusions given based on the data presented?* Perhaps you can remember reading an article or hearing a speech in which individuals discussed their research, stated their data, and then presented a conclusion in which their generalizations were based on their own opinions rather than on the data.

Or take, for example, the advertisements of an automobile manufacturer for the car's low gasoline mileage ratings on tests. The ads mention the miles per gallon obtained on the tests. But they don't say what methods were used to arrive at the rating. Actually, the cars were not tested in regular driving conditions. The cars themselves didn't move. Their wheels were turned on steel rollers. Therefore, such factors as wind or road resistance, which can affect gas mileage, were not taken into account. Thus the test results may not be accurate for driving on roads. The conclusion given is not really based on the data presented.

7. *Are generalizations made beyond what is supported by the evidence?* Human beings have a tendency to overgeneralize. If ten students out of thirty fail an exam, the word often spreads that everybody flunked. There are several reasons for exaggerating or overgeneralizing. In this case those who failed may exaggerate because it is not so humiliating to flunk if everybody else does, too.

Another source of overgeneralization is the making of statements that are based on improperly drawn samples. Samples should be drawn to avoid biases. Suppose you want to know how everyone in the United States will vote for President. If you select only 1,500

How would you go about finding out if the conclusions of an advertisement are based on fact or on opinion?

people to survey, but they accurately reflect the population, you would be able to make a statement about how the American public will vote. If, however, you select a sample of people who are all from the same income group, or the same religion, or the same area, and use your results to make a statement about the whole country, you will be over-generalizing. You do not have a proper sample on which to base your statement. Whenever you are presented with the results of some poll or survey, always ask about the sample on which the results are based.

8. *Is the information consistent with the data of others?* Scientists place great stress on the agreement of other observers before they accept data as fact. If one scientist gets data that are not consistent with the data of others, the scientist often finds that his or her information is wrong. No doubt you have had similar experiences. Suppose, for example, you arrive at an answer of 248 for the third problem in the algebra assignment, and the other twenty-nine members of the class get 276. Would you consider your answer correct and their answer wrong? If you are presented with data that do not agree with the data of others, always examine the information with great care.

9. *Is a cause-and-effect relationship implied when actually there is only an association?* Sometimes we make the error of implying causality when two sets of data are related. For example, if we make a study of boys who drop out of high school and find that most of them own a car, can we say that owning a car caused these boys to drop out of school? Before we can make that statement we need to know how many boys who do not drop out also own cars. Unless the percentage of boys owning cars is significantly higher among the droputs that it is among students in general, we cannot say that owning a car causes the student to drop out.

Also, we would have to be sure that a third factor was not the cause of both owning a car and dropping out of school. For example, low ability to do academic work might be the cause of both. The boy who cannot succeed academically might own a car to achieve some status. The inability to do academic work might also be the major cause of his dropping out of school.

Whenever there is an association between two factors, there are four possibilities for explaining the relationship: A and B are independent and the association is accidental; A causes B; B causes A; or both A and B are caused by a third factor, C.

10. *Does the information appeal mainly to people's reason or to their emotions?* Humans are emotional beings — a fact that advertising people are well aware of. Many products are advertised as giving the individual popularity, sex appeal, status, or happiness. For example, some cigarette ads suggest that smoking a particular brand is like being in the rugged countryside of mountains and high plateaus. However, this comparison is not meant to be judged rationally. After all, smoke, and therefore cigarette smoke, is actually more like the smog of the city than like the clear air of the mountains. The ad is really aiming at the emotional appeal of fresh air and peaceful surroundings, and it suggests that smoking Brand X will give you that same feeling of freshness and peace. Many devices or techniques used in propaganda are directed toward the emotions of the public.

Try to keep these ten questions in mind as you evaluate the many statements you encounter each day. These guidelines also give you an idea of the kinds of questions that scientists ask of their data in evaluating scientific research.

SECTION REVIEW

1. Why is it so necessary to know about the selection process of a sample that is used as the basis for a generalization?

Some leaders, such as Adolf Hitler, have gained support by appealing to people's emotions rather than to their reason.

2. What is the difference between a cause-and-effect relationship and an association?
3. Do most advertisements appeal to people's reason or to their emotions? Give examples of advertisements that appeal to each.
4. It has been said that if a lie is repeated often enough, it will eventually be accepted as fact. What do you think?

KEY TERMS

Give an example of each term.

cause-and-effect relationship	sweeping generality
logical statement	verified information
relationship by association	weasel words

SECTION 4:
What Sociologists Do

Now that you know how sociologists obtain their data, the tools and techniques they use, and the importance of evaluation, let's consider briefly the types of activities involving sociologists. If you were a sociologist, what sorts of things would you be doing? Here are some of the specific activities that engage sociologists.

Teaching. The largest number of sociologists are engaged in teaching at colleges and universities. Now that sociology has become popular as a course of study in the high school curriculum, the number of sociologists teaching in senior high schools is increasing. Along with their teaching, many sociologists, particularly at the larger universities, also are involved in some kind of research.

Research. Research is an essential activity for sociologists, since it is through research that new concepts, generalizations, and theories are added to the field of sociology. For the most part, the concepts, generalizations, and theories taught in the classroom are the result of a great deal of research by many sociologists. The majority of research sociologists work for colleges and universities. But the government, particularly the federal government, is employing increasingly greater numbers of research sociologists. In addition, industry finances some sociological research in such areas as market research, advertising, propaganda analysis, labor-management relations, worker morale, public opinion measurement, and attitude studies.

Administration. A number of sociologists spend most of their time as administrators. They might serve as heads of their departments of sociology in colleges or universities. They might direct a research study for a college, the government, or some industry. Or they might be engaged in the administration and supervision of people in a variety of other situations.

Writing and editing. Many sociologists spend a large part of their time writing or editing books, periodicals, and professional journals. A majority of these writers and editors are also teachers, administrators, or researchers. But for many writing and editing are full-time jobs.

Consulting. Today more and more sociologists are working as consultants. For example, if an industry felt that its production rate was poor because of low morale among the workers, it could call in a consulting sociologist. The sociologist would then make a study of the problem and recommend ways for the company to remedy the situation.

Actuarial work. Actuarial work involves working with statistics. Many sociologists specialize in making statistical calculations. They are concerned with the mathematics of birth rates, death rates, accident rates, crime rates, and other such statistics. From their statistics they may make predictions, determine premium rates for insurance, or advise government and industry. They are often employed by government agencies such as the United States Bureau of the Census, by insurance companies, and by industry.

Social work. It is important to note the difference between sociology and social work. Sociologists are scientists. Their job is to increase our understanding of social phenomena. They organize knowledge about social phenomena into basic theories that make prediction possible. Social workers apply the knowledge of social phenomena to improve social situations. They attempt to help individuals or groups to meet their unsatisfied human and social needs.

Social workers practice their profession in a great variety of settings. They work in family and child welfare agencies. They are associated with courts as probation and parole officers. They practice in hospitals, community centers, schools, and youth centers. They work with people of all ages and needs. They are concerned with welfare planning, research, and individual and group counseling. They often advise governments on the local, state, national, or international (through United Nations agencies) level.

Sociology and social work require different educational programs. The sociologist would carry out graduate work at a university and receive the Master of Arts (MA) or Doctor of Philosophy (PhD) degree. The social worker would attend a graduate school

Drawing by Weber. © 1975, The New Yorker Magazine, Inc.

"In a way, I am kind of famous. But you've probably never heard of me unless you happen to travel in actuarial circles."

of social work to receive the Master of Social Work (MSW) degree.

These, then, are some of the activities of sociologists and social workers. There are also many others that we haven't mentioned. Sociology offers a tremendous number of opportunities to a young person seeking a meaningful vocation. A degree in sociology is also a good background for jobs in civil service or professional religious service, and work with youth organizations, poverty agencies, and community planning groups.

SECTION REVIEW

1. Name the kinds of activities that engage sociologists.
2. Which of these activities would you most want to do?
3. What is the difference between a sociologist and a social worker?

KEY TERMS

Define each term.

actuarial work   social work

1. Design a bulletin board or poster that illustrates the causes and consequences of a specific human relationship.

2. Class project. Divide the class into teams of two persons each. Have each team play several rounds of tic-tac-toe. Then, in a class discussion, analyze the game of tic-tac-toe in terms of structure, functions, patterns, and processes.

3. Look for advertisements that cite the results of research. Judge these advertisements in terms of whether you can know that the research was conducted by the scientific method.

4. Find copies of such sociological journals as *The American Sociological Review, American Journal of Sociology, Social Research, Social Forces, Marriage and Family Living,* and *Social Problems.* Discuss or report to the class on the kinds of research done and the topics that were investigated.

5. Collect articles from newspapers and magazines that involve some problem in human relationships. Then list the variables that would be involved in making an analysis of the problem.

6. Conduct a survey of attitudes of your student body on some current issue. Evaluate the results in terms of your research techniques.

7. Look in the newspapers for reports of research projects that have just been completed. Attempt to determine the specific research techniques and the size of the sample used. Evaluate the results in terms of the sample and research techniques.

8. Set up a situation in which you might observe the reactions of your fellow students. For example, you might wear socks that don't match or comb your hair strangely. Record your observations and discuss.

9. Observe the behavior of drivers at several stop signs. Count the number of drivers who come to a complete stop and those who do not come to a complete stop. Then compare the results to see if there are differences in stopping behavior at the various intersections. If there are differences, could you predict that these differences would continue to occur?

10. Apply the guidelines for evaluating information to a number of advertisements, news articles, and magazine feature articles. What can you say about the accuracy of the information presented?

11. Collect newspaper articles that tell about sociologists and their work. How many different kinds of work do you find?

12. Examine some college catalogs to discover what sociology courses the colleges offer. What is required for a major or minor in sociology?

13. Conduct an interview with a person or persons working in the field of sociology. Ask about the tasks performed by sociologists and the present opportunities in the field.

TOPICS FOR INQUIRY

1. Discuss: The most difficult thing for people to study is other people.

2. Should the primary goal of sociology be the improvement of society? What do you think?

3. Why is it possible for the natural scientist to arrive at laws, when the social scientist can only arrive at generalizations? Explain.

4. How might persons in various occupations use the case study method in their jobs?

5. Discuss the various ways that you might carry out research on each of the following problems: (1) Are teen-agers more liberal in their political views than adults? (2) Are young drivers more skillful in driving cars than adult drivers? (3) Are young people from broken homes more likely to become delinquent than young people from happy homes?

6. What research problems could you study in your school using the technique of participant observation?

7. What are the ethical and legal implications of conducting research by the field study method? Should you obtain permission from persons you observe? Would you use hidden cameras? Do you have the right to invade a person's privacy for the sake of sociological research? Can you be sued for invading an individual's privacy?

8. How do the jobs of the sociologist and the social worker complement each other?

NONFICTION

AMERICAN SOCIOLOGICAL ASSOCIATION, *A Career in Sociology*. Available from the Executive Office, American Sociological Association, 1001 Connecticut Ave., N. W., Washington, D.C. 20036. A pamphlet that answers such questions as: What is sociology? What do sociologists do? What are the educational and training requirements? What is the future of sociology? What is the American Sociological Association?

BART, Pauline and FRANKEL, Linda, *The Student Sociologist's Handbook*. Schenkman, 1971. A guide to writing a sociological research paper, with a good glossary of sociological terms.

BERGER, Peter L., *An Invitation to Sociology: A Humanistic Perspective*. Doubleday, 1963 (pap.). A personalized and lively account of the meaning of sociology.

BIRENBAUM, Arnold and SAGARIN, Edward (eds.), *People in Places: The Sociology of the Familiar*. Praeger, 1973 (pap.). A book of readings stressing sociological analysis of familiar situations.

CHAMBLISS, William J. and RYTHER, Thomas E., *Sociology: The Discipline and Its Direction*, McGraw-Hill, 1975. A critical examination of society and sociology.

CHASE, Stuart, *The Proper Study of Mankind: An Inquiry into the Science of Human Relations*. Rev. ed., Harper & Row, 1967 (pap.). A study of the development of the social sciences and human relations.

CHINOY, Ely and HEWITT, John P., *Sociological Perspective*. Third ed., Random House, 1974. A discussion of basic sociological concepts and perspectives.

COLE, Stephen, *The Sociological Method*. Rand McNally, 1972 (pap.). A concise summary of research methods stressing practical applications.

LIGHT, Donald Jr., and KELLER, Suzanne, *Sociology*. Knopf, 1975. A college textbook that contains a glossary for each chapter.

LYND, Robert S., *Knowledge for What? The Place of Social Science in American Culture*. Princeton University Press, 1969 (pap.). A discussion in which the author urges the application of social research to our most pressing social problems.

MILLS, C. Wright, *The Sociological Imagination*. Oxford University Press, 1967 (pap.). An interesting commentary on intellectual crafts-

22

manship, which takes the position that sociologists work at the inter-section of biography and history.

SAUNDERS, William B. (ed.), *The Sociologist as Detective: An Introduction to Research Methods.* Praeger, 1974. A collection of readings on sociological research methods.

SPEIER, Matthew, *How to Observe Face-to-Face Communication: A Sociological Introduction.* Goodyear, 1973 (pap.). An illustrated account of the methods and values of field work.

FICTION

KAFKA, Franz, *Metamorphosis.* Vanguard or Schocken (pap.). A symbolic portrayal of the breakdown in human relations.

KNOWLES, John, *A Separate Peace.* Dell (pap.). A beautiful but tragic story of a friendship between boys in a private school.

SALINGER, J. D., *Nine Stories.* Little, Brown or Bantam (pap.). Short stories that portray human relations humorously and penetratingly.

SAROYAN, William, *The Human Comedy.* Harcourt Brace Jovanovich or Dell (pap.). An optimistic look at the life of a high-school-age telegram delivery boy during World War II, and his growing awareness of the people around him.

Highlight

How do sociologists study problems?

What do sociologists actually do when they conduct research? What would you do if you were a sociologist faced with a problem or question for which you wanted more information, or a better explanation?

The usual procedure for conducting sociological research is to follow the steps of the scientific method. These steps include isolating the problem, forming a hypothesis, building a research design, collecting the data, analyzing the data collected, and making generalizations.

The first step is to isolate the problem. You may think of a problem as something that is troubling you or society. In terms of the scientific method, however, a *problem* refers to any question for which we seek an answer. It is not necessarily a personal or social problem. It is simply some matter about which we want to know the answer. Sociologists usually choose to research problems that are related to their areas of interest and their particular specialty in the field of sociology.

The next step is to develop a hypothesis. In Chapter I, we defined a *hypothesis* as a tentative assumption, an untested generalization. What is the purpose of a hypothesis? Why waste time with assumptions and educated guesses? The hypothesis is essential because it sets the stage for the research and gives it direction. A hypothesis always states a relationship between two or more situations, events, or factors.

The purpose of the research is to test the hypothesis to see if this statement of the relationship is accurate.

The third step is to build a research design. A *research design* is a set of directions for research. A builder would have a hard time constructing a house without detailed and accurate blueprints. Similarly, a sociologist would have great difficulty in carrying out research without a carefully built research design. To set up a research design, the sociologist must determine the variables and how they will be measured. The sociologist must then decide what sample will be used. Finally, the sociologist must determine what tools and techniques to use in collecting the data. Should observation be used? Or the survey method? Or the case study method?

The fourth step is to collect the data accurately. The collecting process must be done carefully to avoid error. If the data are inaccurate, the results will be useless.

When the data have been collected, the sociologist analyzes them to determine their meaning. On the basis of the data, the sociologist decides whether to accept or reject the hypothesis.

The last step is to decide what generalizations can be made. What can we say about the population on the basis of the sample actually investigated? What conclusions can we draw about the whole on the basis of examining a part?

To see how a sociologist follows these steps, we can look at an actual study. A classic example of sociological research is Emile Durkheim's study of suicide, published by the French sociologist in 1897. Let's examine just what Durkheim did, how he did it, and what he concluded.

The Problem

In Durkheim's France, as in societies today, the question of suicide was one of great popular concern. For suicide represents a problem. It raises not only specific questions for the relatives and friends of the victims, but also larger questions of causation. Why do people commit suicide? Why *don't* some people do it? Why does the rate of suicide vary from place to place? Durkheim noted that suicide rates differed, depending on the society and the conditions. He felt that differences in the rates of suicides suggested that more than individual factors were operating. He thought that suicide must reflect changes in social or environmental circumstances. The problem was to discover the nature of these circumstances and their causes.

The Hypothesis

Durkheim first explored the current explanations for suicide. One explanation was that suicide resulted from individual psychological conditions. Another explanation assigned the cause of suicide to factors in the natural environment, such as the time of year, the climate, or the temperature. After examining case histories and statistical records, however, Durkheim concluded that such explanations were not adequate. In investigating individual psychological conditions, he found that though many of the people who committed suicide were mentally ill, many others were not. Furthermore, no one type of mental illness was always associated with suicide. Neither could he find a clear relationship between alcoholic consumption, or between age, race, or sex, and the suicide rate.

Similarly, such forces as seasonal variation and climate did not cause suicide. When Durkheim separated these environmental factors, he could find no meaningful relationship between them and the suicide rate. For example, if warm weather increased the number of social interactions, and the suicide rate was affected, the important factor was the increased social interactions and not the warmer weather.

By observing available evidence and using reason and common sense, then, Durkheim arrived at his hypothesis that the basic causes of suicide were social in nature. It seemed to him that the main determinants of suicide were such social factors as religion, marital status, and the pace of social change. He therefore hypothesized that the degree of social attachment, or the lack of it, explained the variations in the suicide rate.

The Research Design

To test his hypothesis, Durkheim reasoned that he would need statistics on the number of suicides in given areas at given times. To be able to talk about the *rate* of suicide, he would also need accurate figures for the total population of these areas. Furthermore, he would need all these statistics from a variety of places. Then he could make comparisons between the suicide rate and different social conditions.

He found that most of the European countries, as well as the United States, had relatively accurate statistics on the number of suicides, who committed them, and the total population. All Durkheim had to do was to get at these already existing sources of information.

By comparing the suicide rates of Protestants and Catholics, of urban and rural areas, and so on, Durkheim could test his hypothesis. He could find out if the degree of social attachment determined the rate of suicide, and if suicide was, therefore, a social phenomenon.

Collecting and Analyzing the Data

Building a research design and collecting data are closely related. What Durkheim found was that the data he collected did seem to fit a pattern, and that this pattern confirmed his hypothesis.

He found, for example, that the suicide rates were higher among Protestants than among Catholics. This was so even when he allowed for other differences in the social climate that may have affected the suicide rate. In other words, he did not simply compare the rates of Protestant countries with Catholic ones. Instead, he carefully compared Protestant and Catholic villages within a single area, Bavaria, and still found important differences in the suicide rates.

Similarly, taking other factors into account, he found that single people had higher suicide rates than married ones. Married but childless people had higher suicide rates than people with children. City dwellers had higher suicide rates than people living in rural areas. Men had higher suicide rates than women. And soldiers had a higher suicide rate than civilians.

The Generalizations and Conclusions

From his evidence, Durkheim concluded that the suicide rate *was* determined by the degree of social attachment. He discovered, however, that the relationship was a complex one. Suicide seemed to result from both unusually high levels and unusually low levels of social attachment. From his findings, he was able to generalize that there were three basic types of suicide: altruistic, egoistic, and anomic.

Altruistic suicide occurs when the degree of attachment of the individual to the society is very great. It is not always defined by the society as suicide. Rather, the individuals may be regarded as heroes. This would be the case with soldiers who volunteer for a dangerous mission, in which they are likely to lose their lives, out of zeal for and devotion to their country.

Egoistic suicide, on the other hand, results from a lack of attachment of the individual to the society. The less integrated into society individuals are, and the more they must depend on their own egos or selves, the more likely they are to commit suicide. He found Protestants, who make more theological decisions on their own than Catholics and are therefore less attached to their society, have a higher suicide rate than Catholics. In the same manner single people, city dwellers, and men have higher suicide rates than married people, rural people, and women. They tend to have fewer attachments and responsibilities, more social freedom, and more dependence on their own egos.

Anomic suicide, like egoistic suicide, occurs because the individual is forced to make decisions without any strong social attachments. However, in anomic suicide the individual is unattached because the whole society is undergoing rapid change and the old rules no longer seem to apply. Anomic means normlessness. Anomic suicide occurs during periods of uncertainty, such as times of crisis, revolution, or economic depression.

But it is not Durkheim's conclusions that interest us so much as the steps of his sociological research. His work is an example of a clear, simple, yet thorough application of scientific procedures. Other sociologists continue to use his study of suicide as a model for their own work to this day.

OUR WORLD

Why do you think you have the personality that you have? What influences helped shape your unique personality? Some aspects of your personality were shaped by heredity—the genes and chromosomes you received from your parents. But, for the most part, you are a product of your environment—the natural and social world in which you live. To understand your personality you must understand the culture in which you live. In this unit you can learn how cultural values and rules influence almost every aspect of your life. You can also examine ways in which cultures differ and change, or resist change.

2 Culture

► What is culture?

► Why do cultures vary so much throughout the world?

► What causes a culture to change or to resist changes?

SECTION 1:
The Meaning of Culture

Perhaps you've heard people use the word "culture" to mean refinement and an appreciation of the arts. Sometimes people say that "she needs more culture," or "he really enjoys cultural activities." Sociologically, however, these uses of the term are incorrect. It is also sociologically incorrect to talk of the culturally deprived child. Not all people pick up the same amount of culture. Yet every human being has a culture. Children who are labeled culturally deprived happen not to have the same cultural characteristics as those who do the labeling. But they do have a culture.

What, then, is culture? CULTURE *is the way of life—the shared, learned behavior—of a people.* It includes everything we think, do, and have as members of society. Therefore it includes the ideas, values, beliefs, literature, religion, and philosophy of a people. It also includes the rules by which those people guide their behavior and the material objects that are found among them.

Culture is both shared and learned. The fundamental aspects of a culture are shared by all the people in a given society. However, the more complex the society, the less its culture is universally shared, because it has developed many subcultures. People get differing amounts of culture and have different socialization experiences in our society. For instance, traditionally boys and girls have been raised differently. And there are regional differences in our culture.

Also, not all learned behavior is cultural. A certain (very small) proportion of what we learn is acquired simply through individual experience and is not shared with others or transmitted to them. We might say that all of our behavior that is cultural has been learned. But not everything that we've learned is cultural.

Culture and Society

Culture and society are not the same thing. The sociologist uses the term SOCIETY to refer to *a number of persons living within a certain geographic area who have a common culture and a feeling of unity that helps bind them together into a social unit.* The society is the people who populate a nation. When we speak of the American society we mean all of the people who live in the fifty states that make up the United States. The culture is the way of life of these people. The American culture refers to the shared, learned behavior of the people who are the American society. Every society has a culture. Members of the society transmit the culture from generation to generation as the cultural heritage.

Culture Traits

To understand the meaning of culture more fully, we might examine some of its parts. One part of culture is the culture trait. *A* CULTURE TRAIT *is an individual tool, act, or belief related to a particular situation or need.* Our use of a fork, knife, and spoon when eating is a culture trait. Another trait is the specific way in which we greet people. If you are walking down the hall at school and meet a classmate, you might greet him or her by saying "Hi." However, in other situations the appropriate greeting may be quite different. For instance, if you were selected as a speaker for your class commencement, you would not walk up to the podium and begin your address by saying "Hi." Nor are you likely to say "Hi" when introduced to the personnel manager for a job interview. The greeting you use is related to the particular situation or need.

Thus a culture trait can be a tool, such as a fork, or an act, such as greeting a friend. It can also be a belief, such as the belief that breaking a mirror brings bad luck. Culture traits may be either *material* (tools) or *non-material* (beliefs). They may be simple or highly complex. For example, in lighting a fire we use a match—a simple tool. To get to school you may use a car or bus—highly complex machines.

Culture traits are a part of your everyday life. You are continually choosing the correct culture trait for a specific situation. A person who does not use the accepted culture traits may find that other members of the society begin to avoid him or her. In our culture, if you are taken out to dinner at a restaurant and eat the entire meal with your fingers, you may find that people no longer want to go out to dinner with you.

Culture Complexes

Culture traits combine to form culture complexes. *A* CULTURE COMPLEX *is a cluster of interrelated traits.* For example, the game of football is a culture complex that combines a variety of traits. First, we have a number of material traits, or tools, such as the football, the measuring chain, cleated shoes, helmets, pads, first-aid kits, and warming benches. Second, we have a series of specific acts, such as kicking the ball, passing it, catching it, blocking, tackling, and running with the ball. Third, we have a group of specific beliefs related to the game, such as the belief that the players should be good sports, that certain rules should be followed in playing the game, that penalties should be imposed for violations, and that "our" team must win.

In the modern industrial cultures of today there are thousands of culture complexes. Some other examples in American culture are a school dance, lunch in the school cafeteria, a lab experiment, a business office, a retail store, and a manufacturing plant. Each of these complexes involves culture traits, or specific tools, acts, and beliefs. What other culture complexes can you name?

This culture trait (the way in which people eat) varies, depending on the culture. The tools used for eating in one culture may not be appropriate in another.

Culture Patterns

Culture complexes combine to form larger cultural units called culture patterns. CULTURE PATTERNS *are combinations of a number of culture traits and complexes into an interrelated whole.* For example, the complexes of football, basketball, softball, wrestling, boxing, track, and others all combine to form the American athletic pattern. Other patterns are related to such aspects of the culture as agriculture, manufacturing, education, transportation, and eating. A random list of some culture traits and complexes that make up the American education pattern might include classrooms, textbooks, teachers, students, desks, homework assignments, films, courses, school assemblies, marching bands, senior high schools, parochial schools, and school clubs.

Why Study about Traits, Complexes, and Patterns?

Of what value to you as an individual is this knowledge about culture traits, complexes, and patterns? The point is that you must know about traits, complexes, and patterns if you wish to understand a culture. It is impossible to study objectively a culture as a whole, since it is too large and complex. Instead, you must break it down into its various parts—into traits, complexes, and patterns. Then you can analyze the various traits as they relate to the complexes, and the various complexes as they relate to the culture patterns. Finally, you can analyze the total culture in terms of its patterns. You actually break the culture down into its various parts and then put them back together again to gain an understanding of the structure and function of the various parts and of the total culture.

As you study a culture in this way you come to realize that cultures—all cultures— have a kind of unity about them. That is, the various parts of a culture seem to fit together. The parts of some cultures may seem to fit together much better than others. Yet the traits, complexes, and patterns of all cultures blend to make any particular culture a unified whole.

Ethnocentrism

In studying cultures you will notice that they tend to be ethnocentric. "Ethno" means race, nation, or people. "Centric" means center. ETHNOCENTRISM *is the belief that our own race, nation, or group is central and is the best.* When we are ethnocentric we tend to analyze other cultures by comparing them to our own. For example, we might say that our culture is superior to the Chinese culture because we have better educational opportunities, more freedoms, and a higher standard of living. We are, however, judging the two cultures in terms of our own culture, since the Chinese would consider their culture superior to ours.

Ethnocentrism has a tremendous influence on human relations. When it takes the form of nationalism, it can make world unity and peace very difficult to achieve. The Arab-Israeli disputes are a recent example of disruptions involving nationalistic ethnocentrism. Also, ethnocentrism among members of two schools can lead to strong rivalries. Such rivalries can take the form of healthy competition or, if unchecked by reason, may result in gang fights.

Cultural Universals

The culture has a tremendous influence on the individual. It is an important force in determining what a person thinks and does. Nevertheless, there are wide ranges of behavior within a culture, since the demands of the culture affect the individual in various ways. Also, no one can participate in all of the many aspects of the culture. Everyone is forced to limit his or her participation. Although people vary in their specific forms of participation, every person participates in the culture on three different levels. The first level of participation is in the universals of the culture.

CULTURAL UNIVERSALS *are learned behaviors that are widely accepted and required by a particular society.* They are the general elements common to that society. However, cultural universals do differ from one society to the next. Culture traits that are universals in one society may be unknown in another. For example, a universal in American society is the wearing of clothes in public, a trait unknown to the members of the Suya tribe in the Amazon region of Brazil. Another universal in American culture is compulsory education up to the age of sixteen or more, whereas some cultures have no required formal schooling.

Cultural universals are very important to the individual because they indicate behaviors that are required of all members of the society. If individuals disobey the universals, they are likely to be punished by the society.

Cultural Alternatives

The culture sets up certain universal behaviors that must be followed. But it usually gives the individual a choice about how he or she will meet these universals. For example, our culture demands that we wear clothes in public. But we may choose from a wide variety of colors and styles. A girl might go to the movies wearing slacks or jeans, shorts, a dress, a skirt and blouse, or a pantsuit. Parents are required to send their children to school, but they may choose what kind of school—public, private, or parochial—the children will attend. CUL-TURAL ALTERNATIVES, *then, are the many choices open to individuals for meeting the requirements of the cultural universals.*

Cultural Specialties

The third level of participation for the individual is in the specialties of the culture. CULTURAL SPECIALTIES *are learned behaviors shared by the members of a particular social category but not by the majority of the members of the society.* These specialties involve some activity, skill, or pursuit. They are determined by such factors as age, sex, social class status, occupation, and religion. For instance, children have behaviors not shared by the majority of the society, such as playing hide-and-go-seek or hopscotch. Sex is also responsible for some specialties that particular members of the society share. For example, in our society it is usually boys who learn to play ice hockey, while girls play field hockey. A person's social class status determines many of his or her specialties, such as whether the person plays golf or goes bowling, spends leisure time at the country club or at the local tavern, and buys a yacht or a motorboat. As to occupation, a doctor has developed specialties that are very different from those of a plumber. And the factor of religion determines that the behavior of Roman Catholics during Mass is unlike that of their Baptist or Methodist friends at Protestant services.

Subcultures

The mass media often indicate that teenagers have a subculture all their own. Many sociologists would agree. What does it mean to be a member of a subculture? A SUBCULTURE *is the way of life of a number of people in a society who share the total culture of the society, but also have enough specialties not shared by the society as a whole to make them recognizable and distinct.* A list of some of the traits of the teen-age subculture might include folk-rock and country music, high school, a special vocabulary, long telephone conversations, and specific styles of dress. Other subcultures might be based on race, region, or ethnic background. Because subcultures are distinctive, they sometimes become objects of prejudice and discrimination by ethnocentric members of the society.

At this point you may be wondering how to distinguish a cultural specialty from a subculture. Actually they are very similar. But there is a difference. Electricians have certain specialties related to their job. Sales clerks also have certain specialties related to their job. Aside from their jobs, however, they have most of their learned behaviors in common. Their cultural specialties do not set them apart from the society enough to make them a subculture. On the other hand, when we compare the specialties of the teen-ager with the culture traits of the adults in the society, we find that there are a great many differences. Since so many aspects of a teen-ager's life are different from those of an adult, we can say that teen-agers have a distinct subculture. A subculture exists when a sufficient number of people share a sufficient number of cultural specialties. In other words, specialties combine to make subcultures.

SECTION REVIEW

1. What are culture traits, culture complexes, and culture patterns? How do they relate to each other?
2. What are some effects of ethnocentrism on the culture?
3. List the various alternatives we have in meeting the universals of our culture.
4. Make a list of subcultures you think are present in our society. Then decide what specific cultural specialties apply to each subculture.

KEY TERMS

Define and give an example of each term.

cultural alternative	culture pattern
cultural specialty	culture trait
cultural universal	ethnocentrism
culture	society
culture complex	subculture

SECTION 2:
Cultural Variation

There are many variations in the culture traits of various subcultures within the total culture. Yet these variations seem small when we compare the culture traits of one culture with those of another culture in another part of the world. People all over the world have many of the same basic drives, such as hunger, and are involved in many of the same activities, such as raising crops or animals. But members of different societies go about these activities in different ways. There is a considerable amount of cultural difference, because each culture develops its own particular answers to the same general problems.

Examples of Cultural Variation

What examples of the differences in customs and beliefs among cultures can you think of? The few examples that follow are enough to indicate the enormous range of diversity. For instance, in our culture we believe that when we fight a war we are to kill the enemy. The Aztecs, however, had a completely different concept of war. To them war was a means of obtaining captives for their religious sacrifices. Since they wanted live captives, they believed that killing the

Customs and beliefs about fishing show a great deal of cultural variation. Here you can compare pole fishing in the Indian Ocean with fly fishing in America.

enemy was against the rules of war. When the Spaniards arrived in 1519 and fought to kill, the Aztecs fell back in dismay, and a small Spanish force was able to conquer the Aztec nation.

Another example shows how attitudes about the rules of war vary among cultures. Years ago a European anthropologist was talking with a cannibal from an island in the Pacific Ocean on the topic of war. The European described the effective methods used in killing the enemy in World War I, which was raging in Europe. The cannibal was taken aback at the mass murder of so many people and asked how the Europeans could consume such large quantities of human flesh. The European replied that they did not eat their slain foes. The cannibal looked at him in shocked horror and asked, "What kind of barbarians are you to kill a human being for no good reason?"

There are also great differences in the way cultures view men and women. Traditionally the ideal male in American society has been the man who is aggressive and gets things done. However, Margaret Mead, a well-known anthropologist, found in her studies of societies in New Guinea that the ideal person of both sexes in the Arapesh society was gentle, responsive, and unaggressive. In the Mundugumor society the opposite was true—both men and women were expected to be aggressive, ruthless, and violent. Different, again, was the Tchambuli society, where the sex attitudes were the reverse of our own. The women had the real power. They manufactured goods, fished, controlled the business activities, and made the advances in courting. In marriage the woman tended to be the dominant, managing partner, while the man was submissive and emotionally dependent.

Causes of Cultural Variation

Why are cultures so different? Why don't people throughout the world develop similar cultures, since all people have the same basic needs? Yet some cultures are very simple and others are very advanced in their technology. Why are the rules of behavior in one culture so different from the rules in another culture? To answer these questions we will look at four factors that cause variations among cultures.

Geography. One explanation of cultural variation is the influence of geography. The climate, the topography of the land, and the natural resources all greatly affect the culture. Consider the climate and geography of the Arctic, for example. It seems logical that the Eskimos would build their houses with blocks of ice, use a sled for transportation, make their clothes from animal skins, use seal oil for heat and light, and kill fish and animals for food. They learned to use the natural resources available to satisfy their basic needs for food, clothing, and shelter.

Similarly, the geography influenced the way the early settlers on the great American plains met their basic needs. They built their houses out of strips of sod, used buffalo chips for fuel, and made their clothing from animal skins and homespun cloth. They traveled from place to place on horseback or by wagon, and relied for their food supply on the abundance of wild game and the ability of the soil to produce vegetables and cereal grains.

It seems logical that geography would

cause the inhabitants of a tropical island to have a still different way of life. They would build their homes of bamboo and thatch, travel by canoe, eat fish from the ocean and wild fruits from the jungle, and wear little clothing.

The geographic environment also places different demands upon its inhabitants. The Eskimos had to struggle constantly just to survive in their harsh, threatening natural environment. The settlers of the Great Plains had to plan ahead, since they lived in a seasonal environment. They knew that the summer growing season would be followed by autumn, when they must harvest their crops and lay in supplies for the harsh winter to come. On the other hand, the inhabitants of the tropical island did not have a natural environment that required great preparations. They didn't have to worry about cold weather, for it was always warm. Their basic concern in housing was simply to protect themselves from the rains. They didn't need to store up supplies for the future because fish and wild fruits were always available.

We can easily see the influence of geography on culture if we look at a globe or map of the world. The cultures with advanced, complex technologies are usually not those in which the natural environment is very harsh. Neither are they often found where the natural environment is always pleasant and has an abundance of natural resources. Eskimos had no time to develop an advanced culture. They had to devote their energies to the very act of survival. On the other hand, the inhabitants of the tropical island had no incentive to build a complex technological culture. All their basic needs were supplied by the environment.

It is in the moist continental regions that we find the most advanced technologies. The individuals in this climate zone must plan ahead to be prepared for four distinct seasons of the year. The different seasons and the cycles of storms bring variety and stimulation to the lives of the inhabitants. From these zones have come most of the great inventions that have made advanced technological cultures possible.

Discovery and invention. But many variations in culture cannot be explained by geography. For example, why have some Eskimos lived in igloos and other Eskimos lived in tents made of animal skins? Why did Athens and Sparta, the two city-states of ancient Greece, develop such different forms of government when they both had similar geographical environments? If we look at various cultures that have the same basic geography, we find great differences among them. Surely there must be other reasons for cultural variation.

People living in the same natural environment have the same basic needs. But they do not necessarily find the same solutions for their needs. The Eskimos needed homes for protection from the elements. Some used blocks of ice for building their homes and others used animal skins. Both solutions satisfied the need for protection from the snow and bitter cold. Similarly, people have a need for transportation, but those who lived on rivers, lakes, or oceans did not all design the same kind of water craft. They also devised many different methods to make these craft move. Some constructed oars or paddles. Others built sails to harness the power of the wind. Still others used long ropes attached to animals walking along the river bank who pulled the boats.

It would seem, then, that geographic conditions and resources do not cause variations in culture so much as they limit the kinds of variation that can develop. In other words, the geography sets the stage for finding solutions and provides us with certain natural resources. But sometimes we don't even make use of the many resources around us. For example, some tribes fashioned spear tips from flint when vast re-

sources of iron were available. Although the Greeks had discovered the power of steam, they used it as a toy. Some other societies, however, made excellent use of these natural resources. Later societies used iron to fashion complex tools and implements. Steam was harnessed to provide power for transportation, for operating machinery, and for lifting heavy loads. Why did some societies use their natural resources to advantage while others did not?

At this point we can see the importance of the part played by discovery and invention. DISCOVERY *is the finding of some element or principle not previously known.* Inventions follow discoveries. *An INVENTION is the combination of known elements or principles into some form not previously used.* For instance, members of a society may discover some element or principle not previously known, such as iron ore, the power of wind currents, or the principle of the wheel. They then may combine the known elements and principles into some new form, such as a steel-tipped spear, a sail, or a chariot.

What effect do you think the invention of the incandescent (electric) lamp has had on our lives?

Various societies have made different discoveries of natural resources and principles. They also have invented different ways of using them to solve their needs. An invention in one culture often became the basis for still other inventions in that society, which further increased the amount of cultural variation. The result has been a vast number of different cultures throughout the world.

Isolation. Why is the culture of America more like that of France than like that of the Suya tribe of Brazil? One obvious reason is that the geographic environment of the United States is more similar to that of France than to the tropics of Brazil. Also, both America and France have many discoveries and inventions, whereas the Suya have almost none. But there is another very important factor. Throughout the history of the United States we have had frequent and extensive interaction with the people of France. The two cultures have exchanged ideas, habits, and customs. In fact, many of the original American colonists were from France. But we had no interaction with the Suya. We were not a direct influence on the development of the Suya culture, and the Suya tribe did not have an influence on American culture.

The Suya tribe is an example of a culture living in isolation. ISOLATION *is simply the absence of interaction with other cultures.* In fact, the rest of the world first became aware of their existence in 1959. Because their culture had had no contact with the outside world, members of the Suya tribe were living in much the same way as they did thousands of years ago.

As a result, the Suya culture is one of the simplest found in the world today. The Suya have not developed skills in making pottery and baskets. They obtain these items by trading with neighboring tribes, who have cultures very similar to their own. The Suya catch their fish by putting herbs in the water that cause the fish to suffocate, and then picking up the dead fish. They haven't

If you lived in a culture that was isolated from all technologically advanced cultures, in what ways do you think your present life would be different?

learned how to plow the soil. Their agriculture consists simply of burning off the forest and planting seeds in holes made with sticks.

A third factor in causing culture variation, then, is the isolation of a culture from other cultures. We can say that the more interaction there is among cultures, the more similar they will be. The more isolated the cultures are from one another, the greater the variation. Also, the more interaction between two cultures, the more complex each will become—as in the case of America and France. The less interaction between cultures, the simpler they will remain—as with the Suya tribe.

Basic values. Earlier we asked why some cultures were simple while others had advanced technology. We have seen the importance of geography, inventiveness, and isolation in cultural variation. However, there is a fourth factor—the basic values of the people. BASIC VALUES *are those things which are considered important and good in a particular culture.* The basic values of the people determine their behavior and what they direct their energies toward.

If someone said "ancient Egypt," what would be your first thought? Probably you would think of pyramids. The pyramids are the best single expression of the early Egyptian culture. And they were built without the benefit of modern technology—without power cranes or air chisels. For example, the pyramid of Cheops at Gizeh reaches a height of 481 feet (146 meters) and has a base that covers thirteen acres (5.3 hectares). It contains approximately 2,300,000 blocks of limestone, which weigh about two and a half tons (2.3 metric tons) each. These blocks were cut from quarries forty miles (64 kilometers) away, floated down the Nile on barges, and then dragged up huge ramps into place. The Egyptians used no mortar, but fitted the stones together so perfectly that even today it is impossible to insert a knife blade between many of the joints.

Think of the labor involved during the thirty years of effort required to complete this great pyramid. Why? This cultural variation existed because the people put a high value on achieving immortality for their souls. They believed that they could achieve this immortality by building the pyramids.

After the industrial revolution the Western world directed its energies toward profit-making and a more comfortable life. This emphasis resulted in a complex technological culture with machines to do most of the work. But the Eastern world, until recently, developed no such technology. Why is there such a great difference between the East and the West? One reason is that the energies of the people in the Orient were directed toward aesthetic, philosophical, and religious values rather than toward technology. The Hindus believed in submitting to fate. The Buddhists believed that the supreme goal in life is for the individual to end all earthly desires. And the teachings of Confucius focused on moral and social codes to govern human relationships.

We can see, then, that religious and philosophical beliefs can motivate people to react in different ways to a particular situation. When faced with drought, one society might interpret it as the will of the gods and resign themselves to their fate. Another society would dig wells and build irrigation ditches to water their crops.

But how does an understanding of cultural variation affect you personally? Actually, it gives you a better understanding of the behavior of the individual—of yourself and others. You now know that the behavior of people often attributed to instinct or race is actually the result of the culture in which the individual lives. Race, for example, has not been established as a causal factor in cultural variation. You know that you are the person you are, to a great degree, because of the culture in which you live.

1. What variations in cultures throughout the world have resulted mainly from differences in geography, climate, and natural resources?
2. List some variations in cultures related basically to the differences in discoveries and inventions.
3. Think of some variations in cultures caused mainly by isolation from other cultures.
4. Consider historically the differences between Eastern cultures (such as those of China and Japan) and Western cultures (those of Western Europe and North America). What part has religion played in these differences?

KEY TERMS

Explain how each term affects cultural variation.

basic values	invention
discovery	isolation
geography	

SECTION 3:
Cultural Change

You can easily observe that many changes are taking place in our society. New discoveries are constantly being made in the field of science. New inventions and products are being introduced continually. Styles and fads in clothing change frequently. Old customs are being replaced by new ones. The laws are in a process of adaptation and change. Even the television programs change occasionally.

"Frank Jr. went to Yale, and Alice went to Vassar. Now, Frank III is at Vassar, and Alice Jr. is at Yale, and I'm going to pieces."

Over a period of time the changes are especially evident. For example, if you discuss with a grandparent what life was like when he or she was growing up, you'll realize that quite a few changes have taken place. You can become aware of many changes by watching old movies on television or looking through old magazines. And times will continue to change. Imagine, for instance, what young people in the year 2000 will think of your era!

There are many forces present in a society that bring about change. But there are also forces that oppose change. In every society there is a tension between change, on the one hand, and equilibrium, or balance, on the other. We call the society *dynamic* if the change is very rapid. We call the cultures that are changing very slowly *stable*, because they are almost in a state of equilibrium. But regardless of the pace, change occurs in every society. No society stands still. Some change is always taking place.

Cultural and Social Change

CULTURAL CHANGE *is the process by which new patterns of shared, learned behavior are developed to meet needs not provided by the traditional patterns.* It is a change in the culture. We should, however, make a distinction between cultural change and social change. There is a slight difference between the two. Cultural change refers to a change in the shared, learned behavior of the people. Social change refers to a change in the structure of the social relationships among the people themselves. In reality, though, culture and society are so closely interrelated that a change in one is almost always accompanied by a change in the other. The result is that distinctions between these two kinds of change are often blurred.

The Cultural Base

An important concept in the pace of change is the cultural base. *The* CULTURAL BASE *is all the culture traits of a society at a particular time.* The more culture traits (tools, acts, and beliefs) present in a culture, the more rapidly the culture will change. And every change brings other changes. For example, think of the many changes brought about by the modern automobile. Cars have influenced what we do, where we go, and how fast we get there. We do not have to attend the movie at our neighborhood theater because we can drive to the other side of the city or to the next town, if we prefer the movie showing there. The car has brought more freedom to dating. It also has permitted people to hold jobs many miles from their homes.

In many ways cultural change is like atomic fission—once the process is started it continues to expand, each change causing changes that cause other changes. The story is told about the man who worked for the United States Patent Office in the year 1900.

He resigned his position, saying that the patent office had no future because everything that could possibly be invented had been invented already. But, as you know, the United States Patent Office is very far from going out of business. As our cultural base gets larger and larger, the number of changes in the culture continues to increase.

Factors Influencing Cultural Change

What causes these changes in the culture? Actually there are a great number of causes of cultural change. However, we will limit our discussion to seven specific factors that help explain most cultural change.

Discovery and invention. The most obvious cause of change in American culture is the mass of discoveries and inventions that result from science or technology. As we mentioned earlier, there is a difference between discovery and invention.

Until a number of discoveries had been made, no one could have invented the car. Fire was essential, because it is an ingredient of the internal combustion engine. Harnessing the power of combustion was dependent on the discovery of the principle of the lever, which caused an axle to rotate. This rotating axle was then attached to a form of wheel (the gears), which transferred the power to another axle (the drive shaft). The discovery of the screw was utilized to change the direction of motion from the drive shaft to the rear axle (the differential or rear end). Wheels were then attached to the rear axle to propel the vehicle. Yet even with all of these elements and principles the invention of the car wasn't possible. Friction would overcome all of the movement involved. It was not until oil was discovered and used to limit friction that the automobile could be invented. Thus the automobile involves a great number of discoveries and inventions that were combined to build the very complex machine now so common in our culture.

Some other inventions that were dependent on a number of specific discoveries are the wagon, firearms, ships, the telephone, frozen foods, satellites, and the computer. Each new discovery and invention, if accepted by the people, brings some change in the culture. Some changes, such as "Smile" buttons and bumper stickers, may be very small. Others, such as nuclear weapons, may be very large and affect many societies. Each discovery or invention leads to more discoveries and new inventions, and results in a substantial increase in the size of the cultural base.

Spatial movement of people. People bring about changes in the culture by moving from one place to another. When immigrants arrive in a new country, they bring their old culture with them. Also, a change in the numbers of the population has an effect on the culture. Even the movement of people within a small area causes cultural change. As people move into a town more stores are needed to serve them, more houses are needed, more jobs must be found to support them, and schools must be provided for the education of their children.

We might consider four kinds of population movements. The first is the movement of people from one country or society to another. Some examples are the movement of people from Europe to the new colonies in America, the movement of Jews to Israel, and the movement of people out of South Vietnam in 1975. A second kind of population movement is from one part of a country to another part of that country. In American history we've seen the movement of people westward to the Pacific Ocean. Recently there has been a movement of people from other parts of the United States to Florida and the Southwest. The third kind of population movement is from the rural areas to the cities. It causes great change for the rural areas and the cities as well. One example of

this movement is the recent shift of Black Americans from rural areas in the South to cities as, with the advances in agricultural technology, fewer people were needed on the farms. A fourth kind of movement is from the cities to the suburban areas surrounding the cities. The greatest increase of population in the United States in the last twenty years has occurred in the suburbs.

Diffusion of cultural traits. One of the by-products of the spatial movement of people is cultural diffusion. DIFFUSION *is the process by which one society borrows culture traits from another society and includes them in its own culture.* The American culture has culture traits borrowed from all over the world. For example, we use an alphabet devised by the Phoenicians and Hebrews and modified by the Greeks and Romans. We adopted the seven-day week from Babylonia. The Arabs gave us our commonly used number system. And the Hindus made computations easier by introducing the zero. People living in many parts of the world borrowed from China and the Far East such items as gunpowder, paper, playing cards, porcelain, peaches, apricots, silk, and tea, and made them part of their own culture. The early colonists in the New World brought with them the governmental structures of Europe and, in return, gave to Europe the potato, chocolate, and tobacco. The colonists introduced the horse to the American Indians and accepted from them a new crop—maize, or Indian corn. And in modern times such articles as cars, airplanes, radios, television sets, and Coca-Cola have been diffused so widely that they are almost universal throughout the world.

Social movements. Social movements have also played a very important part in cultural change. A SOCIAL MOVEMENT *is an organized movement to bring about some change in the society.* We are familiar with such movements in America as the abolition movement, the prohibition movement, the women's rights movement, and the civil rights movement.

Social movements usually are led by people who have a special ability to speak out for a specific cause and win followers to the movements. We call this special ability *charisma,* and the leader a charismatic leader. Charisma is, in itself, neither good nor bad. A list of historical charismatic leaders might include Alexander the Great, Julius Caesar, Mohammed, Joan of Arc, Elizabeth I, Adolf Hitler, Fidel Castro, and Martin Luther King, Jr. Because the charismatic leader possesses certain personal qualities that inspire loyalty and enthusiasm, he or she often dominates a social movement in its early stages.

Laws. Most bills introduced into a legislative body suggest a change in some aspect of the society. If these bills are passed and become law they may bring about a change in the society. Not every law passed by a legislative body brings change in the culture, however, since not all laws are enforced.

Not only may new laws bring change but also a different interpretation of an old law by the courts can produce cultural change. A good example is the Supreme Court decision of 1954, which reversed an earlier decision and stated that separate schools for Black Americans actually prevented blacks from being equal. This decision made all segregated schools illegal and launched the current struggle for integration of public schools in America.

Natural disasters. Natural disasters such as droughts, plagues, hurricanes, floods, tornadoes, earthquakes, and tidal waves bring about changes in the culture. They force the people to take some action to repair

One recent social movement for cultural change in our society is the women's liberation movement. It has had an impact on the roles of both men and women.

the damage or solve the new problems created by the disaster. These natural disasters often exact a high toll in lives and money. But they may lead to a more advanced society in the end as the people become united in a common struggle. An example is the San Francisco earthquake of 1906. It cost hundreds of lives and millions of dollars in property damage. But it united the people in rebuilding the area and taking precautions against future earthquakes.

Wars. War probably brings about the greatest change in a society in the least amount of time. War causes the loss of many lives. It causes broken families, as men are inducted into the army. It brings the destruction of a tremendous amount of property and the rise of new cities out of the rubble. It causes changes in the work force, as industry shifts from the production of consumer goods to the materials of war. War also can produce advances in technology and medicine, which carry over to civilian life after the fighting ceases. Another very important factor is that wars bring a mixing of cultures as armies invade new areas. For example, the Crusades introduced the soldiers of Europe to the advanced culture of the Moslem world, and led to the expansion of trade between East and West. The American occupation of Japan after World War II introduced many American culture traits, such as business suits, to Japan. It also brought Japanese culture traits, such as precision-built cameras, back to America.

These are some of the more important causes of cultural change. They are the forces that tend to bring changes in a culture as the people in the society try to adapt to the new situations that face them.

SECTION REVIEW

1. Why is it impossible for a society to stand still?

2. Why is the cultural base so important in determining the speed at which a culture will change?
3. What are the seven causes of cultural change discussed in this section?
4. What other causes of cultural change can you think of in addition to these seven?

KEY TERMS

Explain the meaning of each term.

cultural base
cultural change
diffusion
dynamic society

social change
social movement
stable society

SECTION 4:
Resistance to Cultural Change

Just as there are factors that tend to bring about change, there are many factors present in a society that tend to resist change. Every time someone suggests a change in the social system, others immediately begin to oppose the change. There is the story of a man who was being interviewed by the press on his ninety-fifth birthday. One of the reporters said, "I imagine you've seen a lot of changes in your time." To which the old man replied, "I sure have, mister, and I was agin' every one of 'em."

Factors Influencing Resistance to Change

There are too many factors that cause a society to resist change for us to discuss them all. However, a consideration of the following six factors will help us understand why most new ideas are met with some resistance.

Habit. People are creatures of habit. Once we become conditioned to think or act in a particular way, we find it difficult to change. This is evident when a school that runs on a fixed schedule alters it one day to make time for a special assembly. The change often causes confusion among both students and teachers.

Many customs are carried over from previous generations simply because of habit. They may no longer serve the purpose for which they were originally intended. But still they are continued. For example, shaking hands as a form of greeting is still used today, although the original purpose is gone. Originally people shook hands to show each other that they were not carrying a weapon.

Another ancient custom that has survived long past its usefulness is the tipping of the hat by gentlemen on meeting a lady. This custom originated when men wore armor and their helmets covered part of their faces. A man would then lift his helmet on meeting a lady so that the woman could identify him. Although hat tipping is not universal today in our society, it was a common practice only a decade or two ago and is still practiced by some men. The habit of males walking on the curb side of the walk when with females is also left over from the Middle Ages. At that time townspeople often threw their garbage out of second-story windows toward the street. People nearest the curb were in the greatest danger of being hit. As you can see, even habits that are no longer funcional put up great resistance to change.

Another example of the strength of habit is cigarette smoking in this country. In recent years there has been considerable discussion on the relationship between disease, particularly lung cancer, and the smoking of cigarettes. Although the evidence released by scientists supports a clear relationship between cigarette smoking and diseases, many people refuse to change their smoking habits.

Closely related to habit is a fear of the new or the unknown. For example, people opposed the first railroad because they be-

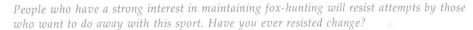

People who have a strong interest in maintaining fox-hunting will resist attempts by those who want to do away with this sport. Have you ever resisted change?

lieved that the human body could not stand movement at speeds as high as twenty miles an hour. Some resistance to change occurs just because it is new and contains an element of the unknown.

Vested interests. The person who is satisfied with the present is never in favor of change. People have a vested interest in preserving things as they are because they like the present and don't know how they would fare with change. For instance, it is not unusual for upper-class persons of considerable wealth, who are faring very well with the way things are, to oppose tax reform, which would result in higher taxes for them. Similarly, some house painters opposed the introduction of spray guns, fearing that the use of spray guns would take away their jobs.

People who have a vested interest in the way things are will resist change. On the other hand, the person who feels that things are so bad at present that any change would certainly be an improvement is likely to accept change. According to this view, a change could not make conditions much worse and might make life a good deal better.

Religious beliefs. People's religious beliefs may cause them to resist changes. Resistance generally occurs when the change clashes with an established religious doctrine. Some members of the clergy condemned the use of ether as an anesthetic after its first public demonstration. They said that to take away patients' consciousness denied these patients their last chance for repentance if they should die during the operation. We are all familiar with the problems faced in India because of the Hindu belief that cows are sacred. Some Hindus will not kill any animal or insect, since it may have a human soul. Sacred cows trample gardens and insects spread disease, but any attempts to change this situation are met with fierce resistance.

Ethnocentrism. Many people tend to take pride in their own cultural heritage and to oppose any idea or product that comes from a foreign country. When foreign-built cars first appeared in America, there was a strong feeling against them. Some people looked on the act of purchasing one as un-American. What other examples can you think of in which ethnocentrism has caused people to resist change?

Cultural lag. It is much easier to convince people to adopt some new tool or invention than it is to convince them to change their religious beliefs or social practices. The homemaker can easily see the many advantages of owning a new automatic washing machine. It is far more difficult to convince that person to practice Buddhism rather than his or her present religion. In our society technological changes are usually accepted faster than changes in other areas, such as social customs or religion. *This situation, in which some aspects of a society change less rapidly than, or lag behind, other aspects of that same society, is called* CULTURAL LAG. Since the material aspects of a society change more rapidly than the nonmaterial aspects, there is a time lag, or cultural lag, until the nonmaterial changes catch up to technological changes. Think of some examples of cultural lag in our society.

One example of cultural lag is the difference between the large advancements made in the weapons of war, and the lack of advancements in the area of international cooperation. Nations now are able to kill millions of people in a very short time. Yet they resist the changes necessary to secure world peace.

The change causes too many problems. Some changes are resisted because they cause more problems than they solve. For instance, we are all aware of the complexity of the English language, particularly in spelling. To solve this problem a student once wrote an essay entitled "How to Simplify

Many people are proud of their cultural heritage and wish to preserve it rather than to change their ways and lose this heritage.

the English Language." The essay showed how we could change the language so that every letter of the alphabet had only two specific sounds, a "high" sound and a "low" sound. No two words sounded the same or had the same meaning. Spelling was very simple, since the word was spelled exactly as it sounded when spoken. It was a brilliant system. But would we accept it in place of the present system? The answer is no. The problems of adopting a completely new system would be too great. To introduce it would mean that the millions of people who now speak English would have to learn a whole new language.

Another example is the new typewriter keyboard designed to make typing much easier. The letters have been rearranged so that the fingers do not move around as much

as on the old keyboard. A person could type more rapidly with much less effort. This new keyboard may sound like a great improvement. But it creates a problem for all those people who have learned how to type by the conventional system and would have to learn to type all over again.

You now know about some of the causes of cultural change and some factors that tend to resist change. Probably you can think of other factors that have not been mentioned. Through our consideration of cultural change you should have a better idea of the tension that exists between change and equilibrium in every society, and more specifically in our own society. From this discussion of the structure and variations of culture, you can now see how important culture is in shaping our behavior.

SECTION REVIEW

1. What are some factors that cause resistance to cultural change?
2. Give examples not mentioned in the text for each of the six factors given.
3. What other factors can you think of that might cause people to put up a resistance to cultural change?
4. Which factors do you feel are most important today in resisting changes in our society?

KEY TERMS

Explain the relationship of each term to cultural change.

cultural lag   habit
ethnocentrism   vested interest

PROJECTS AND ACTIVITIES

1. Discuss the different kinds of foods that are eaten throughout the world. What foods not eaten in one country are considered delicacies in another?

2. Construct a poster or bulletin board that illustrates some of the cultural universals that you've seen presented in television commercials.

3. Do research on various social movements in the past to determine how they've brought lasting changes to the culture.

4. Design and build a game that can actually be played. Then analyze the culture traits involved in playing the game.

5. Have a foreign student speak to your class about the differences between his or her culture and yours.

6. Make lists of cultural specialties related to the following: age, sex, social class position, occupation, and region of the country.

7. Collect some copies of old magazines and bring them to class. Study the magazines and then discuss how the culture traits, complexes, and patterns of today differ from those portrayed in the magazines.

8. Have a panel discussion by persons who have visited other cultures. Have them pick out certain patterns (such as education, eating, transportation, dress) and discuss the differences in the culture traits of the various cultures.

9. Read the novel *Lord of the Flies* by William Golding. Make a comparison between the culture that the boys tried to establish and the one they had come from.

10. Write a short story in which you show how cultural differences can cause conflict.

11. Design a bulletin board showing what life in some other culture is like. You might use such magazines as *National Geographic*.

12. Portray the kind of culture you would like to live in as an adult (or predict what you think it might actually be) through a collage, photo display, drawing, painting, short story, or drama.

TOPICS FOR INQUIRY

1. What are some problems you would face if you were to live in a different culture for a year as an exchange student? What could you do before you left home to help alleviate some of these problems?

2. Which aspects of your behavior may be attributed to the culture? Which cannot be attributed to the culture?

3. Debate or discuss: There is an overemphasis on the material aspects of American culture.

4. Discuss the cultural alternatives and universals that are found in your community.

5. Suppose you were in charge of building a new electronics plant in some other culture. What would you need to know about the culture before building the plant so that you could hire the workers that would be needed? What would you need to know to be able to establish good relationships with both the workers and the community at large?

6. Discuss the positive and negative effects of ethnocentrism.

7. Consider your own community in terms of cultural change. How rapidly is change taking place? Which factors influencing change or resisting change do you feel have been most influential in your community?

8. Considering the importance of the cultural base in social change, what would you predict about the speed of cultural change in the future? In what direction do you think this cultural change will develop?

9. What are some reasons why nations go to war with other nations? Do you think that wars can ever be justified? How would your own life be affected if our nation were involved in a major war?

10. Do you think that teen-agers accept change more willingly than adults? How would you attempt to explain this?

SUGGESTIONS FOR READING

NONFICTION

BENEDICT, Ruth, *Patterns of Culture*. Houghton Mifflin, 1961 (and pap.). A basic book on social anthropology and one of the best known analyses of culture.

GOLD, Herbert, *Fathers*. Random House, 1967 or Fawcett World (pap.). A story of a Russian-Jewish immigrant boy growing up in America and the conflict and misunderstanding he has with his "old-world" parents.

HARRIS, Marvin, *Cows, Pigs, Wars, and Witches: The Riddles of Culture*. Random House, 1974. An anthropologist gives insights into why people behave the way they do.

MCLUHAN, Marshall and NEVITT, Barrington, *Take Today: The Executive as Dropout*. Harcourt Brace Jovanovich, 1972. This book explores the role of human beings in an age of rapid technological change.

MEAD, Margaret, *Sex and Temperament in Three Primitive Societies*. Peter Smith, 1963 or Morrow (pap.). Her famous study of the Arapesh, Mundugumor, and Tchambuli societies in New Guinea.

SEVERIN, Timothy, *The Horizon Book of Vanishing Primitive Man*. American Heritage, 1973. Describes the evolution of prehistoric peoples and explores the societies of the Australian Aborigines, Polynesians, Pygmies, Bushmen, Ainu, and others.

SLATER, Phillip E., *The Pursuit of Loneliness: American Culture at the Breaking Point*. Beacon, 1971 (pap.). A critique of American culture.

TOFFLER, Alvin, *Future Shock*. Bantam, 1971 (pap.). This best seller discusses the problems people face in adapting to the rapid social and technological changes taking place in our society.

TRIPP, Maggie (ed.), *Woman in the Year 2000*. Arbor House, 1974. A collection of twenty-one essays which speculate on what women's (and men's) lives might be like in the year 2000.

WATTENBERG, Ben J., *The Real America: A Surprising Examination of the State of the Union*. Doubleday, 1974. The author gives an optimistic look at American culture through the use of data from such sources as the census, industry, and opinion polls.

WOLFE, Tom, *The Pump House Gang*. Farrar, Straus & Giroux, 1968 or Bantam (pap.). A study of the subcultures formed by motorcyclists, surfers, teen-agers, and others.

WONG, Jade Snow, *Fifth Chinese Daughter*. Harper & Row, 1950. An autobiography by a Chinese girl growing up in contemporary America but forced by her family to maintain the old Chinese traditions.

FICTION

ANAYA, Rudolfo A., *Bless Me, Ultima*. Quinto Sol Publications (pap.). A novel dealing with a young Mexican American's adjustments to the differences between home life and school life.

HERSEY, John R., *A Bell for Adano*. Bantam (pap.). Failure to understand the culture of a small Italian village brings a number of problems for American soldiers during World War II.

HUXLEY, Aldous, *Brave New World* and *Brave New World Revisited*. Harper & Row (pap.). A fictional culture based on the American culture and what might possibly be its final outcome.

POTOK, Chaim, *The Chosen*. Simon & Schuster or Fawcett World (pap.). *The Chosen* portrays the conflicts of two young Jewish boys from opposing sects, and their growth toward humanism and understanding.

SINCLAIR, Upton, *The Jungle*. New American Library (pap.). The culture and society of the immigrant in America are graphically portrayed.

SKINNER, B. F., *Walden Two*. Macmillan (pap.). An idea for a perfect society that involves the control of the individual from birth.

SNEIDER, Vern J., *Teahouse of the August Moon*. Putnam. A story of cultural misunderstandings between the Okinawans and the American occupation forces on Okinawa during World War II.

3 Cultural Values, Norms, and Sanctions

▶ What rules govern your behavior in society?

▶ Can a society exist without rules?

▶ How do societies deal with people who break the rules?

SECTION 1:
The Rules We Live By

Can you imagine living in a society and yet being able to do whatever you want all the time? Actually, everyone must live pretty much according to the rules that the society provides. Usually we aren't aware of many of these rules. We've learned them so well and believe in them so thoroughly that we take them for granted. For example, you get up in the morning and come to school. You wear jeans or shorts when you mow the lawn, and a suit or long dress when you attend a formal dance. If you are driving a car, you stop when the traffic signal is red and go when it is green. If a friend has a camera that you like very much, you don't steal it from him or her—you save money and buy one like it. Every action you make

is governed to some degree by the rules of the society. In fact, without such rules you would find it extremely difficult, if not impossible, even to go about your daily activities. No one could trust anyone else. Life would become utterly unpredictable and insecure.

Cultural Values

The rules of the society are developed from the cultural values. CULTURAL VALUES *are shared assumptions of what is right, good, or important.* They are largely unconscious. If you were asked to make a list of your values on a sheet of paper, you might find it very difficult to do. Yet these same values guide your behavior in most situations of life. All of us have values that channel our behavior. These values come from the cultural values of our society.

Cultural values are different in different societies. What is considered as right, good,

53

or important in one society may be regarded as wrong, bad, or unimportant in another. Also, the cultural values of a particular society may change over time. For example, ten years ago law schools in the United States emphasized preparing their graduates for private practice in such areas as tax, property, securities, and corporate law. Now legal work in public service areas has become increasingly more important and highly valued. The goals of many law students have shifted toward public service-oriented legal careers.

What are some of the basic values of our culture? What values seem to be common to the majority of people who live in the United States? Eight suggested values are given here for your consideration. Remember that they are not fact. They are suggested hypotheses. Do you agree with them? Examine our society to see if these values are actually present.

1. Americans place a high value on *individual endeavor,* on a person working hard to achieve success. The heroes in America are the individuals who use personal initiative and get things done. One example is Benjamin Franklin. In general, it is the enterprising entrepreneur, rather than the priest, teacher, artist, scholar, or soldier, who has gained the higher respect in our society.

2. Americans put great importance on *education.* Many feel that a high school education is a necessity. Often young people also seek some additional type of education, such as vocational or apprenticeship programs, or college courses.

3. Our society puts value on *bigness.* We strive for bigger homes, larger corporations, and higher skyscrapers. We are impressed by

One of the values often found in a heavily technological society, such as in the United States or Germany, is efficiency.

large numbers. We even discuss our art galleries and athletic stadiums in terms of how many people they can accommodate.

4. We value the freedom of *spatial movement*. Americans are constantly on the go, moving from place to place. We drive long distances to attend a particular movie or sports event. We commute for miles by bus, subway, or train to our jobs. And occasionally we move from one community to another.

5. Our society is concerned with *time*. We strive to conquer it by building machines that will do more work per hour, and producing planes and cars that can take us places faster. A watch is a necessity, because every activity must start precisely on time.

6. Americans attach great value to *technology*. We strive to have a machine for every need. We are constantly making technological advances. We not only develop a computer but also continually improve on the original model.

7. The members of our culture are very concerned about their *physical comfort*. However, it is a comfort based not so much on rest and relaxation as on possessions. We work overtime and pinch our pennies so that we can buy a more comfortable home, a newer automobile, more furniture, a color television set, or automatic appliances.

8. In America there is a great emphasis on *self-improvement*. People are encouraged not to be content to remain as they are but to strive constantly to improve themselves. Consider, for example, the popularity of courses in great books, foreign languages, art appreciation, reading faster, or self-improvement. Sometimes this emphasis is carried so far that people study literature, art, or music not for personal enjoyment but to impress others.

Do you find these values reflected in the activities around you? Are the values of teen-agers different from those of the adult population? You can see how the values of other cultures differ from ours by comparing American values with those of various African cultures or Oriental societies.

Social Norms

The cultural values of a society determine the social norms of the society. *The SOCIAL NORMS are the group-shared rules of behavior.* These norms are the expected ways of behaving in the society based on the shared values —the purposes and goals—of that society. For example, because we place some value on physical modesty, we have the social norm of wearing clothes in public. To be accepted members of our society, we must live by the rules which that society imposes on us. When a person doesn't behave according to these norms, he or she is considered a deviant. Someone who walks down the main street of an American city without clothes on is regarded as a deviant, since he or she is not following the standard rules of behavior.

Some norms apply to all persons in a particular situation. For example, in our culture all persons are expected to be quiet in a library, obey the traffic signals, eat with a knife, fork, and spoon, stand during the playing of the National Anthem, and pay their bills. These are just a few of the many norms that every member of our society is expected to follow.

Other norms, however, apply to the individual. They may vary from one person to another. These norms are related to the individual's special role. *A ROLE is the behavior expected of a person because of his or her position in the social structure or group.* Roles are actually specific norms related to the particular position of the individual. They tell people how they are to behave in their particular position in the society or the group. For example, an onlooker and a doctor would have different roles to play if both were at the scene of a serious car crash in which several persons were critically injured. The role of the doctor would demand that he or she give first aid to try to save the lives of the injured. The role of the onlooker might simply require the person to stay out of the way.

People who have a particular position in a group are also expected to follow special norms not expected of the other members of the group. The president of a club is expected to follow norms quite different from those of the treasurer. And both have norms not expected of the other members of the club. In your school band the norms of behavior for the drum major are different from those of the tuba player and the other members of the band. In the family the norms for a parent are different from those of a child.

Thus some norms apply to all individuals in a particular situation, such as all persons in a library. Others apply to individuals who hold specific positions in the society or the group, such as students, musicians, police officers, secretaries, or farmers. An individual might have different norms because of his or her position. But that person is still expected to keep the norms related to specific situations. For example, the musician is expected to obey the traffic signals and so is the president of your student body. Under extreme circumstances, however, the norms for a particular situation are temporarily suspended for a person in a specific position. The police officer is expected to obey the same traffic signals as all other motorists unless he or she is chasing a suspect. In this case the police officer may go above the speed limit and ignore the traffic signals.

Many of the norms are written or explained. However, many are never even stated. We do have signs in the library that say "Silence Please," as well as other signs saying "Yield," "Stop," "No Soliciting," or "No Loitering." But there are no signs telling us to wear clothes, eat with a knife, fork, and spoon, or brush our teeth. As children, we learn many of the norms from the example of others. These norms become so much a part of our lives that we are no longer aware of them. Even the norms that are specifically stated become a part of us so that we obey them automatically. For example, when we're driving and come to a red traffic signal, we don't think about the meaning of that signal. We automatically stop. So it is with most of the norms of our society. They are so much a part of our everyday lives that we take them for granted.

Kinds of Norms

We can categorize social norms according to how important they are in the society and how severe the punishment for violating them is. There are three basic kinds of norms—folkways, mores, and laws. Of these three, the punishment for disobeying folkways is the least severe. The punishment for violating laws is the most severe.

Folkways. FOLKWAYS *are the etiquette and customs of a people that are not of critical importance to the society.* They are important in establishing order and predictability in the many lesser matters of life. Violation of a folkway, however, isn't critical. Take down the American flag before night fall or rain. Don't call the principal by his or her first name. Don't park in the "No Parking" zone. Don't play a trumpet in your home late at night. Be courteous to your elders. All of these are folkways in our society. If you violate one of them you would not endanger the society. And you would not be severely punished. You might receive a reprimand or a parking ticket. You might be considered boorish, thoughtless, or a nuisance. But you would not be regarded as evil or immoral.

Mores. MORES *are rules of behavior that are very important to the society and whose violation would endanger its basic stability.* Do not kill. Do not steal. Do not set fire to

56

The practice of "queuing up," or forming a line, while waiting at a bus stop is a folkway that can be seen frequently in Great Britain.

your neighbor's house. Do not destroy public property. Do not cheat on final exams. These are mores in American society. The violation of any of these mores by a large number of people would endanger the well-being of the society. As a result, the punishments involved are harsh. The person who violates the mores is regarded as immoral. Most people would not even consider violating the mores, though. They have come to think of them as right and proper to the extent that the mores are not open to question. For instance, people do not question whether murder is right or wrong. They believe that murder is immoral and they severely condemn any violators.

Many of the mores are negative. They tell us what we should not do. These negative mores are the "shalt nots" of the culture. Positive mores, on the other hand, tell us what we should do. For example, our cultural norms tell us that if we are present when a person is in danger of losing his or her life, we should offer help. Mores can be positive or negative, depending on how they are stated. For example, the negative rule of Confucius: "What you do not want done to yourself, do not do to others," was stated by Jesus in the positive form: "What you wish that others would do to you, do so to them."

Laws. As the society becomes more impersonal and complex, many of the folkways and mores become laws. LAWS *are norms set up and enforced by the state.* All of the mores listed here are laws except cheating on final exams. How can you distinguish between laws and mores? The laws are set up and enforced by the state. The mores and folkways are set up, maintained, and enforced by public sentiment. For example, if the state legislature made cheating on final exams illegal in your state and you were caught cheating, you would have broken a law. On the other hand, if your state had no policy on cheating but your cheating was in violation of the sentiments of the students, faculty, and administration at your school, you would have violated one of the mores. Laws are formalized norms that specify the rules of behavior and the punishment for violation. They are the most definite of the three kinds of social norms.

1. What values of our culture can you name in addition to the eight mentioned here?
2. How do the norms in our society affect a person's role? Give an example.
3. What are the various kinds of norms and what is the relative importance of each?
4. Describe what a society might be like without some basic norms.

KEY TERMS

Define and give an example of each term.

cultural values	mores
folkways	roles
laws	social norms

SECTION 2:
Internalization, Sanctions, and Social Control

We've seen that every society sets up rules to govern the behavior of its members. Norms are necessary to provide order and prevent chaos. But what makes the people in a society conform to the social norms? There are two basic ways in which norms are enforced—internalization and sanctions.

Internalization

Internalization accounts for most of the norm conformity in a society. INTERNALIZATION *occurs as people come to believe that a particular norm is good, useful, or appropriate. They willingly obey it and expect others to do the same.* The norm becomes internalized. Think of all the things you do because you've come to realize that they ought to be done, got into the habit of doing them, and don't even think about them any more. Imagine if you had to constantly decide when to brush your teeth, or how to wait for the bus, or what to do with a napkin. Instead, we've internalized many of the norms governing routine behavior.

We don't eat with a fork and knife, put shoes on, or drive on the right side of the road because we want a reward, or because we're worried about being punished if we do not follow these norms. In fact, society could not enforce its laws if every citizen obeyed them only because of fear of arrest. There would not be enough police around to catch all violators. And who would watch the police? Instead, we don't even think about laws the greater part of the time— we have internalized them.

Sanctions

But internalization is not sufficient to enforce conformity to all the norms, especially in complex societies such as our own. Imagine a society with a large number of subcultures, each with a somewhat different perspective on the norms. In such a case it is less likely that enough people will internalize a sufficient number of norms to insure an orderly society. Also, everyone does not internalize every norm. Therefore, the society must develop sanctions. SANCTIONS *are the rewards or punishments that the society or group sets up to enforce the norms.* Just as internalization occurs in all societies, every society develops sanctions that accompany norms. The society or group imposes sanctions on members who violate the norms. In this way it protects itself from the chaos that would result if the norms were not obeyed.

Positive and negative sanctions. *The sanctions that are rewards are called* POSITIVE SANCTIONS. Positive sanctions, such as

praise, awards, or bonuses, are used to encourage certain norms of behavior. If people behave in a specific way and are rewarded, they are very apt to behave in the same way again. Their behavior is reinforced by the reward. After they've been reinforced a sufficient number of times, they become conditioned to always respond in the same way. For example, you may study hard during a particular grading period and receive excellent grades. These grades make you feel good. They are a positive sanction, or reward. They reinforce your behavior of studying so that you are likely to work hard during the next grading period to again get high grades. Over a period of time you may learn to always work hard on your assignments. (You may also internalize the norm of studying hard.)

Sanctions that are punishments are called

NEGATIVE SANCTIONS. Negative sanctions, such as ridicule, fines, or imprisonment, are applied to those people who do not conform to the norms. The purpose of negative sanctions is to enforce the social or group norms. Children who hit their playmates may get a spanking. If children are spanked every time they hit a playmate, eventually they stop hitting. The negative sanction, or punishment, has caused them to stop a behavior act. The punishment of a fine for driving on the left side of the road enforces conformity to the norm of driving on the right. After people have been fined one or more times, they usually avoid driving on the left side because they don't want to pay another fine. Or they may always drive on the right side to *avoid* being fined.

Physical and psychological sanctions. Just as sanctions may be classified as positive or

SANCTIONS

	POSITIVE SANCTIONS	NEGATIVE SANCTIONS
PHYSICAL SANCTIONS	candy money gifts trips use of the car bonuses	spanking imprisonment beating death penalty denied use of car fines
PSYCHOLOGICAL SANCTIONS	ribbons, badges, awards personal recognition praise flattery social acceptance promises	name calling ridicule threats fear rejection sarcasm

negative, they may also be classified as physical or psychological. *A* PHYSICAL SANCTION *involves the physical well-being of the individual.* It brings physical pleasure or pain to the person. One example of physical sanction is money. We can use money to pay for a good dinner, or to buy material objects that bring physical pleasure, such as a comfortable chair or a new sweater. In these cases the sanction is both physical and positive.

Physical sanctions may also be negative. Just as money gives us pleasant experiences, the loss of money is a negative experience. It denies us objects that we were going to buy. For example, the person fined by the judge for driving on the wrong side of the road can no longer use that money for his or her own pleasure. Also, the physical sanction itself may be unpleasant or painful, as in the case of a spanking or imprisonment.

A PSYCHOLOGICAL SANCTION *is related to the feelings and emotions of the individual.* Psychological sanctions can make people feel good, because they are accepted, or feel bad, because they are rejected. Psychological sanctions usually apply to the social relationships of individuals. Examples of positive psychological sanctions are ribbons, badges, or awards. These have no physical value to the individual. Instead they are symbols that give the individual status and the admiration of others. Name calling and ridicule are good examples of negative psychological sanctions. To be called an "idiot," "jerk," or "slob" suggests the loss of acceptance by the group. And loss of acceptance, or rejection, is a very effective negative psychological sanction. People are social beings and desire the companionship of others. Therefore, the psychological sanctions exert a great force in bringing about conformity to the norms of the group.

All sanctions are either positive or negative, and also either physical or psychological. The chart above shows the double characteristic of sanctions.

Formal and informal sanctions. All sanctions may also be classified according to a third characteristic, formal or informal. Whether a sanction is formal or informal is determined by whom and how it is administered. FORMAL SANCTIONS *are rewards or punishments used to enforce the laws—the enacted rules—of organizations, institutions, or states, and are carried out by some regulatory body.* Detention after school or suspension are formal sanctions carried out by school administrators. A parking ticket is a formal sanction imposed by law through the municipal judge. Imprisonment or the death penalty are formal sanctions carried out by the state through its judicial system. These examples are all physical sanctions. Formal sanctions are more often physical than psychological. However, formal sanctions may also be psychological. The assistant principal or dean might threaten to expel you from school, which would be a formal negative psychological sanction. Or a judge might threaten you with a large fine or imprisonment if you appeared before him or her again on the same charge. Formal positive psychological sanctions include badges, insignias, and awards given by some formal organization, such as a school, government, business corporation, or the military.

Formal sanctions, such as imprisonment or dismissal from a job, are set down by the state or some other formal organization on an impersonal basis. INFORMAL SANCTIONS *tend to be unwritten and based on personal relations.* Informal sanctions involve both folkways and mores, and are carried out by public opinion. Some common sanctions in this classification are approval, compliments, social acceptance, group rejection, insults, and gossip. Informal sanctions are most often psychological. But informal sanctions may also be physical. For example, the people in the neighborhood could take up a collection among themselves for one of their neighbors in recognition of some achievement or deed. Or a parent may slap the hand of a young child who is reaching for a hot pan on the stove.

Social Control

Thus every social sanction has three characteristics. It is positive or negative, physical or psychological, and formal or informal. The function of every sanction is to enforce the norms of the group or society. The purpose of enforcing the norms is to provide

To realize the importance of social control, think about a situation in which social control has been lost. What happens? Can a society function this way?

social control. Sanctions are used to control the behavior of the members of the group or society. When the norms are enforced to the degree that almost all of the people in the society conform to them, then social control exists. When the sanctions are ineffective and the norms cannot be enforced, control is lost, as in the case of riots. No society can survive for long without some measure of social control. Its members must abide by certain rules of behavior for the society to function smoothly.

The Interrelationships of Values, Norms, and Sanctions

Values, norms, and sanctions are all closely related. In any society there is some agreement as to what is right, good, and important. From this agreement come the basic values of the culture. From these basic values emerge the norms of the culture—the folkways, mores, and the laws. These norms tell the members of the society how they are expected to behave. They are the rules by which the members of the society live together. In every society, however, there are some individuals who refuse to obey the norms and threaten the stability of the society. Therefore, the society sets up a number of sanctions, with which it enforces the norms.

As you can see, the relationship between norms and sanctions is very close. In fact, sanctions are so closely related to norms that sanctions in use become norms. For example, when a parent spanks a child, the spanking, which is a sanction, becomes a folkway. Spanking children is one of the folkways of the American culture. The sanction of offering scholarship awards to students is a folkway. It is one of the ways that students are rewarded in American schools. When an individual is fined for a traffic violation, the fine is a folkway. It is the customary way of dealing with traffic violations in our society.

We should remember, also, that values, norms, and sanctions are all culture traits. We defined a culture trait as an individual tool, act, or belief related to a particular situation or need. Values and norms are beliefs or ideas related to a situation or need. And sanctions, when carried out, are acts.

How do cultural values, norms, and sanctions affect us personally? Obviously, they play a very important part in our daily lives. We were born into a culture that has provided us with a set of ready-made values. From these values come norms, or rules of behavior, which we are expected to follow. In case we might not always follow the norms, the society has established sanctions to try to make us conform. The social norms also define our roles, which determine our group relationships. Every group to which we belong has a set of values, norms, and sanctions for the purpose of maintaining social control in the group. An awareness of these values, norms, and sanctions helps us to be accepted by groups of our peers. It also aids us in our relationships with others in the society.

SECTION REVIEW

1. What happens when a norm becomes internalized?
2. What are the different ways in which social sanctions may be classified?
3. Why is social control so important for a society?
4. How are values, norms, and sanctions interrelated?

KEY TERMS

Define and give an example of each term.

formal sanction
informal sanction
internalization
negative sanction
physical sanction

positive sanction
psychological
  sanction
sanction
social control

PROJECTS AND ACTIVITIES

1. Make a list of the things that you value most in your life. Compare your list with the values of the society. Are there conflicts between your personal list and the values of the society? If so, how might you resolve these conflicts?

2. Conduct an analysis of ads in national magazines to determine what values it promotes in our society.

3. Prepare a collage or photo display that shows some of the many norms of our society.

4. Do research to determine which mores of the Bible have become laws in our society.

5. Make a study of the state laws of your state and the severity of the punishment for breaking these laws. How does the seriousness of the crime relate to the severity of the punishment? Do some punishments seem to be out of proportion to the offense? Explain.

6. Carry a small index card in your pocket or purse and record all of the sanctions that are used on you or by you over a specific period of time, such as a day. Tabulate your results. Which sanctions are used most frequently? Which are most effective? Which are least effective?

7. If possible, interview two police officers, one in a small town and the other in a large city. Ask them about the amount of norm breaking in their communities and the various methods used to establish social control. Then compare the two communities to determine what cultural factors make the difference in social control (if there is a difference) between the two communities.

8. Make a study of social control at your school. What values, norms, and sanctions are involved? Consider these in terms of the administration and faculty and also in terms of the student body. How do they differ?

9. Collect articles from daily newspapers that concern values, norms, sanctions, and social control. Bring the articles (or written summaries of the articles) to class and discuss.

TOPICS FOR INQUIRY

1. Do you think that Americans place too much value on money, material goods, and material success? Explain.

2. What are some problems that you face as teen-agers because of the great emphasis on individualism and individual achievement in our society?

3. In what ways are the values of American society changing? Do you think the changes are desirable or undesirable? Why?

4. Do you think it would be possible to have a society in which all people could "do their own thing"? Why or why not? How might the number of norms in a society relate to the number of people and the complexity of social organization?

5. How do you as an individual find a happy medium between individualism and conformity? For example, if you are too individualistic, you become isolated from society. On the other hand, if you conform completely to all of society's norms, you cease being a unique, growing individual. How might you resolve this problem in your own life?

6. Several American Indians belonging to a tribe that smokes peyote for religious ceremonies were caught smoking it by narcotics agents and arrested. Do you believe that the Indians are guilty legally? Are they guilty sociologically? Should they be punished? If so, how should they be punished?

7. Make lists of positive and negative sanctions used in our society. Which are most common—positive or negative sanctions? How would you explain this?

8. Social control is kept in a society either through internalization of the norms or the application of sanctions. Suppose you were an adviser to the federal government. Your job was to design a program that would bring about better social control. How would you design a program that would provide the best possible social control with the least loss of individual freedom? Discuss various aspects of the programs you might develop.

SUGGESTIONS FOR READING

NONFICTION

BRASCH, Rudolph, *How Did It Begin? Customs and Superstitions and Their Romantic Origins.* McKay, 1966. A book that reveals how many customs and superstitions got started.

FASTEAU, Marc Feigen, *The Male Machine.* McGraw-Hill, 1974. The author sees male role stereotyping as forcing the man into becoming a kind of competitive, unemotional, efficient, and self-contained "machine."

FILENE, Peter Gabriel, *Him/Her/Self: Sex Roles in Modern America*. Harcourt Brace Jovanovich, 1975. Traces the evolution of the self-image and sex roles of middle-class people from the mid-1800's to the present.

HARRIS, Janet, *The Prime of Ms. America*. Putnam, 1975. Deals with the problem of middle-aged, middle-income women whose traditional role is shaken by changing social concepts.

WHYTE, William F., *Street Corner Society: The Social Structure of an Italian Slum*. Rev. ed., University of Chicago Press, 1955. A description and analysis of the behavior of youth in a slum community during the depression of the 1930's. There are excellent discussions of norms and the sanctions that support them.

WHYTE, William H., Jr., *The Organization Man*. Simon & Schuster, 1972 (pap.). A study of the shift in values that accompanied the bureaucratization of American society.

FICTION

LEE, Harper, *To Kill a Mockingbird*. Lippincott or Popular Library (pap.). The values of a small southern town are brought into focus in this novel of prejudice, courage, and understanding.

LEWIS, Sinclair, *Babbitt* and *Main Street*. New American Library (pap.). In these novels Lewis presents a picture of the falseness and pretenses of middle-class America in the 1920's.

O'NEILL, Eugene, *The Hairy Ape*. Random House (pap.). A timeless play that satirizes society's view of itself through the actions of a young sailor who decides he is better than an animal but loses to an ape in the zoo.

PASTERNAK, Boris, *Dr. Zhivago*. Pantheon or New American Library (pap.). Focusing on the conflicts of a young poet in revolutionary Russia, the book makes a general statement about the artist's place in a controlled society.

Highlight

How does your culture affect your life?

In discussing the meaning of culture in Chapter 2, this text makes the point that people are products of their cultural environment. It says that without it, people would not be human. You have every right to be skeptical of this point, however. You might wonder if people don't have certain essential qualities that make them what they are, regardless of the culture in which they live. Aren't you what you are, wherever you may find yourself?

This statement that people become human only within a cultural context is a broad hypothesis. And the broader the hypothesis, the more difficult it is to construct a research design that can be carried out. Nevertheless, social scientists have conducted research studies in an effort to answer this question.

One anthropologist, Professor Ralph Linton, has tackled the problem in a new and useful way. He traced the cultural origins of a large number of everyday artifacts, beliefs, and assumptions that exist in American society. As you read the following excerpt from his work, consider to what extent you think culture affects a person's life.

Our solid American citizen awakens in a bed built on a pattern which originated in the Near East but which was modified in northern Europe before it was transmitted to America. He throws back the covers made from cotton, domesticated in India, or linen, domesticated in the Near East, or wool from sheep, also domesticated in the Near East, or silk, the use of which was discovered in China. All these materials have been spun and woven by processes invented in the Near East. He slips into his moccasins, invented by the Indians of the Eastern woodlands, and goes to the bathroom, whose fixtures are a mixture of European and American inventions, both of recent date. He takes off his pajamas, a garment invented in India, and washes with soap invented by the ancient Gauls. He then shaves, a masochistic rite which seems to have been derived from either Sumer or ancient Egypt.

Returning to the bedroom, he removes his clothes from a chair of southern European type and proceeds to dress. He puts on garments whose form originally derived from the skin clothing of the nomads of the Asiatic steppes, puts on shoes made from skins tanned by a process invented in ancient Egypt, and cut to a pattern derived from the classical civilizations of the Mediterranean. . . . Before going out for breakfast he glances through the window, made of glass invented in Egypt, and if it is raining, puts on overshoes made of rubber discovered by the Central American Indians and takes an umbrella, invented in southeastern Asia. Upon his head he puts a hat made of felt, a material invented in the Asiatic steppes.

On his way to breakfast he stops to buy a paper, paying for it with coins, an ancient Lydian invention. At the restaurant a whole new series of borrowed elements confronts him. His plate is made of a form of pottery invented in China. His knife is of steel, an alloy first made in southern India, his fork, a medieval Italian invention, and his spoon a derivative of a Roman original. He begins breakfast with an orange, from the eastern Mediterranean, a cantaloupe from Persia, or perhaps a piece of African watermelon. With this he has coffee, an Abyssinian plant, with cream and sugar. Both the domestication of cows and the idea of milking them originated in the Near East, while sugar was first made in India. After his fruit and first coffee he goes on to waffles, cakes made by a Scandinavian technique from wheat domesticated in Asia Minor. Over these he pours maple syrup, invented by the Indians of the Eastern woodlands. As a side dish he may have the eggs of a species of bird domesticated in Indo-China, or thin strips of the flesh of an animal domesticated in eastern Asia, which have been salted and smoked by a process developed in northern Europe.

When our friend has finished eating, he . . . reads the news of the day, imprinted in characters invented in Germany. As he absorbs the accounts of foreign troubles he will, if he is a good conservative citizen, thank a Hebrew deity in an Indo-European language that he is 100 percent American.*

* From *The Study of Man* by Ralph Linton, © 1964. Reprinted by permission of Prentice-Hall, Inc., Englewood Cliffs, New Jersey.

From the quotation, it appears that our way of life has many different origins. Almost everything that we say and do, it seems, is related to other cultures. From these other cultures we have put together a combination that is known as American. It is a combination of all these elements that has produced our "100 percent American."

This process of exchanging and distributing cultural traits occurs in all but the most isolated societies. Just as Americans are shaped by cultural traits that they have borrowed from other cultures, people in other societies are shaped by American cultural traits. Try making a list of cultural traits of American origin that have influenced people in other parts of the world. You may have to do some research, since cultural origins aren't always easy to trace. Which list do you think will be longer—the one of traits borrowed by Americans, or a list of traits originated by Americans? Why?

Sociologists do not claim that people consist of only culturally imposed qualities. They do claim, however, that what makes people human, what makes them different from animals, is culture. What you have, what you want, how you act—in short, what you are—stems from the culture in which you live.

4 Deviation from Cultural Norms

▶ What makes someone a deviant?

▶ Why is the amount of deviance increasing in our society?

SECTION 1:
The Concept of Deviance

As you know, every culture has norms to govern the behavior of its people. Groups, too, have their own particular norms that regulate the behavior of the group members. Most of these norms are internalized by the members. But individuals don't internalize every norm. Even sanctions don't bring about complete social control. There are always individuals who violate the norms, who break the rules of the society or group. Individuals deviate from the accepted rules of behavior in all societies.

Who Is a Deviant?

The sociological concept of deviance is a complex one and there are several mis-understandings connected with it. One of these is the common assumption that deviants are in some important way naturally different from nondeviants. This assumption regards deviants as abnormal or as "bad" people who are acting wrongly against "good" people. However, sociologists today don't accept explanations of deviant behavior that assume that deviants are basically different from nondeviants. Rather, they see the difference between deviants and nondeviants as relative, as related to a particular set of norms.

Another problem is that we often think of deviant behavior solely in terms of a single person's actions or behavior. But deviance is not one-sided, it is two-sided. There is norm breaking, but there is also norm enforcement. The situation cannot be one-sided, for if someone breaks a norm that is not enforced then no act of deviance exists, because nobody recognizes that it does. For example, if you belong to a club whose bylaws say that meetings will begin promptly at 8:00 P.M., but you never arrive before 8:30 P.M., and neither does anyone else, you can hardly be called a deviant. In a sociological consideration of deviant behavior we must keep in mind both sides—norm breaking and norm enforcement.

The number of norms in our society is enormous. There are countless informal agreements, cultural mores, and formal laws of all kinds. When we consider the multitude of social norms, and the certainty that everyone will violate some of them, the problem of social deviance becomes complex indeed. Who, then, is a deviant? Since we all violate some of the many norms of the society, are we all deviants? We can't all be deviants, or the concept of deviance would have no meaning.

Sociological Approaches to Deviance

Deviance involves more than just the violation of norms. It depends on which norms are violated, and on who violates them. Suppose, for example, you get a ticket for driving your car too fast. You are not likely to be considered a deviant. But if you continually drive at high speeds and acquire a reputation as a reckless driver, you may be considered a deviant. Similarly, chronic alcoholics, those who publicly violate standards of sexual behavior, and those who are convicted of serious crimes are usually regarded as social deviants.

Social deviance involves interaction between the rule breakers and those making the judgment. This interaction affects not only the labeling of deviants but also the way that offenders perceive themselves. Some rule breakers agree with the judgment of others concerning what is expected behavior and whether they are offenders. People who are stopped for speeding usually recognize the traffic rules and realize that they have violated one of them.

Alcoholics, however, may not view their situation as other people do. They may agree that their drinking is "bad." But they are likely to think that those judging them really do not understand their problem, and that if they did, they would judge differently. Other deviants—such as certain political deviants and some sexual deviants—may believe that their behavior is right and the rest of the world is wrong. Deviants may come to view themselves as being oppressed or persecuted, as being judged by standards made by others and appropriate only for them.

Thus a sociological approach to deviance is concerned with a number of factors and how they relate to one another. These include (1) a norm, (2) a participant or participants, (3) an act, and (4) observers who regard the act as deviant. A norm is not really a standard against which to measure deviance until someone acts in opposition to it. Deviance also requires observers of the norm-opposing act, who judge it to be deviant.

We can get a better understanding of this by considering two distinct theoretical approaches to deviance. The first, the anomie theory of Robert K. Merton, emphasizes how people may deviate from norms to achieve socially approved goals. The second, the labeling theory of Howard S. Becker, stresses the effect on a person of being identified as a deviant.

The anomie theory. ANOMIE *is a state or condition of normlessness.* Merton's theory centers around the various ways in which members of the society relate to the cultural goals or values stressed in the society. Do or don't the members use institutionalized means—socially acceptable ways or norms—to achieve these cultural goals? For example, a cultural goal in our society is to be successful, which is usually defined as material success. The socially accepted way—the institutionalized means—of acquiring wealth and material success is by hard work. For many members of the society, however, this

MERTON'S THEORY OF HOW PEOPLE RESPOND

WAYS OF RESPONDING TO →	CULTURAL GOALS	SOCIALLY ACCEPTED MEANS OF ACHIEVING THEM
1. Conformity	Accept	Accept
2. Innovation	Accept	Reject
3. Ritualism	Reject	Accept
4. Retreatism	Reject	Reject
5. Rebellion	Reject/Replace	Reject/Replace

goal is out of reach. They may not have sufficient education. Perhaps they grew up in the culture of poverty. They may be discriminated against, or be physically handicapped. For whatever reason, they simply cannot acquire enough money to achieve "success." Yet they still are under pressure to succeed. In utter frustration, they may decide to use any means available to reach the goal. When this happens, the norms, the institutionalized means, no longer have meaning. A state of anomie, or normlessness, results.

Merton determined that there are five ways in which members of the society relate to the cultural goals and the accepted means of achieving these goals. Every member of the society uses one of these ways. The diagram above illustrates these five ways of responding: conformity, innovation, ritualism, retreatism, and rebellion.

(1) CONFORMITY. Most individuals in a society accept both the cultural goals and the culturally approved means for achieving them. They may become a part of this category in one of two ways. They may have ac-

cess to acceptable means for achieving the goals. Or they may accept the goals even though they realize the goals are out of their reach. These people are not deviants.

(2) INNOVATION. Some members of the society accept the cultural goals but not the institutionalized means for reaching the goals. They want to be successful in the accumulation of wealth, but find the goal too difficult or impossible to attain by acceptable means. Therefore they innovate. They devise new means for achieving the goals—ways that break the norms. Thus they become deviants.

(3) RITUALISM. Other members of the society also find it impossible to achieve the cultural goals by acceptable means. However, instead of breaking the norms to achieve the goals, they give up the goals. They may label themselves as "honest poor" and be proud of it. They make a ritual of dutifully keeping the norms and obeying the letter of the law. In fact, law and order becomes an end in itself.

(4) RETREATISM. Some individuals reject both the cultural goals and the socially acceptable means to attain them. One recent

One form of "retreatism" is the establishment of a commune by people who choose to reject society's goals and live according to their own rules and goals.

example is the hippie. Hippies believed that the world of work was a rat race and that the acquisition of money didn't really bring much happiness. So they dropped out of society and concentrated on "doing their own thing" in their own way, apart from the rest of the society. Another example is the monastic movement of the Middle Ages. Monks believed that the only way to live a holy life was to escape the evil world and retire to the seclusion of a monastery. Many artists and writers also reject the goals of the mainstream of society and seek their own way of life. Other examples of retreatists are alcoholics, drug addicts, beggars, and psychotics.

(5) REBELLION. These individuals also reject the cultural goals and the socially accept-

able means to attain them. But instead of dropping out of the society, they rebel against it. They want to do away with the cultural goals and acceptable means of the society and replace them with their own goals and means. An example of this would be the Weatherman faction of the Students for a Democratic Society (SDS), who advocated the destruction of the American "establishment" in the late 1960's.

As you know, the conformists are nondeviants. Furthermore, the other four categories of persons are not considered deviant on an equal scale. The ritualists don't really offer any threat to the society. Therefore, they are on the borderline of being regarded as deviants. The retreatists are thought of as deviants, since their life styles are so different. Yet because they are out of the mainstream of society and have little personal contact with others, the retreatists are usually tolerated. The real deviants are the innovators and the rebellious individuals, for they threaten the stable and secure way of life of the society.

The labeling theory. Sociologist Howard S. Becker views deviance from another angle. Instead of focusing on the act of breaking the rules, Becker sees deviance as created by society. It is the society that determines what is norm-breaking behavior. And it is the society that labels particular people who break the norms as deviants, or "outsiders."

Becker points out that we can look at deviance in two ways: 1. according to whether or not individuals have broken the norms, or 2. according to whether or not they are perceived by other people to have broken the norms. The chart on this page shows the relationship between these two factors: 1. the individual's behavior, which is either obedient or norm breaking, and 2. the way others perceive the individual's behavior, as either not deviant or deviant. As you can see, these two factors suggest four categories of individuals, referred to by Becker as the conformer, the falsely accused, the secret deviant, and the pure deviant.

(1) THE CONFORMER is the individual whose behavior is obedient to the norms, and whom others do not perceive as a deviant. Conformers have neither violated the norms nor are thought to have done so by others.

(2) THE FALSELY ACCUSED is an individual whose behavior is obedient to the norms, but who is perceived as deviant by others. Society views some people as deviant, although they have not broken the rules. For example, a teen-ager may get picked up by the police for delinquency, when actually he or she was only a bystander. A college student may be arrested in a marijuana raid, although not one of the users. If our court system is capable of making wrong decisions, then certainly the average person, making informal judgments, is capable of error also. We do not know how many persons are defined as deviants who actually did not commit deviant acts.

(3) THE SECRET DEVIANT is the person who breaks the norms, but is not perceived by others as deviant. This individual violates the norms and gets away with it. Since the norm breaking of secret deviants is not detected, they are perceived as rule abiding and continue to be respected members of society.

(4) THE PURE DEVIANT is the person who has broken the norms and is perceived as deviant. Pure deviants don't get away with breaking the norms. Society views them as rule breakers and may brand them as criminals or sinners.

We can see from this chart that when we talk about deviants, we are referring to those people who break the norms—the secret deviants and the pure deviants. But when we react to deviants, we are reacting to those whom we perceive as norm breakers, the

BECKER'S CATEGORIES OF DEVIANCE

	1. OBEDIENT BEHAVIOR	NORM-BREAKING BEHAVIOR
NOT PERCEIVED AS DEVIANT	the conformer	the secret deviant
2. PERCEIVED AS DEVIANT	the falsely accused	the pure deviant

The individual who tries to commit suicide is a "pure deviant" in our society. That person has broken the norms and is regarded by others as deviant.

falsely accused and the pure deviants, and not the secret deviants. As Becker says, what deviants have in common is not necessarily that they broke norms, but that people regard them as norm breakers.

SECTION REVIEW

1. Why is it so difficult to define deviance?
2. How does Robert Merton's anomie theory explain deviance?
3. Describe Howard Becker's approach to deviance.
4. Do you agree more with Merton or with Becker? Why?

KEY TERMS

Explain the meaning of the following terms.

anomie	labeling theory
conformity	rebellion
deviance	retreatism
innovation	ritualism

Give an example of each of these terms.

conformer	pure deviant
falsely accused deviant	secret deviant

SECTION 2:
The Effects of Deviation

Thus deviance is more than simply the breaking of norms. It involves both norm breaking and the norm enforcer, or the society. In other words, we must consider the deviant in relation to society generally. What are some of the implications of deviation for the individual and for the society?

The Effect on the Individual

If we view a deviant as someone who has been labeled a deviant, regardless of whether that person has actually violated norms, then we may ask what effects such labeling has on that individual. One immediate effect of being labeled a deviant is that the person is no longer accepted in "respectable"—that is, nondeviant—society. His or her associations with other persons are limited, to some degree, to people who are also regarded as deviants. For example, such deviants may be in jail or prison, where they meet real norm-breaking deviants. Even if they are not in jails, prisons, or mental hospitals, they are shut out of the mainstream of society. The label itself usually causes other people to refuse to associate with them.

Because they aren't accepted elsewhere, they are more or less forced to associate with people who share a similar deviant label. Furthermore, these associations influence their future behavior. We know that groups have a strong influence on the behavior of individuals. Since deviants must associate mostly with other deviants, they are much more likely to continue in their deviant pattern of behavior.

This effect applies also to the falsely accused deviant—the person who has been labeled a deviant but who has not actually committed deviant acts. Falsely accused deviants, too, are refused acceptance into respectable society and must confine their associations mainly to other persons labeled as deviants. The result is that once an individual has acquired the deviant label, even if it has been misapplied, he or she is more likely to fall into a deviant pattern of behavior than someone without the deviant label.

Another important factor is the effect of the deviant label on the individual's self-image. A major source of our self-image is how other people view us. We see ourselves through the eyes of others by the way they react to us. When others don't accept us because we are labeled deviants, we soon may come to see ourselves as deviants. We redefine our own self-image to fit the society's definition.

The deviant label also affects the individual's role. In the last chapter we defined role as the behavior expected of a person because of his or her position in the social structure or group. In general, we act the

One of the effects of labeling individuals as deviants is that they frequently live up to the label. Many people who are labeled as criminals and sent to prison commit crimes again when freed.

way others expect us to act. For example, if you know that others (particularly if they are important to you) trust you and believe you to be dependable, responsible, and honest, you are likely to behave in that way. But suppose, on the other hand, you are well aware that others do not trust you, that they believe you to be undependable, irresponsible, and dishonest. How will you behave then? What will your role be? You might well reason that "if anything happens I'll get blamed for it anyway, so I may as well go ahead and do it." It is extremely hard for individuals to remain on the narrow path of conformity when people on all sides are accusing them of nonconformity. Their reasons for playing a conforming role are gone and they may come to accept their role as that of a deviant.

The Distribution of the Deviant Label

The deviant label does not simply become attached to people in a random manner. It is not distributed equally over the population. Certain categories of people are more likely to become labeled deviants than others. For example, sex, class, and race affect the likelihood that a person will become labeled a deviant, regardless of whether or not the person commits any deviant acts. A woman is less likely than a man to be picked up by the police, even when both of them have committed the same act. If picked up by the police, the woman is less likely to be taken to the police station. If taken to the station, she is less likely to be booked. And if booked, she is less likely than a man to be convicted and sentenced. A similar situation occurs when a middle-class boy commits the same deviant act as a lower-class boy—he is less likely to be picked up, to be booked, and to be convicted and sentenced. These circumstances also apply to race. A white man will less often be picked up by the police, booked, convicted, and sentenced than a black man, although the offense is the same.

It is easier, then, to become labeled as a deviant if an individual is male, lower class, and black, as contrasted with being female, middle class, and white. There are, of course, exceptions. One of these exceptions occurs in the case of unlawful sex relationships. If the woman becomes pregnant, she is usually censured and becomes labeled a deviant, whereas the male involved receives a much lighter treatment.

It is also more likely for people to become deviants at some times than at others. For example, the likelihood that the deviant label will be applied increases during official "drives" against a particular type of deviant activity. Suppose, for example, the mayor of the city—perhaps to drum up votes for his or her reelection—declares a drive against vice in the central business district. It suddenly becomes "less safe" to be a prostitute, a pornography peddler, a homosexual, or a drug addict. At the same time it becomes very likely that some people will be falsely accused of such deviant behavior. The result may be to clear the streets, temporarily. But at the same time more deviants may be created, if the misidentified deviants are forced to associate with the real deviants.

The Effect on the Society

How does deviance affect the society? Most kinds of deviance affect only parts of a society, and only in specific, limited ways. Nevertheless, widespread deviance of certain kinds can seriously threaten social order. Consider the following three ways in which deviant behavior may threaten social organization.

First, it may reduce performance in crucial roles to the point where the organization cannot function. For instance, if school administrators, teachers, and athletic coaches became unpredictable about showing up for their activities, schools and athletic teams could not function. Coordinating the teachers' activities throughout the school, the activities of the students in a classroom, and the behavior of the members of a team during practice would become so difficult that progress in these activities would be virtually impossible.

Second, deviance may undermine people's willingness to carry out their parts in an organized activity. Suppose some individuals appear to be well rewarded even though they are "idlers" or "cheats," while those who are devoted to hard work and responsibility see themselves as unrewarded. Those who have been responsible may give up and join the "cheaters," or lose interest in the particular group activity altogether.

The third and perhaps most serious consequence of deviance for organized group activities is its effect on trust. By trust we mean our confidence that others will observe the rules and are committed to obeying them. If distrust of others arises through their deviance, our confidence is shaken and we become uncertain as to what to expect of them. We may then see our own efforts in group activities as wasted, since we don't know whether others will act to make our collective efforts successful. For example, if officials in, say, softball or hockey games were easily bribed so that they would call close, crucial plays dishonestly, players would lose their motivation to play as they do. Extensive breaking of trust by officials would make the game itself impossible. Only through substantial mutual trust in all kinds of social organization can we achieve meaningful personal involvement and social stability.

Of course, all deviance does not threaten social organization. Most, if not all, social organization can tolerate some deviance. Some cheating on exams, an occasional dishonest official, and a certain amount of dishonesty in filling out income tax returns does not destroy schools, athletics, or the Internal Revenue Service. In fact, social organization is frequently set up to cope with a certain amount of anticipated deviance.

A limited amount of deviance may even have consequences that support and reinforce the norms. The norms of any society

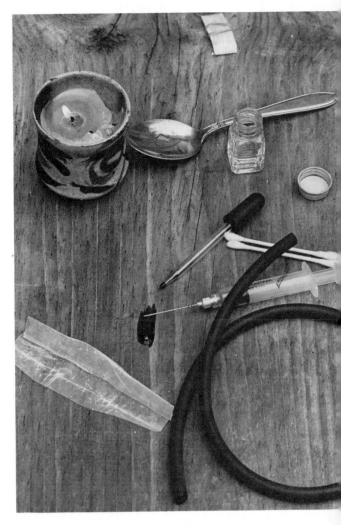

When a society labels drug addicts as deviants, one result is that the norms regarding the use of drugs in that society become more defined.

are rarely, if ever, completely clear by themselves. Most norms are not written down. Even those that are written are not read by many people. And they are always subject to interpretation by the courts. One way that the norms are made clear is through social deviance. When people violate, or are thought to have violated, a norm, they become the focus of attention. They become an

77

example, and receive some punishment. The result is that the norms are clarified for everyone else. This norm clarifying serves to set boundaries, or limits, on role behavior. Without some deviant behavior there would be a general unsureness about what the norms are, which would mean less social stability.

For instance, there are norms in your school which say that students must not cheat in examinations. If no student ever cheated or was known to cheat, it would be difficult for the student body to know the exact meaning of this norm. However, when one student is caught cheating and suspended from school, the norm suddenly becomes quite clear to all students. By defining the norm, this incident of norm violation and punishment helps to set limits on the behavior of every student and thus creates social stability.

Deviance, then, has a variety of functions in society. Social systems are very delicately balanced. Even deviants may contribute to that balance by helping to keep the society stable and intact—although they also create problems for the society.

SECTION REVIEW

1. How does the label "deviant" affect the behavior of an individual?
2. What categories of people in our society are most apt to be labeled deviant? Why is this so?
3. Does deviance have any positive function in the society? Explain.

PROJECTS AND ACTIVITIES

1. Research local newspapers to determine what kinds of deviance present the greatest problems in your community. Do you think the newspapers give an accurate account of the real problems of deviance in your community?

2. Write a personal essay entitled "My Experience with Anomie."

3. Conduct a survey of students in the class to find out what categories of people they perceive as deviant. Have each student write on a sheet of paper five categories of persons he or she considers deviant. Make sure no names are included on the papers. Tabulate the results and discuss.

4. Design a poster that shows cultural areas in which a great deal of deviance is tolerated and also those areas in which very little deviance is tolerated.

5. Do research in current magazines to try to determine what changes in the society have been brought about directly or in-

directly by individuals who would be considered deviant by a large number of people in the society.

6. Interview teachers and students concerning the effects of labeling a student a "troublemaker." How does this label affect the fair judgment of the student by others?

7. Read the novel *Anthem* by Ayn Rand. What does she say about cultural deviance?

8. Do research to determine if there are laws on the statute books of your state that are never enforced. If they are never enforced, are the illegal acts considered as acts of deviance by the people of the state?

9. Using the plot of a television program as a basis, prepare a short story, poem, painting, or drawing that presents the consequences of cultural deviance.

TOPICS FOR INQUIRY

1. When we live in a complex society with many different groups having many conflicting norms, is it possible for a "normal" individual to avoid being considered deviant by some person or group? Why? How does this affect the meaning of the term "deviant"?

2. Do you think that the anomie theory or the labeling theory best explains deviance in our society? Why?

3. Discuss individuals who were labeled as deviant during their lives but were later seen as having served their society.

4. In recent years a number of high government and business leaders have been exposed and punished as "deviants" who broke the norms of our society. Do you think this tends to cause ordinary citizens to be more likely or less likely to break the norms of the society? Explain.

5. Do you think that social deviance is caused by the individuals who violate the norms or by the society? Explain.

6. Will there be more or less deviance in our society in the future? Why do you think so?

NONFICTION

ARENDT, Hannah, *On Violence.* Harcourt Brace Jovanovich, 1970 (pap.). Suggests that violence stems from the frustration of the basic human power to act and is a response to the modern bureaucratic state.

BECKER, Howard S., *Outsiders: Studies in the Sociology of Deviance.* The Free Press, 1963 (pap.). Provides insight into the research and theories of Howard Becker.

COHEN, Albert K., *Deviance and Control.* Prentice-Hall, 1966 (pap.). An important contribution in the field of deviant behavior and its effect on social organization.

ERIKSON, Kai T., *Wayward Puritans: A Study in the Sociology of Deviance.* Wiley, 1966 (pap.). A report of Erikson's research on violating norms.

FINIFTER, Ada W. (ed.), *Alienation and the Social System.* Wiley, 1972 (pap.). A number of studies of alienation and how it relates to the social system.

GRAHAM, Hugh D. *et al* (eds.), *Violence: The Crisis of American Confidence.* Johns Hopkins, 1972 (and pap.). A collection of readings on both violence and crime in America.

KENISTON, Kenneth, *The Uncommitted: Alienated Youth in American Society.* Harcourt Brace Jovanovich, 1965. A study of the social and historical roots of discontentment among a group of college students.

MERTON, Robert K. and NISBET, Robert A. (eds.), *Contemporary Social Problems.* Harcourt Brace Jovanovich, 1976. Part One, entitled "Deviant Behavior," consists of five articles by leading sociologists on five different forms of deviance.

FICTION

DOSTOEVSKY, Feodor, *Crime and Punishment.* Modern Library or Dell (pap.). A hatchet murder starts the story and plunges the main character into a deep psychological drama in which he is pitted against himself and the authorities.

HERSEY, John R., *Too Far to Walk.* Knopf. A college student has an encounter with LSD and becomes the wiser for it.

KEYES, Daniel, *Flowers for Algernon*. Harcourt Brace Jovanovich or Bantam (pap.). The story of a mentally retarded man who becomes a genius through medical means.

MORRELL, David, *First Blood*. Lippincott or Fawcett World (pap.). An anti-war novel that reveals what happens when a highly trained Green Beret tries to return to normal life in the United States.

SILLITOE, Alan, *The Loneliness of the Long-Distance Runner*. Knopf or New American Library (pap.). A reform-school boy gains self-respect through pursuing his own set of values.

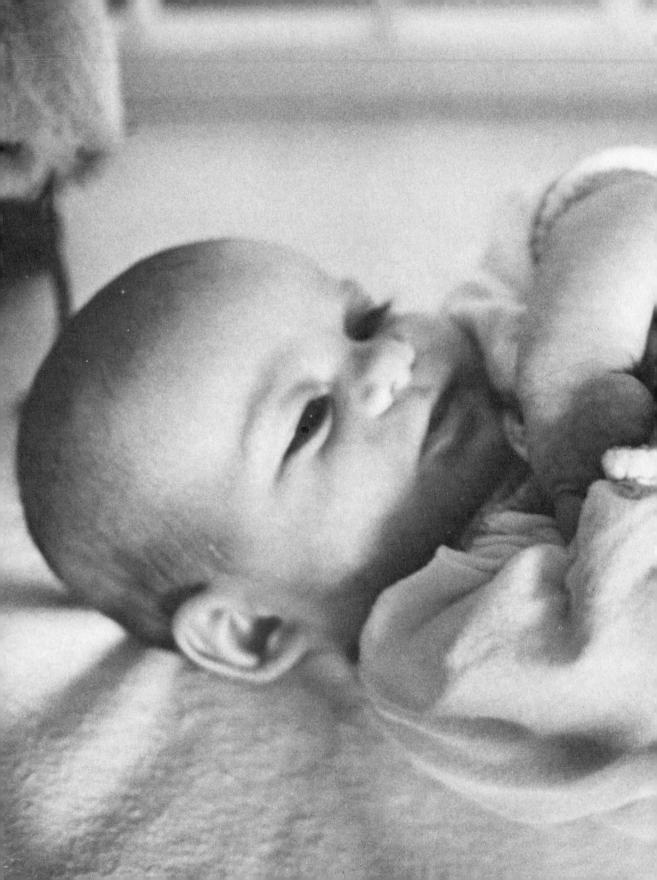

5 Culture and the Individual

► Does anyone have the same personality as you?

► What factors shape your personality?

► How does the culture affect your personality?

SECTION 1:
Culture and Personality

You now know something about culture. You've seen that cultural norms determine the standards of behavior within a given society. And all societies have some persons who are labeled as deviants because they don't obey these norms. But we haven't considered how the culture affects your individual personality. What are the relative influences of heredity and environment in shaping the personality? Indeed, what is personality?

The Meaning of Personality

Often people use the term personality as an easy way of explaining a person's behavior. Someone says that "she is a good sales-woman because she is an extrovert," or "her uncle is hard to get along with because he has an authoritarian personality." Actually, though, the concept of personality does not explain anything about the person's behavior. Instead, the concept of personality is a descriptive one. It relates to specific behavioral traits of an individual. It describes the individual's specific adaptation to his or her cultural surroundings.

We might define PERSONALITY as *the basic organization of people that determines the uniqueness of their interactions with themselves, with others, and with the nonhuman aspects of their environment.* The basic organization refers to the structure of the personality—how it is put together, and the relationships among the various parts. It concerns the total physical, intellectual, and emotional structure of the individual.

The personality structure determines the uniqueness of the individual's interactions. No two personalities are alike. All persons have their own way of interacting with them-

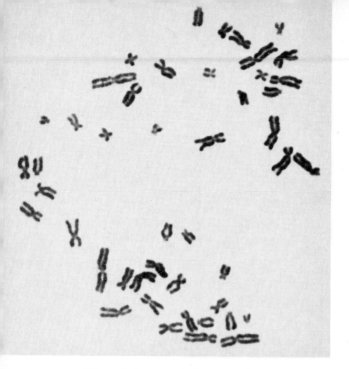

Through the genes in chromosomes (above), people inherit biological characteristics, such as physical size, which can influence their personality.

selves and with their environment. And the way that individuals interact with themselves affects the way they interact with others.

Human interaction always brings about some change in the individual. This change takes place very slowly. It is generally not noticeable from day to day. Nevertheless, the personality is changing constantly. Personalities don't all change at the same rate. For example, the child changes very rapidly in both physical and intellectual aspects of personality. The adult may change very slowly. However, every personality undergoes constant, gradual change as the individual interacts with others.

The personality of individuals—their basic organization—is a blending of all the factors present in their particular social situation with whatever traits they inherit biologically. This brings us to one of the age-old questions: which is more important, hered-ity or environment? There is no simple answer. But we will try to clarify the issue by examining the contributions of both to the developing personality.

The Influence of Heredity

We may define HEREDITY as *the transmitting of genetic characteristics from parents to their children.* These characteristics are innate. They are present at birth. Heredity determines such physical characteristics as hair and skin color. It also regulates the maturation process in the individual, the process by which the individual grows up physically. Biological inheritance is of great importance, since without it we would not even exist.

In addition to being responsible for our existence, biological inheritance provides us with certain basic needs and capacities. For example, human beings have biological drives. The hunger drive makes us want to eat. But drives don't determine our specific behavior. The hunger drive doesn't tell us when to eat, or what to eat, or how to eat. We learn these things from other human beings within the boundaries of our culture. Heredity provides us with certain biological needs. Our environment determines how we meet these needs.

Heredity also plays an important role in shaping human personalities by setting limits on individuals. If you have little aptitude for spatial relations, you are unlikely to be a good architect. If your biological inheritance endowed you with a male 5'5" (1.7 meter) frame, you probably would not become a professional basketball player. On the other hand, you may not become one even if you have a 7' (2.1 meter) frame. The point is that inherited characteristics place limits on what is possible. But inherited characteristics do not determine what an individual will do. Nor do they determine what kind of personality he or she will have.

The Influence of Environment

The ENVIRONMENT *consists of the stimuli and situations, including both natural and social forces, that affect an individual.* The environment is responsible for the acquired aspects of personality. These are the aspects which are not present at birth but which develop as the individual interacts with his or her surroundings. The geographic environment influences the personality, since it affects the overall culture in which the individual lives. The culture greatly determines the social relationships of the individual through the values and norms of the society.

Heredity sets boundaries. The cultural environment establishes the alternatives open to the individual. An individual may have the biological capability to do a great many things. But he or she cannot become a space scientist, for example, unless that alternative is present in his or her culture. Individuals who grow up in the headwater area of the Amazon, for instance, may have the ability but probably will not design toy rockets, much less become space scientists. The alternative of becoming space scientists is not available within their culture. Heredity establishes certain limits. But the final influence on personality comes from the environment.

It is the cultural environment that makes individuals human. It makes them both similar to each other and different from each other. There have been a few recorded instances where children have been raised without the influence of a cultural environment. In one or two cases the children were found with animals. In other instances, the mother isolated the child so that no one would know of his or her existence. In all these cases the result was that the child had no human characteristics except appearance. Such children acquired no reasoning, no manners, no ability to control bodily functions or even to move about like a human being. The evidence seems to indicate that our personality—in fact, our humanity—comes from our cultural environment.

The Effect of Culture on Personality

The culture, then, is a major factor in the personality development of individuals. To find out how much culture affects personality development, consider its influence on the following parts of an individual's personality.

Physical characteristics. The most obvious part of an individual's personality is physical appearance. As soon as we look at a person, we know whether that person is short or tall, fat or thin, has a light or a dark complexion, blond or brown hair, a long or short nose. Of course, the individual has inherited these specific characteristics. However, the individual's physical appearance can be altered by his or her culture. The culture may hold that a dark suntan is desirable, or that certain tattoos or body scars are attractive. Some cultures have believed that long necks, flat heads, or small feet were desirable. As a result, people have made efforts to change the natural physical characteristics of their children to produce these features. Thus the culture may alter in some way the natural physical characteristics provided by heredity.

Temperament. TEMPERAMENT *is the fundamental emotional disposition of the individual.* For example, some people tend to be cool, calm, and collected, and are not easily aroused emotionally. Others seem to have a rather nervous disposition at all times. Temperament is basically innate, or present at birth. But it can be altered by the influence of the culture. Our culture traditionally has encouraged differences in temperament for boys and girls. Suppose a rat runs across the floor of your classroom. If some of the girls become excited and scream or jump up on the chairs, it would be acceptable feminine

The culture influences the kinds of abilities that its members develop. Tribes in the South Pacific, for example, aren't likely to develop an ability in tennis.

behavior. The boys, on the other hand, are not supposed to show any fear of the rat. They are expected to remain calm, collected, and in control, and to protect the girls from the intruder.

Abilities. *An* ABILITY *is the power to carry out some behavior act.* Abilities are skills that are acquired from the culture. For instance, depending on the culture, an individual may develop the ability to play softball or jai alai, to paint or do beadwork, to program computers or use an abacus. Closely related to ability is aptitude. *An* APTITUDE *is the capacity to learn a particular skill or to acquire a particular body of knowledge.* We might say

that aptitudes are related to heredity, but that abilities are always related to the culture. For example, an individual may have the aptitude to be an electrical engineer. But unless members of the culture help him or her to develop the ability, the person can never become an electrical engineer.

Interests. *An individual's* INTERESTS *are those things that he or she finds enjoyment in knowing, feeling, or doing.* The person who has a great interest in music, for example, enjoys learning about music, listening to music, and exercising his or her musical skills. Naturally, people do not all have the same interests. The kinds of things that an individual becomes interested in, however, depend on the cultural alternatives available. You can't become interested in book publishing, for instance, unless your culture includes book publishing companies and thus provides this alternative.

Beliefs. BELIEFS *are those things that the individual accepts as true or actual.* All individuals have beliefs about themselves, their friends, nature, God or gods, work—in short, about all matters that concern them. Their beliefs also include their attitudes, values, preferences, superstitions, prejudices, and knowledge. Some beliefs are based on fact. Others are not. But all beliefs are culturally derived. The individual learns them from others in his or her society.

Habits. HABIT *refers to the regular ways of thinking, feeling, or behaving that an individual has acquired.* Every individual has hundreds of habits related to dress, eating, cleanliness, interactions with others, and daily tasks. Individual behavior acts tell us little about a particular individual. But the regular patterns of behavior that we call habits distinguish one person from another.

Habits, like beliefs, are learned from others. A great many of the habits of any individual represent internalized cultural norms. For example, the norms of our society say that we should drive an automobile on the right side of the road. The individual therefore develops the habit of driving on the right. Almost all habits are related to the culture in some way.

From this discussion of personality parts you can see that no aspect of personality is untouched by the culture in which the individual lives. Suppose, for example, you had been born of the same parents in a completely different culture. You would have the same heredity. But your social environment would be very different. Would your personality be the same as it is now? Most certainly not! You would still have some of the same physical characteristics. Your basic temperament would be somewhat similar. And you would still have the same basic aptitudes. Your abilities, interests, beliefs, and habits, however, would be entirely different. In short, your personality would be very different. You are the personality you are, to a great extent, because of the culture in which you live.

Basic Personality Types

Thus culture affects the development of each individual personality. In addition, it produces a basic personality type in every society. The cultural outlook of a society results in a basic or representative personality type within that society. This doesn't mean that everyone in a given society will have the same personality. The personality characterization may or may not apply to specific individuals. But it does mean that there will be enough basic personality traits in common to recognize people as belonging to one culture or another. It is sometimes difficult to establish personality types in complex societies. Yet, understanding the personality type of a society is helpful in dealing with a people or in anticipating their responses. For personality types can vary considerably from society to society.

We can see the variety of basic or representative personality types in Margaret Mead's study of tribal societies in New Guinea, mentioned in Chapter 2 (pages 35-36). You may remember that the basic personality type for men and women in the Arapesh society was gentle, responsive, and unaggressive. On the other hand, the characteristic personality type among the Mundugumor men and women was aggressive, harsh, and violent. Very different types of personalities can develop in different societies, depending on the cultural patterns of each.

SECTION REVIEW

1. Explain the concept of personality.
2. How is personality influenced by heredity and environment?
3. What are the various parts of our personality? How is each one affected by the culture?
4. In what ways would your personality be different if you had been born and raised in another culture?

KEY TERMS

Explain each of the following terms.

ability	habit
aptitude	heredity
basic personality type	interest
beliefs	personality
environment	temperament

SECTION 2:
The Socialization Process

Now that you know culture influences almost every aspect of personality, you may be wondering how the culture shapes the individual personality. *This process of cultural molding, by which the individual learns the basic skills, values, beliefs, and behavior patterns of the society, is called* SOCIALIZATION. At birth humans cannot talk, walk, feed themselves, or even protect themselves from harm. They know nothing about the cultural norms of the society. Through the process of socialization individuals, human in physical appearance only, are changed into people who have acquired knowledge of their culture and become participating members of their society.

The concept of socialization includes the idea that people are capable of acquiring any number of personal identities or selves. Therefore, which culture we are brought up in, and what stage that culture is in, are critical in determining our identity or self.

The Development of Self

The social self is probably the most important aspect of the development of the individual personality. As you know, personality is the total basic organization of the individual, including both the person's heredity and environment. The social self develops only from the person's social environment. *The* SOCIAL SELF *is the way that an individual sees himself or herself as a result of interacting with others.* From contacts with other people, individuals begin to have a sense of their own selves. The social self involves their wishes, aspirations, and motivations as well as their emotional, ethical, and religious characteristics.

The phenomenon of the social self has been described by the American sociologist Charles Horton Cooley (1864–1929) as the "looking-glass self." Cooley emphasized that we only come to have an image of ourselves when we're able to know what others think of us. We use other people as a mirror. The reflection that we see becomes our self-image.

"Generalized others." A contemporary of Cooley, George Herbert Mead (1863–1931), added to Cooley's theory of socialization and the social self. In Mead's analysis, seeing ourselves as others see us is only the beginning. At this point the child has come to respond to certain "significant others"— people who have a special significance to him or her, such as parents, relatives, and close friends. Children play house and other simple games in which they take on the role of one of these significant persons. Eventually, though, they learn to take on the role

According to Cooley, we can only come to know ourselves and what we are like when we know how others view us and what they think of us.

of more "generalized others"—persons or roles to which they must relate in an abstract way. As they learn to assume the role of the "generalized other," they can put themselves in a number of places at the same time. They can do such complex things as play softball, because they can know what the players in each position expect and are expected to do. Once having learned to respond to the "generalized other," individuals begin to develop a sense of community or society. They become aware of how society relates to them and they to it. At this point they have become socialized. They are now thinking, reasoning human beings.

Transactional Analysis. A more recent theory gives further insight into how we develop a sense of self. This theory, known as Transactional Analysis (TA), emphasizes "transactions" between people. *A TRANSACTION consists of a stimulus from one person and a response from one or more other individuals.* It is through transactions that we become socialized. As children, we may have

experienced unpleasant, traumatic transactions, or "negative strokes." At the same time we received recognition and love, or "positive strokes." The balance between negative strokes and positive strokes greatly influences a person's sense of self.

As children grow and develop, their experiences tend to reinforce one of four "life positions." These life positions are:

1. I'm not O.K. — You're O.K.

2. I'm not O.K. — You're not O.K.
3. I'm O.K. — You're not O.K.
4. I'm O.K. — You're O.K.

Young children usually feel dependent and inadequate. They are often in life position 1. They feel that they are not O.K., but adults are. If children experience mostly negative strokes, position 1 becomes position 2. This position is mainly one of withdrawal—"I'm not O.K. but neither are you, for you've hurt me by not loving me." If children are often mistreated, they will probably move into the third position: "I'm O.K. but you're not O.K., and I'm going to get even with you." If the child receives a sufficient number of positive strokes (love, affection, recognition), he or she can move into the fourth position: "I'm O.K.—You're O.K."

The socialization that occurs from childhood transactions is usually negative in our society. It therefore leads young children to feel and value themselves as not O.K. But as they grow older, they begin to deal with themselves and their environment as independent, mature individuals rather than as dependent, immature children. They discover that they can overcome negative childhood experiences. This enables individuals to see themselves as being free to discontinue functioning as not O.K. They can choose to resocialize into the more satisfying life position of being O.K. and seeing others as also being O.K.

Being O.K. doesn't mean that people are without fault, or have risen above all their faults, imperfections, and emotional problems. It simply implies that the person is growing toward what he or she really wants to be and has a positive sense of self.

The Agents of Socialization

These explanations of the self are theoretical looks into the socialization process. We will now consider some specific forces and agencies that shape socialization experiences. What, for instance, is the influence of the family, the peer group, and the school in developing the social being?

The family. The family is the main agent in socialization, especially during the early stages of an individual's life. Studies comparing the development of children in family situations with children raised in hospitals, orphanages, and foundling homes show the importance of the family as a socialization agency. Babies and young children who don't have the benefit of a family develop more slowly in all respects—in mental ability, in motor ability, and emotionally. Even when nurses or others sing them lullabies and rock them to sleep, this attention doesn't seem to take the place of the love and attention of a family. Family situations give children a variety of experiences that develop their social selves and prepare them to become effective members of society.

Two kinds of socialization activities take place within the family: deliberate or intended ones, and unconscious or unintended ones. Deliberate socialization experiences are those in which the parent purposefully tries to guide the behavior or outlook of the child. The mother may tell her children about the importance of being truthful or of being considerate of others. The father may instruct his son to avoid fighting, but, if he cannot, then to fight to win. Parents are constantly carrying out deliberate attempts to mold their children. They want to prepare children for the future, for being on their own.

Unconscious or unintended socialization seems to have an even greater overall effect on the child than deliberate socialization. Suppose, for example, the father deliberately tells his child about the importance of being polite, but acts impolitely himself. The child is likely to follow what the father does rather than what he says. The unconscious, unintended socialization also occurs more often than the deliberate kind. For every time that a parent deliberately tries to influence his or her child, there are many others in which unintended messages get across subtly and effectively.

The peer group. Another important agent of socialization is the peer group. *A* PEER GROUP *consists of individuals who are equals, usually close friends and associates who are about the same age.* To have friends and be

One of the most important and influential agents of socialization is the peer group—especially in adolescence. How do your peers influence your behavior?

accepted in the society, we must win the acceptance of our peers. To win their acceptance we must behave in ways that conform to their standards. Our personality is shaped by the peer group, as we try to be the kind of person the group wants us to be. Think of some times when your peer group has influenced your behavior.

The school. The school also plays a major role in socializing children and youth. Much of the socialization process performed by the school is deliberate. Class activity is planned for the purpose of deliberately teaching reading, writing, arithmetic, and other skills. Extracurricular activities, such as school dances, clubs, and athletic events, are also provided to train the student for life in the society. In addition, the school deliberately attempts to transmit cultural values, such as patriotism, responsibility, and good citizenship. As with the family, within the school

a large amount of unintentional socialization occurs. For example, the school provides a place for students to meet and develop their own set of skills and values. And some of the unintentional socialization may also be the opposite of the intended. Teachers, like parents, may sometimes say one thing but give the opposite impression through their actions.

Other agents of socialization. While the family, the peer group, and the school are probably the most important socialization agents, there are others as well. Religious institutions certainly play a role, especially in the area of values and morals. Agencies such as the Boy Scouts, Campfire Girls, and 4H clubs also contribute to the socialization of the individual. For those who are employed, a job adds another whole dimension to the socialization process.

The mass media—newspapers, magazines,

books, television, radio, films—also serve as socialization agents. They, too, communicate values and standards of behavior that influence the individual. The mass media are growing in importance. But at present they are still not as effective as the more immediate socialization agents.

Another kind of socialization agent is the reference group. *A* REFERENCE GROUP *is any group with whom a person identifies and whose attitudes and values he or she tends to adopt.* People usually act out their social role with reference to some group or groups. They may not even belong to the group. Yet as long as they identify with its standards and attitudes, the reference group is influencing their behavior and providing socialization experiences. Honorary societies or school clubs serve as reference groups for some high school students. A social class, such as the upper-middle class, is another reference group for some people. Also, individuals may change their reference groups, particularly as they adjust to changing social conditions.

One of the difficulties of the socialization process, especially in a complex and rapidly changing society, is that often the socializing influences conflict with one another. For example, the family and the peer group may make conflicting demands on the individual. Each may present the person with a different set of values and demand conformity to those values. How an individual copes with such conflicts and inconsistencies depends on the extent of these pressures and on his or her particular personality development.

Both socialization and personality development are lifelong processes. Socialization at an early age is more significant than later on, and brings about greater changes in the individual personality. Nevertheless, socialization is gradually changing us from the day we are born until the day we die.

SECTION REVIEW

1. What is socialization?
2. Do you agree or disagree that the only way you can see yourself as you are is through the way others relate to you?
3. Explain the Transactional Analysis theory of the development of the self.
4. What are the agents of socialization that influence the developing personality?

KEY TERMS

Define each term and provide an example of each from your own life.

"generalized others"   socialization
"looking-glass self"   social self
peer group   transaction
reference group   Transactional
"significant others"   Analysis

PROJECTS AND ACTIVITIES

1. Do a research report on the influence of heredity on personality.

2. Conduct research on a famous person who was physically handicapped. Try to discover how his or her personality was affected by the handicap.

3. Make a list of your interests and then analyze how you happened to become interested in each.

4. Design a bulletin board or poster that illustrates various factors that make up an individual personality.

5. Read the play *Death of a Salesman* by Arthur Miller. Show how Biff's personality is molded by his father and his peers in school.

6. Make a list of your beliefs and try to determine how you developed each belief.

7. Being as objective as possible, analyze your abilities. Attempt to explain how you developed these abilities and how you might use them to best advantage.

8. Carefully observe television commercials for the way male and female personality traits are imposed on you by your culture.

9. Construct a collage that shows the cultural influences on personality.

10. If possible, use a movie camera to document a particular socialization process.

11. Analyze a television series based on family relationships. Can you see the effects of these relationships on the individual personality?

TOPICS FOR INQUIRY

1. Discuss the extent to which a newborn baby has an individual personality.

2. Compare the amount of influence that parents have on the personalities of their children through: (1) the genes and chromosomes they pass on to their children, and (2) the relationships that they have with their children.

3. Give examples of how people develop a sense of self as a result of the way others have related to them.

4. Discuss reasons why a two-year-old child might get the feeling of being "not O.K."

5. Describe some of the traumas we experience as children. What effect might they have on the development of our social self?

6. Discuss the relative influence of the family, the peer group, the school, the church, youth organizations, and the mass media as

agents of socialization during different periods of an individual's life from infancy to adulthood.

7. Explain how the socialization process tends to help individuals to become different as much as it helps them to become similar.

SUGGESTIONS FOR READING

NONFICTION

ALLPORT, Gordon W., *Pattern and Growth in Personality*. Holt, Rinehart and Winston, 1961. A basic book on personality that includes an approach to personality, development of personality, structure of personality, assessment of personality, and understanding of personality.

ARONSON, Elliot, *The Social Animal*. Viking, 1972 or W. H. Freeman (pap.). A basic introduction to social psychology that covers such topics as conformity, self-justification, aggressiveness, prejudice, and attraction to others.

BRIM, Orville G., Jr. and WHEELER, Stanton, *Socialization After Childhood: Two Essays*. Wiley, 1966, or Krieger (pap.). The first essay is on "Socialization Through the Life Cycle" and the second discusses "The Structure of Formally Organized Socialization Settings."

HARRIS, Thomas, *I'm OK— You're OK: A Practical Guide to Transactional Analysis*. Harper & Row, 1969 or Avon (pap.). An easy-to-understand book that gives the basic principles of Transactional Analysis.

HUNT, Robert Cushman (ed.), *Personalities and Cultures: Readings in Psychological Anthropology*. Natural History Press, 1967 (pap.). A book of readings that explore the role of personality in shaping culture and show how individual, regional, and group personality traits affect the patterns of culture.

MEAD, Margaret, *Sex and Temperament in Three Primitive Societies*. Peter Smith, 1963, or Morrow (pap.). A study of personality characteristics in three primitive societies: the Arapesh, the Mundugumar, and the Tchambuli.

STRAUSS, Anselm (ed.), *George Herbert Mead on Social Psychology*. University of Chicago Press, 1964. Selected papers of George Herbert Mead. Parts III through VII deal with mind, self, and society.

FICTION

BUTLER, Beverly, *Captive Thunder*. Dodd. Unhappy in her home and school situations, Nancy Essen runs away to Milwaukee, where she finds a purpose in life through involvement with Project Head Start.

MAUGHAM, W. Somerset, *Of Human Bondage*. Doubleday or Pocket Books (pap.). A boy with a congenital deformity—a club foot—becomes a man, although not without a great deal of pain.

NARAYAN, R. K., *The Vendor of Sweets*. Viking or Avon (pap.). A nonconformist from East India returns home after receiving an American education and faces conflicts between tradition and progress.

Highlight

What is the difference between culture and society?

All of the concepts that you are discovering in your study of sociology can be included under two main headings—"Culture" and "Society." These two categories are central to sociology. You have been learning about cultural concepts in this unit. In the next unit, you begin the study of society. Thus at this point it might be useful to examine more closely what these two important categories mean and how they differ from each other.

You may remember the definitions of both terms. In Chapter 2 we defined *culture* as the way of life of a people—the shared, learned behavior of the members of a society. We defined *society* as a number of people living within a certain geographic area who share a common culture and have a feeling of unity that binds them together. We said that a society is the people who live in a specific geographic area, while culture is the shared, learned behavior of these people.

As you can see, there is a good deal of overlap between these two categories. There cannot be a culture except within a particular society. We can talk about the culture of a society that no longer exists, such as the culture of the ancient Romans. But the fact is that when Roman culture was developing, there was a Roman society. Similarly, we cannot talk about a society except in terms of its culture. Try describing a particular culture without using the context of its society. Or describe a specific society without referring to its culture. What happens?

But despite this interdependence of the two categories, we can distinguish between them. There is a difference between cultural aspects and social relationships. If we observe the behavior and relationships of human beings, we can sort out the cultural factors and the social factors. Before we discuss the difference between cultural and social factors any further, though, take a look at the following list. Into which category—cultural or social—would you put each of these ten items?

1. The idea of progress
2. A guard on a basketball team
3. The belief in God
4. A teacher leading a classroom discussion
5. The custom of shaking hands when meeting
6. An automobile assembly line
7. The value of friendship
8. The organization of the White House staff
9. The latest model Chevrolet
10. Shoppers in a supermarket

Some of the items on this list refer to the cultural categories of ideas, norms, and things. The outstanding characteristic of cultural factors is that they deal with *meaning.* What we think and what we do makes sense because it has meaning to us. It has meaning that is not unique to our own personality. It is shared with others in our society. Such meaning is attached to ideas, relationships, and things. It is the essence of culture.

Other items on the list primarily involve people relating with other people. They are mainly *relationships*—two or more people in interaction. We can say that relationships are social events, while the meaning of such relationships is cultural.

To explore this distinction between the two categories further, we can compare their differing effect on human beings and on animals. Many animals, like human beings, have social relationships. Take dogs, baboons, and ants, for example. They each (in their natural state) participate in social relationships. But can we say that those relationships have meaning? Are they cultural in the human sense? The world of people has conscious meaning. The world of animals does not. This difference helps distinguish human beings from animals.

How is it that human social action is cultural, while animals appear to have social relationships without cultural meaning? The answer to that question lies in the difference between the nature of human beings and animals. Most animals are born with "instinctual imprints." That is, what they are interested in, and what they will do about it, is largely or entirely "programmed" into them according to their nature. Their behavior is "triggered" by their environment. A dog, for instance, reacts to its environment like a dog. Try to imagine a dog acting like a cat. Wouldn't it seem strange and out of character? Animals follow their instincts. And if those instincts require social behavior, animals will behave in a social way. Wild dogs run in packs because they are by instinct programmed that way. Cats are solitary hunters for the same reason.

Human beings, however, are not programmed for any particular type of social behavior. They must learn their behavioral patterns, including the number and kinds of social relationships they are involved in. Because such relationships are not programmed into people, the meaning that they have attached to their social relationships can differ from culture to culture. For example, a football game has a certain meaning in contemporary American culture. It does not have the same meaning in Brazil. On the other hand, soccer has a special meaning in Brazil that is not present in the United States.

Now look again at the list of ten items. In light of what you've just read, identify once more which items are primarily cultural and which are mainly social. You will find that some are not clear-cut. Number 2 (a guard on a basketball team), for example, illustrates that relationships and their meaning are interconnected. A guard on a basketball team is part of a social relationship—a basketball team—that has a distinct meaning in our culture.

As you go through the list, pick out the purely cultural items. Then pick out those that involve relationships and are, therefore, social. How does your selection compare to the choices you made the first time? Next, explain the cultural aspects of the social items. Also, indicate what can be added to the purely cultural items to make them social.

As you continue reading through this book, bear in mind that sociology deals basically with only two topics—culture and society. Or, to put it another way, sociology focuses on the study of cultural meaning and social relationships. Can you think of any examples that do not fit into either one of these categories?

UNIT TWO

THE ORGANIZATION OF SOCIETY

Our culture influences our personalities. In fact, the values and norms of our society regulate our entire lives. Since our society is so important in our lives, have you ever wondered about its organization? How do you think social groups are organized? How does the social class structure affect our lives? How does the placement of minorities in the social structure affect everyone in the society? And what about the effects of the geographic distribution of people in a society?

6 Social Groups

▶ In what ways do you interact with others?

▶ How much of your time do you spend in groups?

▶ How does participation in groups affect your life?

SECTION 1:
Interaction in Groups

The human social group is the main object of investigation for the sociologist. It is in the group that human relationships take place. Every individual participates in groups and is influenced by the other members.

What Is a Group?

We may define a GROUP as *two or more individuals who interact with one another and are together physically*. The interaction is what makes the group a unit. What, then, is interaction? HUMAN INTERACTION *is the action of one individual causing another individual or individuals to act*. Interaction takes place when two or more persons are mutually influencing each other.

Human interaction may be either physical or symbolic. *Physical interaction* occurs, for example, when one person kisses another person on the cheek and is kissed in return. The two individuals are mutually influencing each other in a very physical way. *Symbolic interaction* accounts for most of our interactions, however. We communicate with each other through the use of symbols. The most commonly used symbols are those of language. If your teacher asks you a question and you respond with an answer, symbolic interaction has taken place. Symbolic interaction also includes the use of such symbols as gestures and facial expressions. The catcher on a baseball team gives a gesture or signal to tell the pitcher what kind of ball to throw. A certain expression on your mother's face tells you that she disapproves of what you just said.

Some form of human interaction is essential for a group to exist. But how much interaction is necessary for individuals to be considered a group? If people are talking to

101

each other, or fighting, they are interacting. But suppose two people are in a railroad station at 3:00 A.M. waiting for a train. They are alone in the station, sitting at opposite ends of a long bench. Neither is looking at the other, but each is aware of the other's presence. Are they a group? To determine whether or not they are in interaction, we might ask ourselves another question: "Do I always act the same when I'm aware of another's presence as I do when I know that I'm alone?" Some of us might talk to ourselves, or whistle softly, when we know we are alone. But if we're aware of another person's presence, we aren't likely to do these things. We don't want others to think that we're a bit odd. We might, therefore, consider the two people as a group because their awareness of each other probably affects their behavior. We can say, then, that the criterion of interaction is met if the people are aware of each other's presence.

The second requirement for persons to be a group is the criterion of being together physically. Let us say that if the individuals are physically close enough to communicate verbally and can see each other, then they meet this criterion. Thus two people talking on a telephone would not be a group because they are not together physically, even though they are in interaction.

You can see from this discussion some of the difficulties of making useful definitions. We need careful definitions, though, for uniformity. Sociologists must have specific definitions for accurate measuring in research studies.

Categories. These, then, are the requirements for group membership. We now have the problem of how to label group-like situations that do not meet these requirements. There are two kinds of categories of people who have something in common but are not in interaction or together physically. The first category consists of any two or more people who are not particularly conscious of what they have in common, and who do not necessarily interact with one another. Examples of this category would be all persons who have ever had the chickenpox, or all individuals between the ages of eighteen and sixty-five, or everyone who has ever been in Yankee Stadium. We can call these *statistical categories* because they are based on merely the statistical fact of existence. They lack the element of consciousness of kind—they don't know what they have in common.

The second category is similar to the first in that physical presence and interaction are not required of those included in it. It differs in that the members are aware that they belong to a special category. For example, black people in the United States are not a group because they are not all together physically and in interaction. Yet they certainly have consciousness of kind. We can call this category a *social category*. It includes such groupings as race, sex, occupation, and nationality. Italian Americans, golfers, and teen-agers are all social categories.

Associations. There is another type of human grouping that does not fit our requirements for group membership. Large organizations that have been formed for a specific purpose do not get all of their members together physically, nor are all of the members in interaction. But such organizations usually consist of many individual groups, which meet and interact both among themselves and with other groups in the organization. Even though these organizations do not fit our definition of a group, they are more than just a category.

Sociologists refer to such specific-purpose organizations as *associations*. Labor unions, corporations, political parties, factories, and fraternal lodges are all associations because they are organized for a specific purpose. Although they are not groups, they are composed of many smaller groups. Your own high school might be considered an association. It is formally organized for a specific

This bar mitzvah is one example of a transitory group. The people involved are meeting together for this one occasion, which lasts a relatively short time.

purpose, the education of youth. Yet it is beyond the definition of a group because rarely, if at all, can the total population of the school—the students, the faculty, and the administrators—meet together and interact. Your high school is an association composed of many groups, such as individual classes, administrative officers, and the cafeteria staff, which have various degrees of interaction among them.

Kinds of Groups

There are a number of ways of dividing groups into kinds or types. We can divide groups on the basis of time—of how long they exist and how often they meet.

Transitory and recurrent groups. TRANSITORY GROUPS *are temporary groups which meet only once for a relatively short time.* The three most common transitory groups are crowds, audiences, and mobs. In a crowd the individuals are together physically but the interaction among the total group is very minimal. This is the case with a group of people waiting for the traffic light to change so that they can cross the street. An audience is a temporary group being subjected to a common stimulus, such as students in the assembly hall being addressed by the assistant principal. In a mob the members are highly emotional and united in purpose. An example is an angry group attempting to take over an embassy building.

We spend a limited time in transitory groups. And the interaction that takes place

103

is mostly impersonal. Therefore, transitory groups have much less influence on the individual than recurrent groups.

RECURRENT GROUPS *are rather permanent groups in which persons interact over and over again for a long period of time.* There are two basic types of recurrent groups, formal ones and informal ones. FORMAL GROUPS *are those which have an official structure or formal organization.* They are formed to achieve a specific purpose or goal. A good example is a club. A club is a formally organized group. It usually has a specific set of officers and sometimes a formal constitution and bylaws. And its members share in a number of activities together. In your school you may have a camera club, an international relations club, or a science club. Such clubs are formally organized, with a number of specific functions, and are centered around a particular activity.

The other type of recurrent group is the informal group. INFORMAL GROUPS *are those which do not have an official structure or deliberately formed organization.* That is, they have no charter of formal bylaws or regular meeting hours. They include *peer groups,* or individuals of about the same age and position, and *congeniality groups*—individuals who get together because they enjoy one another's company. Examples of informal groups are neighborhood play groups of children, the very close friendship groups of adolescents, and families who often get together to go to movies or sports events. The characteristics of these groups are that they are informal and that the members do things together because they like one another.

Dyads and triads. Another way to divide groups is by the size of the group. *A two-person group is called a* DYAD. In a dyad, each member of the group has direct control over the group's existence. If one member leaves the group, the group ends. Furthermore, decision-making in a dyad can be awkward. If both members fail to agree, one member must convince the other, or the group will cease to exist. Think of some two-person groups in your own experience. How stable are they?

A major change in groups seems to occur when the size increases from two to three. *A three-person group is called a* TRIAD. In a triad, the group can assume a life of its own, independent of any particular member. No one person can disband the group. Also, decision-making in a triad is easier than in a dyad, since two people against one are more persuasive than one against one.

Group Relationships

Despite all these labels for groups, human relationships often do not fit into a rigid category. Therefore social scientists have set up a description of two opposite extremes. Between the two extremes runs a scale they call a *continuum.* Group relationships can then be arranged on this continuous scale between the two extremes so that the continuum shows the range of relationships. One such scale is the primary-secondary continuum.

The primary group relationship. *In the* PRIMARY GROUP RELATIONSHIP *the entire personality of the individual is taken into account. The relationships are intimate and face-to-face. Communication is deep and intensive. And personal satisfactions are of primary importance.* Family relationships are probably the most primary of all our group relationships. Your parents and siblings (brothers and sisters) react to your entire personality, not to just a part. The relationships are very intimate and personal. And you are important for your own personality rather than for what you do. For example, you may not have the most perfect features, and may get an occasional low grade in school, but your parents will still love you. An important aspect of the primary relationship is that since each individual is contributing his or her unique

Have you ever been part of a triad—a three-member group? If so, what advantages and disadvantages do you find in being with this number of people?

personality to the relationship, he or she can't be replaced by another person.

The secondary group relationship. On the opposite end of the continuum is the SEC-ONDARY GROUP RELATIONSHIP. *This relationship involves a reaction to only a segment of the individual's personality.* The person's importance to the group is not his or her unique personality, but the specific function that he or she performs in the group. The relationship tends to be casual, temporary, and limited in personal involvement. It is functional. And the individual can easily be replaced by anyone who can carry out the same function.

For example, suppose you were employed to unload sacks of cement from railroad cars. Your employer is not concerned about your entire personality, whether you attend church regularly, what your I.Q. is, or if you have gleaming white teeth. His or her concern is about only one segment of your personality—can you unload the bags of cement? If he or she discovers that you can't do the job, your employer may simply fire you and hire someone else who can do the job.

These examples of family and employment fall near the extreme ends of the continuum.

THE CONTINUUM OF PRIMARY-SECONDARY RELATIONSHIPS

PRIMARY RELATIONSHIPS		SECONDARY RELATIONSHIPS		
Family	Congeniality Group	School Club	Classroom	Job

Most of our relationships are somewhere between the two. The primary-secondary continuum might appear as shown on this page. In this continuum of our society the family is the most primary and the job the most secondary. The congeniality group is more primary than secondary. And the school club is about as much primary as secondary. The relationships in your classroom may be more secondary than primary but not nearly as secondary as your job. Remember that these placings are only hypothetical. In real life each would depend on the individual as well as the specific group. But perhaps this continuum will help you understand what is meant by primary and secondary relationships.

The in-group relationship. Two other group relationships studied by sociologists are the in-group and out-group relationships. *The* IN-GROUP RELATIONSHIP *is one in which we have a sense of loyalty, friendliness, solidarity, and identification.* In-group relationships are usually ethnocentric. There is a strong "we" feeling, in which we speak of "our school," "our club," or "our gang." Often members of the in-group adopt certain symbols of identification, such as emblems, badges, or a style of dress, to set them off from others.

The out-group relationship. *The* OUT-GROUP RELATIONSHIP *is one in which we feel a sense of disinterest, distrust, scorn, avoidance, competition, fear, or in some cases, hatred.*

The "we" feeling does not apply to the out-group. Rather, the out-group is "they." In fact, in-group and out-group relationships are determined by who is viewed as "we" and who is viewed as "they."

We must realize, though, that who is in the in-group and out-group changes, depending on the criterion. For example, in international relations all Americans are an in-group, while the rest of the world is an out-group. In school affairs, however, the members of the school community are the in-group, and everyone else is the out-group. In family matters, the family members are the in-group, and everyone outside the family is the out-group. Actually, as you can see, in-groups and out-groups are not really groups at all. They are relationships based on concepts of belongingness.

SECTION REVIEW

1. What criteria must be met for a number of people to be a group?
2. How do categories and associations differ from groups?
3. What are the differences between transitory groups and recurrent groups? Between dyads and triads?
4. What is the primary-secondary group continuum and how is it used?
5. What is an in-group relationship? An out-group relationship? Can you belong to an out-group?

106

KEY TERMS

Define and give an example of each term.

association	peer group
congeniality group	physical interaction
continuum	primary group
dyad	relationship
formal group	recurrent group
group	secondary group
human interaction	relationship
informal group	social category
in-group	statistical category
relationship	symbolic interaction
out-group	transitory group
relationship	triad

SECTION 2:
The Recurrent Group

Recurrent groups are relatively enduring. They develop observable structures, functions, patterns, and processes. Thus the sociologist is able to observe them over a long time and analyze them carefully.

Characteristics of Recurrent Groups

Sociologists have noted the following characteristics of recurrent groups. As you read about these characteristics, decide if they are found in the recurrent groups in your life.

Group goals. Recurrent groups develop goals. These goals may be objects, situations, or satisfactions. For example, the goal of a basketball team might be to win the league trophy — an object. The goal of a local chamber of commerce might be to provide a playground for the community — a situation. The goal of your family might be to achieve pleasant and personality-building relationships — a satisfaction.

Group goals may be formal or informal. *Formal goals* are clearly stated and understood by all of the group members. They might be stated in a constitution or set of bylaws of the group, as in the case of a science club, photography club, or student council.

Informal goals are not officially stated by the group and not consciously recognized by the members. For example, a congeniality group of close friends usually does not have any written goals. In fact, if you were asked to name the goals of your congeniality group you probably couldn't do so. You know only that you like one another's company and enjoy doing things together. Informal goals are usually related to the values of the group. The members of the group have similar feelings about what is right, good, or important. Persons who do not share the same values are not likely to join the group, or are apt to drop out after a short time.

Group roles. After a group has existed for a period of time, specific group roles begin to emerge. In the case of formally organized groups this may occur very soon, such as through an election of officers. In the informal group roles develop much more slowly. But some division of labor usually takes place as different members begin to accept and carry out specific responsibilities. This division of labor within the group is called *role allocation.* The leader in a group allocates the roles so that every member has some meaningful function to perform. The leader then sees that the members carry out their roles. Group roles can also be self-allocated, as is usually the case of the leader's role.

Since we defined a role as the behavior expected of a person because of his or her position in the group, a particular role cannot exist by itself. There must be another person in another role doing the expecting. This situation, in which each role has an opposite

This ballet class is a recurrent group. What are the group goals of a ballet class? The group roles? The role behavior? Some group norms and sanctions?

or reciprocal role, is referred to as the *reciprocal nature of roles*. In the family, for example, a man cannot be a husband by himself; he must have a wife. The two roles cannot be separated. Neither the husband nor the wife can be a parent without a child. Nor can the role of uncle exist without a niece or nephew. In your classroom, your teacher cannot perform the role of teacher unless he or she has students to teach. In any group a leader can only exist if he or she has followers. Supervisors in a factory cannot play their role unless they have some workers to supervise.

The reciprocal nature of roles is related to rights and duties. Actually, all roles have both rights and duties. A *right* is an opportunity or privilege allowing the person to act. A *duty* is the obligation of others to permit the act to take place. In other words, a right is an opportunity to act that is recipro-cal to the duty of another person or persons to permit the act. The role of the group leader is to lead the group. But the leader can do this only if the group members permit him or her to lead them. Individuals cannot carry out their roles unless the people in reciprocal roles allow them to do so.

Role behavior. The group roles are the behavior expected of the various group members because of their position in the group. *Role behavior* is the actual behavior of each person in carrying out his or her role. We are well aware that the members of a group do not always carry out their roles. The president may fail to give real leadership to the group. The secretary may fail to keep up the minutes of the meetings. The treasurer may lose some of the group's funds. When there is a significant difference between the group roles and the role behavior of the group members, the unity and efficiency of the group are threatened.

Group norms. Within the group there is a specific set of norms that governs the behavior of the members. For example, if a girl is to be a member of the basketball team, she must abide by a specific set of norms. She must not break the rules of training set up by the coach and the team members. In a formal group these norms may be specifically stated. In an informal group they are often just generally understood.

If the group is to continue to exist there must be *group consensus* of the norms. This means that the majority of the members regard the norms as appropriate and important enough to conform to them. The amount of conformity the group will demand depends on how the norm contributes to the purpose of the group or how deeply it is rooted in sentiment and tradition. Without consensus the group cannot survive for any length of time.

Group sanctions. When a member of the group does not conform to the norms of the group, the group applies *sanctions* (rewards or punishments—in this case, punishments) to the nonconforming member. A member of the football team who breaks training rules may be suspended from the team. By applying sanctions the group can control the actions of its members.

Communication. Communication among the members of the group is necessary for the successful operation of any group process. Imagine the chaos that would exist if the members of the football team could not communicate. The methods of communication commonly used within the group are language and gestures.

Structure, function, pattern, and process. Recurrent groups characteristically have structures, functions, patterns, and processes. Groups develop a particular *structure* or organization as roles are given to the individual members. Sociologists determine this structure by observing the events that occur among the members of the group.

Very closely related to the group structure is *function*. Sociologists study the function of the group itself, which is related to the group goals. They also study the particular functions that the various members carry out in their specific roles.

Groups also develop certain *patterns of behavior,* acts that are repeated over and over. For example, some groups develop certain rituals or ceremonies that are carried out each time the group meets, such as reciting the Scout Oath and Law. Or they participate in the same type of activities, such as football plays.

There are also various *processes* present in groups. Through group processes, change takes place in a specific way. The most basic process is interaction, since it is involved in all human group relationships. Change occurs through interaction, as the members of the group are mutually influencing each other.

Studying Small Groups

The following three approaches to the study of small groups have helped social scientists in their investigation of the structures, functions, patterns, and processes of small recurrent groups. The study of small groups is the particular activity of the social psychologist, whose basic concern is the individual as part of the group. Yet sociologists often engage in research on the small group.

Sociometry. Sociologists have searched for techniques to study interpersonal relations. A pioneer in this was a socially oriented psychiatrist, J. L. Moreno. He developed a technique called *sociometry*. This technique examines the patterns of interaction in an informal group structure, such as subgroup and friendship patterns. It considers the position of each individual in relationship to the others. Suppose, for example, we wanted to determine the informal group structure of ten boy scouts. We could ask each boy to name by secret ballot his first, second, and third choice of members with whom he would most like to share a pup tent. When all of the secret ballots are in we can make a *sociogram,* a diagram which shows the relationships. Our sociogram might look like the diagram below.

Usually some group members are admired and accepted by many in the group, while others tend to be rejected and isolated. From this sociogram we can quickly see who is the most popular member of the group, who is unpopular, and which members are most friendly with each other. Can you pick out the three boy scouts who form a clique (prefer each other) within the group?

Group dynamics. *Group dynamics* is concerned with the meaning the group has for its members and how participation in the group changes the individual's behavior. Group dynamics developed out of the work of Kurt Lewin, a social psychologist. During World War II, when many foods were in short supply, he carried out research on how to change the food habits of individuals. He used one group in which group discussion took place and another group in which the more traditional lecture method was used. He found that ten times as many women changed their habits in the first group as in the second group. After considerable research with individuals in group and nongroup situations, Lewin concluded that it is easier to change individuals in a group situation than it is to change any of them separately. As a result of Lewin's research, many sociologists are now focusing on the group dynamics of a given situation.

Interaction process analysis. *Interaction process analysis* is more concerned with the types and methods of interpersonal behavior than with the contents or results of group action. The emphasis is less on what is said than on how it is said. This approach was developed by Robert F. Bales. Bales conducted investigations of such group situations as committee meetings, leadership training meetings, and competitive games. His technique of research was to give group members a problem to solve. He then observed the kinds of group reactions, rather than the actual solutions, through a one-way screen. Bales found that the same kinds of reactions occurred over and over again.

SOCIOGRAM SHOWING FIRST, SECOND, AND THIRD CHOICES OF PUP TENT PARTNERS FOR TEN BOY SCOUTS

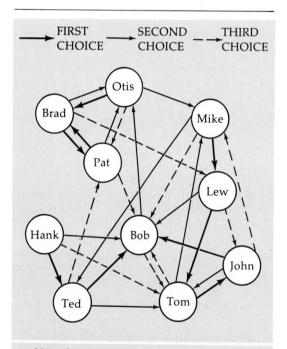

Note that Bob is most popular and is chosen seven times. Hank is a social isolate as he is never chosen. Observe also the close relationship of Pat, Brad, and Otis.

Similar roles, such as that of leader, joker, and silent member, usually emerged. His contribution was to place the emphasis on the interpersonal reactions as a means of analyzing small-group behavior.

SECTION REVIEW

1. What are the characteristics of recurrent groups? Describe a specific recurrent group in terms of each characteristic.
2. How would you use sociometry to study a small group?
3. According to Lewin, what is the best way to change people's behavior?
4. Robert Bales stressed what aspect of small groups?

KEY TERMS

Explain and give an example of each term.

duty	pattern
formal group goal	process
function	reciprocal nature
group consensus	of roles
of norms	right
group dynamics	role allocation
group sanctions	role behavior
informal group goal	sociogram
interaction process	sociometry
analysis	structure

SECTION 3:
Universal Social Processes

Social processes are types of group interaction. Whenever people get together and interact, they interact in one or more of five basic ways—they are in conflict, they compete against one another, they cooperate with one another, they accommodate one another, or they assimilate a person or persons into the group. Since these five types of social processes, or group interaction, are found in all societies and in all interaction, they are called *universal social processes.* Let's examine each of the processes—conflict, competition, cooperation, accommodation, and assimilation—in detail.

Conflict

CONFLICT *is the deliberate attempt to coerce, oppose, harm, or resist the will of another person or persons.* It may range from the extreme of killing an enemy to the deliberate slighting of an associate. Usually conflict is physical. But it can also be psychological. Conflict may be personal or corporate. *Personal conflict* is conflict between two or more members within a group. For example, there was personal conflict between Hitler and several of his German generals, who eventually tried to assassinate him. *Corporate conflict* is conflict between groups within a society or between two or more societies. The most common example of corporate conflict is war. Here each nation is attempting to break, oppose, harm, or resist the will of the other nation or nations.

Corporate conflicts within a society may take the form of labor-management conflicts, race conflicts, or conflicts between rival business organizations. In each case one group wants to break or resist the will of the other group. Physical violence may break out in labor-management or race conflicts and result in the destruction of property and the loss of people's lives. Conflict between rival business organizations may take the form of price cutting or attempts to force the rival into bankruptcy. Whichever method is used, the purpose is to harm or destroy the business rival.

Conflicts can occur in transitory groups as well as in recurrent groups. If you were walking down a dark street and a masked person emerged from the shadows, placed a gun in your back, and demanded your purse or wallet, the two of you would be an example of a personal conflict within a transitory group.

The effects of conflict. Personal conflict within a group makes group consensus impossible. It greatly limits the effectiveness of the group to perform some task. Unless the conflict can be quickly resolved and consensus restored, the group will not be able to survive.

On the other hand, corporate conflict tends to strengthen the group. The in-group members develop a strong feeling of unity as they struggle to oppose the out-group. For example, before the United States entered World War II the nation was divided by a great variety of attitudes toward the war. But after the bombing of Pearl Harbor and our declaration of war, Americans became firmly united in the war effort against the Axis Powers.

Competition

COMPETITION *occurs when two or more groups or persons oppose each other to achieve a goal that only one can attain.* Although at first conflict and competition may seem very much alike, there are three major differences. The basic difference between them is that conflict places the emphasis on harming or destroying the opponent, while competition places the stress on achieving the goal. A second difference is that conflict always involves an awareness of the opposition but competition may occur without any knowledge of the opponent. For example, when two members of a group are in conflict, each knows that the other is his or her opponent.

A track meet illustrates the social process of competition, in which two or more people strive for a goal that only one person can win.

This is often not true in competition. If you are applying for a scholarship, taking an exam, or applying for a job, you do not know against whom you are competing. A third difference is in the norms. Conflict usually has no clearly defined norms, whereas competition is governed by specific social norms. For instance, in war there are no basic rules and no referees to enforce them. However, when you play a softball or basketball game, specific rules of behavior are followed. And officials are on hand to impose sanctions on the parties who break the rules.

What begins as competition sometimes ends as conflict. Two business managers compete with each other to see who can make the most sales. As they become more and more emotionally involved in the competition, they are no longer interested in making the most sales. Each wants to destroy the other. Or two men competing for the affection of the same girl may lose interest in winning the girl and focus only on the idea of harming or destroying the opponent.

Cooperation

COOPERATION *occurs when two or more persons or groups work together to achieve a goal from which all the members will benefit.* For example, the members of a softball team cooperate in order to win the game. If the team wins, each player shares in the glory. When the junior class members work hard on their class project and win more points than the seniors or sophomores, all juniors, even those who did nothing, share in the reward. We might consider cooperation the process that gets things done. For no group can achieve any goals without cooperation among the members of the group.

Competition and cooperation. In our society it is common to find both cooperation and competition in the same situation. One group cooperates among themselves to win the competition with another group. For ex-

ample, the members of a hockey team cooperate with one another when they compete against the opposing team. Also, we use competition to build cooperation. The individual members of the hockey team compete against each other to determine which players cooperate best and should be on the first team or the starting lineup. We find cooperation and competition working together not just in sports but in all aspects of American life—in education, business, politics, religion, and small groups, to name a few. In American society cooperation and competition go hand in hand.

Accommodation

ACCOMMODATION *is a state of balance between cooperation and conflict, achieved through a conscious attempt by the conflicting parties to reach an agreement.* The conflicting parties do not intend to cooperate with each other. They are simply going to tolerate each other so that both can make some progress toward their individual goals. Both parties know that if they continue the conflict, they will greatly harm themselves. To avoid such wasteful destruction, they reconcile or settle their conflict. Their accommodation may take any of the following forms.

Coercion. *In* COERCION, *accommodation is brought about by force or restraint.* Coercion implies the existence of a weak party and a strong party. The weak person or group must accept the restraint of the strong, for the weak party is powerless to resist. An example of balance caused by coercion would be the Pax Romana, the years of peace and stability within the Roman Empire from 27 B.C. to 180 A.D. The real reason for the peace was that Rome had conquered the other countries in the Mediterranean area and held them in submission so that no conflict was allowed to develop. The same situation can take place within a group if one member is so strong that none of the other group mem-

Secretary of State Henry Kissinger held a number of talks with Egypt's President Anwar Sadat (left) in 1975 in order to achieve a compromise on the Middle-East situation. For this compromise, both Egypt and Israel had to make some concessions.

bers is willing to oppose him or her. Accommodation by coercion may occur in athletic, racial, religious, or industrial conflicts — in fact, in almost any kind of conflict.

Truce. *A* TRUCE *is an accommodation in which the conflicting parties agree to stop the conflict for a period of time so that negotiations may take place.* It is quite common for armies to accept a truce to allow time for the two sides to negotiate an armistice or surrender.

Compromise. *When a* COMPROMISE *is made, each side agrees to give up some of its demands for the sake of resolving the conflict.* The Missouri Compromise of 1820 is a good example. Representative James Tallmadge of New York had proposed an amendment to Missouri's application for admission as a state. This amendment stated that the further introduction of slaves into Missouri would be prohibited and that all children born into slavery after its admission would be freed. The House, where the North had a majority, voted for the amendment. But the Senate, where the southern bloc was very powerful, rejected it. Congress became deadlocked. At this point Henry Clay of Kentucky proposed

a compromise that would bring Maine into the Union as a free state and admit Missouri as a state with no restrictions on slavery. Both sides accepted Clay's compromise, which became known as the Missouri Compromise. The crisis between North and South was accommodated for a short time.

Arbitration and mediation. Arbitration and mediation are actually devices used in bringing about compromise. *In* ARBITRATION, *the two conflicting parties agree to accept the decision of a neutral third party, who settles the dispute. In* MEDIATION, *the third party has no power, but acts as an adviser and counselor in helping the conflicting parties come to an agreement.* Both arbitration and mediation are commonly used in industrial conflicts to settle deadlocked negotiations between labor unions and management.

Toleration. TOLERATION *is a form of accommodation without formal agreement. The conflicting parties avoid conflict by developing an attitude of "live and let live," by informally agreeing to disagree.* An example is the attitude of "détente" between the United States and the Soviet Union. The two nations have not signed a formal declaration of this attitude. They simply exist side by side, watching each other and trying to avoid a face-to-face conflict.

Accommodation can occur between nations, organizations, groups, or individuals. Many of our interactions take the form of accommodation. We refuse to cooperate with the other party. Yet conflict is too costly. So we simply develop a working arrangement with them.

Assimilation

ASSIMILATION *is the process by which two previously distinct groups blend into one unified group.* This fusion of two previously separate groups is brought about through the sharing of attitudes, values, and skills. Assimilation may take place on a small scale or on a very large scale. For example, assimilation occurs when you accept a new student into your school. On a very large scale, assimilation has occurred in American society as immigrants from all over the world have come to the "melting pot" and made it their new home. When these immigrants have become so much a part of American life that

they are not considered "foreigners," complete assimilation has taken place.

Complete assimilation of people into a society involves amalgamation and acculturation. AMALGAMATION *is acceptable intermarriage between previously distinct groups.* ACCULTURATION *is the intermixture of the shared, learned behaviors of both groups.* Actually the process of acculturation is the same as that of cultural diffusion. Both involve a borrowing or exchange of culture traits. The results may be a relatively equal exchange of traits. Or one culture may practically absorb the other. Or the two cultures may merge into a completely new culture. Complete assimilation requires that the separate, distinct groups become so much like each other that they are no longer distinguishable as separate groups.

Not all immigrants to America have become fully assimilated. In some cases only accommodation has taken place, as with groups that are tolerated only if they stay in their section of town. In some cases amalgamation has taken place but acculturation has not. For example, some of the immigrants from Western Europe have intermarried to

Assimilation, or the blending of two sets of values, attitudes, and beliefs, is likely to occur when an American family adopts a child from another culture, such as a Vietnamese child (shown here).

the extent that we cannot tell if their national background is German, English, Irish, Dutch, French, Swedish, or Danish. Yet at the same time they have maintained some of the shared, learned behaviors of their native lands, which makes them distinguishable from other Americans. On the other hand, there are some cases in which acculturation has taken place but not amalgamation. This has been true of many immigrants to the United States who are not of the Caucasoid race. For example, the Japanese and blacks have in many instances become so acculturated that their shared, learned behaviors cannot be distinguished from those of other Americans. Yet the mores of American society have not encouraged their fusion through intermarriage.

Although not usually considered with the five universal social processes, there are several other social processes that are of great importance in human relationships. We will discuss two of these—stratification and differentiation—in the next chapter.

SECTION REVIEW

1. What is the difference between conflict and competition? Can one lead to the other?
2. Why do cooperation and competition often occur together?
3. What are the various forms that accommodation might take?
4. What is necessary for complete assimilation to take place?

KEY TERMS

Explain each term and use it in a sentence.

accommodation	conflict
acculturation	cooperation
amalgamation	corporate conflict
arbitration	mediation
assimilation	personal conflict
coercion	toleration
competition	truce
compromise	universal social process

PROJECTS AND ACTIVITIES

1. Using a camera, take pictures and make a slide set or photo display that illustrates as many different kinds of groups as possible.

2. Try to determine some of the statistical and social categories to which members of the class belong.

3. Pick a television show that has a group as its main set of characters. Then analyze the group and the relationships among group members.

4. Develop and present a sociodrama (play) that illustrates both in-group and out-group relationships.

5. Attempt to join a dyad with the intention of making it a triad. Interview the other two members concerning the differences that emerge in the group's structure as a result of your entry.

6. Draw or cut out pictures of groups and set up a chart explaining the relationships of the people in the groups.

7. Make up a questionnaire and distribute it to members of a particular group, such as members of an athletic team, to determine their feelings about roles, norms, and sanctions in their particular group. Keep the questionnaire anonymous.

8. Divide the class into groups of three to five students each and attempt to have them communicate with one another using only nonverbal communication. As a result of this experience, how important would you say that verbal communication is in the group?

9. Construct a display that graphically illustrates the use of symbols in human interaction.

10. Read a short story of your choice and make a sociogram of the characters in the story.

11. Design a task that may be done in small groups in your classroom. Then observe and, if possible, use a videotape recorder to record the groups as they go about completing the task. Analyze the tape (or your observation) in terms of the social processes involved.

TOPICS FOR INQUIRY

1. Could an association actually become a group for a short period of time? If so, how? Give examples.

2. Analyze your class as a recurrent group, using the characteristics of recurrent groups mentioned in the chapter.

3. Can a recurrent group continue to exist if it does not have all of the following: group goals, group roles, some role allocation, group norms, group sanctions, and communication? Which of these are most important? Which are least important?

4. Make a list of groups at your school and then attempt to place each group on the primary-secondary relationship continuum. Do students all agree on where each group should be placed? Why or why not?

5. What do you see as the advantages and disadvantages of each of the methods of studying small groups: sociometry, group dynamics, and interaction process analysis? Why?

6. Discuss: Whenever humans interact, at least one of the five universal social processes is present.

7. Do you think that complete assimilation of all persons will ever take place in American society? Explain your answer.

SUGGESTIONS FOR READING

NONFICTION

BERNE, Eric, *What Do You Say After You Say Hello?* Grove, 1972 or Bantam (pap.). A psychological examination of group processes by the author of *Games People Play.*

HARE, Alexander Paul, *et al.* (eds.), *Small Groups: Studies in Social Interaction.* Knopf, 1965. A book of readings on the interaction of small groups.

MILLS, Theodore M., *The Sociology of Small Groups.* Prentice-Hall, 1970 (pap.). A discussion of the study of small groups, such as families, work crews, and legislative committees.

NYE, Robert, *Conflict Among Humans.* Springer, 1973 (and pap.). Nye emphasizes the psychological dimension in conflict and other group processes.

OBERSCHALL, Anthony, *Social Conflict and Social Movements.* Prentice-Hall, 1973. Contains a good summary of various theories of conflict and provides historical references.

REEVES, Elton T., *The Dynamics of Group Behavior,* American Management Association, 1970. A primer in applied group dynamics with an emphasis on personal problems.

SCHUTZ, William C., *Here Comes Everybody: Body-Mind and Encounter Culture.* Harper & Row, 1972 (pap.). A lighthearted encounter-group manual by the director of the famous Esalen Institute.

TIGER, Lionel, *Men in Groups.* Random House, 1969 (and pap.). The author emphasizes the importance of biological motivation in human social groups, and how "maleness" affects group behavior.

FICTION

DOS PASSOS, John, *The 42nd Parallel.* New American Library (pap.). Part of Dos Passos' trilogy *U.S.A., The 42nd Parallel* is concerned with the interaction among a variety of social levels across the 42nd parallel in the United States.

GOLDING, William, *Lord of the Flies*. Putnam (pap.). A group of boys tries to establish a society on an island. The story moves from humor to horror as the society seems doomed to self-destruction.

MILLER, Arthur, *All My Sons*. Viking. The story of a family unit faced with internal conflict as the father tries to avoid the fact that he was indirectly involved in the death of his oldest son.

————, *Death of a Salesman*. Viking (pap.). A play about a family struggling to determine its identity.

7 Social Stratification

- ► What determines your status?

- ► How does your social class status affect your life?

- ► How can you change your social class status?

SECTION 1:
Class Structures

The social process of stratification is an important part of the organization of society. The term stratification comes from the words "strata," meaning layers, and "ify," meaning to make into or to form. SOCIAL STRATIFICATION *refers to the layering of social categories into higher or lower positions of prestige or respect.*

Status

These higher or lower positions are called statuses. STATUS *is the individual's position in the social structure.* For example, some people are Supreme Court Justices, and others are doctors, lawyers, bankers, teachers, carpenters, or garage mechanics. Each of these persons has a particular status, or position,

in the society. A person's status is his or her position in the society in relation to other positions. Status does not deal with the individuals themselves but with the social category (position) into which they've been placed. Status isn't Dr. Jones the doctor, Mrs. Smith the banker, or Mr. Green the carpenter. In other words, it does not refer to the personality of the individuals involved, but only to the position of a doctor, banker, or carpenter in society. In Chapter 6 we discussed the position of a person in the group. Not only do people have a position in each group to which they belong, they also have a position, or status, in the structure of the society.

How do people get their status? It happens in two ways. ASCRIBED STATUSES *are assigned by society on the basis of some fixed category, without regard to a person's abilities or performance.* You have the status of a teenager simply because you were born at least thirteen years ago. You have no choice about the status ascribed to you. The son of a king

121

One basis of differentiation into social categories is age. For instance, entry into first grade in a public school is related to your birth date.

is a prince merely by the fact of his birth. You belong to a particular social class in our society because of your family background. You did not have the opportunity to choose your parents. You do not determine your ascribed statuses. For the most part you simply learn to live with them, for you cannot change them yourself.

ACHIEVED STATUSES *are earned by the individual through competition with others.* You are a junior or senior in high school because you've met certain educational requirements. You have status as an outstanding basketball player because you've averaged twenty points in your last ten games. With achieved statuses, you yourself choose the particular statuses you want to earn. Your teachers have their statuses because they decided to attend college and complete the necessary requirements to become certified as teachers. They teach in your school be-

cause they were selected from a number of applicants for the job. In your day-by-day interactions with others, you are constantly achieving various statuses.

Statuses, then, are essential to the process of stratification. But, before social stratification can take place, there must be differentiation.

Differentiation

DIFFERENTIATION is another social process. *It involves describing people in terms of certain personal characteristics and then classifying them into specific social categories on the basis of these characteristics.* Every person is classified according to such characteristics as sex, age, occupation, education, religion, race, and intelligence. The person is then placed in a social category along with all others in the society who have the same characteristics. Each social category becomes ranked according to its relative position with other social categories. The people in a given social category are then regarded as belonging to a particular social class level. The hierarchy of social classes that results is called a *social class structure.*

Kinds of Social Class Structures

Social class structures may be rigid or flexible. A rigid class structure is called a caste. *A* CASTE SYSTEM *is a social class structure in which individuals must remain in the social class of their birth.* A well-known example is the caste system of India. In India, most individuals cannot move from one social class to another. They live according to the regulations of the caste, or social class, into which they were born.

An OPEN-CLASS SYSTEM *is a social class structure in which individuals may move from one class to another.* In an open-class system, a person's parents or family background are not as important as the characteristics of the particular individual. A person may advance to another social class by displaying various abilities and achievements. The United States has, for most people, an open-class system. The system is flexible and permits a good deal of movement—both upward and downward. Many people in our society do not end up in the same class position as their parents.

The Vocabulary of Social Stratification

To examine social class structure and stratification the sociologist uses a specific set of terms. For us to understand social stratification, we must be familiar with some of these terms.

Status. Status has already been defined as the individual's position in the social structure of the society.

Prestige. Not all statuses are equal. Some are ranked higher than others. PRESTIGE *is the evaluation of status.* In the United States people regard the status of doctor or lawyer as higher than the status of carpenter or garage mechanic. This evaluation of the various statuses is called prestige.

Role. In Chapter 6 we defined a role as the position of an individual in relation to the group. Here we will rephrase the definition in terms of status (although actually the definitions are the same). *A* ROLE *is the specific behavior expected of an individual because of his or her status.* We might say that a person's role is the part he or she plays in the group or the society. Shakespeare summed it up in the play *As You Like It:*

> All the world's a stage,
> And all the men and women merely
>   players.
> They have their exits and their entrances,
> And one man in his time plays many
>   parts. . . .

We might say that we are all actors in the drama of life. Our stage is the society in which we live. We play a particular role based on our status in the society. For example, the role of the student is to study, that of the teacher to teach, the doctor to heal, the parents to provide for their children, the children to obey their parents, and the president to preside. Every individual plays different roles in different groups and situations. Your role in this class is that of student. However, you may also play the role of cheerleader, or end on the football team, or singer in the glee club, or editor of the school newspaper. At home your role is that of an adolescent. When you shop at a store, you play the role of consumer. If you have a part-time job, you play the role of employee.

Role conflict. Sometimes we find conflicts among the various roles we play. For example, you may find that the school newspaper, for which you are a reporter, is hold-

Some people, like research scientist Jonas Salk (left), have attained both esteem and prestige. Salk is esteemed for his work in controlling polio. And his status as a scientist has prestige.

ing a meeting at a time when you are supposed to be at work. Your glee club may be performing on the same evening that your parents want you home for a family celebration. We all experience role conflicts as we become involved in many different groups in society.

Role behavior. In Chapter 6 we said that role behavior is the actual behavior of the individual in carrying out his or her role. Although the role of the student is to study, all students do not perform this role in the same way. Some work very hard to learn all they possibly can. Others work hard enough to get an average grade. Still others try to get by with as little studying as possible. Each individual carries out his or her role in a specific way related to his or her own personality.

Esteem. As we carry out our roles in our own specific way, we are being evaluated— judged—by others. *The evaluation of role behavior is called* ESTEEM. The amount of esteem we earn depends on how well we carry out our roles. The student who studies hard, makes the honor roll and the National Honor Society, and is awarded a scholarship to college achieves high esteem. The student who fails without having made an effort has little or no esteem among those who value scholastic success.

We must distinguish between prestige and esteem. *Prestige is the evaluation of status.* In ranking status, the individual as a person is not important. For example, a doctor has high prestige because of the status of the position. A sanitation worker, on the other hand, has rather low prestige. Yet it is possible for the sanitation worker to have high esteem and the doctor to have low esteem. The sanitation worker may be highly esteemed because the worker performs the job quietly, thoroughly, and efficiently. The doctor may have low esteem because he or she has diagnosed the illnesses of many patients incorrectly.

Investigating Social Stratification

There are three basic approaches used by sociologists in studying stratification. These are the objective approach, the subjective approach, and the reputational approach. These approaches help sociologists determine which social class levels exist and how people are placed in them. Which approach is best for a specific study depends on the particular kinds of data that the scientist needs to test his or her hypothesis. Each approach will provide different kinds of data.

The objective approach. In the objective approach sociologists observe certain people, studying their interests and interactions to determine the criteria used to divide these people into social classes. In searching for the criteria, sociologists derive a number of indicators, such as income, occupation, housing, or education. The study is objective because it relies on these indicators, which can be measured. However, to be meaningful, the indicators must accurately reflect the situation that actually exists in the community. Also, for the analysis to be objective, the sociologist should not be emotionally involved in community affairs.

The subjective approach. This approach does not use objective indicators. Instead, it relies on the feelings that people have about where they belong in the class system. In the subjective approach the sociologist asks the individuals where they place themselves in the social class structure.

There are several advantages to this approach. The first is that it is relatively easy to carry out. The sociologist simply devises a questionnaire that gives individuals the opportunity to rate themselves as to their social class status. A second advantage is that it is usually possible to obtain a fairly large sample, since questionnaires can reach many people. A third advantage of this method is that it shows an important aspect of class status that is not revealed by the other methods. The other methods are based on how someone else ranks the individual person. Yet it might be very important, from the standpoint of the social interaction of the individual, to know how the person rates himself or herself, as well as to know how he or she is rated by others.

This individual is using the subjective approach to determine the social stratification system in Peru. He is going from house to house asking people where they would place themselves in the existing social class structure.

A major disadvantage of the subjective approach is that the results are often influenced by the specific choices given to the individual. Two subjective studies of the social class structure in the United States may get different results because of the questions they choose to ask. For example, in one study, the Institute of Public Opinion asked this question: "To what social class in this country do you think you belong—the middle class, the upper, or the lower?" It obtained these responses:

Upper class	6%
Middle class	88%
Lower class	6%
Total	100%

In another study, the term "working class" was included. These interesting results were obtained:

Upper class	3%
Middle class	43%
Working class	51%
Lower class	1%
Don't know	1%
Don't believe in classes	1%
Total	100%

Clearly, it is important for sociologists to choose their questions very carefully when using this approach.

The reputational approach. In the reputational approach the people of the community themselves classify individuals into social class levels. They rate each individual on the basis of his or her reputation in the community. The sociologist simply asks the people how they classify each other, what classifications they use, how they evaluate each individual, and how they rank the various classes. This approach can only be used in communities that are small enough for people to know one another fairly well. To carry out the research the sociologist chooses a number of persons—usually long-term residents of the community who know many people—to serve as judges. Each of these judges then rates all of the persons he or she knows. Enough judges are selected so that virtually every person in the community can be ranked. The ratings of the judges are then averaged to determine the social class structure of the community.

One of the great values of this approach is that it is closely related to what actually takes place in the community. The people in the community are constantly ranking one another. The sociologist simply questions a sufficient number of people in the community (who thereby serve as judges) to find out their rankings.

SECTION REVIEW

1. What is the difference between ascribed status and achieved status?
2. How do prestige and esteem differ?
3. What is role conflict? Give examples in your own life.
4. What are the three approaches used by sociologists in studying social stratification? Name the advantages of each approach. What are some disadvantages of each approach?

KEY TERMS

Define and give an example of each term.

achieved status	reputational approach
ascribed status	role
caste system	role behavior
differentiation	role conflict
esteem	social class structure
objective approach	social stratification
open-class system	status
prestige	subjective approach

SECTION 2:
The American Social Structure

How many social classes do you think there are in America's complex society? Do definite social classes even exist in this country? These questions are difficult to answer, since we have an open-class system and no traditional class categories. In the 1800's Karl Marx developed the view that social classes are based on production, or the way the economy is organized. He believed that society was divided into two social classes: the bourgeoisie, or capitalists, and the proletariat, or workers. Fundamental to Marx's theory of class is the concept of class consciousness. It means that members of a particular class have a sense of identification, belonging, and attachment to their class, and would act to protect the interests of their class.

There is little evidence that either this kind of class consciousness or Marx's clear-cut class distinctions have actually developed in modern societies. Instead, social classes seem to be based on differences in status. And these status differences relate more to life style, occupation, family background, and educational differences than to Marx's class consciousness.

Our society is not divided into the two social classes described by Marx. But we do have social classes. In 1941, W. Lloyd Warner and his associates did a famous study of a New England town that they called "Yankee City." From this study Warner generalized that all communities have social class structures that have some similar features. The social class structure that he found probably comes closer than any other to being accepted by sociologists as *the* basic social class structure that exists in America.

The Distribution of Social Classes

Warner found six special social classes: upper-upper, lower-upper, upper-middle, lower-middle, upper-lower, and lower-lower. He also found that although most people rate themselves as middle class, the result is different when they rate each other. Most people are rated in the lower class. If we break Warner's distribution of the social class structure down into three classes—the upper, middle, and lower—we find that only 3 percent are in the upper class. Thirty-eight percent are in the middle class. The great majority, or 59 percent, are in the lower class. Warner's study is more than thirty years old, and it is of a single community. As a result, his figures are not accurate for American society today. Nevertheless, his findings that, in general, the classes get larger from top to bottom, still apply to our class structure. (See page 128.) And his concept of six social classes is still used today.

Criteria of Class Placement

To examine the distribution of persons in the class structure of "Yankee City," we must consider the criteria that Warner used in placing persons in the specific classes. Warner used the reputational approach in his "Yankee City" research. From that study he developed a set of criteria to use in objective stratification studies, which he called the "Index of Status Characteristics." This index consisted of the following four criteria:

(1) OCCUPATION   (3) HOUSE TYPE
(2) SOURCE OF INCOME   (4) DWELLING AREA

There are certain factors that determine the status of each of these four criteria. OCCUPATIONS are given high status on the basis of such factors as power, prestige, security, dignity, and the amount of educa-

127

DISTRIBUTION OF THE POPULATION OF "YANKEE CITY" INTO THE SIX SOCIAL CLASSES

Three Upper Classes 13%	UPPER-UPPER: 1.4%	Upper Class 3%
	LOWER-UPPER: 1.6%	
	UPPER-MIDDLE: 10%	Middle Class 38%
Three Lower Classes 87%	LOWER-MIDDLE: 28%	
	UPPER-LOWER: 34%	Lower Class 59%
	LOWER-LOWER: 25%	

tion required. You may have thought that the most important fact about occupation was the amount of salary the job paid. This, however, is not necessarily true. Although an electrician might make a larger salary than a college instructor, the electrician is not given a higher status.

The status attached to INCOME is related to how the person obtains the income. Warner placed the sources of income in a hierarchy according to the status that they give to people.

1. *Inherited wealth:* The people live on money left to them by an earlier generation.

2. *Earned wealth:* The people have earned enough money to be able to live on the income they receive from their investments (such as stocks and bonds).

3. *Profits and fees:* The people receive their income from capital investments and from fees for rendering professional services. A consultant, doctor, lawyer, or architect would be in this category.

4. *Salary:* The people work for someone else and are paid a certain salary each year. This suggests that they are paid for ability rather than for what they actually do.

5. *Wages:* The people are paid a specific amount per hour for the time they are actually working. This suggests that they are paid only for what they do.

6. *Private assistance:* The people depend on assistance given to them by relatives or friends.

7. *Public assistance and nonrespectable income:* The people depend on welfare payments or income derived from illegal activities.

The criterion of HOUSE TYPE refers to the kind of home the person lives in. The status of the home is based on the cost of the house, its design, the number of rooms, and how well it is kept up.

The criterion of DWELLING AREA involves the neighborhood in which the home is located. The factors that determine the status of the home also determine the status of the neighborhood. A neighborhood, however, may have a few homes that do not fit in with the rest.

Warner used these four criteria of class placement to describe his six social classes.

The upper-upper class

(1) OCCUPATION. These people are the "aristocracy of birth and inherited wealth." They might be called the leisure class, for many of them don't work. They receive all of the money they need from inherited wealth. Members of this class who do work often are involved in some aspect of investment and finance. Others may enter politics — such names as Roosevelt, Harriman, Rockefeller, Scranton, Stevenson, and Lodge are familar to most Americans.

(2) SOURCE OF INCOME. Since their wealth is inherited, most income comes from dividends on stocks, interest on bonds, and other investments in business and industry.

(3) HOUSE TYPE. The upper-upper-class people live in very large and elaborate houses, which may have belonged to their family for generations.

(4) DWELLING AREA. The upper-upper-class people are likely to have homes in more than one place. They may have a town house, a country estate, and vacation retreats. Their houses are all built in very exclusive areas, which are recognized as upper-upper-class neighborhoods.

The lower-upper class

(1) OCCUPATION. Most individuals of the lower-upper class have only recently become wealthy and do not have a distinguished family heritage or inherited wealth. This class consists of self-made millionaires, very successful business, professional, and financial people, and famous entertainers and athletes.

(2) SOURCE OF INCOME. Their income comes from investments, from profits in business

This summer "camp" on a lake in the Adirondack Mountains belonged to the wealthy Vanderbilt family. Members of the upper class usually own more than one home.

and industry, fees (in the case of professional people), and contract salaries (for entertainers and athletes).

(3) HOUSE TYPE. The lower-upper-income people live in expensive homes, which may be very elaborate or ornate. Their homes sometimes cost more than those of the upper-upper class.

(4) DWELLING AREA. The lower-upper-class people live in exclusive neighborhoods, but these areas do not have the long-established traditions of the upper-upper-class neighborhoods. The basic criterion which separates the two classes is time—the time that has enabled the upper-upper-class families to establish a heritage and tradition.

The upper-middle class

(1) OCCUPATION. The upper-middle class is composed of somewhat successful businesspeople and respected professional persons such as doctors, lawyers, architects, college professors, and members of the clergy.

(2) SOURCE OF INCOME. Their income comes largely from fees, business profits, and salaries.

(3) HOUSE TYPE. The upper-middle-class people live in spacious, fairly expensive homes.

(4) DWELLING AREA. They live in the "better" suburbs or in comfortable apartments. Their houses are well cared for, generally have large yards, and are not crowded together.

The lower-middle class

(1) OCCUPATION. This class consists of small businesspeople, white-collar workers, managers, and skilled craftsworkers. In this class are such occupations as accountants, carpenters, office workers, and salespeople.

(2) SOURCE OF INCOME. Salaries, wages, and business earnings.

(3) HOUSE TYPE. These people live in small, neat houses, well cared for and usually conventional in style, or in relatively small city apartments.

(4) DWELLING AREA. The lower-middle class often lives in tract developments in the suburbs, or in the less expensive apartment areas in the city.

The upper-lower class

(1) OCCUPATION. The members of the upper-lower class are employed as skilled or semiskilled factory workers, service workers, and small shop owners. They are considered to be hard-working people.

(2) SOURCE OF INCOME. The basic source of income for almost all these persons is wages earned from their jobs.

(3) HOUSE TYPE. The upper-lower class may live in houses or apartments quite similar to those of the lower-middle class, although the condition of their dwellings may not be as good.

(4) DWELLING AREA. Upper-lower-class people live in the less desirable sections of the city, town, or suburb.

The lower-lower class

(1) OCCUPATION. In this class the people are unskilled workers, migrant workers, the unemployed, and those who depend on public assistance.

(2) SOURCE OF INCOME. Income is from wages or assistance payments.

(3) HOUSE TYPE. The lower-lower-class people are the slum dwellers, living in city tenements or substandard houses.

(4) DWELLING AREA. They occupy city slums or ghettos, or run-down rural areas.

The Effects of Social Class Status

How is the individual's life affected by his or her social class? Sociologists have found class to be one of the most important factors in predicting a person's life chances, attitudes, and patterns of behavior.

Life chances. The term "LIFE CHANCES" *refers to the probability that a person will have certain experiences.* Many of our experiences are greatly influenced by our social class status. The following are some experiences or life chances that are related to class position. Remember that these data refer to groups and that individuals can improve their life chances.

1. *Mental health.* Since persons in the higher classes can afford the cost of psychiatric treatment, they usually get better treatment for mental illness. In addition, persons in the higher classes are more likely to recognize mental illness and to seek treatment.

2. *Life expectancy.* Because of such factors as better physical and mental health services, nicer homes, less dangerous jobs, and more leisure-time activities, life expectancy is longer in the upper classes.

3. *Education.* There is a close relationship between years of schooling completed and social class. Among the students who attend college, those from the higher classes are more likely to attend the "Ivy League" colleges or other well-known liberal arts colleges. Those from the lower classes are more likely to go to a state university or local community college. Nearly all aspects of education are influenced by social class.

4. *Vacations and travel.* Persons from upper classes travel widely. As we move down the class levels, individuals travel less and less.

5. *Group membership and activities.* Both the kinds of groups belonged to and the amount of participation are very much class-related. For example, youths from upper classes are much more apt to participate in sports activities, youth organizations, and religious organizations than are youths from lower classes. Upper classes tend to join professional organizations and clubs. Members of the lower-middle class often belong to fraternal lodges. And the lower classes seldom join clubs.

6. *Occupation.* The occupation that a young person enters is closely related to the social class status of his or her family. The children of people at the top of the social class system

Social class status affects the kinds of vacations that people take. There is a difference in the style in which members of different social classes travel.

are much more likely to get top jobs than are those from the lower classes.

Attitudes and behavior. Social class status also influences the attitudes and patterns of behavior of individuals. Some important social behavior affected by class status is summarized here:

1. *Childbearing.* Although less true today, there has been a relationship between social class and the number of children born to a family. The lower the social class, the greater the average number of children born per family.

2. *Childrearing practices.* Lower-class parents tend to be more rigid, more authoritarian, and more apt to use physical punishment. However, they exert less supervision over their children. Middle- and upper-class

parents are thought to be more permissive and less authoritarian, but to exert greater supervision over their children.

3. *Kinship relationships.* Kinship is extremely important in the upper classes, where family background and ancestry are emphasized. It is quite important in the lower classes, where it forms a basis for socializing, visiting, and economic assistance. The middle classes place very little emphasis on kinship.

4. *Politics.* There is a relationship between social class and political affiliation. The higher the social class, the greater the percentage of Republican voters. The relationship is not simple, however. For example, the upper classes and the upper-middle class tend to be conservative regarding economic

policy and government action, but somewhat liberal on questions of civil liberties and civil rights. The working class tends to be liberal with respect to economic policy and government action, but somewhat conservative concerning individual liberties.

5. *Values and norms.* The various social classes have different values and norms. One sociologist has concluded that upper-class youths tend to be oriented toward the past, because they have no hopes of doing better than their parents. Middle-class youths tend to be oriented toward the future, intent on achieving even more than their parents. Lower-class youths tend to be oriented toward the present, since for them the future may seem to hold little promise.

6. *Tastes.* The individual's tastes in clothing, art, music, literature, home decoration, leisure-time activities, movies, and many other areas are closely related to his or her social class status.

7. *Style or way of life.* Each social class can be regarded as a subculture. The way that people live their day-by-day existence, the things they know and think about, what they do, and what they have are all related to class.

SECTION REVIEW

1. What are Warner's criteria of social class placement?
2. What six social classes did Warner find in "Yankee City"?
3. What percent of the population of "Yankee City" were in each social class level?
4. What are the effects of social class status on the individual?

KEY TERMS

Define each term.

class consciousness
life chances
lower-lower class
lower-middle class

lower-upper class
upper-lower class
upper-middle class
upper-upper class

There is also a difference in the tastes and way of life among the social classes. An interest in polo, for instance, is usually associated with the upper classes.

SECTION 3:
Social Mobility

As you know, the United States has an open-class social system. In an open-class system a person can change his or her social position. The process by which people change their social class position, and also the process by which the social structure itself changes, is called social mobility. SOCIAL MOBILITY *is the movement of individuals and groups within the social class structure.* It is important to distinguish social mobility from physical mobility—movement from one place to another place within a social system. To illustrate, an example of physical mobility is the movement of a family from Philadelphia to Denver because the husband or wife was transferred to Denver by the company. Social mobility may become involved, however, if the person who is being transferred also receives a substantial promotion.

Types of Social Mobility

People may change their social class position in one of two ways. They may move from one position to another within their class. Or they may move into another class.

HORIZONTAL MOBILITY *is movement of the individual within a social class level.* If a man quits his job as a carpenter to become a garage mechanic, he remains in about the same social class status. The two jobs have about the same occupational status. Both require about the same amount of training, pay similar wages, and have a similar amount of prestige. The individual has been horizontally mobile.

VERTICAL MOBILITY *is movement of the individual between social class levels.* This movement may be either up or down—the in-

dividual may either rise in the social structure or fall to a lower class level. For instance, suppose the carpenter did not become a mechanic. Instead, he arranged substantial loans and became a building contractor. After a few years he has a successful business. He employs more than a hundred persons as carpenters, masons, plumbers, electricians, office staff, estimators, and salespeople. Now he would probably be considered as belonging to the upper-middle class, especially if his social behavior—his life style and his friends and associates—were acceptable to upper-middle-class people.

Vertical mobility may be downward also. For example, suppose the successful building contractor becomes an alcoholic. As his drinking problem increases he is less able to manage his business, and his company begins to lose money. At the same time he is no longer invited to social affairs, where he once was an active participant. Eventually he is forced into bankruptcy, and loses his home and business. He may try to work again as a carpenter. But he may have difficulty holding a steady job, since he is often absent due to his drinking. In time, he may be forced to work as an unskilled laborer. As he is now unemployed frequently and has acquired a reputation as an alcoholic, he may at this point be considered as a member of the lower-lower class. He has been vertically mobile downward, having dropped several levels in social status.

Social mobility can take place in several different ways. One way occurs as a result of changes in an individual's career. This kind of mobility, CAREER MOBILITY, *is related to a change in jobs of the individual.* By looking at the person's employment history, a sociologist can determine if his or her change in jobs has brought about social class gains or losses. The carpenter in our example experienced mobility as a result of changing his occupational status.

A second kind of mobility is intergenerational. INTERGENERATIONAL MOBILITY *occurs as a result of changes in status between parents and children.* If the father is a carpenter, but his son goes to college and becomes a lawyer, intergenerational mobility has taken place. Studies of fathers and sons show, however, that sons tend to enter occupations that are similar in social status to the occupations of their fathers. That is, a higher percentage of sons enter an occupation with a status similar to that of their father's occupation than enter any other occupational level. Sons of fathers who have blue-collar occupations are more likely to enter blue-collar occupations. And sons of fathers who have white-collar occupations are more likely to enter white-collar occupations.

Group mobility is a third kind of mobility. GROUP MOBILITY *is the movement of an entire group, class, or caste in relation to the whole social class system.* For example, as a group black people in the United States have been moving up compared to the total population. In any complex society there is a continual shifting up and down of the relative positions of the various segments of the population.

Social Mobility in the United States

In the American social class system much more horizontal mobility than vertical mobility takes place. In career mobility, most persons who change jobs change from one semiskilled job to another semiskilled job, or from one sales job to another. It is more difficult to move between blue-collar and white-collar jobs — between manual and non-manual employment.

Although many children experience some mobility, intergenerational mobility is usually limited to movement into the social class level immediately above or below. Americans like to think that their society is espe-

Less intergenerational mobility takes place among farmers than among many other occupations. The children of farmers often enter the same occupational level as their parents.

cially mobile in this way. But studies indicate that the rate of intergenerational mobility is about the same here as in other highly industrialized countries. Approximately 25 percent of the children move into a social class level that is different from that of their parents.

The mobility ethic. In the United States a special kind of emphasis has been placed on upward mobility. There is a MOBILITY ETHIC, *which is the belief that the individual not only has the right to succeed but has the duty to* *succeed as well.* It involves more than simply regarding upward mobility as "good" and downward mobility as "bad." In America the person who rises in the social class system is regarded as a good person and the individual who has not been able to rise in the social class system, or is actually downwardly mobile, is regarded as less worthy. Also part of our mobility ethic is the belief that all mobility is the direct result of our personal efforts or lack of effort. This serves to reinforce the view that those in the lower classes lack ability and ambition, and therefore deserve their low status and esteem. At the same time, however, the mobility ethic has spurred people to work toward social advancement. The "rags to riches" notion that hard work pays off in social rewards has had special importance in America.

The fact that America has never put great emphasis on family background (except in the upper class) has opened the door to the possibilities of individual success. The mobility ethic is probably strongest today in the middle classes. There people are proud that they do not have any great family heritage. They like to say that they "lifted themselves up by their own bootstraps," or that they are "self-made." However, being born into a middle-class family makes it comparatively easy to "pull oneself up by one's bootstraps" in our society. Middle-class young people have the opportunities to succeed. They are expected to go to college and obtain good jobs. It is not quite so easy for those starting out in a lower position, although their opportunities to succeed are increasing.

Causes of upward mobility in America. The existence of the mobility ethic itself is a cause of upward mobility. The ethic provides basic motivation to advance in our social class structure. It discourages downward movement, and favors improving class position. Several other factors also have contributed to the existence of upward social movement in our society.

1. *Technological innovation.* Industrialization and technology have increased the number of upper-level positions and decreased those at the lower end. Advances in technology have caused a steady increase in the number of technical, professional, managerial, and white-collar jobs, and a steady decrease in the number of unskilled and semiskilled jobs. Continued upward mobility is needed simply to staff the increasing numbers of upper-level statuses, and to provide places for those in the decreasing lower-level statuses. For example, there has been a great change in the labor force brought about by the introduction of credit purchasing. Thousands of white-collar workers have been needed to determine the amounts due, send the bills for payment, and record and deposit the payments. Also, increased competition in business and industry and the development of new products have added employment in both wholesale and retail sales. Job opportunities then increase in advertising, public relations, personnel agencies, insurance, investments, and entertainment. All of these, and others, open up new higher statuses — and sometimes close off lower ones.

2. *Immigration.* The great numbers of immigrants coming to America have helped the upward movement of native-born workers. Immigrants were generally forced to start at the bottom of the social ladder. This resulted in increasing the opportunities and raising the statuses of many native-born workers.

3. *The differential birth rate.* As we said earlier, the lower classes have tended to have a higher birth rate than the upper classes. The upper classes don't always reproduce themselves in sufficient quantity to fill the upper-level statuses. Therefore, openings exist for persons from lower classes to move up and enter the ranks of the higher classes.

4. *Downward mobility.* Any mobility that is not the result of filling vacant statuses must result from some interchange of ranks.

In other words, there must be a move down for every move up, and a move up for every move down. Because there is some downward mobility, because some people, like our alcoholic carpenter, move down the social class ladder, a space is opened up at the top for someone else to move into.

How does the individual move upward? What are the avenues by which people can move up the social class ladder? We can isolate at least four basic ways in which young people might achieve a higher social class status than their parents.

1. *Education.* Perhaps the most obvious avenue of upward mobility is education. The amount of education a person has helps to determine the kinds of jobs he or she can get. And the occupation of the individual is the most important factor in determining social class status. In general, the jobs that are associated with high social class status require the most amount of education.

Increased education also helps upward mobility by providing socialization experiences connected with middle- and upper-class life. To attain membership in a social class the individual must be able to act as an equal. The farther a person progresses in our educational system, the higher the average social class position of the students. By continuing their education, therefore, lower-class students have a chance to learn the appropriate behavior—as well as the characteristic dress, attitudes, beliefs, and tastes—of the higher classes.

As the years of education completed by the population rise, more education is required to achieve a high status. For example, the status of a high school education is not as high as it was a generation ago, because so many more people have high school diplomas.

2. *Marriage.* Another avenue for upward mobility, especially for women, is marriage.

137

A child's status is based on the status of his or her parents, especially the father. Later on, boys usually go out into the world and maintain or achieve their own status. Traditionally, however, the status of a girl in adult life has been largely determined by the man she married. For the status of the husband generally determined the status of the couple. Now, though, there is an increase in our society of women who work and achieve status on their own.

Actually, women are much more apt to marry upward than are men. Although a man also may achieve upward mobility if he marries a woman from an upper class (especially if the woman's father gives him a high status job), this is relatively rare.

3. *Ability and talent.* The person with outstanding ability and talent in such areas as the arts, sports, science, or mathematics may achieve upward mobility. This is especially true of individuals who are successful in the sports or entertainment fields.

4. *Extra effort and hard work.* Lacking other avenues of upward mobility the status-seeking individual can sometimes rise through plain hard work, especially in the areas of business and industry. People who work eagerly at their job and do the best they can are likely to be promoted to jobs of higher status.

However, efforts directed toward upward mobility are more likely to come from those above the bottom than from those at the bottom itself. Once an individual has made some upward movement, he or she begins to appreciate what mobility can mean. Also, those who are not in the lowest class have more time and energy available to direct toward upward mobility. They don't have to devote such a large proportion of their energy simply to staying alive.

Status insecurity. Upward mobility in the United States is often accompanied by status insecurity. When people are moving up the social class ladder, they often don't know

Stevie Wonder (left) has been widely recognized as a talented singer and musician. One way to attain upward social mobility is through ability and talent.

what is appropriate behavior in their new class. To make sure that they are fully accepted as members of this class, they sometimes overdo what they think is acceptable behavior. They may adopt overly formal speech or dress. Or they may spend a lot of money in a showy manner. Status insecurity is especially common among the lower-upper class. This all-out effort to prove that they are really upper class may keep upper class people from accepting them.

SECTION REVIEW

1. What types and kinds of social mobility are there?

2. What is the mobility ethic?
3. What factors have caused upward group mobility in America? Can you think of any factors not mentioned here?
4. How might an individual achieve upward mobility?

KEY TERMS

Explain the meaning of each term.

career mobility	intergenerational
differential	mobility
birth rate	mobility ethic
downward mobility	social mobility
group mobility	upward mobility
horizontal mobility	vertical mobility

PROJECTS AND ACTIVITIES

1. Drive, walk, or bicycle around your community and try to determine which neighborhoods are upper-upper, lower-upper, upper-middle, lower-middle, upper-lower, and lower-lower class. Can you tell with any degree of accuracy? What problems are involved in attempting to rate neighborhoods according to social class?

2. Construct a collage that shows the style of life in the various social classes.

3. Follow the society page in your local newspaper for information about the style of life of the upper classes in your community.

4. Conduct a survey of middle-class adults to determine their attitudes toward the upper classes and lower classes.

5. Study the advertisements and articles in several magazines and then rate the magazines in terms of the social class status of the persons to whom each magazine is most likely to appeal.

6. Compose a song that deals with some aspect of social class in America.

7. Study television commercials to determine what, according to the commercials, gives status in our society.

8. Conduct research to determine how technological innovation has affected social stratification in America.

9. Write a drama or short story that illustrates the injustices of social stratification.

10. Obtain the latest copy of the U.S. Bureau of the Census, *Statistical Abstract of the United States.* Look up statistics about the occupations, income, and education of Americans. What do these statistics tell you about stratification in America?

TOPICS FOR INQUIRY

1. Debate: To the average American, status is achieved by the ownership of the "right" material goods in sufficient quantities.

2. Discuss examples of Americans who have achieved high social status. How did they achieve their high status?

3. What aspects of a caste system can be found in the American open-class system?

4. Do you agree with the statement that "we can become anything we want to in America if we just work for it"? Why or why not?

5. Discuss your own observations of the mobility ethic in America.

6. How have your own attitudes and behavior been influenced by the existence of social classes in America?

7. Do you think that it would ever be possible to have a classless society? Why or why not?

SUGGESTIONS FOR READING

NONFICTION

ARONOWITZ, Stanley, *False Promises,* McGraw-Hill, 1973 (and pap.). A historical and contemporary analysis of working-class consciousness.

BIRMINGHAM, Stephen, *The Right People: A Portrait of the American Social Establishment.* Little, Brown, 1968. An interesting discussion of the upper classes in America today.

HOLLINGSHEAD, August B., *Elmtown's Youth: The Impact of Social Classes on Adolescents*. Wiley, 1949 (pap.). A report of carefully carried out research to determine how an adolescent's life is affected by his or her social class status in the community.

HOWELL, Joseph T., *Hard Living on Clay Street*. Anchor, 1973 (pap.). Case studies of several blue-collar families.

LYND, Robert S. and LYND, Helen M., *Middletown in Transition: A Study of Cultural Conflicts*. Harcourt Brace Jovanovich, 1963. A famous study of the importance of social class in the life of a community.

MAYER, Kurt B. and BUCKLEY, Walter, *Class and Society*. Random House, 1970 (pap.). A discussion of social stratification, class, power, and social mobility in American society.

MILLS, C. Wright, *The Power Elite*. Oxford University Press, 1956 (and pap.). A study of the power of the upper classes in America.

———, *White Collar*. Oxford University Press, 1951 (and pap.). A classic study of the American middle classes.

PACKARD, Vance, *The Pyramid Climbers*. Fawcett World, 1971 (pap.). Packard discusses the problems faced by business executives as they strive for success in our nation's huge corporations.

———, *The Status Seekers*. McKay, 1959 or Pocket Books (pap.). An analysis of class stratification in the United States.

SEXTON, Patricia Cayo and SEXTON, Brendan, *Blue Collars and Hard-Hats*. Random House, 1971 (and pap.). A political analysis of working-class America.

WARNER, W. Lloyd, *Social Class in America: The Evaluation of Status*. Harper & Row, 1960 (pap.). A study of the American social class structure.

FICTION

FITZGERALD, F. Scott, *The Great Gatsby*. Scribner (and pap.). The problems faced by one man as he attempts to achieve social mobility in the 1920's.

GARDNER, Herb, *A Thousand Clowns*. Random House. A television writer decides that he has had enough of social class status.

HAWLEY, Cameron, *Executive Suite*. Popular Library (pap.). A group of men are being studied for a new position. The values of each show up in his quest for status.

HINTON, S. E., *The Outsiders*. Viking or Dell (pap.). Teen-agers from the ghetto try to develop a values system and come into conflict with teen-agers from the upper social classes.

LEWIS, Sinclair, *Babbitt*. Harcourt Brace Jovanovich or New American Library (pap.). A satirical look at middle-class life in the United States.

ORWELL, George, *Animal Farm*. Harcourt Brace Jovanovich or New American Library (pap.). A satire on life in a communistic society which practices total equality for all.

Highlight

How do you measure social mobility in a society?

What would you do if you were a sociologist who wanted to investigate the amount of social mobility in a society? How would you find out if there is more or less social mobility than there used to be?

You might approach this problem by comparing statuses in the society over a period of time to see if any change has taken place. First you would need to know how the members of the society rank the various positions in their society. What do they regard as high and low statuses? Then you would have to know who occupies these statuses, and who occupied them before.

One way of comparing statuses over time is to compare the occupations of sons and daughters to those of their parents. Occupation is a central status in our society, and it probably says more about relative social ranking than any other status. We can assume that if sons and daughters tend to have the same kinds of jobs as their parents, there is not much social mobility. If, however, sons and daughters tend to have higher rated occupational statuses than their parents, we can assume that the society is experiencing upward mobility. Or if sons and daughters are occupying lower ranked positions than their parents, we can assume that the society is undergoing downward mobility.

You might want to use your class as a sample for investigating social mobility.

(Remember, however, that unless your class is a representative sample of the society, you won't be able to conclude much about our society as a whole.) You might start out by collecting data on the occupation of your father and your father's father, or of your mother and her mother. Following is a ranking of occupations in the United States obtained in a national poll by three sociologists at the National Opinion Research Center. You can use the ranking chart to determine if your father experienced social mobility as compared to his father, or if your mother was socially mobile compared to her mother. If you combine the findings of each member of your class (keeping each person's data anonymous), you can learn about the presence or absence of social mobility.

To determine the amount of mobility, you might consider that your father was upwardly mobile from his father if he rose six points or more, or your mother showed upward mobility from her mother if she rose six or more points. You might say that no mobility took place if there was a change of five points or less in either direction. Downward mobility will have occurred if your father's occupation is six or more points below that of his father, or your mother's occupation is six or more points below that of her mother.

THE RATINGS OF OCCUPATIONS

OCCUPATION	SCORE
U.S. Supreme Court Justice	94
Physician	93
Nuclear physicist	92
Scientist	92
Government scientist	91
State governor	91
Cabinet member in the federal government	90

OCCUPATION	SCORE	OCCUPATION	SCORE
College professor	90	Electrician	76
U.S. Representative in Congress	90	Railroad engineer	76
Chemist	89	Owner-operator of a printing shop	75
Diplomat in the U.S. Foreign Service	89	Trained machinist	75
Lawyer	89	Farm owner and operator	74
Architect	88	Undertaker	74
County judge	88	Welfare worker for a city government	74
Dentist	88	Newspaper columnist	73
Mayor of a large city	87	Police officer	72
Member of the board of directors of a large corporation	87	Reporter on a daily newspaper	71
Minister	87	Bookkeeper	70
Psychologist	87	Radio announcer	70
Airline pilot	86	Insurance agent	69
Civil engineer	86	Tenant farmer—one who owns livestock and machinery and manages the farm	69
Head of a department in a state government	86	Local official of a labor union	67
Priest	86	Manager of a small store in a city	67
Banker	85	Mail carrier	66
Biologist	85	Railroad conductor	66
Sociologist	83	Traveling salesperson for a wholesale concern	66
Captain in the army	82	Plumber	65
Accountant for a large business	81	Barber	63
Public schoolteacher	81	Machine operator in a factory	63
Building contractor	80	Owner-operator of a lunch stand	63
Owner of a factory that employs about 100 people	80	Playground director	63
Artist who paints pictures that are exhibited in galleries	78	Corporal in the regular army	62
Author of novels	78	Garage mechanic	62
Economist	78	Truck driver	59
Musician in a symphony orchestra	78	Fisher who has own boat	58
Official of an international labor union	77	Clerk in a store	56
County agricultural agent	76	Milk route driver	56
		Streetcar driver	56

OCCUPATION	SCORE
Lumberjack	55
Restaurant cook	55
Singer in a nightclub	54
Filling station attendant	51
Coal miner	50
Dock worker	50
Night guard	50
Railroad station attendant	50
Restaurant waiter	49
Taxi driver	49
Bartender	48
Farmhand	48
Janitor	48
Clothes presser in a laundry	45
Soda fountain clerk	44
Sharecropper—one who owns no livestock or equipment and does not manage farm	42
Sanitation worker	39
Street sweeper	36
Shoe shiner	34

Source: From "Occupational Prestige in the United States, 1925–1963" by Robert Hodge, Paul Siegel, and Peter Rossi from *American Journal of Sociology*, November 1964. Reprinted by permission of the University of Chicago Press.

What did you find out about social mobility? Are you able to draw any conclusions from your findings as to the amount of mobility in our society?

To find out more about social mobility in our society, we can also examine changes that are taking place in the proportion of males and females in various occupations. Here is a table of the percentage of men and women employed in the major occupational categories during the years 1960, 1970, and 1975. Notice what changes have taken place, and in which categories, during these years. Can you draw any conclusions about the social mobility of men and women in our society based on occupational statuses?

OCCUPATION AND SEX	SELECTED YEARS		
	1960	1970	1975
Professional and Technical Workers			
Male	64%	61%	58%
Female	36%	39%	42%
Managers and Administrators			
Male	84%	84%	81%
Female	16%	16%	19%
Salespeople			
Male	60%	57%	58%
Female	40%	43%	42%
Clerical Workers			
Male	32%	25%	22%
Female	68%	75%	78%
Craft Workers			
Male	97%	97%	95%
Female	3%	3%	5%
Operatives			
Male	72%	69%	70%
Female	28%	31%	30%
Service Workers			
Male	35%	34%	38%
Female	65%	66%	62%
Farm Workers			
Male	82%	83%	87%
Female	18%	17%	13%
Nonfarm Laborers			
Male	98%	96%	91%
Female	2%	4%	9%

Source: U.S. Bureau of the Census, *Statistical Abstract of the United States, 1975.*

8 Minorities in the Social Structure

► Who decides who is a minority?

► How are minorities treated in our society?

► What are some reactions of minorities?

SECTION 1:
Minorities and Their Development

In the last chapter we described the social class structure of the United States. This description is closest to the class structure of the "dominant" members of the society. Other members don't have full access to this social class structure and have structures of their own. These people who are to some degree separate from the dominant structure are called minorities, or members of a minority category.

A MINORITY, *then, is a category of people who are discriminated against or made a subclass in the social class structure because they are considered different from the dominant members of the society.* The word "minority" means less than half. Usually social minorities make up less than one half of the population. In a few cases, however, the population of the minority category is numerically larger than that of the dominant members. For example, in South Africa the white Europeans make up less than 20 percent of the total population. Yet all persons who are not white Europeans are minority members under the system of apartheid—racial segregation and discrimination. In all cases the determining factor is not the number of people but the category of people who control the society. If the dominant category, the people in power, discriminates against other categories in the society, then the other categories are social minorities.

A category of people may be considered different from the dominant category for a number of reasons. They may have a physical appearance, such as height or skin color, which sets them off from the others. Their language may be different. They may observe different customs, or practice a different religion. Or they may be poor.

Kinds of Minorities in American Society

The table on this page shows the percent distribution of the various minority categories in the United States. Notice that in the United States the minorities are a small percentage of the total population. Only about 13 percent of the American population are not Caucasoids, or members of the white

---

SOME CATEGORIES CONSIDERED MINORITIES IN THE UNITED STATES

SOCIAL CATEGORY		PERCENT OF TOTAL U.S. POPULATION
Total White Population (figure includes Jews and other white foreign born)		87.5%
Total Nonwhite Population		12.5%
Black	11.1%	
American Indian	.4	
Japanese	.3	
Chinese	.2	
Filipino	.2	
All Other	.3	
	12.5%	
Total Foreign Born (both white and nonwhite)		4.7%
Jews (both native born and foreign born)		2.8%

Source: U.S. Bureau of the Census, *Statistical Abstract of the United States: 1975,* and the *American Jewish Yearbook,* 1974–75.

---

race. Of this small group of nonwhites, almost 90 percent are black. Most of the rest are members of the Mongoloid races and have various national backgrounds. Also, only about 5 percent of the American population are *foreign born,* or immigrants (both white and nonwhite) from other countries.

Racial minorities. RACIAL MINORITIES *are those categories of people who have a different physical appearance from the dominant category.* Actually, the physical characteristics of race are biological rather than social. Physical anthropologists have classified human beings into three general races—Caucasoid, Negroid, and Mongoloid—on the basis of a number of specific physical characteristics. Anthropologists agree, however, that these classifications are somewhat arbitrary. For physical differences within a given racial group are often greater than the average differences between racial groups.

Perhaps you've heard people speak of "Negro blood" and "white blood." But no one can distinguish between the blood cells of a Negro and a Caucasian on the basis of race. The blood of all human beings, regardless of race, falls into one of four blood types: A, B, AB, and O.

Many attempts have been made to prove that one race is superior to another in ability and intelligence. However, scientific data do not support such beliefs. Careful investigations have found no differences which could, with certainty, be due to race. Social scientists believe that the causes of differences in ability or intelligence are the cultural background and the socialization of the individual, not race.

Although race is a biological term, it has become a social concept as well because people have chosen to make racial distinctions in their relationships. If persons of other races were not treated differently, race would not be a social concept.

Ethnic minorities. ETHNIC MINORITIES *are those categories of people who have a culture*

This Vietnamese mother and child and this Navajo youth are examples of racial minorities in American society. Are they also examples of ethnic minorities?

or subculture that differs from that of the dominant members. The different culture or subculture may involve language, values, norms, customs, religion, or a combination of these. Most ethnic minorities in the United States have a different national background from the dominant group in society. They may be foreign-born immigrants or the children of immigrants. These persons may continue to preserve many of the values, norms, and customs of their native countries. Other Americans then observe that these people are different, and often discriminate against them. The Bureau of the Census uses the term *foreign white stock* to refer to immigrants born in a foreign country of non-American parents as well as to people born in the United States of foreign-born parents. Those

classified as foreign white stock make up about 15 percent of the total population. The table on page 150 shows what percent of these people came from each of the various countries of origin.

Americans also distinguish minorities on the basis of religion. Probably the best-known religious minority in America is the Jews. However, almost any religion can make its believers a minority if they live in a community in which the majority of persons practices another religion. For example, Roman Catholics or Baptists living in certain parts of Utah would be an ethnic minority, since most of the people are members of the Church of Jesus Christ of Latter Day Saints. For an idea of where in America the Jews live, see the table on page 150.

FOREIGN WHITE STOCK, BY COUNTRY OF ORIGIN

COUNTRY OF ORIGIN	PERCENT OF FOREIGN WHITE STOCK
United Kingdom	7.3%
Ireland (Eire)	4.3
Norway	1.8
Sweden	2.4
Denmark	1.0
Netherlands	1.1
Switzerland	.7
France	1.0
Germany	10.8
Poland	7.1
Czechoslovakia	2.3
Austria	2.9
Hungary	1.8
Yugoslavia	1.3
U.S.S.R.	5.8
Lithuania	1.0
Greece	1.3
Italy	12.6
Other Europe	3.6
Asia	5.2
Canada	9.0
Mexico	7.0
Cuba	1.7
Other America	2.9
All Other and not reported	4.1

Source: U.S. Bureau of the Census, *Statistical Abstract of the United States:* 1975.

SPATIAL DISTRIBUTION OF JEWS IN THE UNITED STATES

GEOGRAPHIC REGION	JEWS (PERCENT)
Northeast	60.1%
North Central	12.6
South	14.1
West	13.2
	100.0%

Source: The *American Jewish Yearbook,* 1974-75. Reprinted by permission of The American Jewish Committee and The Jewish Publication Society of America.

equal in amount of intellectual capacity. Yet top positions in almost all fields in our society are filled by men. The only explanation is that women have traditionally played a minority role in our society. They've been discriminated against in the job market.

Similarly, age categories sometimes have the effect of placing certain people in a minority position. The very old in our society generally are assigned to a low status. For instance, how easy is it for people over sixty-five years old to find employment?

Attitudes Toward Minorities

Minorities are social categories because of the attitudes of the dominant members of the society. If some individuals were not considered as different, and reacted to as different, minorities would not exist in the social structure. No one is born with attitudes that brand certain individuals as minority members. All such attitudes are learned. As the song in *South Pacific* states: "You've got to

Other minorities. Sex and age often serve to distinguish people from one another in much the same way as race and ethnicity. We know, for example, that men and women are

be taught to hate." Through the socialization process the children in a society are taught to react to different persons in different ways. They tend to adopt the attitudes of their parents toward members of minorities. Such attitudes may take the form of prejudice, stereotyping, and discrimination.

Prejudice. *A* PREJUDICE *is a rigid emotional attitude, a preconceived opinion about others.* It can take the form of a tendency to respond negatively toward all members of a particular group or social category. For example, if children are told many times that all members of a certain minority are lazy, ignorant, and dirty, they may come to believe this as fact. Yet they may never have met a member of this minority category and have no basis for this belief.

Stereotyping. Very closely related to prejudice is stereotyping. STEREOTYPING *is a process by which we tend to treat all members of a particular category as being alike.* It is usually the result of overgeneralization. We may have an experience with one person who belongs to a particular social category. Then we overgeneralize by thinking that all others in the category are just like that person. We see several sailors drunk while on leave and we overgeneralize that all sailors drink to excess. We develop the stereotype of the drunken sailor. Some other common stereotypes that have developed in our society are the hot-tempered Irish, the tight-fisted Scot, the formal, aloof English, and the emotional Mexican. Many jokes are based on the stereotypes that exist in a society.

What does this cartoon suggest about the attitudes of the dominant members in our society toward hippies?

Drawing by W. Miller;
© 1970 The New Yorker Magazine, Inc.

When we've had experiences with a number of persons of any social category, we know that we can't really stereotype individuals. Each individual is a unique person. Moreover, these stereotypes have some influence on the persons who are stereotyped. If told enough times that they have a particular quality, people tend to develop that quality. They believe it is normal for them to have it. This is known as the *self-fulfilling prophecy*. The expectation brings about the prophesied result. The individual behaves in the way that other people expect him or her to behave.

Discrimination. DISCRIMINATION *is behavior toward another person that is different from the individual's usual behavior toward others.* Generally the difference in treatment occurs because the other person is a member of a particular social category. The individual is not reacting to the person but to the social category that he or she represents. In our society discrimination takes place in such areas as education, voting, employment, group membership, and housing. In some cases it leads to open conflict in which individuals attempt to do harm to the person or destroy the person's property simply because of his or her membership in a minority category.

Usually prejudice and discrimination go together. The person who is prejudiced also discriminates. They may, however, operate separately. A person who is prejudiced may not discriminate. People may be prejudiced against Jews but still rent their apartment to a Jewish person because they don't want to be fined for violating the civil rights laws. A person who discriminates may not be prejudiced. People may have no prejudice against Jews but may decide not to rent their apartment to a Jew for economic reasons. For example, they may know that their present tenants are prejudiced and would move out if they rented to a Jewish person.

How Minorities Develop

What makes a person a member of a minority? Why, for instance, is a black person a member of a minority category? Black Americans aren't minority members because they are black. They're minority members because black people are considered a minority in our society. People aren't members of a minority category because of their race. They are minority members because of *social definition,* or the way their society defines their race. A black person born in Kenya is not a member of a minority category, since his or her race is the social category that is in control of the society in Kenya. The important factor in minority membership is not race or birth—it is social definition.

There are three basic ways in which minority definitions develop.

Migration. One cause of minorities is migration. Blacks are a minority in our society because they migrated here from Africa. Actually, blacks are an example of involuntary migration—they were brought here by force as slaves. Some others who are minorities because of migration, such as the Jews, Irish, Italians, and Greeks, arrived through voluntary migration—they came because they wanted to. All are minorities because they are now living in a country where they are not members of the dominant category.

Colonialism. Some persons are members of minorities in their own country, without ever leaving their place of birth. During the last century many peoples became minorities because of colonialism. Today the blacks in South Africa are a minority in their own country even though they far outnumber the European whites there. Since the whites have political and social control of South Africa, they are the ones who make the social definitions. And they have defined the black South Africans as inferior.

More than half of the American Indians live on reservations. These reservations are located mainly in Arizona, New Mexico, Utah, South Dakota, Montana, and Wyoming.

A similar situation took place in our own country. The American Indians have become a minority and have been relocated on reservations in some of the most arid and unproductive sections of the United States. Indians on the reservations are free to leave and enter the mainstream of American society. But assimilation into the white people's society is not easy. Whether they live on a reservation or in the white people's society, American Indians are faced with discrimination.

Annexation, cession, and military conquest. A people may become a minority when their country is annexed to another nation either voluntarily or involuntarily. For example, when Texas was admitted to the Union in 1845, the Spaniards, Mexicans, and Indians living there became minorities. Many areas have been added to nations through military conquest or the threat of conquest and have resulted in making the inhabitants into minorities. Some examples might include the many peoples subdued by the Roman Empire, by Germany in World War II, and by the Soviet Union after 1945.

SECTION REVIEW

1. How do racial minorities and ethnic minorities differ?
2. What is the difference between prejudice and discrimination? Do they always go together?
3. What is stereotyping? Is stereotyping always involved in prejudice?
4. How do social categories become minority categories?

KEY TERMS

Define and give an example of each term.

discrimination	prejudice
ethnic minority	racial minority
foreign born	self-fulfilling prophecy
foreign white stock	social definition
minority	stereotyping

SECTION 2:
The Behavior Patterns of Dominant Members and Minorities

The presence of minorities in a society means that the dominant categories of people must deal with them in some way. When some people in a society look upon others as being different and inferior, the behavior patterns of everyone involved are going to be affected. How do the dominant members of the society relate to the minorities? How do the minorities react to the dominant members of the society? What patterns of human relationships develop between social categories?

Behavior Toward Minorities

We may classify the behavior patterns of the dominant members of a society toward its minorities into five basic types: extermination, expulsion, segregation, integration, and assimilation.

Extermination. Dominant members have tried various approaches toward minorities. One approach is EXTERMINATION—*getting rid of the minorities by destroying them*. It is the most harsh of all treatments of minority people. Yet there have been a number of cases of extermination. One example of a minority category that was dealt with by extermination is the American Indian. Although there was no official government policy to exterminate the Indian tribes, Indians were in the way of westward expansion. Many settlers along the frontier felt that the Indians had to be exterminated. Treaties that the United States government made with Indian tribes were often broken by settlers who wanted more land. The attitude of many of the white settlers toward the Indian was expressed in a common phrase of the time: "The only good Indian is a dead Indian." Some of this extermination, however, was indirect. As white people killed off the great herds of buffalo and deer, many Indians were no longer able to survive because they did not have a well-developed system of agriculture. In any case, the strength of the Indian tribes was weakened. And they were unable to resist the masses of settlers who moved into the western lands.

Some cases of extermination have been the result of anti-Semitism, or hatred of the Jews. For example, after the assassination of the Russian czar in 1881, the Jews became the scapegoats of the Russian government. Pogroms were organized against the Jews—situations in which huge numbers of Jews were massacred. The official policy of the government was to force one third of the Jews to emigrate, to convert another third to Orthodox Christianity, and to destroy the other third. The most familiar example of anti-Semitism, though, is the mass extermination of approximately six million Jews by Hitler's Germany during World War II.

Expulsion. The American Indians who survived extermination were later dealt with by EXPULSION, *or the removal of the minority from the society*. The Indians were rounded up like cattle and shipped off to reservations that had been set aside for them. Most of these reservations were in areas where the land was largely worthless—land on which white settlers could not make a living. Also, during World War II Japanese Americans in the United States were removed from society and kept in detention camps until the end of the war. Another example is the expulsion of the Jews and Moors (Spanish Moslems) from Spain during the early Middle Ages. If you've read Longfellow's poem "Evangeline," you are familiar with yet another example of expulsion of a minority. In the poem the Acadians, a French-speaking mi-

Many Japanese Americans were treated unjustly during World War II. About 110,000 Japanese Americans were rounded up and confined to camps, such as this one.

nority, were expelled from British Nova Scotia.

Segregation. SEGREGATION *is the spatial separation of the minority category from the dominant members of the society.* The ghetto is a segregation device first used in Europe in the Middle Ages to separate the Jews from the rest of the society. The ghetto was a section of town surrounded by high walls within which the Jews were forced to live.

In America, segregation has been used to keep blacks and the dominant white population separated. For many generations Black Americans have been forced to live in certain sections of town. Their children have been forced to attend segregated schools. In the southern states, blacks were required to use drinking fountains and restrooms that

had been specifically set apart for them. They attended special theaters for blacks only. And they swam at beaches set apart from those used by white southerners. The famous *Brown v. Board of Education of Topeka, Kansas* decision by the Supreme Court in 1954 marked the beginning of the end to legal segregation in the United States. Yet today white and Black Americans still live largely segregated in separate communities.

Segregation is a very common method of dealing with minorities. It is present to some degree in most societies that have minority populations. Also, segregation is always accompanied by discrimination. The separation of people on the basis of their membership in a minority category results

155

NEGATIVE BEHAVIOR PATTERNS   POSITIVE BEHAVIOR PATTERNS

Extermination   Expulsion   Segregation   Integration   Amalgamation   Assimilation

All behavior of the dominant social category toward the minority categories
falls somewhere between the two extremes of extermination and assimilation.

in differential treatment toward those who have been segregated.

Integration. INTEGRATION *is the process by which the dominant and minority social categories function as equals.* It does not necessarily mean that the social categories will cooperate together. But it does imply that some form of accommodation will take place. Many of the barriers that have separated the various categories are broken down. Yet some informal and unofficial barriers may remain.

In America the goal of the civil rights movement has been to remove the restrictions that have kept minorities from exercising their rights as American citizens. This goal includes the right of minority members to buy a house in any community they choose, limited only by their financial ability. It includes being able to send their children to the same schools to which other parents send their children. And it includes competing for a job on the basis of ability and experience rather than skin color.

Assimilation. ASSIMILATION *takes place when two previously distinct social categories blend into one unified social category.* Assimilation requires that the features of the original categories are no longer distinguishable. When complete assimilation has occurred, the previously distinct categories have been thoroughly combined. Only the characteristics of the new unified social category are present.

The difference between integration and assimilation is one of degree. Integration requires only that all citizens be allowed to exercise their rights with no restrictions due to race, religion, national origin, or sex. Complete assimilation requires *amalgamation,* or the acceptability of intermarriage between the previously distinct social categories, and *acculturation,* or the intermixing of the shared, learned behaviors (see page 115). Both complete amalgamation and acculturation take many years. Also, assimilation cannot take place until integration has occurred.

We can place all the patterns of behavior that we have just discussed on a sort of continuum. At one end of the continuum we would put the most harsh, negative relationship between social categories, extermination. At the other extreme we would put the most positive relationship, assimilation. Expulsion and segregation would be rated somewhere along the negative side of the continuum. Integration, amalgamation, and acculturation would be somewhere on the positive side. The continuum would look like the diagram on this page.

In the United States the patterns of behavior toward minority categories vary greatly depending on the particular minority involved. The dominant group's behavior toward Black Americans ranges between segregation (although a few people propose expulsion) and integration (although some go as far as amalgamation). Acculturation has been limited. The culture of black people in America is basically the same as that of the dominant white majority. But centuries of segregation have resulted in the development of a distinctive subculture. Some foreign white stocks such as the English, Swedish, Dutch, German, and French have been completely assimilated. There are no distinctive differences between them and the dominant social category. Behavior toward the various other minorities in our society falls somewhere between the two extremes on the continuum.

Minority Behavior Toward the Dominant Category

The behavior of minorities toward the dominant category may be classified into six types: acceptance, accommodation, rationalization complex, voluntary segregation, organized protest, and aggression.

Acceptance. People may just accept the fact of their minority status. In this way they're able to get along well with the dominant category, who assigned them that status. They are the people who "know their place" and stay there. They've come to accept the existing system as it is, which may include believing in their own inferiority. In our society until very recently many women accepted an inferior social position.

Accommodation. Minority members resent their minority status. They may even hate the members of the dominant category. But they can't afford to protest. They may have too much to lose. They may not have any opportunity to resist because of the strength — such as physical or political power — of the dominant category. By preserving an outward appearance of accepting the situation, they may be able to achieve a tolerable existence.

Rationalization complex. Some minority individuals develop a kind of rationalization complex. They come to believe that they would be successful and wealthy if only they were not members of a minority. All personal failures can be blamed on the fact that they suffer from discrimination. Other causes of their problems are not examined. A convenient "ready-made" explanation thereby exists for anything that happens.

Voluntary segregation. A sort of "voluntary" segregation may take place in which the members of a minority separate themselves from the dominant categories. In this way they avoid many unpleasant relationships with dominant members. Jews, for example, have been called "clannish" because they tended to cluster together in a particular section of the city. The Chinese and the Italians have voluntarily formed a "Chinatown" and a "Little Italy" in some American cities. The movement of some black people toward a separatist black nationalism is another example.

Organized protest. The purpose of organized protest is to bring about a change in the situation. It also serves to give the protesters a sense of participation and accomplishment. Of the American minorities, blacks have taken the lead in organized protest. Organizations such as the NAACP (National Association for the Advancement of Colored People), CORE (Congress of Racial Equality), SCLC (Southern Christian Leadership Conference) and SNCC (Student Non-Violent Coordinating Committee) have sponsored such protest activities as boycotts, sit-ins, and marches. These activities have caused the American public to focus on the civil rights problem, and thus have brought about the passage of important laws related to civil rights.

The response of organized protests and demonstrations by minority members in the 1960's and 1970's helped produce greater rights and opportunities for minorities.

Aggression. Not all persons who resent their minority status are able to conceal their feelings. They find an outlet for their frustrations in the form of aggression. The aggression may be vented toward the dominant category, another minority, or against one another. Aggression toward the dominant category may take many forms, ranging from gossip to acts of petty sabotage to major riots. Members of some black activist movements have been willing to express their aggression toward the dominant category through violence, if necessary, to emphasize their desire for liberation. In some areas of mixed racial and ethnic categories, minorities take out their aggressions on other minorities. For example, some Spanish Americans may show strong prejudice against Mexican Americans. The Mexican Americans may then take out their aggression on blacks. Black Americans, lacking a scapegoat, may vent their aggression on other blacks.

SECTION REVIEW

1. In what ways have the dominant members of society reacted to minorities?
2. Which ways do you think are the most common in our society today? Answer this question in terms of the various minorities.
3. In what ways have the minorities related to the dominant members of the society?
4. Do the various minority categories in our society use basically similar or basically different behavior patterns in reacting to the dominant members?

KEY TERMS

Define and give an example of each term.

acculturation   extermination
amalgamation   integration
assimilation   segregation
expulsion

PROJECTS AND ACTIVITIES

1. Do a historic study of a particular minority in America.

2. Examine the lyrics of current popular songs for indications of protests against prejudice and discrimination.

3. Using a newspaper, make a study of what is being done to obtain equal rights for minorities.

4. Make a field trip to a community center, church, welfare center, or other organization in a minority community. What services are provided?

5. Carry out research on one of the protest organizations.

6. If you are a member of a minority category, write a newspaper feature article, editorial, short story, or poem on what it is like to be part of a minority in the United States.

7. Do research by field observation to determine if there is discrimination in housing, employment, and education in your area.

8. Construct a collage that illustrates relations between a minority category and the dominant members of the society in America.

9. Obtain the most recent edition of the U.S. Bureau of the Census, *Statistical Abstract of the United States*. Look up the statistics on the number of various minorities in the United States and compare with the data given in the chapter. How have the numbers of the various minorities changed? Which minorities have increased in numbers? Which have decreased? Have the numbers shifted in any geographic area?

TOPICS FOR INQUIRY

1. Why is it impossible to define minorities simply in terms of actual numbers?

2. Debate: White persons of foreign birth are so well accepted in our American society today that they can no longer be considered minority members.

3. What minorities are present in your community? How are they generally treated?

4. List examples for the three different ways that minority definitions develop. Why can't we simply say that people are born members of minorities?

5. Debate: Minorities do not really want integration but prefer to associate with members of their own category.

6. Which minority category in America do you think has been most unjustly treated by the dominant members of the society? Support your answer.

7. Do you think that eventually amalgamation will take place to the point where we will have complete assimilation in the United States? Explain your answer.

8. What proposals would you suggest to help alleviate prejudice and discrimination against minorities in America?

SUGGESTIONS FOR READING

NONFICTION

GOLDSTEIN, Rhoda (ed.), *Black Life and Culture in the United States.* Crowell, 1971 or Apollo (pap.). A book of readings focusing on distinctive characteristics of black American culture.

GRIFFIN, John H., *Black Like Me.* Houghton Mifflin, 1961 or New American Library (pap.). The author tells how he blackened his skin and traveled through the Deep South, experiencing the prejudices against Black Americans.

HOSOKAWA, Bill, *Nisei: The Quiet Americans.* Morrow, 1969 (and pap.). The official story of the Japanese in America for the Japanese American Association.

KINLOCH, Graham, *The Dynamics of Race Relations: A Sociological Analysis.* McGraw-Hill, 1974 (pap.). A theoretical framework is suggested for the study of race relations.

MARTIN, James and FRANKLIN, Clyde, *Minority Group Relations.* Merrill, 1973. A college textbook which studies intergroup relations, focusing on racial, ethnic, and religious groups in contemporary American society.

SAGARIN, Edward (ed.), *The Other Minorities.* Xerox College Publishing, 1971 (pap.). Discusses women, homosexuals, the poor, and others as minorities.

SKLARE, Marshall, *America's Jews.* Random House, 1971 (pap.). A historical and contemporary study of American Jews by a renowned scholar in Jewish studies.

SPIEGEL, Don and KEITH-SPIEGEL, Patricia, *Outsiders, USA.* Holt, Rinehart and Winston, 1973. Twenty-four original essays on outgroups in American society.

SUNG, Betty Lee, *Mountain of Gold: The Story of the Chinese in America.* Macmillan, 1967. The story of the struggle of the Chinese for survival, acceptance, and full participation in American life from the Gold Rush days to the present.

TEAGUE, Bob, *Letters to a Black Boy.* Walker, 1968. The writer describes in detail his bitter experiences as a black in America.

THOMAS, Piri, *Down These Mean Streets.* Knopf, 1967 and Vintage (pap.). A description of the problems faced by a Puerto Rican boy growing up in Spanish Harlem (New York City).

WAGNER, Nathaniel and HAUG, Marsha, *Chicanos: Social and Psychological Perspectives*. Mosby, 1971 (pap.). A book of readings concerning psychological and sociological studies of Mexican Americans.

WAX, Murray L., *Indian Americans: Unity and Diversity*. Prentice-Hall, 1971 (and pap.). Dramatizes the American Indians' struggle against the white settlers, emphasizing the current Indian condition.

FICTION

BRESLIN, Jimmy, *World Without End, Amen*. Viking or Avon (pap.). A twenty-nine-year-old New York City cop visits Ireland and begins to realize the brutality of survival among minority groups.

FAULKNER, William, *Intruder in the Dust*. Random House (and pap.). A story of racial inequality directed against blacks in the South.

HANSBERRY, Lorraine, *A Raisin in the Sun*. Random House or New American Library (pap.) A black family buys a home in a white neighborhood so they can have a yard and grass and trees, but they are faced with a white committee who offer to buy their house.

HOFFINE, Lyla, *Carol Blue Wing*. McKay. Having just finished her junior year at college, a young Indian girl suffers conflict between her love for her own people's homelands and her wish to teach in the white society's school.

LEE, Harper, *To Kill a Mockingbird*. Lippincott or Popular Library (pap.). The experiences of a white lawyer in the South after he takes the case of a black person.

MARQUES, Rene, *The Oxcart*. Scribner (pap.). A Puerto Rican leaves with his family for New York and a better life, only to be destroyed by the values of a mechanized society.

PAPASHVILY, George and PAPASHVILY, Helen, *Anything Can Happen*. Harper & Row. The hilarious story of the experiences of a Georgian (Russian) immigrant to the United States.

SCHWARZ-BART, Andre, *The Last of the Just*. Atheneum or Bantam (pap.). A Jewish boy finds himself at the mercy of the youth of Hitler's Germany.

SHULMAN, Irving, *West Side Story*. Pocket Books (pap.). A portrayal of two gangs in the heart of New York City. Two people cross the lines of prejudice and cause several deaths.

STEINBECK, John, *The Pearl.* Viking or Bantam (pap.). A horrifying tale about the way a town treats a Mexican pearl diver and his family after the diver finds an enormous pearl.

VASQUES, Richard. *Chicano.* Doubleday. The saga of a Chicano family who leave Mexico for the United States, where they suffer the prejudices all too common to Chicanos.

9 Population and Human Ecology

▶ What determines the size of a society's population?

▶ How does overcrowding affect human behavior?

▶ What are some characteristics of large and small communities?

SECTION 1:
Population Characteristics

A POPULATION *is the total number of people living in a specific area.* The organization of a society and the relationships of its people are very much affected by the characteristics of its population. Take, for instance, the characteristic of population size. Many people today are concerned about overpopulation. The rapid world population growth in recent years is unparalleled in human history. How will societies and people's lives be affected by such an increase in population? There are those who predict that as the population of the world increases, the standard of living will decrease. Eventually there will be mass starvation all over the world. Are these only wild threats of extreme pessimists? Or do we really face the threat of mass starvation in the near future?

To answer these questions, we must have some knowledge of basic concepts of population. We have to know about the factors that determine how many people will make up the population of any specific society or the world in general. Every society is constantly adding and subtracting people to its total population. Persons are added to the population either by births or by movement into the society. They are subtracted either by deaths or by movement out of the society. Since every society has a different total population to which persons are added and subtracted, population data are usually given either as rates per thousand people or else in percent.

Population Increase and Decrease

POPULATION INCREASE *is the percentage increase in total population during a year.* Since population increase figures are given in percent, it is possible to compare the growth

165

rates of countries of all sizes. A population increase of 1 percent means that the population will double in approximately seventy years. A 2-percent increase means the population will double in approximately thirty-five years. A 3-percent increase means it will double in only twenty-three years.

Birth and death rates. *The* BIRTH RATE *is the number of births per 1,000 members of the population over a period of a year. The* DEATH RATE *is the number of deaths from all causes during the year per 1,000 persons alive at the middle of the year.* A birth rate or a death rate by itself is practically meaningless. Both must be considered. If the society has both a high birth rate and a high death rate, the population will remain basically stable. Many countries, however, have a high birth rate and a low death rate. For the world as a whole, the birth rate is 34 and the death rate is 15. Births greatly outnumber deaths. Why?

Advanced technology tends to lower both birth and death rates. But it tends to lower death rates much sooner than it lowers birth rates. People accept ways of living healthier and longer lives much more quickly than they accept ways of limiting the number of children they will have. The result is a population explosion. The real cause of the population explosion is not the high birth rate—it has never been lower. The cause is people living longer and thus greatly lowering the death rate.

Life expectancy. One factor that influences the death rate is life expectancy. LIFE EXPECTANCY *is the average number of years an individual can expect to live.* If people live longer, the death rate will be less. It is a common belief in our society that if every couple had only two children, then the population would remain stable. The idea is that every person would only be replacing himself or herself. This would work in practice if every couple replaced themselves with two children by the age of twenty-five or so, and then died. But they don't. Modern tech-

nology makes it possible for them to live to the ripe old age of approximately seventy years. They replace themselves, and then stay around to watch their children replace themselves—and almost stay long enough to see their grandchildren replace themselves. When life expectancy increases and generations overlap in this way, population growth is much more rapid.

Population movement. In addition to birth and death rates, a nation's population growth is influenced by the migration of people in and out of a country. IMMIGRATION *refers to the movement of people into a country.* Immigration can provide a society with a larger labor force, or new knowledge and skills. The immigrants to the United States in the 1800's, for instance, provided America with inexpensive labor and more consumers. EMIGRATION *is the movement of people out of a country.* The term NET IMMIGRATION *refers to the number of people who come in minus those who leave.* For instance, if 1,000 people move in and 100 move out, the net immigration is 900. Net immigration in the United States usually accounts for about one fifth of our population growth.

Population base. *The* POPULATION BASE *is the total number of people in a society at any one time.* This is the figure to which the birth rate and net immigration are added to get the latest population total. The larger the population base is to start with, the greater the number of people who will be added, even when the birth rate is the same. A society of 100,000 persons increasing at the rate of 2 percent a year will gain 2,000 people in one year, while a society of 200,000,000 persons increasing at the same rate will gain 4,000,000 people during that year.

Also important in determining the population total are the age and sex distributions of that population. Only women bear children, and in our society they usually have them when they are in their twenties and thirties. Therefore, a large number of women

With the increase in life expectancy, the generations overlap each other more and more. Now older people often live to see their great-grandchildren.

of that age in a population can increase the number of births, even though the birth rate stays the same. In the United States today, due to an increase in number of babies in the late 1940's to mid-1950's, we have a very large population of women of child-bearing age. If these women have children, there will be an increase in the number of births, even though the actual birth rate—the number per 1,000 people—is dropping.

Population and Human Behavior

How does living in a crowded area affect human relationships? Why are there more single women than single men in the United States? What happens when capable people in good health are forced to retire at age sixty-five? Is there a relationship between the number of children in a family and where the family lives? These are a few of the many questions we might ask about population and human behavior.

Population density. Human behavior is affected by crowding. One of the ways of measuring the amount of human crowding is by population density. *The POPULATION DENSITY is the number of persons per square mile, or per 2.6 square kilometers, of land area.* Population density varies greatly throughout the United States and the world. For example, the population density of the United States is 58. For India it is 455, and for Japan it is 753. There is also a considerable difference among the various states in our country. The population density of Alaska is 0.5. Wyoming is 3, Ohio is 260, New Jersey 953, and the District of Columbia 12,402. For an idea of a dense population area within a state, consider that the borough of Manhattan in New York City has more than 67,000 persons per square mile (or per 2.6 square kilometers) of land.

Perhaps in reaction to the problems of high density areas, some people have been moving from high density urban areas to low density spacious areas.

Population density figures are useful for understanding some basic problems, such as feeding, housing, and clothing many people living in a small area. Some nations have a very low standard of living because of a high density of population. Others, such as Japan, have a high standard of living under very crowded conditions because of their advanced technology.

Population density is also related to social problems such as crime, juvenile delinquency, poverty, mental illness, and drug addiction. Research indicates that as people become more crowded, they tend to become more alienated from one another and more aggressive. Large cities with high population densities are reporting a number of cases where citizens watch others being mugged, raped, or murdered and offer no

help. These bystanders simply say that they don't want to get involved.

Sex ratio. *The* SEX RATIO *is the proportion of men to women in a population.* It is stated as the number of males to 100 females. A sex ratio of 100 would mean that the sex distribution is equal. For the United States the sex ratio is approximately 95, which means that there are 95 males to every 100 females. Actually, it varies according to age. A few more males are born than females. But males have a higher death rate than females. As a group, they tend to do more physically dangerous activities than females, such as fighting in wars. Males also seem to be less durable physically than females. The result is a shortage of men in relation to women. As the woman grows older the shortage becomes even greater, for men tend to marry women younger than themselves. Also, women live longer than men. Many women spend their last five or ten years single after the deaths of their husbands.

Age composition. The ages of the citizens of a society are very important. In the United States most people under twenty-one, as well as people sixty-five and over, are dependent on the society. It is the category of persons in their twenties through sixty-four years who must support the rest of the society, since the young are in school and most people over sixty-five are retired. A larger proportion of young and old places a greater burden on the middle age category of citizens. If a society has a large number of children, it is burdened by the financial cost of providing education for these children.

The age factor affects the economy of a nation in other ways. The age composition of the population influences the kinds and number of products made. People at different ages require different products. For example, teen-agers provide a large market for transistor radios, records and tapes, cosmetics, clothing, entertainment, and automobiles. A high birth rate has a positive effect on the economy as the growing children's needs change from baby food and diapers to larger-size clothes and bicycles, and then to cars and new homes. A change in the birth rate forces the economy to make changes in the goods that it produces. A change in the death rate also brings changes in the economy. With the longer life span of Americans now, we are seeing an increase in the goods and services provided for the elderly by our economy.

Differential fertility. FERTILITY *is the actual reproduction that occurs in a population.*

Teen-age girls own twice as many record players as Germany has VW's.

Different members of the population do not reproduce at the same rate. We might consider a few differentials to illustrate this concept.

● The fertility rate tends to be higher in rural areas than in urban areas.

● It tends to be slightly higher for non-whites than for whites.

● The more education women have, the fewer children they have. Women with less than eight years of education, for example, have about one third more children than do women with four years of college or more.

● The fertility rates of Roman Catholics are generally higher than those of Protestants. And the fertility rates of fundamentalist Protestants tend to be higher than for Protestants in general.

● As the social class position of families goes up, the fertility rate generally goes down.

These, then, are some of the important concepts of population. They are necessary for understanding the population explosion problem and the many other ways in which population affects human behavior and social relationships.

SECTION REVIEW

1. Why is population increase (or population decrease) the most important concept for comparing future population trends of several countries?
2. How does population density affect human behavior?
3. Suppose a society has a sex ratio of 110. What does this figure mean? What are some implications for the society of having such a sex ratio?
4. What are some problems for a society with a large proportion of children and elderly persons in the population?
5. Give some examples to illustrate the concept of differential fertility.

KEY TERMS

Explain each of the following terms.

birth rate
death rate
differential fertility
emigration
fertility
immigration
life expectancy

net immigration
population
population base
population density
population increase
sex ratio

SECTION 2:
Human Ecology

Where people live has an effect on their relationships with others. Their activities and social relations will be different depending on whether they live in Manhattan, in a suburb of Chicago, on a small farm in Alabama, in a town in Iowa, on a 100,000-acre (40,486-hectare) ranch in the Nebraska sandhills, or in a beach house in California. Both the geographic and social environments exert a strong influence on all aspects of a person's life. *The area of sociology that investigates and analyzes the causes and consequences of the spatial distribution of human population is* HUMAN ECOLOGY. It is the study of how the spatial arrangement of people on the earth affects human relationships.

Ecology and population are very closely related because ecologists obtain much of their data from population statistics. Human ecologists are concerned with such phenomena as density of population, population movements in space, and the different characteristics of communities and neighborhoods. They study how these phenomena influence the basic patterns of human relationships. How, for instance, do communities affect the lives of those who live in them?

How are your human relationships affected by your geographic and social environment? Human ecologists are studying many aspects of this question.

Communities

A COMMUNITY *is a number of people who live in a certain geographic area and have a social structure that provides for their physical and social needs.* A community may be a village, town, city, or metropolitan area. The important criterion of a community is not the size but the interaction of the people with each other in their day-to-day activities. Even a large metropolitan area may be a community, if there is interaction among many of the individuals. For example, workers from the suburbs may commute to the core city every weekday, while other workers living in the city may be employed in a factory in the suburbs. Much interaction among individuals in a metropolitan area may occur on the job, through organizations, shopping, attending school, visiting friends, and during leisure-time activities. There is also a good deal of interaction among persons when they are caught in a traffic jam in one of our metropolitan areas!

Rural and urban communities. *An* URBAN COMMUNITY *is one that has a population of 2,500 inhabitants or more. A* RURAL COMMUNITY *has a population of fewer than 2,500 inhabitants.* Rural communities consist of persons who live on farms, or in towns or vil-

171

What characteristics of a rural community are illustrated in this picture?

lages that add up to a total of less than 2,500 people.

Rural communities differ considerably from one another, as do urban areas. There is, therefore, a good deal of overlap in specific characteristics of rural or urban communities. The best way to describe rural and urban communities, then, is on the basis of a continuum. On one end of the continuum we can list the characteristics that are most rural in nature. On the other end we would put the characteristics that are most urban. We can then describe individual communities in terms of where they fall on the continuum. Let's look at some characteristics.

Characteristics of rural communities in the United States:

1. Rural communities tend to be *small in size* in both population and land area.

2. *The population density is low,* much lower than in urban areas. There may be only two or three houses per block. Often each family has a large garden. Many rural communities also are quite isolated from other communities.

3. *The people tend to be homogeneous,* or very much alike. Usually they are of the same race or national background. Often subcultures do not exist within rural communities. There may be a great difference in incomes among families in the community. Nevertheless, the style of life of the people is more homogeneous and class consciousness exists less than in the city.

4. *Housing is generally single-family.* Apartments are rare. If more than one family lives in a dwelling, they are likely to be related. Most of the houses are comfortable but not elaborate.

5. *The interactions of the people tend to be primary.* Since the number of people is small, most individuals know almost everyone else and are on a first-name basis. When a stranger comes into the community, he or she is immediately recognized as an outsider.

172

How do the characteristics of a metropolitan community (shown here) differ from the characteristics shown on the opposite page?

6. *Group membership usually overlaps* in the rural community. Because of the size of the community, most of the organized groups have the same people as members. Therefore, there is a good deal of interaction among the same people as they participate in such activities as work, shopping, social affairs, and leisure-time activities.

7. *Social control is informal.* Since everyone knows everyone else, the individual is strongly motivated to conform to the norms of the community. Gossip is a very important factor in social control. An individual who breaks the norms knows that everybody will hear about it in a very short time. The formal sanctions of the police and the courts are often not needed to settle minor disputes. People know one another well and can settle many conflicts among themselves.

Characteristics of urban and metropolitan communities in the United States:

1. Urban communities are *large in size,* both in area and in population. For example, Los Angeles contains a land area of 464 square miles (1,206 square kilometers) and has a population of nearly 3 million. Houston, Texas has a land area of 434 square miles (1,128 square kilometers) and a population of about 1.25 million.

2. *Urban areas have a high density of population.* Brooklyn, New York has a density of about 37,000 persons per square mile (per 2.59 square kilometers). Chicago has a population density of 15,000. In Jersey City, New Jersey, there are more than 17,000 persons per square mile (per 2.59 square kilometers).

3. *The people who inhabit the urban areas are heterogeneous,* or different from each other. There are differences in race, national background, religion, social class, and family income. There is also a great variation in neighborhoods—some are slums, some are new, some are expensive, some have only one ethnic category, and some have several ethnic categories. The people in urban areas generally belong to all levels of social classes,

and class distinctions between levels may be quite evident.

4. The typical urban area has *a great variety of housing*. There are exclusive neighborhoods with expensive homes, areas of housing developments in which the houses are very much alike, areas of two-family houses, high-rise apartment districts, and slum areas. Some of the housing is very old and some is new. Some of the housing is surrounded only by concrete or bare earth.

5. *A higher proportion of human interaction is impersonal in the urban area.* Many relationships are secondary in nature. Except for some close friends, the individual reacts to people on a no-name basis. The individual may walk down the streets of the city and not meet a single person he or she knows.

6. *Group membership does not overlap very much.* A person might be a member of five

THE RURAL-URBAN CONTINUUM

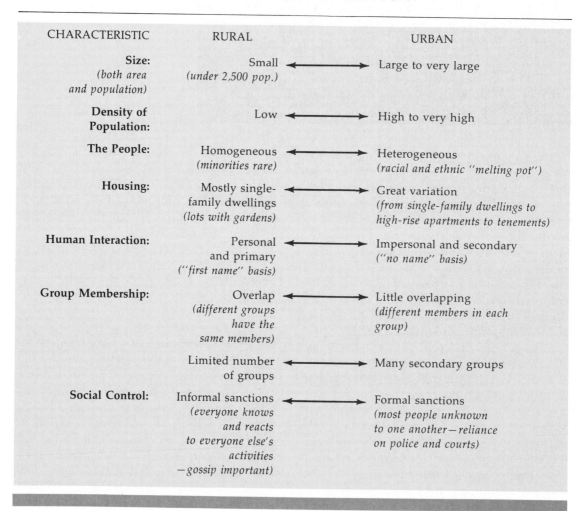

CHARACTERISTIC	RURAL	URBAN
Size: *(both area and population)*	Small *(under 2,500 pop.)* ←——→	Large to very large
Density of Population:	Low ←——→	High to very high
The People:	Homogeneous *(minorities rare)* ←——→	Heterogeneous *(racial and ethnic "melting pot")*
Housing:	Mostly single-family dwellings *(lots with gardens)* ←——→	Great variation *(from single-family dwellings to high-rise apartments to tenements)*
Human Interaction:	Personal and primary *("first name" basis)* ←——→	Impersonal and secondary *("no name" basis)*
Group Membership:	Overlap *(different groups have the same members)* ←——→	Little overlapping *(different members in each group)*
	Limited number of groups ←——→	Many secondary groups
Social Control:	Informal sanctions *(everyone knows and reacts to everyone else's activities — gossip important)* ←——→	Formal sanctions *(most people unknown to one another — reliance on police and courts)*

What characteristics of a suburban community do you see in this picture? In what ways are suburban communities different from both rural and urban communities?

different groups and none of the same people would be in any of the five groups. The typical city has a multitude of secondary groups to which the individual may belong.

7. *Social control is formal.* The police may be called in to settle minor disputes between neighbors. Since individuals often don't know one another in a metropolitan area, they are not controlled by gossip and ridicule. Instead, the police and the courts control people's behavior by the administration of formal sanctions.

Of course, few, if any, communities have all of the characteristics of a rural or an urban area. Rather, every community has each of the characteristics to some degree. Every community could be placed somewhere between the extremes of the continuum for each of the seven characteristics. For instance, a community may be more rural in some characteristics and more urban in others. The figure on page 174 is a continuum that summarizes the characteristics just discussed.

The suburban community. A third kind of community is the suburb. *A* SUBURB *is a smaller community related to but beyond the limits of the core, or central, city.* The Bureau of the Census usually classifies suburbs as part of a metropolitan area. But the characteristics of many suburbs place them somewhere near the middle of the continuum.

There are great variations among suburbs. Some suburbs have many of the same characteristics as urban communities, differing only in size and location. Other suburbs have more characteristics that are rural in nature. Many suburban communities tend to be more urban than rural because of their large increase in population in recent years and their close association with the core city. Most suburbs are dependent on the core city for such functions as jobs, distribution of goods, services, utilities, museums, entertainment, and recreation. The table on page 176 presents a number of census statistics that make it possible to compare suburban residents with city dwellers and the farm population.

These, then, are some of the character-

SELECTED STATISTICS OF THE POPULATION ACCORDING TO RESIDENCE

ITEMS	SUBURB	CORE CITY	FARM
Median family income	$11,771	$9,519	$7,296
Median school years completed for all persons 25 and over	12.3	12.0	10.7
% of all persons 25 and over having 4 years of college or more	14.4	10.9	4.6
% of families receiving public assistance income	3.4	7.2	3.7
% of persons 65 and over	7.6	10.5	10.5
Mean size of family	3.61	3.47	3.64
% of families with income less than poverty level	5.2	11.0	15.8
Fertility rate (births per 1,000 women)	2,035	1,943	2,567
% of households lacking some or all plumbing	1.4	2.9	16.4

Source: U.S. Bureau of the Census, *1970 Census of Population, General Social and Economic Characteristics.*

istics of rural, urban, and suburban communities. Where does your community fit on the continuum? How would your life be different if you lived in one of the other kinds of communities? Which kind of community would you prefer to live in, if you had a choice? Why?

Ecological Processes

Ecological processes involve movements of the population. Ecologists are concerned with the movement of people from one region to another. But they are even more concerned about movements from one type of ecological area to another. The following ecological processes deal with population movements between ecological areas.

Urbanization. URBANIZATION *is the movement of people from the farms to the cities.* A great deal of urbanization has taken place in the United States. Until recently, there was a continuing movement of population from nonmetropolitan to metropolitan areas. Up until 1970, the percentage of the population living in urban areas increased steadily in this century, and the percentage in rural areas decreased. The farm population has shrunk from 30 percent of the total population in 1920 to less than 5 percent today.

You might wonder how the cities are able to absorb large numbers of people. Some cities have built skyscrapers—tall office and apartment buildings that hold many people and take up little land space. Other cities have annexed more territory. In general, cities that are completely ringed by incorporated municipalities, and therefore can't annex more territory, have not been showing population gains.

Most of the recent population gains in metropolitan areas have been due to the settling of immigrants from other countries in the cities. Since 1970, however, more people have moved out of the cities than have moved in. There has been a shift in the population movement. For the first time in many, many years, nonmetropolitan areas are growing faster than metropolitan areas.

Suburbanization. SUBURBANIZATION *is the movement of people from the core city to the surrounding suburbs.* As the cities have gradually expanded, the suburbs have expanded much more rapidly, until now a larger percentage of the population lives in the suburbs than in the core city. In 1970 the suburbs became the largest sector of the population, with more people than either the core cities or all the rest of the country outside metropolitan areas.

Segregation. SEGREGATION *exists when only one category of people lives in a particular neighborhood.* Some cities have neighborhoods known as "Little Italy," occupied by Italians, or "Chinatown," occupied by Chinese people. These are segregated neighborhoods, where one category of people chooses to live in the same area. In reality, most neighborhoods are not occupied totally by only one category of people. There are usually some families belonging to another category living in that neighborhood. A segregated ecological area, however, contains an overwhelming majority of one particular category. (See other examples on page 155.)

Invasion. INVASION *is the movement of one social category into an area occupied by another social category.* For instance, if only Italians live in a neighborhood, and several Mexican American families move in, the process of invasion is taking place.

Succession. SUCCESSION *occurs when a new group succeeds, or takes over the neighborhood from, the previous group.* Suppose that when Mexican Americans begin to move into an Italian neighborhood, most of the Italian

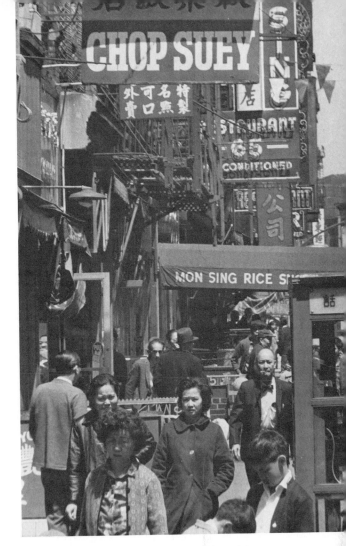

A number of cities have areas, such as this one, that are inhabited mainly by one category of people. This situation is known as voluntary segregation.

families begin to move out. If their homes are sold to Mexican American families, who now move into the neighborhood, succession has taken place.

Actually, the processes of invasion and succession take place slowly over a number of years. There are examples of invasion and succession in most large urban areas. Which of the five ecological processes just described appear to be taking place in your own community?

SECTION REVIEW

1. What does an ecologist study?
2. What is the rural-urban continuum and how is it used?
3. Compare the characteristics of rural and urban communities in the United States.
4. What are the characteristics of the suburban community?
5. Explain the five ecological processes mentioned in the chapter.

KEY TERMS

Explain and give an example to illustrate each term.

community
human ecology
invasion
rural community
rural-urban
  continuum

segregation
suburbanization
suburbs
succession
urban community
urbanization

PROJECTS AND ACTIVITIES

1. Collect articles from your local newspaper on a particular problem in your community that is directly related to population. What solutions to the problem are suggested? What solutions would you recommend?

2. Obtain the latest edition of the U.S. Bureau of the Census, *Statistical Abstract of the United States.* Look up data on the number of births, deaths, net immigration, and population base for the latest year. Then compute these data to find the percentage of population increase.

3. Do research to find the population changes in each state since 1970. Which states show the greatest increase (in percent)? Why is growth greatest in these states? Do any states show a decrease in population? If so, why? Which states show the smallest increase in population? Why?

4. Interview three individuals of similar age—one who has lived in an urban area, one in a suburban area, and one in a rural area. Compare their views of what life is like in each area.

5. Prepare a photo exhibit or slide presentation that illustrates the various ecological areas.

6. If you live in a city, visit its urban renewal office to find out what has been done in the past and what the plans are for the future of your city.

7. Obtain copies of farm magazines, read them, and write a short report on what you learned about farm life.

8. Visit a realty office in your community to determine how the value of a home is affected by the neighborhood in which it is located.

9. Do research on the various farm organizations and what services they offer to farm families. Consider the following: the Grange, the American Farm Bureau Federation, the National Farmers' Organization, and various farm cooperatives.

10. If you live in a metropolitan area, obtain the census tracts for it. (They are usually available at the city library.) Study the statistics for selected districts throughout the metropolitan area. Then visit the districts and compare what you observe with the statistics.

TOPICS FOR INQUIRY

1. In the middle 1970's approximately 20 percent of the population growth in the United States was due to immigration. Some have suggested that we should limit immigration. What do you think? Why?

2. Statistics from the World Health Organization indicate that the United States has shown less increase in the life expectancy of adult males over the last twenty years than most other member nations. In fact, close to twenty nations have a higher life expectancy for males. How do you account for this? Consider such factors as accidents, overeating, and emotional stess.

3. How would your own personal life change if there were: (1) a doubling of the population density? (2) a lowering of the sex ratio from ninety-five to seventy-five? (3) a great increase in the number of people over age sixty-five?

4. How would the social and economic areas of our society be affected by a tremendous drop in the birth rate?

5. Animal studies indicate that when crowding occurs, the animals become hostile and aggressive. What effects do you think crowding might have on humans?

6. Discuss your own community in terms of the rural-urban continuum, placing it on the continuum in each of the seven characteristics.

7. Debate the advantages and disadvantages of living in a suburban home vs. living in a high-rise apartment in a major city.

8. Many persons feel that the rural environment is the most desirable in which to live and that cities, although necessary, are basically undesirable. What do you think? Which environment would you prefer? Why?

BANFIELD, Edward C., *The Unheavenly City Revisited*. Little, Brown, 1974 (and pap.). Deals with the problems of cities and the growth and distribution of populations.

BIRD, Caroline, *The Crowding Syndrome*. McKay, 1972. An optimistic approach to learning to live with too much and too many.

BROWN, Harrison and HUTCHINGS, Edward Jr., *Are Our Descendants Doomed?* Viking, 1972 (pap.). An inquiry into technological change and population growth.

EHRLICH, Paul, *The Population Bomb*. Sierra Club Books, 1969. Deals with the problem of the "population explosion."

FETTERMAN, John, *Stinking Creek*. Dutton, 1970 (pap.). A study of life in a rural village in southern Appalachia.

JOHNSON, Stanley, *The Population Problem*. Halsted, 1973. A very comprehensive coverage of the population problem.

KAHN, E. J., *The American People; the Findings of the 1970 Census*. Penguin, 1975 (pap.). Points out the relevant similarities and differences among Americans in such aspects as race, mobility, status, money, sex, and migration.

LEINWAND, Gerald, *The City as a Community*. Pocket Books, 1970 (pap.). An account of life in the city.

――― (ed.), *Governing the City*. Pocket Books, 1971 (pap.). Discusses the problems of city government.

LINDSAY, John V., *The City*. Norton, 1969 or New American Library (pap.). New York's former mayor reports firsthand on the struggle to preserve and improve the quality of city life.

LISTON, Robert A., *Downtown: Our Challenging Urban Problems*. Delacorte, 1970 or Dell (pap.). A discussion of the problems of the cities and how they are being solved through the cooperation of government, business, and individual citizens.

MUMFORD, Lewis, *The Urban Prospect*. Harcourt Brace Jovanovich, 1968 (and pap.). The author discusses the problems of urban life.

NATIONAL GEOGRAPHIC SOCIETY, *Life in Rural America*. National Geographic Society, 1974. Covers the virtues of rural life. Discusses small towns, work, leisure, fellowship, and so on.

WALLS, Dwayne E., *The Chickenbone Special*. Harcourt Brace Jovanovich, 1973 (pap.). The story of the largest migration in history— from rural America into the city—told by blacks who moved north.

180

UNIT
THREE

COLLECTIVE BEHAVIOR

No doubt you've watched scenes of violence and rioting on television news. As you observed them, did you sometimes wonder if the people involved had gone crazy? How does violence get started? What causes the participants to behave as they do? Sociologists are very much concerned with this kind of social behavior. They want to know the causes and consequences of such unstructured behavior as violence and riots. They also study such relatively unstructured social behavior as rumors, fads, fashions, and propaganda. These are all examples of collective behavior.

10 Unstructured Behavior

► Why do rumors and fads spread?

► What causes us to "lose ourselves" in a crowd?

► How does unstructured behavior get started?

SECTION 1:
Structured vs. Unstructured Behavior

Have you ever watched an audience that is "carried away" by a performance of a rock group? At the end of a song members of the audience may scream, jump up and down, cry—a few may even faint. After the performance a part of the audience may mob the performers, trying to get their autographs or a lock of their hair. These emotional group reactions are spontaneous and relatively unstructured. They are examples of collective behavior. In sociology, the term COLLECTIVE BEHAVIOR *refers to the study of relatively unstructured situations, such as crowds, riots, panics, fads, fashions, and social movements.* These phenomena are characterized by behavior that is not fully controlled by cultural norms and structured social relationships. Although the term "collective" is the usual title given to such behavior, perhaps a better word to describe this kind of behavior is "unstructured."

Examples of unstructured behavior often make newspaper headlines. But the drama of these events is less important than the effect of these situations on the life of the individual and the culture of the society. For example, religious revivals can change the lives of many individuals and also bring about great social changes in the society. The small religious club started by John and Charles Wesley at Oxford University in 1729 developed into a separate religious denomination, the Methodists, and brought about social changes in England. Panics may lead to the loss of lives, as when people trample each other to get out of a burning building. Or they may lead to a crisis in the society, as during the stock market crash of 1929. Fads and fashions that offer variety in the lives of individuals may remain as specific culture

This is an example of structured behavior, in which group values, group norms, and group roles are present, and each person has a sense of self.

traits of the society, such as collars on men's shirts or wearing wristwatches. Rumors very often lead to mass behavior that results in individual distrust, group conflicts, or a lowering of group morale. Each one of us participates in many temporary and recurrent groups that are structured. But we also are constantly involved in group situations that are unstructured.

Before analyzing unstructured behavior, though, it is necessary to examine structured behavior. The root "un" suggests that unstructured behavior is missing something that structured behavior has. Basically, STRUCTURED BEHAVIOR *is group behavior that is controlled by some type of group structure,* such as common values, group norms, and specific role relationships. Unstructured behavior takes place in social situations where these characteristics are absent. In UNSTRUCTURED BEHAVIOR *the usual values, norms, and roles that control the behavior of the individual in the group situation are missing.*

The Structured–Unstructured Continuum

Actually there is no fine line that divides structured behavior from unstructured be-

havior. Structured group situations vary greatly from those that are rigidly structured to those that are loosely structured. At the same time completely unstructured group situations do not occur, for some structure exists in all social relationships. To understand structured and unstructured group situations, let's think again in terms of a continuum. In the continuum structured and unstructured would be at opposite extremes, and all social situations would fall somewhere in between. Social behavior would have a degree of structure ranging from a very rigid structure to basically no structure. What, then, are the characteristics of those two extremes of social behavior?

Characteristics of structured behavior. We will examine the characteristics of structured behavior as they apply to a basketball game, a rigidly structured group situation.

1. *Group values are present.* In the structured behavior of recurrent groups common values play a large part in group structure. In a basketball game, for example, we would find such values as "our school is best," "our team is best," or "our team must win." At the same time fair play and being a good sport are highly valued.

2. *Group norms are present.* These norms

may be formal or informal, rigid or flexible. In a high school basketball game the norms are formal and rigid. Before the game there is often the presentation of the colors and the singing of the National Anthem. The team captains always shake hands. There are norms that specify the value of a field goal, the time limits, what is considered a foul, and the specific penalties for any violations of the norms. Some norms also apply to the spectators and their behavior.

3. *Group roles are present.* In structured behavior the roles of the individuals are quite obvious and specific. There are a great many roles in a basketball game: coach, team captain, forward, guard, center, scorekeeper, timekeeper, cheerleader, substitute player, member of the band, and spectator. Every individual involved in the social situation of a basketball game has a well-defined role to play.

4. *The individual has a sense of self.* The individual has a distinct concept of self related to his or her role in the social situation. Basketball players, for instance, clearly understand what they are supposed to do in the various game situations, and they judge how well they are doing it. Individuals are also conscious of the values and norms of the group and of their responsibility to carry out their assigned role. They are very conscious of themselves and they feel responsible for their actions.

Characteristics of unstructured behavior. We are describing the extremes of a continuum. Therefore the characteristics of unstructured behavior will be exactly the opposite of those for structured behavior.

1. *No group values have developed, or those which have developed are questioned by many group members.* For example, a crowd of people looking at a display in a store window has no group values. Neither does a crowd of people waiting for the traffic light to change, or a crowd milling about at a carnival. Instead of common group values the

members of a crowd have individual values, which may be quite different.

When a group has common values that are seriously being questioned by many group members, the structure of the group is weakened. If the group changes from a structured group to an unstructured group, it will not exist long. It has no unity to hold it together.

2. *There is an absence of group norms, or failure to obey the norms.* A crowd of people waiting for the light to change, watching a window display, or milling about is not aware of any specific norms related to that particular situation. People who watch but do nothing as an individual is being robbed or murdered before their eyes are experiencing a new situation to which no group norms apply. In an unstructured situation, without group norms, people may do nothing.

These people in the pool illustrate unstructured behavior, in which there are few or no group values or norms, and little or no role allocation.

Drawing by Henry Martin.
© 1975 The New Yorker Magazine, Inc.

"As we move toward a more structured society, I suppose we'll see fewer and fewer days when clouds are scattered lazily across the afternoon sky."

In some cases the norms are present but are considered to no longer apply to the situation. A crowd of people waiting for the traffic light to change is aware of the norm that no one should cross the street when the light is red. However, if no cars are coming from either direction, some individuals may ignore the red light and cross the street. Since no cars are coming, they consider that the norm no longer applies.

In a crisis situation the norms may seem to have no application to the situation. Yet they may still be the best guides to behavior. If the building is on fire the ordinary rules of etiquette would seem inappropriate, since the problem is one of self-survival. Yet in some crises these rules of etiquette, or norms, are still needed. For example, in the tragic Coconut Grove fire in Boston on November 28, 1942 a total of 491 persons were killed. When the famous night club caught fire, the persons inside panicked and ran for the doors, which became jammed with people. After the fire was over, hundreds of bodies were found piled up behind each jammed door. Had the crowd walked out in an orderly fashion, no one might have died.

3. *There is no role allocation.* Individuals do not have specific roles to play. Nor is there any specific leadership. The crowd of people waiting for the traffic light to change has no allocation of roles. No one is the leader. Instead, leadership must develop in unstructured groups. If one person goes across on the red light and others follow him or her, that person becomes the leader. Studies indicate that people will tend to follow a well-dressed person, such as a business executive, across the street on a red light. But they may not follow someone who appears to have a low status, such as a person dressed like a blue-collar worker.

The outcome of many critical unstructured situations depends on whether or not a leader emerges. For instance, suppose a crowd begins to gather at the scene of a car accident in which several persons have been injured. No police officers are present. No one in the crowd is experienced at giving first aid. Who will administer first aid? Who will call for a doctor and an ambulance? Who will contact the police? Who will direct traffic and hold back the crowd? Since no roles have been allocated in this situation, the leaders must emerge from the crowd. One or two persons may emerge and take leadership and keep the situation well in hand. Or no leaders may emerge and chaos may result.

In many critical situations an individual has assumed leadership and prevented a panic. Molly Brown earned the title "Unsinkable" because she prevented a panic among the persons in her lifeboat as their ship, the *Titanic,* was sinking, after it hit an iceberg. However, more than 1,500 persons did lose their lives in this disaster of 1912.

186

THE CONTINUUM OF STRUCTURED-UNSTRUCTURED BEHAVIOR

STRUCTURED BEHAVIOR	UNSTRUCTURED BEHAVIOR
Characteristics	*Characteristics*
1. Presence of group values	1. Absence of group values
2. Presence of group norms	2. Absence of group norms
3. Presence of group roles	3. No role allocation
4. Individual has sense of self	4. Individual may lose sense of self

All group situations fall somewhere on the continuum between the two extremes.

4. *Individuals may lose their sense of self.* They may become anonymous as individuals by losing their identity in the group. Since they have no specific role in the group, it is very easy for individuals to go along with the crowd. They do whatever the crowd does. Research has shown that individuals will perform actions in a crowd situation that they would never even think of doing on their own.

The individual's experiences in the crowd situation may lead to feelings of shame or guilt afterward, as the person recalls what he or she has done as a member of the crowd. On the other hand, such experiences may increase the individual's identity with a particular group or category, such as his or her school, gang, race, or ethnic category.

The figure on this page is a continuum that summarizes the basic characteristics of structured and unstructured group behavior.

Emotional Contagion

Emotional contagion is involved to some degree in all human relationships. But it is particularly important in unstructured situations. EMOTIONAL CONTAGION *is the rapid communication of a strong emotion, such as fear, among persons until almost everyone present is showing the same emotion and the same type of behavior.* Just as a contagious disease spreads from person to person, a particular emotion spreads from person to person until almost everyone is experiencing the same emotion. Each person is affected by his or her perception of how others feel. As individuals see the emotions and behavior of others, they change their own feelings and actions to conform with the emotions and behavior of those around them. Since there are no specific norms or roles to be followed in an unstructured situation, the persons involved are easily swayed toward a particular kind of behavior.

In structured group situations, emotional contagion is important in building group unity and morale. The basic function of the cheerleaders at an athletic event is to arouse emotional contagion that will develop into a strong group spirit in support of the team.

In unstructured social situations, emotional contagion may lead to chaos and disaster. If, when a slight tremor of the building occurs, a few persons scream "earthquake" and run for the doors of the movie theater,

other individuals are likely to run also. Soon there is mass confusion and disaster, as some people are trampled.

The end result, however, is dependent on whether or not an individual emerges as the leader, and what kind of leadership he or she exerts. For the leader is the person who can best guide emotional contagion in a specific direction. Suppose, for example, after a high school basketball game the students from both schools are in the parking lot heading for their cars. One student makes an unflattering comment about the other school's team. A student from the other school responds. One comment leads to another, and emotional contagion begins to build. The situation is relatively unstructured. Emotions heighten. At this point the crowd could easily change into a group brawl or a free-for-all fight between the students of the two schools. Suppose, then, a rather level-headed student, realizing the seriousness of the situation, emerges as a leader in the other direction. The student points out that the game was well played by both sides and was won fairly by the other school. The student suggests that fighting would accomplish very little. It certainly would not change the score. Instead, they should wait and attempt to defeat the other school in their next regularly scheduled game. Suppose, at the same time, a leader emerges who claims that the other team did not deserve to win and should be beaten now. Whether or not a fight will develop depends on the ability of either leader to win the support of the other students. If the student pushing for a fight can develop the greater emotional contagion, a fight will result. If the student suggesting that they not fight can develop the greater emotional contagion, a fight will not result.

188

Emotional contagion in an unstructured social situation tends to make the persons involved more open to suggestions. They are less concerned about weighing alternatives or considering the outcome of suggested actions. And they are less restrained in performing socially unacceptable acts. As a result, the behavior of the individual and the group in these situations is much less predictable than in a structured situation.

SECTION REVIEW

1. What are the characteristics of structured behavior?
2. What are the characteristics of unstructured behavior?
3. Why is the structured–unstructured continuum useful?
4. How does emotional contagion influence people?

KEY TERMS

Explain and give an example of each term.

collective behavior   structured behavior
emotional contagion   unstructured behavior

SECTION 2:
Kinds of
Unstructured Behavior

Unstructured behavior may be divided into two basic categories, according to the closeness of the personal relationships. In one of these categories the persons involved form a face-to-face group, such as a crowd. In the other category the persons involved engage in a particular kind of mass behavior apart from one another. This is the case with such forms of collective behavior as fashions, fads, and social movements. First let's consider collective, or unstructured, behavior in face-to-face situations. Then we will investigate nonface-to-face situations.

Crowds

A CROWD *is a large number of people gathered together in one place.* Crowds fit the description of unstructured situations. There is little development of group values, group norms, group roles, and individual sense of self. Also, crowds are easily caught up in emotional contagion. Crowds do, however, differ greatly in their structure and in the amount and intensity of interaction.

Casual crowds have no real structure and have a very low amount and intensity of interaction. They usually arise spontaneously. Examples of casual crowds are the people who stand in front of a department store watching a window display, the gathering of "sidewalk superintendents" observing a building under construction, or a gathering of students waiting to go to class. There is little common feeling in a casual crowd. But the possibility of developing unity of behavior by spreading emotional contagion certainly exists.

An *audience* is a group of people exposed to a common stimulus. The audience has some structure, since particular norms and roles are involved. But a strong structure can't develop because of the short-term nature of an audience. The degree of interaction may vary greatly. For example, in a movie or a lecture the interaction is one-way and of a low intensity. On the other hand, the interaction in a class discussion may be quite high, if all students are participating. Audiences also are targets for emotional contagion. For instance, comedians usually try to bring forth laughter and make it contagious among members of their audiences.

Some crowds are more active, engaging in

What kind of crowd do these people represent? A casual crowd? An audience? A mob? A panic? What characteristics shown here determined your decision?

some type of physical activity, such as dancing or playing a game. When the activity is oriented toward a particular objective or goal, emotions can run high. Such crowds can be unstable and very changeable, because of the high state of emotion involved. They may become mobs.

A MOB *is a crowd that focuses on an intent involving aggressive behavior,* such as lynching, beating, or destroying property. Mob behavior is very often impersonal in nature. It is directed toward any and all members of some particular group or category. If the real object of aggression is not available, the mob often takes out its frustration on an innocent bystander. When the mob reaches a high emotional pitch, it may direct its aggression on any and all persons who happen to be present. Mobs usually depend on leadership to direct their aggressive behavior.

When more than one mob is involved, and when the intent is less focused, the crowd is engaged in a riot. *A* RIOT *is a situation in which a number of mobs are acting in a randomly destructive way.* Rioting usually expresses generalized resentment and rebellion rather than having any definite purpose or goal. For example, riots have occurred in American cities in which mobs of Black Americans, often touched off by an incident between blacks and police officers, have expressed their resentment by randomly looting and destroying property. Examples of riots involving minorities or students or laborers may be found both in America's recent and distant past.

Or the behavior of crowds may take the form of an orgy. *An* ORGY *is a situation in which the usual taboos and restraints are relaxed, and the group members indulge their appetites.* This type of crowd behavior sometimes occurs among soldiers under battle conditions. For example, during World War II members of the Medical Corps performed operations on the wounded in temporary tent hospitals set up near the battle lines. They often worked around the clock for days. They were trying to save the lives of those so badly wounded that they could not be moved from the battle zone. The tensions, fatigue, and emotional pressures under these conditions became unbearable. When a break in the fighting brought a brief pause to their work, some would find release from their pressures by indulging in a drinking orgy. After they sobered up, they could return to treating the wounded under the same tense conditions.

Crowds may also express themselves in the form of a panic. *A* PANIC *occurs when a group, in the face of immediate danger, is retreating from the threatening situation.* The danger usually involves physical survival. The threatening situation might be a sinking ship or a burning building. In a panic, emotional contagion is extremely important. It can increase the sense of danger far beyond the actual danger involved and lead to disastrous results. For example, too many people may jump into the same lifeboat and capsize it, drowning everyone. The panic itself, rather than the danger that brought it on, then becomes the cause of a disaster.

Aside from unstructured behavior in face-to-face groups, there is unstructured behavior among people apart from one another. Now let's look at some of these forms of behavior.

Fashion

FASHION *consists of the short-term, socially approved variations in specific aspects of the culture, such as in clothes, art, furniture, or car design.*

Sometimes the change in fashion is introduced by a subculture, and then spreads to the culture. In the late 1960's the hippies generally wore jeans, T-shirts, and long hair. These styles then became the acceptable attire for all young people.

In a free enterprise system, fashion is very important. Manufacturers must compete for their share of the market. They are constantly introducing new merchandise to gain a greater volume of sales. With modern advertising techniques, we have even come to expect a constant change in styles and fashions. Fashion exists in many areas, including clothing, cars, and popular music.

Women's fashions. Women's fashions in clothes change constantly. The new fashions originate with designers, who are located in a few major cities such as Paris, Rome, and New York. After deciding on the new trends, designers conduct fashion shows to display their new styles. Usually the first of the new fashions to appear are sold at high prices by expensive stores. Originals continue to command a high price. But slight variations of the original design often are mass produced for the competitive market. European designers also sell original designs to large department stores, which then have the right to reproduce as many copies as they want.

Women's fashions tend to go in cycles. Skirt lengths go up and down and then up again. Skirts change from narrow to full and back to narrow again. Colors, shoes, and accessories also vary from year to year. Currently almost any fashion is in style. Perhaps never before have we had such a variety of styles in clothes at the same time.

Men's fashions. In the past, men's fashions have not changed as rapidly as women's. In recent years, however, men have become more aware of fashion and style in clothes and grooming. There has been an emphasis on the casual look, with more variety in shirts and shoes and brighter colors. Hair

styles have tended to be longer. Mustaches and beards have been popular with some men. As with women's fashions, it is a time in which almost any style in clothing and grooming is acceptable.

Cars. Styles in cars also change from year to year. Today they are available in a great variety of models, makes, styles, and sizes. There has been a trend in the past few years toward cars that are smaller and get better gas mileage. Styles have also been affected by new safety laws. For instance, the convertible has disappeared in recent years. And small decorative bumpers have been replaced by massive functional bumpers.

Some features of automobile styling go in cycles. For example, almost all cars in the 1940's were fastbacks. During the 1950's they

disappeared, only to return as the new look in styling in the late 1960's.

Popular songs. The specific songs that make the "top ten" vary constantly. When a particular song makes the "top ten," it usually remains there for only a few months at the most and then disappears. However, it may reappear a number of years later. Some popular songs of the 1940's and the 1950's became popular again, with slight variations, in the 1970's. Sometimes old songs are re-arranged to fit current tastes.

Not only the individual songs but also the type of popular music may change. In the 1960's, folk-rock music was the rage. In the mid-1970's, country music gained nation-wide popularity.

Fads

A FAD *is the spread of some fairly unimportant and external pattern of behavior.* Some fads, such as bingo, may become a fashion, custom, or habit. Most fads, however, are short-lived. They reach a peak of popularity and then fade rather quickly. Examples of such fads are hula hoops, ankle bracelets, and dancing the "twist." Some fads are local in scope, while others spread over an entire nation or even many nations.

Sometimes fads are sparked by very successful movies or TV programs. Examples of these would be the Bonnie-and-Clyde and the Godfather fads. In the early 1970's the movie *The Great Gatsby* brought a return to the styles of the 1920's for a short time. What are some fads that are popular in your community today?

Crazes. CRAZES *are fads that are much more emotional in nature.* They are feverish, all-consuming activities that spread very rapidly. Perhaps you've heard about the crazes of the 1930's, such as the dance marathon, goldfish swallowing, and flagpole sitting. The great craze of the mid-1970's was streaking, or running through a public place

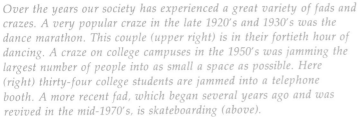

Over the years our society has experienced a great variety of fads and crazes. A very popular craze in the late 1920's and 1930's was the dance marathon. This couple (upper right) is in their fortieth hour of dancing. A craze on college campuses in the 1950's was jamming the largest number of people into as small a space as possible. Here (right) thirty-four college students are jammed into a telephone booth. A more recent fad, which began several years ago and was revived in the mid-1970's, is skateboarding (above).

dressed only in sneakers. Many bumper stickers appeared during this craze, such as "Streakers tan more evenly."

Sometimes crazes spring up around a particular popular singer or movie star. There have been crazes over Elvis Presley, Robert Redford, the Beatles, and the Rolling Stones, to mention a few.

Booms. *A* BOOM *is a craze that is related to a "get rich quick" scheme.* Usually booms expand rapidly like a bubble and then burst. Some examples of booms are the California Gold Rush of 1849-50, the Florida land boom of the 1920's, and the chain letter craze of the 1930's. And in the 1970's there was the land boom. People were told that land would become less and less available as the population expands. They were encouraged to buy a plot of land, say, in the mountains. The idea was that it would be worth a large sum in the future. Some money was made on land. But at the same time many people lost on the deal. Much of the land was sold sight unseen. And many owners found that they could only reach their land by donkey or by backpacking. The result was that Congress passed laws making it possible for buyers to get their money back if they visited their property within a year and were unhappy.

Social Movements

Social movements are another kind of unstructured, or collective, behavior that falls in the category of persons apart from one another. *A* SOCIAL MOVEMENT *is a collective attempt to bring about a change in society.* Most social movements have a unity of purpose. They are dedicated to an ideal. They have a desire to achieve change through action. And they include a number of different groups. Social movements usually are of longer duration than fashions and fads, and are more organized. A few movements use revolutionary means to overthrow existing conditions, such as fighting the American

Revolution to achieve independence. But most social movements propose to improve existing conditions. Many prison reform movements, for instance, want to change the treatment of prisoners and improve the conditions in jails. They do not propose to overthrow the whole system.

There are examples of social movements throughout history. One that was under way in the early 1970's was the ecology movement. Many organizations tried to bring attention to the rapid destruction of our environment by air and water pollution and overpopulation. By the mid-1970's, the movement had been slowed down by the energy crisis and the economic recession. Another social movement in the 1970's was women's liberation. The National Organization for Women (NOW) and a number of other groups worked for greater freedom and opportunities for women. Interestingly enough, this movement had a countermovement. Some women organized themselves to oppose women's liberation because they liked their present roles and felt the suggested changes were undesirable.

The success of a social movement often is related to whether or not the social change becomes institutionalized or widely accepted in the larger society.

Rumors

One other form of behavior in a relatively unstructured social situation is the rumor. RUMORS *are stories or information passed from person to person without confirmed evidence to support them.* Rumors are not necessarily false, but they tend to be distorted because of the emotionalism and lack of structure in the situation.

There are always a number of rumors going around in any community. Most of them are trivial. But some are influential and can have serious consequences in human relationships. These are the rumors that are of interest to sociologists and social psychologists. They are usually related to situations of anxiety or stress. And they usually deal with topics of importance to the members of the community, such as details of a murder, strike, or riot. In the school situation rumors sometimes circulate about a particular assignment or the final exam.

The first pioneers in research on rumor, psychologists Gordon Allport and Leo Postman, concluded that the more important a subject is to the individuals involved, the more rumors there will be about it. They found also that the number of rumors increased in relation to the uncertainty of the information. War is a situation that illustrates their hypothesis. War is of extreme importance to people. Yet censorship usually limits the amount of legitimate information available. As a result, many rumors spread among troops as they are waiting for specific orders. Also, rumors about encounters with the enemy often spread among civilians before the factual reports are available.

SECTION REVIEW

1. What are the various kinds of crowds and what are the characteristics of each?
2. Give some examples of your own of fashion as unstructured behavior in our society.
3. What different kinds of fads are there, and what are the characteristics of each?
4. What is a social movement? How do social movements develop?
5. Why do sociologists study rumors?

KEY TERMS

Define and give an example of each term.

audience	mob
boom	orgy
casual crowd	panic
craze	riot
crowd	rumor
fad	social movement
fashion	

PROJECTS AND ACTIVITIES

1. Carefully study an unstructured situation, such as a crowd milling about at a carnival, or the people in a city park on a Sunday afternoon. To what degree are the four characteristics of unstructured behavior present? Is emotional contagion involved? Does any leadership emerge?

2. Look in newspapers for examples of unstructured behavior in social situations. Attempt to make some generalizations about unstructured behavior from these articles.

3. Do a sociodrama of one or more of the following unstructured situations: an automobile accident, a person fainting on the sidewalk, a holdup, a building on fire, or a child caught in a fence.

4. Carefully observe the behavior and interactions of an audience in three situations: (1) at a theater, (2) at an athletic event, and (3) at a lecture. How do they differ? How do you explain the differences?

5. Study emotional contagion and how it works at several swimming, track, basketball, or ice hockey events. What are some factors that increase the influence of emotional contagion?

6. Make a bulletin board display or poster that illustrates the many aspects of a riot.

7. Interview a police officer to find out how the police are trained to handle riot situations.

8. Locate old magazines that date back to the 1930's or 1940's. Design a project that illustrates the changes in clothing fashions over the years.

9. Write a short story based on a recent fad.

10. Carry out research on some historical or current social movement.

TOPICS FOR INQUIRY

1. What proportion of your time is spent in unstructured situations compared to the amount of time you spend in structured situations? How has the proportion changed over the last ten years of your life? How do you think it will change in the future?

2. Why is it that some people scream, cry, and even faint when watching certain performers, but show very little emotion when watching other performers? What are the characteristics of the performer that bring on these emotional outbursts?

3. Discuss in terms of your own experiences: Individuals will perform actions in a crowd situation that they would never think of doing on their own.

4. Have you ever observed a mob in action? If so, describe and analyze the characteristics of the mob that you remember most vividly.

5. Discuss your observations of behavior at an athletic event, party, or rock concert. Where would you place the behavior on the structured-unstructured continuum?

6. What kinds of situations most often lead to rumors among teenagers? Why?

7. Discuss panic situations that you've experienced. What did you do? Was your response similar to or different from the responses of others in the situation?

8. Discuss: American advertising is based on the phenomenon of fashion. Give examples.

9. What are some fads and crazes that are popular today? What is your basis for deciding which are fads and which are crazes?

SUGGESTIONS FOR READING

NONFICTION

KLAPP, Orrin E., *Collective Search for Identity*. Holt, Rinehart and Winston, 1969 (pap.). This book analyzes modern humanity's search for identity in terms of mass behavior and movements. It views the problem as a symptom of advanced technology and urbanized societies that have lost symbolic balance.

MONTE, Anita and LEINWALD, Gerald, *Riots*. Simon & Schuster, 1970 or Pocket Books (pap.). A complete coverage of riots, their causes and consequences. It includes readings.

SHIBUTANI, Tamotsu, *Improvised News: A Sociological Study of Rumor*. Bobbs-Merrill, 1966 (and pap.). A report of sociological research conducted on the phenomenon of rumor.

THOMAS, Piri. *Down These Mean Streets*. Knopf, 1967 or New American Library (pap.). An autobiography set in Spanish Harlem (New York City) that describes the author's survival of drug addiction and prison.

VON HOFFMAN, Nicholas. *We Are The People Our Parents Warned Us Against*. Quadrangle, 1968 or Fawcett World (pap.). The impact of the hippie movement is depicted in this view of the Haight-Ashbury district of San Francisco.

FICTION

CAMUS, Albert, *The Just Assassin*. Random House (pap.). A play that illustrates what happens to a group when the individual goals differ from those of the group.

CLARK, Walter V., *The Ox-Bow Incident*. Peter Smith or New American Library (pap.). A psychological study of a small group that decides to hang two men without a trial.

SHUTE, Nevil, *On the Beach*. Apollo or Ballantine (pap.). A novel about the ways people react when they are faced with the crisis of imminent death from radioactive fallout.

Highlight

What happens in unstructured situations?

How do you decide what to do in a situation? If you think about it, you will probably conclude that you cannot decide what to do unless you know where you are, and who you are. You must have some social location, and you must have a role. In most situations you do know these things. And you act according to them. When you are in school in the role of a student, for example, you automatically follow certain behavioral norms. You go to classes, sit at desks, carry books, and answer teachers. When you are at home in the role of a son or daughter, you follow other norms. In most cases, as soon as you are aware of your social location, and your position within that location, what you are to do comes almost naturally. This is structured behavior. The structure comes from norms applied to social position. It saves you from always having to figure out what to do.

But suppose you are in your classroom. An earthquake occurs, causing the walls to crumble, the door to be blocked, and half the students to be badly injured. What would you do then? Would you panic? Would you assume a leadership role and somehow guide the survivors to safety? Would you scream and yell? What *would* you do?

The point is that you really don't know what you would do. You have never been in such a situation and your socialization experiences have not prepared you for such a role. The situation lacks structure. At least, it is seriously lacking in the kind of structure that would give you a ready-made set of responses to follow.

Let's consider another situation. Your school football team is engaged in a hard-fought battle for the Conference leadership. Your team is leading 7–6. It is the fourth quarter, last play of the game, four seconds on the clock. The opposing quarterback throws a long pass into the end zone that appears to be incomplete. However, the referee calls pass interference and awards the touchdown. The call is a questionable one, highly subjective. Your team is enraged. In the stands, fighting breaks out all around you. What do you do? What rules or norms can you follow?

Or imagine that you have completed high school, gone off to college, studied hard, and graduated. You majored in Elementary Education. Now you find that the job market in your field is flooded with applicants. There are few, if any, vacancies. You had a fortunate upbringing, a large share of good luck, you put a lot of time and effort into preparing yourself, and you lived by all the rules. Yet you find no reward at the end. You can't get a job. What action can you take? Do you go back to school for further training? Do you pressure people who might be able to help you into using their influence in your behalf?

These situations all have one element in common. That element is the lack of a predictable structure. The expected norm-role relationships are not present. The people involved are forced to act or respond according to their own basic egos. Unstructured behavior occurs, then, when the usual guideposts of social position and role are missing.

There are several ways in which you can find out more about the reactions that occur in unstructured situations. One thing you can do is to act in some situation in a way that is different from how you are expected to act. For example, suppose you went home after school and acted toward the other members of your family as you would toward strangers or new acquaintances. You might make some polite small talk. You would avoid the usual assumptions about your rights, privileges, duties, and obligations. What might be your family's reaction at the dinner table, say, if you reacted to them as though you had never met them before? And how do you suppose they would react to you?

Another thing you can do is to interview someone who has lived as a civilian in a place that went through an extended period of warfare or civil strife. A person who lived in Central Europe during World War II would be a good example. So would some-one who lived in Northern Ireland during the recent civil war there. Or someone who was in Lebanon during the 1975-76 civil crisis. Ask them questions about how they coped with the unexpected. You may even be able to get such persons to come and speak to your class about their experiences.

One other thing you could do is to conduct some library research on living conditions in relatively unstructured situations. You might focus particularly on how the people involved dealt with unexpected changes in these living conditions.

From your own ideas, talking to people, and doing research about reactions in unstructured situations, you might try drawing up a list of the various responses people have to such situations. How many of these reactions do you think *you* might have to an unstructured situation?

Complete New E
Cape Cod
Standar
SPRINGFI
ORCESTER TE
Spain
THE WOON
Grain Shipper
Pawtuck
Maine Mall
ttleboro
UNION STAR
Schenectady teachers
53-week year?
Knickerbo
sterdam Even
THE EV
TIMES
THE REPORTE
HERALD ST
Franco dies:
an era ends
in Spain
sale of no
may delay
U.S. officials plotted
5 world leaders

11 Mass Communication

▶ What effects do the mass media have on our society?

▶ How do the mass media influence you as an individual?

▶ How much of mass communication is propaganda?

SECTION 1:
The Mass Media

Without communication there could be no collective behavior. COMMUNICATION *is the transmission of information, ideas, and emotions by the use of symbols,* such as words, pictures, figures, graphs, or gestures. Through communication people make themselves known and learn about others. Communication is an essential part of all social interaction. In a large, complex society, much of the communication involves many people in scattered locations.

MASS COMMUNICATION *is the simultaneous exposure of a large number of people to stimuli transmitted by impersonal means from an organized source.* Mass communication is not a group phenomenon. There are no face-to-face relationships. Individuals presenting a

show on radio or television, for example, don't have direct contact with the people tuned in to their program. They simply do the show in front of a microphone or television camera. Unless there is a studio audience, they are not performing in the presence of an audience. They present their show to an unseen public.

The Communications Revolution

Today the world is witnessing what has been called the "communications revolution." There have been more technological changes in communication during the past fifty years than during the previous 5,000. Recent developments in communication technology have made it possible to reach more people in more places in less time than ever before. Human beings have communicated with one another for millions of years. They have used written symbols for the past 6,000 years. But only during the past 100 years have

Are records and tapes examples of mass media? How many kinds of mass media can you name?

there been enough literate people world-wide to make mass communication of the printed word possible. And only in the past fifty years or so has technology made communication among the vast majority of people in many societies both possible and practical. The advances in methods of communication have brought great changes in human relationships. People are now exposed to the ideas, activities, inventions, and traits of diverse cultures throughout the world.

Today much of the communication that takes place is mass communication. The sources of mass communication are the mass media. *The* MASS MEDIA *consist of the many stimuli to which large numbers of people are* exposed, such as newspapers, books, magazines, pamphlets, billboards, radio, television, and movies.

Mass communication is big business. And it is growing continually in size and scope. Because of the large-scale endeavors, the big sums of money, and the many people affected by mass communication, the problems are also vast. We will consider three basic problems—the control of the mass media, the content of mass communication, and the probable effect on society.

Control of the mass media. There are many examples in history of individuals gaining tremendous power over people through the control of the mass media. In the United States the mass media are a part of the free enterprise system. Control is related to supply and demand and the amount of competition. But what about situations in which the mass media have no competition, such as in parts of our country where there is only one newspaper or one television channel? Even in larger metropolitan areas the competition is limited in that many of the mass media are controlled by large syndicates, such as Scripps-Howard, the Hearst Corporation, Time-Life, Inc., and the National Broadcasting Company (NBC). The source of most news other than local information is one of the two news services—Associated Press (AP) and United Press International (UPI).

The government provides some control. Many of the mass media are regulated to some degree by government agencies. The Federal Communications Commission (FCC), for instance, regulates interstate and international communications transmitted by wire and radio, including TV. One way in which the FCC can exercise its control is by issuing or withholding licenses to operate radio and television stations.

The people also have some control over the mass media. It may seem as if the advertisers have a good deal of control in television, since they decide which programs they want to sponsor. Actually they are likely to buy time primarily on programs that large numbers of people choose to watch. Studies are conducted to determine how many probable viewers are watching each television program. On the basis of these studies, the various programs are given "ratings." If the rating of a program remains low, the network will cancel that program and try something else. The fees that networks charge advertisers are directly related to the number of viewers of that program. Therefore the networks spend a great deal of effort to produce programs that people want. Ultimately, then, it is the viewers who determine what kinds of programs appear on commercial television.

Control of the mass media is a controversial issue. One point of view claims that Constitutional guarantees of free speech and free press prohibit control of the media by the government. Another group says that government regulation of the mass media is necessary to provide representation of all points of view. Others think that such mass media as radio and television use the air waves, which belong to everyone, and therefore the people should have some control.

Content of the mass media. Much of the content of the mass media is designed to provide entertainment and spread information. Some of the content also has tremendous educational value.

The people influence content by what they choose to read, listen to, or watch. The mass media are concerned about producing a profit. They may resort to sensationalism, and stress violence, to sell more copies or air time. If a youngster helps an elderly women across the street, the event is not newsworthy. But if the same person knocks her down and grabs her purse, the press has a story that will sell newspapers.

We might also ask if movies portray life as it really is in the society or if they tend to stress the life of the deviant person, such as the gangster or the alcoholic. Or the mass media may present life as people would like it to be. Romance is often stressed in novels, movies, and television programs.

Effects of the Mass Media

The most important questions deal with the influence of the mass media on the people of the society. For example, do the mass media cause great changes in the society? We know that new products advertised on television and in magazines and newspapers often become accepted almost immediately. Various fads and ways of thinking are also spread rapidly by the mass media. We are continuously creating a mass culture in the form of sports, popular music, movies, television programs, and the comics.

But do the mass media actually bring about a change in the norms of a society? For example, movies are rated by the movie industry as "G" (general audiences—all ages admitted), "PG" (parental guidance suggested), "R" (restricted—under seventeen must be accompanied by parent or adult guardian), and "X" (adults only). Yet movies that were originally classified as "X" have been reclassified to "R" only a few years later. Many "R" movies have later been changed to "PG." This suggests that the norms of the society have changed. Citizens accept scenes of sex and violence that they would not accept only a few years ago. But did the mass media bring about this change in morality, or are they only reflecting the public's changed views? What is your opinion?

The effect on politics. The mass media also play a part in the American political process. The success of a political candidate in getting elected is related to the kind of press coverage the individual gets. If the press coverage is good, the individual is much more likely to be elected.

The public image of the candidate as created by the mass media is important. This

Thousands of Horses Are Being Starved To Death Because Owners Can't Afford to Feed Them

Cancer-Causing Drug Still On Market

Prominent Doctor Claims . . .

Amazing 'Youth Diet' Could Add 20 Years to Your Life

Private Lives Of Hollywood Wives

Sometimes the mass media, such as newspapers and magazines, use sensationalism to catch the attention of their readers and increase their sales.

The mass media can have a tremendous effect on political careers. It is through the mass media that most political candidates develop their public image.

includes how the candidate looks on television. Therefore candidates are often made up like movie stars before they appear on television. Many political experts have written about the role of television in the presidential election of 1960. They believe that a major factor in the victory of John F. Kennedy over Richard M. Nixon was that Kennedy presented a much better image during their television debates.

The mass media allow the American public to be informed on the political process and politicians. All Americans can, in a sense, participate in the national political conventions as they watch the proceedings on television. They can also keep a close watch on the politicians through the mass media. Some newspaper columnists concentrate their energies on exposing wrongdoings by elected and appointed officials of government. Articles written by these columnists exposed the Watergate scandals that toppled Richard Nixon from power in the mid-1970's.

The effect on individuals. The mass media tend to give a certain amount of status to those people whom they feature in their coverage. In the minds of the citizens, these people must be important or they wouldn't be covered by the mass media. As a result, persons who want status for one reason or another often work very hard to keep their names and faces in the various mass media.

The effect on social problems. It has been suggested that the mass media create social problems by calling attention to certain dramatic forms of deviance. Consider, for instance, the effect of coverage by the mass media of the use of drugs. In the early 1970's, articles, books, television programs, and films made almost every citizen in America familiar with the various kinds of drugs and their uses. Did this publicity lead persons to try drugs who might never have heard of them, had it not been for the mass media?

Consider the hippie movement. We have always had a small segment of the population who follow offbeat life styles. We have called them "Bohemians" or "beatniks" or "hippies." However, in the 1960's the hippie movement was picked up by the mass media. Every newspaper and magazine had articles about hippies and hippie life. Television specials presented pictures of life in the Haight-Asbury district of San Francisco or on a hippie commune. The real question is this: Did the portrayals in the mass media glamorize hippie life to the extent that young people (and some not so young) from all over the country joined the hippie movement? Would the hippie movement have grown to any degree if the mass media had not kept it before the public's eyes?

Another aspect of this is whether the presence of television cameras creates or expands social problems. Do they cause people to behave differently than if no cameras were present? For example, the television cameras may inspire a peaceful group of demonstrators to become more militant to publicize their cause. What do you think?

The effect on forming public opinion. PUBLIC OPINION *is the pattern of combined judgments of people exposed to a particular issue of importance to them.* Are people's opinions formed by the mass media? Actually, most studies indicate that the mass media are more likely to reinforce attitudes and opinions that people already have than to change their attitudes and opinions. People tend to select material from the mass media that is consistent with their existing attitudes and opinions. The individual who feels that Jones is the best candidate for public office will probably listen to Jones's campaign speeches and believe every word. On the other hand, the individual who does

How much of what you read in the newspapers do you believe? How effective do you think newspapers are in forming public opinion?

not like Jones will tend either not to hear what Jones says or to believe that all of Jones's statements are lies.

Campaigns designed to change people's behavior have only a limited chance of success, according to research studies. Campaigns by the mass media to get people to stop littering, for example, generally reach the people who already are convinced that they should not litter. The people who litter seem to pay little, if any, attention to such appeals. Campaigns to get people to drive more carefully also have little effect on the way people drive. Most drivers rationalize that they already are good drivers. They feel that the appeal is meant for other persons, who are "bad" drivers.

Some research on communication through the mass media indicates that other people have more effect than the mass media on the formation of public opinion. This research suggests that communication goes through two steps. First, there are a number of per-sons who pay attention to the mass media and become informed on issues. They have been called "opinion leaders." Second, these leaders share their opinions with the many people who do not follow the mass media directly but rather depend on others for their information. This kind of communication process emphasizes the importance of social relationships in the acceptance of new ideas or ways of action. Individuals are more likely to adopt a new idea or way of action when they hear about it from another person whom they know personally or respect. Thus the greatest influence of the mass media may be indirect rather than direct.

One interesting issue is whether the mass media mislead public opinion by biased reporting of the news. This bias could be deliberate or unintended. For example, almost all of the newsworthy events reported on the evening news occur over a much longer time span than can be presented on the news program. The segment of the event chosen to show on the news program can make a big difference in the formation of public opinion. Of all the film that the news photographer took, which one- or two-minute segment will be shown to the public? Will the news editor select the segment that is most spectacular? Or the one that supports his or her own particular bias? Whatever part is chosen, it represents an interpretation of the event.

Consider also the many demonstrations by yippies (Leftist activists) and others at the Democratic National Convention held in Chicago in 1968. Almost all of the television coverage showed the brutality of the police as they pushed back the crowds or loaded demonstrators into police vans. Public opinion seemed to form against the Chicago police. Yet sociologists who were present reported that under the circumstances, the police controlled themselves very well. They spent long hours on the line. (They were on twelve-hour shifts.) And they had to deal with obscene behavior from the demonstrators, which was never shown on television. Were the Chicago police unfairly judged?

SECTION REVIEW

1. What is mass communication and what are the mass media?
2. Pick one form of the mass media and discuss how much you think it should be controlled and by whom.
3. What are some of the effects of the mass media on politics, individuals, social problems, and public opinion?

KEY TERMS

Explain the meaning and the importance of each term.

communication
communications
  revolution

mass communication
mass media
public opinion

SECTION 2:
Propaganda

In recent years propaganda has become a major form of social control. The development of the mass media and the communications revolution have made it possible to spread propaganda on a large scale. Today we are confronted with propaganda daily, in political campaigns and advertising slogans, in publications and radio and television programs, on billboards and in speeches.

In the United States the term "propaganda" generally has a negative association. People talk of propaganda spread by the "other side" or the "opponents," but never by themselves. The implication is that propaganda consists of lies and distorted facts. Actually propaganda may be factual truth. PROPAGANDA *is the presentation of biased ideas to influence group attitudes, opinions, or behavior.*

Propaganda generally presents only one side of an issue. Nevertheless, the presentation may be true or untrue, good or bad. For example, the Environmental Protection Agency sponsors advertisements about the dangers of littering and polluting the environment. By our definition these ads are propaganda. Yet they are not necessarily bad. On the other hand, many people view the biased presentation spread by Hitler's Minister of Propaganda, Goebbels, during the rise of Nazism in Europe as bad and untrue. In other words, the term "propaganda" is neither good nor bad, but neutral. It is the content of the propaganda that may be good or bad, depending on who is evaluating the information.

The presentation is expressed through symbols as found in writings, speeches, pictures, and gestures. Along with the growth of the various mass media to spread propaganda, a number of specialized professions have developed. Members of these professions include the press agent, the lobbyist, and advertising, publicity, and public relations people. There are also part-time propagandists, such as reporters, cartoonists, artists, authors, and teachers.

Basically the aims of propaganda are short-term, situational, and immediate. Propaganda usually relies on an appeal to the emotions to unite people with different interests in some short-term response to a particular situation. Possible goals of propaganda might be to elect a candidate to public office, start a riot, increase the sales of a particular product, pass a bill in Congress, or improve the public image of a person, organization, or institution. Long-term aims are less common. It is more difficult to keep up an emotionally based response or a changed attitude over a period of time.

How Propaganda Works

Two general approaches are used in the spreading of propaganda — the psychological approach and the sociocultural approach.

The psychological approach. The psychological approach assumes that individual behavior is influenced by subconscious and unconscious motivations. It spreads propaganda by appealing to some of the unconscious elements of the human personality.

The psychological approach has been used to motivate people by disturbing the balance of their personalities, making them feel uncomfortable, then offering them some course of action that will end this uncomfortable feeling. In the past, in-depth studies found that some American homemakers may have felt guilty because they didn't work as hard at household duties as their mothers did. If labor-saving home appliances were advertised as giving the homemaker more time for bridge, golf, or other leisure activities, this only increased the feelings of guilt. Because homemakers felt guilty, they were un-

Are these signs propaganda? Why or why not?

comfortable. The balance of their personality was disturbed. They became possible customers for any item that relieved their guilt and restored their balance. They were likely to buy some home appliance if they believed that the purchase would free them to spend more time with their children and therefore be a better parent. In this case, then, efforts to motivate homemakers to buy a certain product would try to lessen their unconscious guilt feelings.

In his book *The Hidden Persuaders,* Vance Packard reports that the depth merchandisers, who use the psychological approach, have found ways to increase sales by appealing to human subconscious cravings and needs. Packard suggests that sales can be increased by satisfying the needs for: (1) emotional security, (2) feelings of self-worth, (3) ego gratification, (4) creative outlets, (5) love objects, (6) a sense of power, (7) a sense of roots, and (8) immortality.

The psychological approach assumes that behavior, such as voting or buying, is affected by the psychological factors operating within the individual. These psychological factors become the target of the propaganda.

The sociocultural approach. This approach spreads propaganda by defining the norms that are guidelines for the behavior of groups. It takes place most easily in unstructured situations, where the norms have not yet been formed. For example, in a riot situation the leaders may define the norms, convincing the masses that under present conditions the appropriate behavior is to set fires, destroy property, kill people, or loot stores.

The sociocultural approach is more difficult in situations in which the norms are already present and must be redefined. The civil rights movement, for instance, involves propaganda to change the behavior of the white population. The nonviolent approach advocated by the late Dr. Martin Luther King, Jr., is a good example of the sociocultural approach. Dr. King's attempts to redefine the norms were very difficult because norms already existed that were based on emotional attitudes of long standing. The bus boycotts were attempts to redefine the norms to permit Black Americans to ride in buses without discrimination. The restaurant sit-ins were attempts to redefine the norms to allow black people to eat at any public restaurant. Marches were held to try to redefine the norms relating to voting rights, housing, education, and employment.

An important factor in the sociocultural approach is the participation of people who have a certain social status. Because they have some influence in the society, they are special definers of the situation. The civil rights movement gained many such definers as white people joined in the boycotts and demonstrations, wrote books and articles, gave speeches, painted pictures, drew cartoons, and sang songs that emphasized the redefined norms.

For the most part the nonviolent movement involved the sociocultural approach. But it also included some elements of the psychological approach. For instance, sometimes violence broke out and the members of the movement who were attacked did not fight back. They then placed the guilt for violence on their attackers.

Public Relations

The basic task of public relations people is to develop ways of presenting their clients or organizations favorably to the public. One noted early public relations person was Ivy Lee. He changed the stereotype of John D. Rockefeller from that of a robber baron to a philanthropic old gentleman who enjoyed giving away money to worthwhile causes.

The work of public relations people becomes evident if we examine a specific

The right way to use an aluminum can is to use it again.

YES WE CAN
ALCOA

This is a public relations ad by Alcoa. It is encouraging the collection and recycling of aluminum cans throughout the country, thereby creating an image of the company as concerned about America's natural resources.

organization, the Cigar Institute of America. By the end of the 1930's the sales of cigars had declined markedly. Cigar smoking had developed a bad public image. It was often associated with the bootleggers, gangsters, gamblers, and racketeers of the "Roaring Twenties." To improve this image, the Cigar Institute of America was founded. A public relations man was hired to give advice. He first suggested that the Institute offer prizes to news photographers for the best published photographs of people smoking cigars. Pictures of famous people from all walks of life smoking a cigar began to appear in newspapers. Another campaign to improve

the public image of cigar smoking promised the motion picture industry free advertising on 25,000 cigar counters for every movie that presented a positive image of cigars. Within a few years over forty movies had scenes in which the heroes rather than the villains puffed on cigars. Sales of cigars rose rapidly. An estimated million and a half additional men became cigar smokers between 1952 and 1955.

In the 1950's in-depth research carried out by public relations people revealed that the cigar was one of the most powerful symbols of masculinity in America. When the new father passed out cigars, he was really bragging about his masculinity. Research showed that young men felt uneasy smoking cigars. Perhaps they considered cigars such virility symbols that they felt inadequate trying to smoke them. Other studies indicated that cigars appealed both to men who were very strong and to those who were weak and small. Evidently small men felt robust and virile when they smoked cigars.

Many advertisements in newspapers and magazines and on television are really public relations advertisements. Examples of these are the Bell Telephone System and public service company ads. These companies don't have any major competitors. If you want gas and electricity in your home, you get it from the public service company that serves your neighborhood. You aren't likely to have a choice of companies. These companies are advertising, then, not to increase their business so much as to create a favorable public image. Some other large companies also have advertisements that do not attempt to sell a particular product. Their ads simply show how great the company is and what wonderful things it is doing to make life better for you, the consumer.

After the Arab oil embargo of 1973, all of the major oil companies directed their ads toward public relations. The public was aware that the oil companies' profits had jumped as much as 150 percent in one quarter and that the government was investigating the companies for various kinds of fraud carried out during the oil crisis. So the oil companies produced ads to improve their public image. Instead of suggesting that the consumer use more of their particular brand of gas, their ads described ways that the consumer could cut down on his or her use of precious oil. At the same time, their advertising stressed the things that the companies themselves were doing to cut down on their use of energy. And their ads mentioned the large amounts of money and

personnel they were devoting to the search for more energy for the future.

Investigate the advertising found in newspapers and magazines and on television today. Which ads are really directed toward building a good public image for some company? Do you think that ads *should* be used to build the public image of a company?

Advertising

Advertising is a booming business in America. The purpose of advertising is to increase the sales of a product. Therefore the target group, the group of people toward whom the ads are aimed, is very important. A different approach is used, depending on whether the target group consists of children, teen-agers, men, women, the upper class, the lower class, intellectuals, and so forth. The type of approach used is also affected by whether the goal is to obtain new customers or to build loyalty to the product in the old customers. Some of the ads for American cars, for example, emphasize the new styling and new features of the latest model, to attract new customers. Ads for some foreign cars encourage loyalty to the product by stressing the advantages of their car, regardless of the model or year.

To see how advertising works, consider the approaches used to sell two different brands of toothpaste. In the mid-1950's Crest, which contained fluoride, was introduced as a "milestone of modern medicine." The ads for this product stressed scientific studies in which one group brushed with Crest and another group brushed with other brands. The results showed that the group using Crest had X percent fewer cavities.

At about the same time another new toothpaste appeared—Gleem, with GL 70. The ads for Gleem did not stress the special abilities of GL 70. Instead they used the psychological approach. In-depth research had shown that most people felt guilty be-

"**Dear American Tourister:** **My luggage says first class even though my ticket says coach.**"

Ann Citron, Florida

American Tourister

The Verylite

©AMERICAN TOURISTER. WARREN. R.I.

Why is this an example of advertising and not a public relations ad? Compare this with the institutional ad on page 211. How do they differ?

cause they did not brush their teeth after every meal. Therefore the ads for Gleem used the slogan "For people who can't brush their teeth after every meal" (which includes most of the population). First people were made to feel guilty because they didn't brush after every meal. Then they were presented with a way to overcome their guilt, brushing with Gleem. The campaign was successful and Gleem sales soared.

Because of the nationwide advertising given to both products at that time, it seemed as if two rival companies were engaged in a struggle for top sales. This impression was immediately corrected by reading the labels on Crest and Gleem. The labels showed that both were produced by the same company.

After a few years the approach used by Gleem was changed slightly to increase sales. The ads had been telling people that they needed to brush their teeth only once a day when they used Gleem. The new advertising campaign suggested that brushing your teeth with Gleem once a day was good for your teeth. But three brushings would be that much better. The idea behind the campaign was to sell three times as much toothpaste.

As you can see, advertising and public relations are very similar and are closely related. The main difference is that public relations campaigns are trying to promote the public image of the client, whereas advertising campaigns are trying to sell a product. However, public relations and advertising people work together in many situations. Public relations persons may design a program to promote the public image of a company, product, or habit. Then the advertising people may use this public image in their campaign for selling the product.

2. How does the sociocultural approach differ from the psychological approach?
3. How do public relations people use propaganda?
4. How is propaganda used in advertising?
5. How do the goals of public relations differ from those of advertising?

KEY TERMS

SECTION REVIEW

1. What are the basic aims of propaganda? Is propaganda necessarily false or misleading information?

Define and give an example of each term.

advertising
propaganda
psychological approach

public relations
sociocultural
approach

PROJECTS AND ACTIVITIES

1. Analyze at least thirty advertisements in magazines, making generalizations about the propaganda techniques and devices used.

2. Conduct research on politicians who have been exposed by news columnists as having engaged in illegal or inappropriate behavior while in office. How much of a role did the mass media play in changing their lives?

3. Analyze a daily newspaper in terms of the types of features that are included. Is there something for everybody? If not, who is left out?

4. A substantial portion of the income of many actors and actresses is from the production of television commercials. Conduct research on what is involved in the filming of these television commercials.

5. Construct a collage that shows how an individual's life is affected by the mass media.

6. Examine a varied selection of magazines (perhaps at the public library) to determine the various interests served by magazine publishers. Make a list of these interests and of the ways in which they're expressed.

7. Through a mural, drawing, painting, poem, or short story, illustrate the process by which a news story makes its way into a newspaper. Note the opportunities for changes or error as the story passes from one person or department to another.

8. Write a report on the field of motivational research (research designed to determine how people are motivated to buy certain products).

9. If possible, interview an individual in the advertising department of one newspaper and one magazine to find out the cost of ads in each and the importance of advertising as a source of revenue to each. How do your figures on newspaper and magazine advertising compare? What factors determine the costs of advertising in each case?

10. Create an advertising campaign to promote some product. What methods will you use to influence public opinion? Which of the mass media will you use?

TOPICS FOR INQUIRY

1. According to our definition of propaganda, what are some of the occupations in our society that could be classified as professional propagandists? Discuss each occupation in terms of how it relates to the spreading of propaganda.

2. Discuss or debate: The government should have more control over the various mass media, regulating content and advertising.

3. What are the current methods used by the film industry to draw larger crowds into the movie theaters? Discuss these in terms of causes and consequences.

4. An old saying is: "Necessity is the mother of invention." For example, in a free enterprise system the manufacturer, to be successful, would have to come up with a product that is needed by the people. Today some are suggesting that the phrase has changed to: "Invention is the mother of necessity." In other words, the manufacturer comes up with a product that provides a good profit margin and then engages the advertising people to convince the public that they need it. What do you think?

5. Discuss the relative merits of the psychological approach vs. the sociocultural approach in propaganda. Which approach appears to be used most often? How would you explain this?

6. Debate: Advertising serves no useful purpose for the consumer, since the majority of advertisements tell the public practically nothing about the product or service presented.

7. Discuss reasons why public opinion is so important in a democratic society.

NONFICTION

BAKER, Samm S., *The Permissible Lie: The Inside Truth About Advertising*. Beacon, 1971 (pap.). A discussion of advertising by an ex-advertising executive. He stresses that deceptive advertising is not only accepted but is also encouraged by many advertisers and agencies.

HAMPTON, Max, *Throw Away the Key*. Bobbs-Merrill, 1966. An autobiographical story about the adventures of a public relations director for a chain of international hotels.

JACOBS, Norman (ed.), *Culture for the Millions: Mass Media in Modern Society*. Beacon, 1964 (pap.). In this book of readings many experts debate the influence of the mass media on American culture.

MCLUHAN, Marshall, *Counter-Blast*. Harcourt Brace Jovanovich, 1969 (and pap.). A rather unusual approach to the understanding of the "electric information environment" in which we live.

————, *Understanding Media: The Extensions of Man*. McGraw-Hill, 1964 (and pap.). A discussion of how the new media of the electronics age have created a totally new environment for human beings.

MANDELL, Maurice I., *Advertising*. Second ed., Prentice-Hall, 1974. A discussion of the history and organization of advertising, and the relation of advertising to marketing management.

PACKARD, Vance, *The Hidden Persuaders*. McKay, 1957 or Pocket Books (pap.). A study of motivational research in which the author discusses the various ways used in advertising to stimulate people to buy a product.

SEIDEN, Martin H., *Who Controls the Mass Media: Popular Myths and Economic Realities*. Basic Books, 1974. A readable and thought-provoking book on the mass media and their power over people.

FICTION

DAVIDSON, J. and MARTIN, W., *What I Tell You Three Times Is True*. Dutton. This novel shows the influence of the media on the average person.

ORWELL, George, *1984*. New American Library (pap.). The author reveals his view of the future, in which all human actions and thoughts will be controlled by Big Brother.

UNIT
FOUR

SOCIAL
INSTITUTIONS

If you and a hundred other people were shipwrecked on an island, how would you organize yourselves? What would you do to make sure that your essential needs were fulfilled? In this unit we will consider what the essential needs of a society are, and how people meet these needs. First we'll determine what social structures or institutions all societies develop to regulate the fulfilling of the basic needs. Then we'll investigate five universal social institutions in detail: the family, education, religion, economy, and government.

12 The Importance of Social Institutions

▶ What are the fundamental needs of a society?

▶ How do societies regulate the fulfilling of these needs?

▶ What characteristics do all social institutions have in common, regardless of the time, place, or culture?

SECTION 1:
Meeting Basic Needs

Have you ever referred to your high school as an institution? What did you mean? In our society we hear the word "institution" used in many ways. The term may refer to prisons, mental hospitals, children's homes, or homes for the aged. We also speak of welfare, the General Motors Corporation, the Supreme Court, or the Roman Catholic Church as institutions. However, when sociologists use the term they have a specific definition in mind.

What Is a Social Institution?

A SOCIAL INSTITUTION *is an enduring cultural structure that meets certain fundamental needs of the society and establishes social con-* *trol.* By "enduring" we mean that social institutions exist over a considerable time. In fact, they are quite permanent. By "cultural structure" we mean a complex collection of values, norms, and roles that are common to everyone in the society and that regulate human relationships. In Chapter 1 we discussed structure as the way something is put together, its organization. A social institution is the way these values, norms, and roles are put together or organized. Social institutions have a function. Their function is to meet the fundamental needs of the society. By "fundamental" we mean that if these needs were not met, the society would not survive.

Of course, social institutions have no physical structure and cannot be seen. We cannot observe values, norms, or roles except as they are reflected in the way people behave. Also, social institutions do not themselves carry out the fundamental needs of the society. Instead, they regulate the way in which individuals, working sepa-

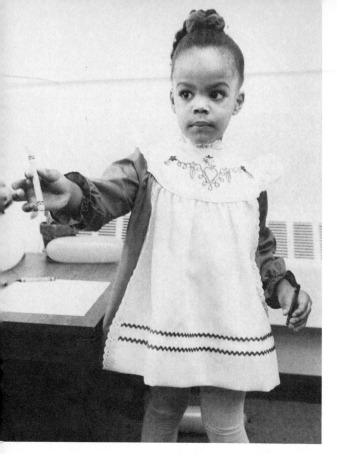

What special characteristics of human beings, not common to other species, are shown in this picture? Human beings also have certain special needs, which the family helps fulfill.

rately and in groups, will meet the fundamental needs. By "social control" we mean that social institutions regulate human behavior in the society.

Thus prisons, hospitals, and schools do not fit our definition of a social institution. What are they, then? For our purposes, we can refer to them as associations or organizations. As you may remember from Chapter 6, associations are special-purpose organizations. Schools, colleges, hospitals, and prisons fit this description. Thus a particular school is an association. But education itself is an institution. For education is a cultural structure that meets a fundamental need of the society.

The Fundamental Needs of a Society

What are the basic needs of a society that must be met if the society is to continue to exist? These needs are very important, since the survival of the society depends on them. We will consider five fundamental needs for which a society must develop social structures—social institutions—if the society is to survive.

Replacing members. Without new members to replace the old members as they die, no society can survive for long. Members of the population may be replaced by immigration. But the basic means of replacing old members is through sexual reproduction.

Human beings have particular biological characteristics that make them different from other species. These characteristics help determine the cultural structure that they have created to replace members. What are these special biological characteristics? First, human beings have a highly developed brain, which makes them capable of complex thought processes. They can learn the meanings of symbols and can combine these symbols to develop complex ideas. A second important factor is that humans walk upright, which gives them the free use of their hands. A third difference between human beings and most other species is that humans have grasping hands. Because their thumb is opposite the fingers, they can grasp small tools, such as pencils, and use them with great precision. A fourth advantage is that people have voice boxes that permit them to make a large variety of sounds. As a result, they have been able to develop a tremendous number of words in a great variety of languages. A fifth difference is that human beings are born as weaklings and require a longer period of time to mature than most other species. They are born with few, if any, instincts and must acquire abilities through learning. Therefore newborn humans are extremely dependent on others for the first few years of their lives. A sixth difference is that the sexual appetite in humans is continuous rather than cyclic, and is present from puberty through old age.

What do these differences between humans and the other species have to do with the reproduction of new members for the society? The answer is that these differences enabled people to consider the special needs of human beings in reproducing themselves and to develop a social institution to meet these needs. Humans had to consider such factors as their continuous desire for affection, and a child's needs for care and training over a long time. Norms developed that provided for some kind of marriage in which a man and woman would live together in a family situation. This arrangement supplied people's needs for affection, support of the family, and care of the offspring. It also made possible a division of labor so that both men and women could provide for their own needs.

The resulting family is *not* a social institution. The social institution of the family is the totality of all values, norms, and roles related to sexual reproduction. The institution is not visible except through the human relationships of family groups.

Socializing new members. If the society is to exist, the new members (whether immigrants or children) must be taught the cultural heritage and the skills and knowledge they need to become a part of that society. Infants must be taught how to feed themselves and how to protect themselves from the dangers of the environment. They must be taught the language so they can communicate with others. As they grow older, they must learn how to find their place in the division of labor so they can provide for their needs.

A number of values, norms, and roles have developed around the socialization of the new members of society. It is these that make up the social institution of education. As we stated earlier, a school is not an institution. It is an association. The institution of education is the totality of values, norms, and roles that regulate the socialization of the new members of the society.

A sense of purpose. If a society is to survive, its members must have a sense of purpose so they feel that their lives are worth living. The suicide rate tends to be high among people who feel hopeless and see no point in life. The cultural structure

Some people have a desire to help others as their sense of purpose and their overriding goal. This doctor is dedicated to the goal of helping improve the health of American Indian children.

that has most provided a sense of ultimate purpose is the institution of religion. People may find a sense of purpose outside of religion—say, from a philosophy of life or devotion to a cause. But throughout history humans have generally defined the meaning of existence in terms of religious beliefs. Religion helps explain certain phenomena that people wonder about, such as injustice, suffering, and death. It also gives people hope for the future. Religion is related to a belief in the supernatural, in a creator, or in some supreme power or powers.

As you may realize, a church is not a social institution. It is an association connected with the institution of religion. The institution of religion is the totality of values, norms, and roles related to religious beliefs.

Producing and distributing goods and services. If human beings are to survive, they must have food, water, and shelter from the elements. The system created to supply these needs may be very simple or very complex, depending on the particular society. For example, in a tribal society the father may provide food for his family by hunting or fishing. In a capitalistic society there are many secondary groups, such as canning companies, that produce and distribute food. Every society, however, has some division of labor. If there were no division of labor, every individual would have to supply his or her own needs. Yet some people in the society, such as the infant, the elderly, and the ill, are unable to supply their own needs.

People in a society are dependent on one another for certain essential goods and services. The social institution that meets these needs is the economy. The economic institution is all the values, norms, and roles related to the production and distribution of goods and services.

Maintaining order and security. To survive, a society must be able to keep order among its members. This involves the distribution of power in the society. The society cannot exist unless it maintains some orderly control over the sources and distribution of power. There must be an ultimate authority to resolve conflicts between members of the society and to sanction those who violate the norms. The structure that provides this function is the institution of government.

The history of our existence on earth reveals numerous and continuing conflicts between different societies. Since people haven't learned to live in peace with other societies, some means of protection from outside attack is essential. It is through the institution of government that a society provides for the protection of its citizens from other societies.

The institution of government is the totality of values, norms, and roles for maintaining order within the society and protecting the society from other societies. There is an aspect of government that sets it off from all of the other social institutions, however. It has the power of formal sanction. It has norms that provide for the administration of sanctions on those who violate the laws of the society. Government is the only institution that provides for formal sanctions. Therefore it is the government that applies sanctions to those who violate norms related to the other social institutions. For example, in the United States norms relating to the family, such as marriage and divorce, are enforced by government. The government applies negative sanctions to those who are continually absent from school. The government guarantees individuals the right to worship freely. It has the power to punish those who try to interfere with these rights. The government also regulates various economic activities, such as interstate commerce and fair trade practices, and enforces these regulations with sanctions.

Social Institutions and Fundamental Needs

Each social institution is concerned with regulating the human relationships that develop in meeting a specific fundamental human need. Each social institution also regulates some human relationships associated mainly with the other social institutions. For example, the need to socialize the new members is related to the social institutions other than education itself. The family plays a very important part in the early socialization of the child. Religion also carries out many educational functions through Sunday schools, religious classes, and other special programs. From the economic institution people learn about products and services. They are socialized as workers when they hold jobs, and as consumers when they purchase the goods and services. The government supplies many educational functions and opportunities to learn about the society, and controls education indirectly. Furthermore, government has the power of sanction to enforce the laws requiring youth to attend school. The diagram on this page shows the interrelationships between social institutions and fundamental needs.

To summarize, every society must meet all of its fundamental needs if it is to continue

INTERRELATIONSHIPS BETWEEN THE SOCIAL INSTITUTIONS AND THE FUNDAMENTAL NEEDS OF SOCIETY

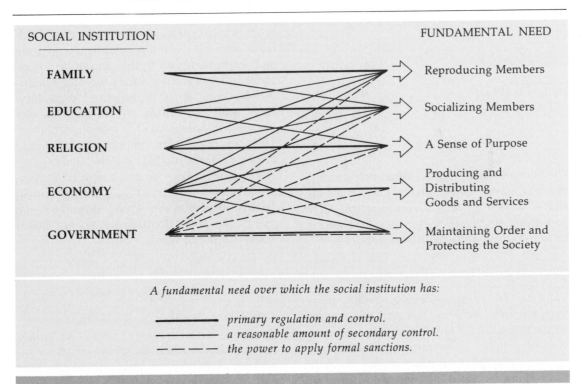

SOCIAL INSTITUTION

FUNDAMENTAL NEED

FAMILY

EDUCATION

RELIGION

ECONOMY

GOVERNMENT

Reproducing Members

Socializing Members

A Sense of Purpose

Producing and Distributing Goods and Services

Maintaining Order and Protecting the Society

A fundamental need over which the social institution has:

——————— *primary regulation and control.*
——————— *a reasonable amount of secondary control.*
— — — — *the power to apply formal sanctions.*

to exist. Therefore every society has values, norms, and roles related to each of these fundamental needs. The values, norms, and roles make up enduring cultural structures, known as social institutions.

SECTION REVIEW

1. What is a social institution?
2. Describe the fundamental needs of a society and the social institution that regulates each need.
3. How are the social institutions and fundamental needs interrelated?

KEY TERMS

Define and give an example of each term.

enduring cultural
  structure
fundamental need

social control
social institution

SECTION 2:
Characteristics of
Social Institutions

Although there are great differences among the five major social institutions, they all share certain general characteristics. Can you think of any characteristics that might be common to all social institutions?

Social Institutions Are Universal

As far as we know, every society, from prehistoric to modern, has had some form of these five social institutions. We assume that all societies in the future will also have these five social institutions, although their forms may be quite different from those of today. The actual forms depend on the time,

place, and culture. But the functions of social institutions are universal.

Social Institutions Are Related to Fundamental Needs

The primary function of a social institution is to regulate human relationships related to a specific social need. The family regulates sexual relationships and reproduction. The educational institution regulates the socialization of the new members. The government regulates the keeping of order within the society. The basic function of the social institution is called the primary function. *The PRIMARY FUNCTION is the intended or expected function of the social institution.*

Each social institution, however, regulates other human relationships not related to its primary function. For example, the primary function of education is to socialize the young. But in addition it also provides an economic function—it prevents the youth from entering the labor market immediately and competing with the adults for jobs. Since this is not the primary function of education, we call this function secondary. SECONDARY FUNCTIONS *are the unintended or unexpected functions of a social institution.* They are often quite important and should not be underestimated.

Remember that social institutions perform these functions of regulating the human relationships that are related to fundamental needs. But social institutions do not themselves fulfill the needs.

Social Institutions Provide Values, Norms, and Roles

Social institutions regulate human relationships through values, norms, and roles. As we stated earlier, we can't see *values* except through the behavior of people who react to these values.

Norms, for the most part, also are not

Every social institution has secondary functions. A secondary function of the economic institution is to introduce new products, which affect our lifestyles.

visible. For example, we can't see the folk-ways and mores of the society except by observing human beings who are guided by these norms. We observe the effects of the norms in action as they influence human social relationships. We can, however, see formal norms or laws to some degree. We can observe a sign that says "Stop," "No Parking," "Speed Limit 55," or "No Unauthorized Personnel Admitted." We can also observe some laws of the society by looking at the United States Constitution, the statute books of a state, or the local ordinances of a city or town.

We can only see *roles*, though, by observing human beings as they interact with one another. Roles such as father, mother, child, employer, employee, police officer, tourist, or student are visible only through the human relationships.

Social Institutions Set Up Patterns of Interrelated Roles

Most of the roles we play as members of our society are related to institutions. For example, in the family we find such roles as husband, wife, father, mother, child, uncle, grandmother, brother, sister, and nephew. In education we find such roles as principal, counselor, student, teacher, coach, and professor. In religion we have the roles of minister, priest, rabbi, Sunday school teacher, altar boy, and missionary. In the economic institution there are roles such as employee, employer, manager, farmer, banker, and consumer: The institution of government also provides a great number of roles—President, justice of the Supreme Court, representative, senator, cabinet member, police officer, and judge, to name only a few.

Actually, every individual plays some role in each of the five major institutions. For example, every individual plays some role in the family. All of you play the role of son or daughter in relation to your parents. Similarly, every person plays some role in education, whether he or she is a professor, teacher, student, graduate, or dropout. Since you are in school, you have the role of student. At the same time every individual plays some role in religion. For instance, if you belong to a church or synagogue, you are a churchgoer. If you have never been involved in any religious activity, you are playing the role of nonbeliever. If you once went to church but do not now attend, you are playing the role of former churchgoer. The institution of religion has a role for everybody, ranging from heathen to convert to believer.

If you have a part-time job after school, you play the role of employee. If you don't have a job, you are unemployed. You play the role of consumer in relation to the economic institution even if you do no more than buy a hot dog occasionally. Since a governor cannot play his or her role without people to govern, you play the role of the governed in relation to your state governor. When you are eligible to vote, you become a constituent—a person represented by your elected officials. As you can see, you play a role in each of the social institutions.

Sometimes role conflicts develop among the various social institutions. The individual's role in one institution conflicts with his or her role in another institution. For example, suppose it is late afternoon and your father wants you to mow the lawn. But you need to study for a test tomorrow at school, your church youth group is having a meeting, you are supposed to report for work on your part-time job, and you have a summons to appear in traffic court that day. You are faced with a conflict of roles among all five institutions. Although such a predica-

ment is rare, it is not unusual to have conflicts between your roles in two or three institutions at the same time.

Social Institutions Are Related to Most Social Activities

Social institutions are the main vehicles through which society carries on its activities. Most of the social activities we participate in have some relation to one of the social institutions. Most activities are related to the family, school, religion, the economy, or the government. Even our recreational and leisure-time activities relate to the family, school, or religion. With the existence of so many commercial recreational facilities, such as theaters, bowling alleys, country clubs, restaurants, night clubs, miniature golf courses, and television and radio stations, a great many of our leisure-time activities also involve the economic institution. What activities do you participate in that are not related to any of the social institutions?

Social Institutions Involve Culture Traits

Each social institution includes both material and nonmaterial culture traits. For example, in the institution of the family we find the material culture traits of houses, furniture, home appliances, home decorations, dishes, and silverware. We also find such nonmaterial traits as love, affection, respect, devotion, memories, and wishes.

One material culture trait that institutional organizations and associations usually have is some kind of building, such as a house, school, church, synagogue or mosque, office or retail store, and capitol building. There are also symbols related to the various institutions, such as a family crest, school colors, religious symbols, brand names, and national flags.

Is bicycling related to any of the social institutions? If so, which one or ones? And how is it related?

Among the nonmaterial culture traits are the rituals or ceremonies related to each social institution. Some examples of these rituals and ceremonies are Sunday dinner at the grandparents', school assemblies, a worship service, the office party, and Presidential receptions for the heads of states of other countries.

Social Institutions Resist Change

Since social institutions are more stable and better organized than other aspects of the society, they tend to be very resistant to change. A major reason for their organization and stability is their concern with the basic functions of social order, such as reproduction and socialization.

Because social institutions change very slowly, they help give stability, order, and security to life. Rapid changes in a society can result in instability, the loss of order, and insecurity. Social institutions tend to offset the rapid changes in other aspects of the society and help maintain stability, order, and security.

Society Protects Social Institutions

To be sure that the major social institutions will continue to exist from generation to generation, societies arrange for their protection. Usually social institutions are protected through the institution of government. For instance, the family is protected and preserved by a great number of formal laws, which relate to such situations as marriage, divorce, rape, adultery, prostitution, and bigamy.

The educational institution is preserved through local, state, and federal regulations. Traditionally the reponsibility for providing

227

The judiciary is part of our government. It is through the judicial system that government protects social institutions by punishing those who violate the norms.

schools has been with the local school boards of the many school districts found in each state. State governments have set up minimum standards for schools and have also provided laws requiring attendance by all youth under a particular age. There are also recent efforts in some state legislatures to have the money collected by local school districts divided up on a state-wide basis. The purpose is to provide a fairer share for the poorer school districts. The federal government also provides a good deal of aid to states and local districts for the improvement of their public schools.

The government of the United States has no laws that demand or require the existence of religion. But in the First Amendment the Constitution definitely states that "Con-gress shall make no law respecting an establishment of religion, or prohibiting the free exercise thereof. . . ." In other words, Congress can in no way interfere with the social institution of religion. In its rulings the Supreme Court has protected this freedom of worship by erecting a wall of separation between church and state.

The United States government protects and preserves the economic institution in many ways. It has passed legislation to protect the economic system from monopoly, unfair management practices, or undue control by organized labor. The government also tries to preserve the free enterprise system of capitalism by exerting controls to prevent such economic disasters as depressions and runaway inflation.

Most of all, the government of the United States has protected and preserved itself. Through the establishment of the federal system, with its three branches of government—legislative, executive, and judicial—and its built-in system of checks and balances, provision has been made for the continuing stability of the United States government.

SECTION REVIEW

1. What is a primary function? What is a secondary function? What are the primary and secondary functions of social institutions?

2. State the characteristics common to all social institutions. Can you think of any characteristics of social institutions not mentioned in the text?

3. What groups can you name that are not related to one of the five major social institutions?

KEY TERMS

Explain and give an example of each term.

primary function   secondary function

PROJECTS AND ACTIVITIES

1. Analyze a current magazine in terms of the needs of the society that are most often represented in the magazine.

2. Examine several news magazines and identify as many roles, values, and norms as you can in our society. Group these roles, values, and norms under the five social institutions. Discuss your findings.

3. Do a report on the five major social institutions in some tribal culture.

4. Read the poems "Richard Cory" and "Miniver Cheevy" by American poet Edwin Arlington Robinson, and comment on what protests or problems each character had with his own set of social institutions.

5. Select a social institution. Then, using daily newspapers, show how that particular social institution breaks down or fails to perform ideally. Discuss how that institution might be improved so that it operates more nearly ideally.

6. Draw a comic strip episode that illustrates a pattern of inter-related roles set up by social institutions.

7. Choose some social activity and write a short report on how that activity is related to the various social institutions.

8. Do research into some specific attempt to change one of the social institutions and the difficulties involved.

9. Design a bulletin board or photo exhibit showing the non-material culture traits in our culture that are related to one of the social institutions. Include a paragraph explaining your display.

10. Write a newspaper editorial entitled "Why and How Our Social Institutions Must Be Preserved."

11. If possible, interview a government official or political leader to find out in what ways government protects and preserves social institutions in the United States. Prepare a list of questions before the interview.

TOPICS FOR INQUIRY

1. As societies become increasingly more complex and technological, what happens to the formality of the social institutions? What explanations for this can you give?

2. What do you think life in the United States would be like if the five major social institutions were destroyed?

3. Consider a prison as a separate society. Are the five basic needs present in a prison society? How are these five basic needs met in a prison?

4. How can the need for a sense of purpose be provided for by means other than religion? Give examples.

5. When social critics refer to "the establishment," they are often referring to the five major social institutions of the society. They generally imply that "the establishment" is against change. What are the advantages and disadvantages of the resistance to change of social institutions? Cite specific examples.

6. How might efforts toward change be channeled through institutions?

7. Discuss: In the United States the government is a kind of super institution that regulates all of the other institutions in addition to carrying out its own functions. Do you agree or disagree? Are you in favor of this arrangement or would you change it? If so, how?

NONFICTION

BENNIS, Warren G. and SLATER, Philip E., *The Temporary Society.* Harper & Row, 1968 (and pap.). An analysis of what the authors see as a weakened institutional structure in America.

BERGER, Bennett M., *Looking for America: Essays on Youth, Suburbia, and Other American Obsessions.* Prentice-Hall, 1971 (and pap.). A series of essays focusing on particular aspects of American society.

GOODWIN, Richard, *The American Condition.* Doubleday, 1974. Examines American institutional structure in terms of its effect on individualism.

PRESTHUS, Robert, *The Organizational Society.* Random House, 1962 (pap.). A study of bureaucratic forms and how they relate to the culture and social institutions.

SLATER, Philip E., *Pursuit of Loneliness: American Culture at the Breaking Point.* Beacon, 1971 (and pap.). A critical analysis of American institutions and their effects on cooperation and individual action.

WILLIAMS, Robin M., Jr., *American Society: A Sociological Interpretation.* Third ed., Knopf, 1970. An analysis of the major institutions in our society.

FICTION

GREEN, Hannah, *I Never Promised You a Rose Garden.* Holt, Rinehart and Winston. A story about a young schizophrenic girl's adjustment to life in a mental institution and her slow, agonizing process of reentry into the outside world.

Highlight

What keeps social institutions going?

By now you know that to survive, all societies, everywhere, must find ways to sustain themselves. They must devise ways of providing for new members. They must find ways of transmitting their cultural heritage. They must develop a means of explaining and justifying their way of life. They must also devise a system for exchanging goods and services, and for keeping order.

All societies meet these needs by developing institutions. Institutionalization is a process that makes activities patterned, regular, and predictable that otherwise would require much planning, thought, or attention. The bell system in most schools is an example of institutionalization. It causes each class to occur at a regular and predictable time. As a result, no one has to do much conscious thinking about it. Imagine what would happen if each class had to be rescheduled every day. Institutionalization provides ways of doing things that seem natural and ordinary—that do not require deliberate thinking in every situation.

But institutionalization can't exist by itself. What keeps social institutions going? How are they maintained? A society develops institutionalized practices that fit into the framework of the culture and that support the culture. The society then maintains these institutionalized practices partly through ritualization. The society provides these practices with a religious, ethical, or intellectual justification. And it often sustains them by a system of rewards or incentives.

Here is an anthropologist's observations of certain institutionalized practices in the Nacirema society, a North American people living between Canada, Mexico, and the Antilles. From this description you can see how ritual helps maintain the institutionalized practices of a society.

While much of the people's time is devoted to economic pursuits, a large part of the fruits of these labors and a considerable portion of the day are spent in ritual activity. The focus of this activity is the human body, the appearance and health of which loom as a dominant concern in the ethos [habits and beliefs] of the people. While such a concern is certainly not unusual, its ceremonial aspects and associated philosophy are unique.

The fundamental belief underlying the whole system appears to be that the human body is ugly and that its natural tendency is to debility [weakness] and disease. Incarcerated [imprisoned] in such a body, a man's only hope is to avert these characteristics through the use of the powerful influences of ritual and ceremony. Every household has one or more shrines devoted to this purpose.

. . . The focal point of the shrine is a box or chest which is built into the wall. In this chest are kept the many charms and magical potions without which no native believes he could live. These preparations are secured from a variety of specialized practitioners. The most powerful of these are the medicine men, whose assistance must be rewarded with substantial gifts. However, the medicine men do not provide the curative potions for their clients, but decide what the ingredients should be and then write them down in an ancient and secret language. This writing is understood only by the medicine men and by the herbalists who, for another gift, provide the required charm.

The charm is not disposed of after it has served its purpose, but is placed in the charm-box of the household shrine. As these magical materials are specific for certain ills, and the real or imagined maladies of the people are many, the charm-box is usually full to overflowing. The magical packets are so numerous that people forget what their purposes were and fear to use them again. While the natives are very vague on this point, we can only assume that the idea in retaining all the old magical materials is that their presence in the charm-box, before which the body rituals are conducted, will in some way protect the worshiper.

Beneath the charm-box is a small font [bowl for water]. Each day every member of the family, in succession, enters the shrine room, bows his head before the charm-box, mingles different sorts of holy water in the font, and proceeds with a brief rite of ablution [washing]. The holy waters are secured from the Water Temple of the community, where the priests conduct elaborate ceremonies to make the liquid ritually pure.

In the hierarchy of magical practitioners, and below the medicine men in prestige, are specialists whose designation is best translated "holy-mouth-men." The Nacirema have an almost pathological horror and fascination with the mouth, the condition of which is believed to have a supernatural influence on all social relationships. Were it not for the rituals of the mouth, they believe that their teeth would fall out, their gums bleed, their jaws shrink, their friends desert them, and their lovers reject them.

. . . The daily body ritual performed by everyone includes a mouth-rite. . . . It was reported to me that the ritual consists of inserting a small bundle of hog hairs into the mouth, along with certain magical powders, and then moving the bundle in a highly formalized series of gestures.

In addition to the private mouth-rite, the people seek out a holy-mouth-man once or twice a year. These practitioners have an impressive set of paraphernalia [equipment], consisting of a variety of augers [drills], awls [tools for making holes], probes, and prods. The use of these objects in the exorcism of the evils of the mouth involves almost unbelievable ritual torture of the client. The holy-mouth-man opens the client's mouth and, using the above-mentioned tools, enlarges any holes which decay may have created in the teeth. Magical materials are put into these holes. . . . The extremely sacred and traditional character of the rite is evident in the fact that the natives return to the holy-mouth-man year after year, despite the fact that their teeth continue to decay.*

Notice how some of the institutional practices of the Nacirema are maintained. How do they justify their body rituals? Is there a system of rewards or incentives to sustain their practices? Some of these practices may sound familiar to you. What is Nacirema spelled backwards?

Most societies have an extensive network of institutionalized activities that are practiced without conscious thought. All societies have to meet certain fundamental needs and accomplish certain goals if they are to survive. To attain these ends, they must have institutional practices. And these practices are usually sustained through rituals.

*From "Body Ritual Among the Nacirema" by Horace Miner from *The American Anthropologist*, Vol. 58, No. 3, 1956. Reprinted by permission of the American Anthropological Association and the author.

13 The Family

► How are families organized?

► What are the functions of the family?

► What are some characteristics of American family life?

SECTION 1:
Family Structures and Functions

What values, norms, and roles make up the structures of the social institution of the family? In our discussion of family structures we won't label values, norms, or roles as such. Instead, we'll consider six aspects of structure: forms of marriage, marriage restrictions, family organization, family residence, authority, and kinship. However, you should be able to pick out the values, norms, and roles involved in these six areas.

The Family Social Structure

How many wives may a man have? How many husbands may a woman have? The number of marriage partners that an individual is permitted to have determines the form of marriage involved.

Forms of marriage. The norms of American society permit only one marriage partner at a time. *The marriage of one man to one woman is called* MONOGAMY. ("Mono" means one, and "gamy" means marriage.) Monogamy is the most common form of marriage. It is found all over the world. It generally prevails in societies such as Western cultures, in which the numbers of men and women are nearly equal.

Some societies, however, permit POLYGAMY, *or marriage to more than one partner at the same time.* ("Poly" means many.) Polygamy can take the form either of polygyny or polyandry. POLYGYNY *is the marriage form in which a man is permitted to have more than one wife.* Historically, polygyny has been more the norm than monogamy. Polygyny sometimes occurs in societies that have a large majority of women, or where women play an important role in the family economy. But it may occur for prestige reasons, also. For example, in some pastoral tribes in Africa, the status of the man is

related to the number of wives and children he has. Therefore, he is encouraged to have as many wives as he can afford. The first wives often "push" their husband to take more wives because it gives the entire family unit more status. It also elevates the first wives, since earlier wives have more status than later ones. Furthermore, these African wives welcome the extra help with the work. The more wives a man has the larger his farm can be, for the wives do the farm work.

In this system each wife has her own room or hut, where she and her children live. The husband rotates among his wives. He is not allowed to show any partiality, living with each one for a twenty-four hour period. As the husband gains status through a greater number of wives and children, and improves his economic position, each of the wives shares in his status. Observers of this system have reported that it functions to the mutual benefit of all.

Polygyny is practiced today among some peoples of Africa, Asia, and the Arab world. The Moslem religion, for instance, allows a man to have up to four wives, if he can support them. Even though the norms of a society may approve of polygyny, not all the people in that society may practice it. Even in a polygynous society a great number of people practice monogamy. For most societies do not have enough women available to provide several wives for each eligible man.

The other form of polygamy is POLYANDRY, *which occurs when one woman has more than one husband.* Although this form of marriage has never been very common, it has always existed in a few societies. Today it is practiced by some of the Arctic Eskimos and some societies in central Asia, India, and the Marquesas Islands.

Polyandry is generally found in societies that have a high proportion of males. For example, in Jaunswar Bawar, in the Himalayas of India, a society of 60,000 people practices polyandry. Men outnumber women four to one. When a girl marries one man, she automatically marries all of his brothers. The women who live with their several husbands are called "rantys." If a "ranty" divorces her husbands she then returns to live with her parents and is called a "dhyanty." If a "dhyanty" chooses to marry again she is likely to end up with another set of brothers because her new husband must pay a sum, determined by the village council, to her first set of husbands. Since the sum is usually more than one individual can pay, the cost is shared with his brothers, who thereby become husbands, too. Although the women of the society protest against the system and the government of India has tried to stop the practice, the men of Jaunswar have strongly resisted changing it.

In addition to monogamy, polygyny, and polyandry, there is a fourth form of marriage, usually called GROUP MARRIAGE, *in which there is more than one partner of each sex.* This arrangement of plural wives and husbands is rare. Some utopian communities have practiced it, however. In the 1800's a utopian community, the Perfectionists, of Oneida, New York, allowed each adult to have sexual relations with any other adult. Some hippie communes have also practiced what might be called group marriage, although without cultural approval.

Marriage restrictions. In every society there is some restriction as to whom an individual is permitted to marry. These restrictions are of two types: exogamy and endogamy. EXOGAMY *requires that a person marry someone outside of the immediate family, clan, village, or tribe.* ("Exo" means outside.) Exogamy is closely related to the incest taboo. The *incest taboo* prohibits sexual relations between persons of opposite sexes who are very closely related. In almost every society the norms prohibit marriage between close relatives, such as father–daughter, mother–son, brother–sister, and first cousins. In many tribal societies marriage must be outside of the clan, village, or tribe.

On the other hand, ENDOGAMY *requires that a person marry someone within the tribe, race, social class, or religion.* ("Endo" means within.) Endogamy is particularly important in a caste system, which permits only persons within the same caste to marry. Until recently, many states in the United States prohibited marriage between persons of different races. Although now legal, interracial marriages are not encouraged by the society. In America most marriages are between persons of similar social class levels. Also, although now socially acceptable, marriages between persons of different religions, such as between Protestants and Jews, were at one time frowned upon, and still are often discouraged by the families of each prospective partner.

Types of family organization. The size of the family unit may vary greatly from culture to culture. In many tribal societies the family size is determined by blood relationship and common ancestry. *This type of family organization, in which several generations of blood relatives live together, is called an* EXTENDED *family.* If the society traces descent through the father, when the son marries he and his wife would live with his parents, as would his brothers and their wives and children. The grandparents might also live with the family. In this case membership would include four generations: the grandparents, the parents, the sons and their wives, and their children. This type of family existed in pre-Communist China, and can be found today in parts of India, rural Japan, Africa, Turkey, and Iran.

The other basic type of family organization, in which membership consists only of the married couple and their dependent children, is called the NUCLEAR *family.* This is the accepted form in the United States, where children generally move away from their parents' household when they marry. Whereas the extended family is based on

Some families in our society, such as this one, have several generations of blood relatives living nearby. They all get together often. Are they an extended family, or not?

blood relationship, the nuclear family is formed by marriage.

Family residence. There are three common rules of residence concerning where the young married couple will live. *When the son and his wife move in with or reside near his parents at marriage, the type of family residence is called* PATRILOCAL. ("Patri" means father, and "local" means place.) The son and his wife may move into his father's household, or may live nearby. In some African tribes, for example, the son builds his house some distance from his father's house but still within the father's "kraal" or family village.

In some societies the husband moves in with or resides near the wife's family, a system called MATRILOCAL ("matri" meaning mother). This system has been common in some of the American Indian societies, such as the Hopi, Iroquois, and Navajo.

A third type of family residence is the one found in American society. *In the* NEOLOCAL *type* ("neo" meaning new), *the married couple moves completely away from both sets of parents and establishes a new household.* As you might expect, the neolocal residence is related to the nuclear family, and the patrilocal and matrilocal residences occur with the extended family.

Authority. *When the father has the authority in the family, the family is* PATRIARCHAL ("arch" meaning rule). Patriarchal norms are common in many societies. In strictly patriarchal households the wives have no authority whatever. The male head has complete control over his wife and children. In other societies the reverse is true. *When the society is* MATRIARCHAL, *the authority in the family is in the hands of the wife and mother.* Matriarchal societies also tend to be matrilocal, as in the Hopi and Navajo tribes.

238

A *third form of family authority is* EQUALI-TARIAN. Here the power is shared by the husband and wife.

Kinship. Kinship is determined by the society's rules of descent. There are three basic types. *When the descent is traced in the father's line, it is* PATRILINEAL. *When it is traced in the mother's line, it is* MATRILINEAL. *In a third system,* BILATERAL, *descent is traced on both the father's and mother's sides.* This is the system found in the United States. Although the wife usually takes the last name of her husband, as do the children, the society recognizes relatives on both sides and the children trace their ancestry through both parents.

A society that is patriarchal is likely to be patrilineal. In other words, when the father is the ruler, the descent is also traced

Drawing by John Saxon,
© 1973 The New Yorker Magazine, Inc.

"This is not a debate, a discussion, a man-to-man talk, or a meeting of minds. I'm telling you something!"

through the father. Similarly, matriarchal and matrilineal systems are often found together. When the control is equalitarian, the kinship is usually determined bilaterally.

Functions of the Family

In the last chapter we discussed the fact that social institutions have primary and secondary functions. In the following discussion of the various functions of the family, consider which are primary and which are secondary. Also, think about the values, norms, and roles related to each function.

Reproduction. Every society has norms establishing the family as the unit for producing offspring. Although familial patterns vary from society to society, as do the norms for premarital sexual relations, in all societies the family performs the function of reproduction. The social institution of the family defines the terms on which sexual reproduction will take place and establishes some form of marriage as the approved social relationship. Marriage provides the physical and psychological environment necessary for the survival and growth of children.

Socialization. The family transmits the culture to the new generation. Through the family, children learn the values and norms of the society. They learn about the roles they must play through the example of their parents and through the sanctions applied when they misplay their role. Because the family group tends to be relatively stable and enduring from the infant's birth through his or her years of growing up, the family provides for the development of the mature personality.

Providing ascribed statuses. The family gives the child a status. When babies enter the world, they receive a status from their parents. Although this status is apt to be an achieved status for the parents, it is ascribed for the child, since children have no opportunity to choose their parents. Research studies have shown that an individual's ascribed status, based on his or her family's standing, is the most important single factor in determining the person's eventual social class standing.

This function may be more important for girls than for boys. When boys become adults, they may go out into the world and achieve their own status. Girls, on the other hand, sometimes face social barriers to achieving their own status. Traditionally, a married woman's status has been related to the status of her husband, regardless of her own achievements. If a woman does not marry, she may establish her own achieved status. Yet her opportunities may be limited, since in some areas she may not be permitted to compete on equal terms with men. Such barriers can be, and are being, overcome. In addition, for both men and women the "platform" from which they step out into the world is of utmost importance in determining their eventual position.

Providing companionship, affection, and intimacy. An individual needs companionship, affection, and intimacy with another human being or beings for his or her physical and psychological well-being. Through the primary family group these needs are provided. In the family group an individual finds love and affection and a sense of belonging, without having to prove his or her worth. Of course, all families do not provide this environment, but the norms suggest that they should.

Regulating sexual relations. The norms of the family define conditions under which sexual relations may occur. Although complete conformity to these norms is never achieved, the social institution of the family does exert strong control over sexual relations. One of the questions being debated by social critics today, however, is whether or not the control of the family over sexual relations is weakening. What do you think?

Providing social control. The family group provides a form of social control over both parents and children. The children are influenced to conform to the norms of the society because they don't want the disapproval of the parents. At the same time, the parents are influenced to conform to the

The family performs the function of providing a certain amount of physical and psychological protection for its members. Is this a primary or a secondary function?

social norms because they don't want to bring scandal and disgrace to their family.

The economic function. In some societies the family is the basic economic unit. Every member of the household performs some duty that provides for the economic well-being of the family. For example, the father might tend to the farming, the mother might make clothes and prepare food for the family, and the children might help out in the fields or in the home.

In American urban society the family has lost this function, although in rural farm areas some households still work on the farm as a family unit. In most cases economic productivity in the United States today takes place outside rather than within the family unit. However, the family does contribute to the division of labor between the sexes. The family provides some specialization and division of the various tasks necessary for meeting individual needs.

The transmission of private property. A last function that we will consider is the transmission of private property from one generation to the next. Almost every society has norms relating to what happens to an individual's property at his or her death. And usually these norms are based on the family. If there is no will, most states in the United States have laws specifying that the property of the deceased shall be divided between the wife or husband, if living, and the individual's children. In some African tribes the property of the mother is passed on to the daughters and the property of the father is passed to the sons.

SECTION REVIEW

1. What are the various forms of marriage?
2. What are the two types of family organization? Which is most common in our society?
3. What are the three types of family authority? Are all three found in our society?

4. Name the functions of the family. Which are primary and which are secondary?

KEY TERMS

Explain the meaning of each of these terms.

bilateral system	matrilocal system
endogamy	monogamy
equalitarian household	neolocal system
	nuclear family
exogamy	patriarchal household
extended family	
group marriage	patrilineal system
incest taboo	patrilocal system
matriarchal household	polyandry
	polygamy
matrilineal system	polygyny

SECTION 2:
Patterns and Processes in American Family Life

Now that we've examined the structure and functions, we are ready to consider the patterns and processes of the American family. First, however, let's review what is meant by patterns and processes. Pattern is the repetition of behavior that makes prediction possible. Process is change taking place in a specific way or number of ways. Our concern here will be with the processes in structures, functions, and patterns of American family life.

What are some of the basic characteristics of the American family? What changes are taking place in the American family? To answer these questions let's look at some statistics on marriage and divorce rates, age at marriage, size of families, and the changing role of women.

MARRIAGE AND DIVORCE RATES IN THE UNITED STATES FOR SELECTED YEARS 1900-1974

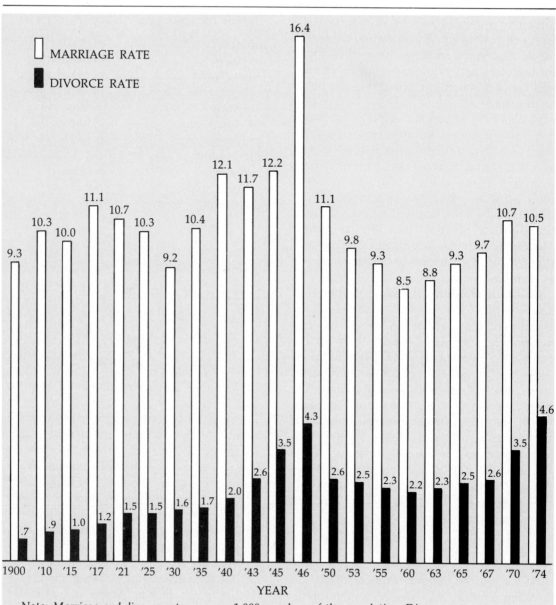

☐ MARRIAGE RATE

■ DIVORCE RATE

YEAR

Note: Marriage and divorce rates are per 1,000 members of the population. Divorce rates include annulments.

Source: U.S. Bureau of the Census, *Statistical Abstract of the United States, 1975*.

Marriage and Divorce Rates

DIVORCE *is the legal termination of an officially recognized marriage.* In considering the number of marriages and divorces, we will examine the rates rather than the actual numbers. The advantage of using rates is that they allow for changes in population, since they give the number of marriages or divorces per 1,000 population. These statistics are shown in the graph on page 242. The figures for most years contain some estimated data, since complete data are usually not available. Notice that the data are for selected years rather than an equal interval scale of years.

As you analyze the data, consider the following questions: (1) Can you see the influence of wars, depressions, and periods of prosperity in the data? (2) Are cycles evident that show the influence of one generation on the next generation? (3) Do the marriage and divorce rates tend to vary together? If so, how?

We can see from the graph that the divorce rate has been increasing since 1900. Not only has the divorce rate increased but also the percentage of divorced persons in the society has grown a great deal. For example, in 1940 only 1.8 percent of the women who were eighteen years of age and over were divorced. By 1974 the figure had increased to almost 5 percent. For men the percent divorced grew from only 1.4 percent in 1940 to 3.5 percent by 1974.

Will the rate of divorce increase or decrease in the future? The fact that young people today are more inclined to marry for love, affection, and companionship than for economic security might lead to more divorce, if these psychological needs and expectations are not met. Also, the fact that many women can support themselves today and therefore do not need to depend on a man for economic support could contribute to an increased divorce rate.

On the other hand, the present trend toward later marriage could tend to lower the divorce rate. It is now estimated that about one out of two marriages in which the couple is under twenty years of age fails. For all marriages, the failure rate is about one out of three. So the trend toward later marriage might help reduce the divorce rate. Also, many married women are now employed. Their salaries increase the family income and may help prevent financial difficulties, which can be a cause of divorce.

You might look for articles in periodicals and statistics on divorce to obtain the most recent figures on the divorce rate. What do you think will happen to the marriage and divorce rates in the future? Why?

Divorce laws. A divorce may be granted only after court action. The laws vary greatly from state to state. In some states, one member of the couple must file a suit with the court (this person is called the *plaintiff*), charging the other member (called the *defendant*) with some violation of the law. The plaintiff's charges must be an act or actions that the state recognizes as legal grounds for divorce. Some of the more common grounds for divorce are adultery (voluntary sexual relations with someone other than your spouse), imprisonment, physical and mental cruelty, desertion, drunkenness, nonsupport, insanity, or living separate and apart. The grounds used to obtain the legal divorce often are not the real reason for problems in the marriage. Perhaps the husband and wife have found that they cannot get along and both want a divorce. If one member files for divorce, the defendant can simply not show up to contest the petition. Usually the judge will then grant the divorce and the defendant is considered guilty as charged.

More and more states are now adopting what have been called "no-fault" divorce laws. The no-fault divorce laws do not put the blame on one partner, requiring one person to be guilty of grounds for divorce.

Instead, one party (called the *petitioner*) files a suit asking that the marriage be dissolved. The petitioner has only to state that the marriage is finished. The other spouse (called the *respondent*) may agree or may reply that the marriage should not end. In this case the judge may postpone action on the suit for sixty days (in some states) and either recommend or order the couple to undergo marriage counseling. After the sixty-day period is over, the judge must grant the dissolution of the marriage, if either party still wants it. The court's primary function is to insure that property is divided in a fair way and that, if there are children, their custody and support are provided for.

Other ways of breaking up marriages. In addition to divorce, a marriage may be broken because of death, separation, desertion, or annulment. Death is a common cause. However, our basic concern here is with families in which both husband and wife are still living, but are not together.

SEPARATION *is a situation in which the husband and wife are legally married but are not living together by common consent.* Separation is usually an informal step leading to a formal divorce. However, it may also be a formal arrangement, legally recognized. It is often used by couples whose religion prohibits divorce.

DESERTION *is a situation in which one spouse simply abandons the other.* Deserting partners don't let their spouses know where they are going, since frequently they want to escape from their family duties and responsibilities. Desertion has been called a "cheap divorce" because it costs nothing and involves no financial obligation (unless the individual is arrested under a court order and forced to pay). Desertion is most common among spouses with low incomes.

In both separation and desertion the couple are still legally married, so neither is free to remarry. A marriage can be legally terminated only by court action in the form of a divorce or an annulment.

ANNULMENT *is a court decision that declares a marriage null and void because of some legal flaw.* This flaw might consist of coercion, being under age, bigamy, insanity, fraud, marriage performed by an unauthorized person, or unwillingness to consummate the union. The most common reason is fraud related to some kind of false representation. For example, annulments have been granted when an individual stated that he or she never used drugs but was found to be an addict, a woman failed to disclose that she had an illegitimate child, or a man concealed knowledge of his sterility, or inability to produce children. After an annulment each partner returns to his or her original status before the wedding took place, since an annulment is legal recognition that no marriage existed.

Age at Marriage

Age at first marriage has declined since 1890. In 1890 the median age at which men first married was twenty-six. The age for women was twenty-two. By 1950 the median age for men had decreased to approximately twenty-three, with women marrying at age twenty. In 1974 the median age at marriage for men was still twenty-three, but the median age for first marriage for women had increased to twenty-one. Recent trends indicate that both men and women are now waiting still longer before first marriage.

Another trend is that the percentage of both men and women who are marrying has begun to drop. For example, in 1960 approximately 76.4 percent of the males eighteen years and over were married. But by 1974 the figure had decreased to 73.7 percent. For women it changed from 71.6 percent in 1960 to 67.6 percent in 1974.

These are some of the many different ceremonies with which people begin marriage. Shown here is a Roman Catholic wedding (upper left); a Japanese ceremony (upper right); an informal outdoor wedding (lower left); and an Orthodox Jewish wedding (lower right).

Think of some factors that a couple should consider in deciding how many children to have. Is cost a factor? What about time? What are some others?

Size of Families

The American family is slowly shrinking in size. The size of the average American family had grown to 3.7 members in 1965, as couples tended to have more children. But by 1974 the average family had declined to 3.4 persons. This may not seem to you to be much change. Yet when you consider that a family always has two members to begin with, this is a significant change.

A number of factors have led to smaller families. The recent emphasis on problems of ecology and the population explosion has no doubt caused some families to have fewer children. The economic recession of 1973–75 may have been a factor. Certainly the cost of raising children to adulthood has in-creased tremendously. Couples simply can't afford to have so many children today. At any rate we can probably expect an even greater decrease in the size of the average American family, as many young couples now tend to want either no children or only one or two.

The Changing Role of Married Women

Today couples are having children sooner —or not having them at all. The average married woman today has her first child at twenty-two, her last child at twenty-six, and has them all in school when she is thirty-one or thirty-two. By the time she is forty-three, the last child has left home. Since the average woman in America lives to the age of about seventy-five years, this means that she has approximately thirty-two more years after her children have left home.

Several other factors have greatly altered the role of the married woman in our society. One is the new technology that fills our homes with a large number of labor- and time-saving machines and devices. This makes it easier for the married woman to enter the labor market, since she has more time available outside the home. Another factor is the influence of the Women's Liberation Movement. Because of Women's Lib, women today have many options open to them that were not even thought of a few years ago.

The number of women with jobs has been increasing steadily. Today, there are more than 36 million women in the labor force. In fact, nearly 50 percent of all women over sixteen years old are a part of the labor force. They represent close to 40 percent of the total American labor force. Of these women, only about 23 percent are single, approximately 62 percent are married, and just under 15 percent are widowed or divorced.

Married women may choose to work in the labor force for a number of reasons. Many probably work to give the family a higher standard of living or to help put the children through college. Others may work because they need the creative outlet for their talents and abilities. No doubt more and more married women will be a part of the labor force in the future. It is also very likely that many will be entering fields of work that were previously occupied primarily by men.

Women play an essential role in our economy. About 23 million of the women in our labor force are married. The largest category of employed married women, after clerical work, is that of professional and technical work.

SECTION REVIEW

1. How have marriage and divorce rates changed since 1900? What are some factors that influence changes in the marriage and divorce rates?
2. What are no-fault divorce laws?
3. At about what age do American men and women first marry today? At what age did they marry in 1890?
4. What factors have influenced the size of American families today?
5. How has the role of married women in the United States changed in the last few years?

KEY TERMS

Explain the meaning of each term.

annulment
desertion
divorce

no-fault divorce laws
separation

PROJECTS AND ACTIVITIES

1. Do research to find examples of cultures that practice the three forms of marriage not common to the Western world today: polygyny, polyandry, and group marriage. Do these marriage forms function well in these societies? Why do these societies practice these forms of marriage? Are the marriage practices in these societies changing? If so, how are they changing?

2. Contrast family life on a farm with family life in the city.

3. Conduct a survey of the students in the class to determine patterns of authority in the family, and analyze the results.

4. Have class members survey their parents to find out how far apart from each other the husband and wife grew up. Ask the individuals whether they grew up in (1) the same neighborhood, (2) different neighborhoods in the same city, (3) different towns or cities in the same state, (4) in different states, or (5) in different countries. Discuss the generalizations that can be made from the survey.

5. Conduct an interview with an employee of a marriage-matching or computerized dating service. What are the advantages of such matchmaking? What do you see as disadvantages?

6. Do a sociodrama in which a young girl tells her parents that she wants to marry a boy of whom they do not approve.

7. Write a short story or drama that portrays your view of the ideal family.

8. Make a survey of the students in the class to determine what specific responsibilities they have in the home—what tasks they are required to do. Discuss your findings in terms of the functions of the family in American society today.

9. Follow a television series based on a family and comment on the patterns and processes implied. How realistic is the series? How do the ideas of the family presented in the series coincide with your ideas of family life?

10. Do research to find out what grounds for divorce are legal in your state. Which grounds are most commonly used in obtaining a divorce?

11. If possible, sit in on divorce court proceedings and observe a number of cases. What did you learn about the causes of divorce and the effects of divorce on the individuals involved?

TOPICS FOR INQUIRY

1. Discuss the advantages and disadvantages of the four types of marriage: monogamy, polygyny, polyandry, and group marriage. How would the sex ratio in the society affect the practicality of each type?

2. Which of the functions of the family discussed in the chapter do you think is most important in our society today? Why?

3. In what ways has your family helped you determine your values, norms, roles, and goals?

4. How do you think the American family will be affected by the changing sex roles (toward equality of the sexes) in our society? Do you approve or disapprove of these changes? Why?

5. Discuss how the relationships in the family are affected by the wife working outside the home.

6. If the wife works outside the home, should the husband do approximately half of the housework? Why or why not?

7. What do you think the trend will be in the future in terms of age at first marriage? Why?

8. Debate: One reason for the growing divorce rate is that the mass media give young people such a distorted concept of "love" that they enter marriage with exaggerated expectations.

9. Debate: Traditional marriage and family is the most important characteristic of a civilized society.

SUGGESTIONS FOR READING

NONFICTION

BLOOD, Robert O. Jr., *Marriage*. Second ed., The Free Press, 1969. A college textbook that covers all aspects of marriage and includes the findings of many research studies on marriage and the family.

DeCARAVA, Roy D. and HUGHES, Langston, *The Sweet Flypaper of Life*. Hill & Wang, 1967 (and pap.). A first-person account of life and values in Harlem (New York City).

FARBER, Bernard (ed.), *Kinship and Family Organization*. Wiley, 1966 (pap.). A book of readings that presents various sociological approaches to the relationships between family and society and indicates the role of kinship in each.

FILENE, Peter Gabriel, *Him/Her/Self: Sex Roles in Modern America*. Harcourt Brace Jovanovich, 1975. A study of sex roles in America and how they've changed over the years.

HESS, Robert D. and HANDEL, Gerald, *Family Worlds: A Psychosocial Approach to Family Life*. University of Chicago Press, 1974 (pap.). Case histories of five families in terms of how they function.

KELLEY, Robert K., *Courtship, Marriage, and the Family*. Second ed., Harcourt Brace Jovanovich, 1974. A textbook on the patterns and purposes of courtship, the adjustments of marriage, and the development of family life in the United States.

LEVENSON, Sam, *Everything but Money*. Simon & Schuster, 1966 or Pocket Books (pap.). A true story about a family rich in everything but money. A nonfiction best seller.

MEAD, Margaret and HEYMAN, Ken, *Family*. Macmillan, 1965. A book of Margaret Mead's thoughts and observations of family relationships all over the world, illustrated with Ken Heyman's photographs.

QUEEN, Stuart A. and HABENSTEIN, Robert W., *The Family in Various Cultures*. Fourth ed., Lippincott, 1974 (pap.). A study of fourteen family systems in fourteen cultural and historical settings throughout the world.

250

FICTION

AGEE, James, *A Death in the Family*. Bantam (pap.). A penetrating portrayal of a family's reaction to the death of the father.

BALDWIN, James, *The Amen Corner*. Dial. A woman minister's unsavory past life is discovered by her son.

BUCK, Pearl, *The Three Daughters of Madame Liang*. John Day or Pocket Books (pap.). The story of a heroic Chinese woman whose three daughters have been educated in America, and the changes in the family produced by Communism.

LEWITON, Mina, *The Divided Heart*. McKay. A fifteen-year-old girl learns how to face her parents' divorce.

O'NEILL, Eugene, *Long Day's Journey into Night*. Yale University Press (and pap.). Drugs threaten to destroy a family.

ROTH, Henry, *Call It Sleep*. Avon (pap.). A Jewish immigrant family struggles to survive in the city.

SARTRE, Jean-Paul, *No Exit*. Knopf. An existentialist play concerning people's need for love and communication in a false society.

14 Education

► What functions does the educational system perform?

► How is American education structured?

► What changes are occurring in American education?

SECTION 1:
Educational Structures and Functions

The socialization of its new members is a task that must be accomplished if a society is to continue to exist. The values, norms, and roles related to this task make up the social institution of education.

Informal Educational Structures

In some societies the socialization of new members is carried out in a very informal way. In most tribal societies, for instance, the basic task is to teach the child the values, folkways, and mores of the society as well as the basic skills necessary to take part in the division of labor. This teaching is usually done by members of the family, clan, or village. The women instruct the girls in the skills necessary to become a good wife. The men teach the boys how to hunt and fish and provide for a future family. In these societies the socialization process is carried out through informal groups. There is no formal (legally imposed) educational structure.

Formal Educational Structures

In other societies the family and other groups continue to play a role. But a good part of the socialization process is carried out by a complex, formal educational structure made up of many specific organizations and associations. The early societies of Babylonia, Egypt, Persia, India, China, Greece, and Rome had formal educational structures. They did not, however, have universal education as we know it in the United States. In the early societies formal education was limited to the upper classes, who had the leisure time necessary to pursue knowledge.

During the Middle Ages in Europe almost all education was provided by the Roman Catholic Church. Instruction was centered around the monasteries and later around the universities founded by the Society of Jesus (the Jesuits), a religious order begun by Ignatius Loyola in 1534. At one time all the rulers of Europe were educated either in schools operated by the Jesuits or by Jesuit tutors. People who were not members of the ruling classes had little opportunity to become educated. Gradually, though, through the influence of the Renaissance, Reformation, and Industrial Revolution, formal education became more secular and began to include the middle and lower classes.

Educational structures in the United States. In America the first schools were religious. They were usually for the purpose of educating the clergy. Since it was not considered necessary for girls to become educated, the early schools were for boys only. To insure that its inhabitants could read the Bible, the Massachusetts government passed a law in 1647 requiring that all towns of more than fifty householders set up schools for their children. Other states also began to provide elementary schools. By the early 1800's, though, these schools were inadequate. A movement for free, tax-supported schools succeeded in establishing a system of free public elementary schools in most northern cities by the 1850's. Then demands grew for free high school education and, eventually, for public universities.

Along with the growth of public schools in America came state laws for compulsory (required) attendance. States began passing compulsory attendance laws in the second half of the 1800's, starting with Massachusetts in 1852. Today almost every state has a compulsory school attendance law. Most of the states require attendance in school from the age of six or seven to age sixteen.

Because of the importance of educating its citizens, the United States has developed an extensive formal educational structure. Today children may begin their formal education at the age of two or three, if their parents enroll them in a nursery school or day-care center. They may go to kindergarten at about age five. At the age of six, children enter the elementary school, where they will stay for either six or eight years. Under the six-year system they will enter a junior high school for three years and then go to a senior high school for three more years (called a 6–3–3 system). Or they might go to a junior high for two years and a senior high for four years (6–2–4 system). Under the eight-year system the elementary school goes to the eighth grade, followed by four years of high school (an 8–4 system).

Individuals may stop their formal education when they graduate from high school or pass the age of compulsory attendance. On the other hand, they may decide to continue their education. They may choose to enter a four-year college or university, a junior or community college, a technical school, a vocational school, a business school, or an apprenticeship program in one of the skilled trades. If they receive their bachelor's degree, they may then go on to graduate school to work toward a master's or doctor's degree. After receiving the doctor's degree, they may continue their education in postdoctoral study and research. The formal structure of American education is shown in the diagram on page 255.

Other educational structures. Not all socialization occurs through the schools. As we discussed in the last chapter, the family plays a very important part in the socialization of the child. The family starts the socialization process and teaches the child the basic values and norms of the society. In addition to the family, the groups to which the individual belongs, such as the neighborhood play group, church youth groups,

THE AMERICAN EDUCATIONAL STRUCTURE

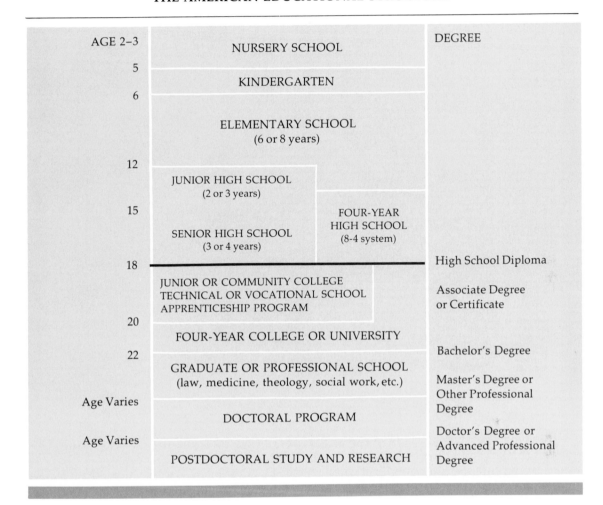

AGE 2–3	NURSERY SCHOOL	DEGREE
5	KINDERGARTEN	
6		
	ELEMENTARY SCHOOL (6 or 8 years)	
12	JUNIOR HIGH SCHOOL (2 or 3 years)	
15	SENIOR HIGH SCHOOL (3 or 4 years) / FOUR-YEAR HIGH SCHOOL (8-4 system)	
18		High School Diploma
	JUNIOR OR COMMUNITY COLLEGE TECHNICAL OR VOCATIONAL SCHOOL APPRENTICESHIP PROGRAM	Associate Degree or Certificate
20	FOUR-YEAR COLLEGE OR UNIVERSITY	
22	GRADUATE OR PROFESSIONAL SCHOOL (law, medicine, theology, social work, etc.)	Bachelor's Degree
Age Varies	DOCTORAL PROGRAM	Master's Degree or Other Professional Degree
Age Varies	POSTDOCTORAL STUDY AND RESEARCH	Doctor's Degree or Advanced Professional Degree

congeniality groups, and Little League teams, contribute to the socialization process. Other sources for the socialization of children in many societies today are the mass media, such as television, radio, the movies, books, and newspapers. The experiences of the individual that are related to the economic institution are also important as the person plays the role of consumer and, later, of employee. And contact with governmental processes help socialize the individual.

The Primary Educational Function

The primary, or intended, function of educational structures is the socialization of new members. In a complex society there are many aspects to the socialization process. We might include the following eight aspects of socialization in a complex society:

1. Teaching basic skills in the use of the symbols of the society, such as reading, writing, and arithmetic.

One of the primary functions of the educational structure is to teach certain basic skills. What problems might you have if you didn't learn the basic skill of writing?

2. Helping the student develop skills in abstract thinking and problem solving.

3. Transmitting the cultural heritage, from which individuals may develop pride in their society.

4. Communicating to children the current basic values of the culture.

5. Teaching the special aspects of the culture, such as art, music, literature, drama, science, technology, and sports.

6. Teaching some vocational skills so that the individual can take his or her place in the job market.

7. Training citizens for life within the political structure of their particular societies.

8. Preparing children to live among and interact with other human beings.

Secondary Educational Functions

In addition to socialization, the primary function, the institution of education carries out a number of secondary functions. Secondary, or latent, functions are those functions that are unintended or unexpected. We will consider seven secondary functions.

Keeps children and youth occupied. The school system provides the function of assuming responsibility for the children for a certain number of hours each day. Because children are occupied in school, their mothers are able to get jobs, or do volunteer work, or see friends. At the same time the function of keeping youth occupied means that many adolescents are kept busy in school. Young people who otherwise might find that they have a lot of time on their hands are attending junior and senior high school.

Keeps many young people out of the labor market. Because of compulsory school attendance laws, most young people under the age of sixteen are kept from competing with adults for available jobs. The great number of students attending college are also kept out of the labor market. For example, imagine what would happen if all teen-agers over fourteen years of age suddenly left school and began looking for jobs. There are nearly 25 million people between the ages of fourteen and nineteen enrolled in school who would become available for the labor market. The fact that they are in school makes more jobs available to others.

Provides a vehicle for social mobility. The recognized means of upward social mobility in the United States is through education. A particular educational degree gives the individual achieved status, regardless of what his or her ascribed status might have been. By going to college, children from upper-lower-class families may become lower-middle or even upper-middle class. The rela-tionship between education completed and income shows how education is a vehicle for social mobility.

For example, consider the table on this page, which shows the relationship between income and years of school completed for employed men twenty-five to sixty-four years old. From this table you can see that median income increases as education increases. For instance, there is a difference of $1,500 in median income between graduation from high school and the completion of one to three years of college. A college degree and postgraduate degrees further increase an individual's income. Actually, there is no real proof that increased education is necessary to perform high-paying jobs. But there is evidence that education is helpful in obtaining them.

Not only does education help provide the learning and skills necessary for upward mobility, but it also provides experience in middle- and upper-class life styles. This training in behavior patterns, such as what to wear, how to speak, and what to say, is probably at least as important as the formal learning in achieving upward mobility.

MONEY INCOME BY YEARS OF SCHOOL COMPLETED

EDUCATION COMPLETED		MEDIAN INCOME (1974)
Elementary:	Less than 8 years	$ 6,619
	8 years	8,598
High School:	1 to 3 years	9,659
	4 years	12,255
College:	1 to 3 years	14,680
	4 years or more	18,351

Source: U.S. Bureau of the Census, *Statistical Abstract of the United States, 1975.*

A secondary function of the educational institution is to bring you together with people whom you might never know otherwise. Such contacts can have a lasting impact on your life.

Serves as an instrument of social change. Education at the high school and college level introduces new ideas to students at a time when they are becoming independent of their parents and are developing their own views. The influence of high school tends to be less than that of college. Most high school students are still living with their parents, who may follow closely the activities of the school. But when students go to college, they usually leave their parents. Their thinking becomes challenged by professors who, because of the academic freedom that most of them enjoy and the knowledge they have in a specialized field, often encourage new approaches and new solutions to problems. Students begin thinking in terms of new concepts and ideas. This freedom to express new ideas serves to loosen the bonds of tradition and to spur social change.

Provides recreational and social activities for the community. The school provides recreational and social activities for the adults as well as for the students. One example is the athletic events, which are an important part of the activities of any high school. At these events the adults of the community may participate by cheering. They may become involved in remembering the "good old days" when they were in high school. In addition, they may participate in social events through the PTA and other school-related groups.

Provides opportunities to meet new people. In school and college, students become acquainted with many new people they would not otherwise meet. These acquaintanceships and friendships may continue throughout the individual's life. They may later serve as contacts for business, or may provide social contacts for the individual who moves to a new area.

Serves as a marriage market. High schools and colleges, with their many dating activities, play a very important part in the meeting of future marriage partners. Proof that schools perform this function is shown by the large number of married couples who first met as students in high school or college. In fact, the acknowledged aim of some college students is to obtain a spouse as well as a bachelor's degree.

SECTION REVIEW

1. How is the American educational system organized?
2. How has the formal educational structure developed historically?
3. What is the primary function of the educational system? What is included in this function?
4. What are some secondary functions? How are they carried out?

SECTION 2:
Patterns and Processes in American Education

What are the basic characteristics of American education? What changes are taking place in the patterns of American education? To answer these questions, we will look at some statistics.

The Growth of Education in America

First we will examine the patterns in the number of schools in America, the school enrollment, and the number of graduates. Although the number of secondary schools and colleges has increased since 1930, the number of elementary schools has decreased greatly. In 1930 there were approximately 238,000 public elementary schools in the United States. The number has been diminishing steadily since then, until today there are fewer than 63,000. The reason for this decrease is the change from the typical one-room school of rural America to the present large elementary school in urban areas and the consolidated school in rural areas.

The number of secondary schools has increased slightly since 1930. In that year there were approximately 27,000 public and private secondary schools. Today there are about 29,000. Actually, the number of secondary schools in America reached a peak in the later 1960's and has been declining slightly since then. Looking at higher education, the number of colleges and universities, including both public and private institutions, has increased since 1930—from about 1,400 to more than 2,700 today.

For the period between 1930 and 1970, the figures for school enrollment show a substantial growth. When we consider the total enrollment of persons at the elementary, secondary, and college levels, we have a figure of over 29 million students in 1930 compared to nearly 59 million students in 1970. If we look at the approximate number of students per school, we find that the average enrollment per elementary school changed from about 86 in 1930 to about 400 in 1970. The change was even greater for secondary schools and colleges. In other words, the data indicate that American schools are getting larger. At the same time, the number of elementary schools has decreased and the

School enrollment figures are changing. What effect might the decline in enrollments have on individual schools? On the whole community?

The Financial Support of the Educational System

The cost of supporting the vast number of schools and colleges makes education one of the largest businesses in the United States. From an annual expenditure of slightly over 3 billion dollars in 1930, total expenditures for public and private education have climbed to more than 110 billion dollars. The expenditures for public schools alone are over 90 billion dollars. Even though the value of the dollar is much less than it was in the 1930's, the amount of money involved in education is staggering.

Where does this great sum of money come from? Who pays for the public schools? The answer is that the taxpayers provide the money for the operation of the nation's public schools. This money is allocated on three different levels. Traditionally, most of the support for the schools has come from the taxpayers in the local school districts. A second source of funds is from state revenues. A third source is the federal government. We can see from the table on page 261 that the source of funds is gradually shifting from local sources to state and federal revenues. This situation is occurring because of the current attempts to equalize educational opportunities.

In the past, there have been extensive variations in the amounts of funds available from local sources, and therefore in the quality of education available. For example, one school district may have a great deal of taxable property, such as a manufacturing plant, railroad yards, or warehouses. The district next to it may have only very modest homes as the tax base. Since schools are supported at the local level primarily by property taxes, these two districts will differ in their ability to support schools. In addition, the district that has the high tax base is likely to have few children to educate, since it is not a residential area. The residential area, on the

number of high schools has not increased enormously. They just became larger to take care of the increased enrollment.

A dramatic change is taking place in the school enrollment figures for the 1970's, however. Due to a lowering of the birth rate in the mid-1960's, the number of students enrolled in elementary school began to drop about 1970. This decline in the school population is expected to reach the high schools around 1980. And the continued rise in college and university enrollments is projected to level off by the mid-1980's.

REVENUE OF PUBLIC ELEMENTARY AND
SECONDARY SCHOOLS, BY SOURCE OF FUNDS

| SCHOOL YEAR (ending) | SOURCE OF REVENUE | | |
	FEDERAL	STATE	LOCAL
1940	1.8%	30.3%	68.0%
1950	2.9	39.8	57.3
1960	4.4	39.1	56.5
1966	7.9	39.1	53.0
1970	8.0	39.9	52.1
1973	8.7	40.0	51.3

Source: U.S. Bureau of the Census, *Statistical Abstract of the United States, 1975.*

other hand, is apt to have a great number of children but no real tax base.

Funds for schools that come from the state tend to provide more equality among the local districts. In a few states (such as New Jersey) there has been an attempt to replace the property tax with state funds allocated to local districts according to their needs. Federal funds tend to equalize education among the states, since states differ in their ability to support education. Although more and more funds are coming from the state and federal governments, over 50 percent of the support still comes from the local districts.

Support of public schools is often stated according to the amount per student. In 1975 the average expenditure per pupil was $1,250 for the United States as a whole. In other words, it cost the taxpayers, such as your parents, an average of well over a thousand dollars a year to support your public school education. The amount, of course, varied from state to state. In one state the amount per pupil was $2,005; in another, it was $871.

Federal Aid to Education

The federal government has increased its aid to public education considerably in recent years. Federal funds have been used to introduce more and more programs that give special aid to schools and promote national equality of education. Some of the programs for elementary and secondary education are the Teacher Corps, assistance for educationally deprived children, American Indian education programs, aid provided by the National Defense Education Acts, money for school library materials and vocational education, and emergency school assistance. A good deal of federal aid also goes to higher education in the form of research facilities, training grants, grants to colleges for buildings and equipment, support for veterans' education, and loans to colleges, universities, and students.

In addition to support for the public schools and higher education systems, the federal government provides financial assistance to a number of other educational programs. Large amounts of federal funds are used for applied research and development, school lunch and milk programs, the military academies, library services, international educational programs, educational television, and education in federal prisons. The amount of federal support is sizable, and continues to increase each year.

One result of the increased federal aid is concern that the federal government may be gaining too much control over individual schools through its financial support. The control comes through requiring local districts to meet certain regulations in order to receive federal funds. For example, school districts must be "in compliance" with the desegregation regulations in order to qualify for federal funds. It is true that the federal government has gained some control over the local schools. But at the same time the schools have been able to improve their programs. Perhaps your school is one of the many that have received federal aid for new equipment, textbooks, library books, or construction.

Community Control

Another dimension to the control of American public schools is now in process—decentralization, or community control. Traditionally, as we have mentioned, localities have retained the main control over educational policies (within the guidelines laid down by the state departments of education). This policy has permitted parents in small towns and suburban areas to have some influence in running schools. But in very large districts, such as New York City, local control has only recently begun. Large city districts have been divided into a number of smaller ones in cities such as New York and Chicago so that the local residents of a community have more opportunity to participate and exercise some influence. The

practicality or success of community control of school systems in large cities is being evaluated at the present time.

Private Schools

Public schools are supported by tax money and are open to any resident of the school district. Private schools are supported by a means other than tax money, such as tuition fees, church support, or donations. Usually private schools offer something that is not available at the public schools, such as religious training, special activities, small classes, or tutoring. The people who send their children to private schools are paying for the public schools through their taxes at the same time. They send their children to private schools because they feel that the benefits gained make up for the additional cost.

The enrollment in private schools in the United States is small, except at the nursery school and college levels. Around 75 percent of the children attending nursery school are at a private school. About 15 percent of children in kindergarten, 10 percent of elementary school students, and less than 8 percent of high school students are in private schools. However, nearly one fourth of all college students attend a private college.

Special Education

In American education today there is an emphasis on meeting the needs of each student. Accordingly, more and more special schools and classes are being provided for exceptional children. An exceptional child is an individual who differs in some way from the average child. Exceptional children may have speech defects, be emotionally disturbed, or be unusually gifted. The highest number of special schools and classes are for children with speech impairments, the next

This is one of approximately 1,700 Catholic high schools in America. About 75 percent of the students enrolled in private high schools are attending Catholic schools.

highest are for the mentally retarded, and the third highest are for gifted children. But there are also schools for the emotionally and socially maladjusted, for crippled children, for the deaf, and for visually handicapped children. Today there are more than 3 million special schools and programs for exceptional children.

SECTION REVIEW

1. What has happened to school enrollments over the years? What will probably be the situation in the future?

2. How are public schools financed? What changes are taking place with regard to the source of funds?

3. How has federal aid helped to improve education?

4. What are some differences between private schools and public schools?

5. What are special schools?

KEY TERMS

Define each term.

community control   public school
private school   special education

1. Do library research on the activities of fourteen- to eighteen-year-olds in several other societies to find out which societies enforce school attendance, what kinds of schools exist, and whether some type of work is done in place of going to school.

2. Spend an evening watching television and evaluate the programs in terms of their educational value.

3. If you attend a public school, arrange interviews with persons (administrators, teachers, and students) connected with a private or parochial school. If you attend a private or parochial school, interview persons connected with a public school. Then compare your school with the other school. What is the difference in emphasis in the two schools? How do the curricula compare? What are the advantages and disadvantages of each?

4. Draw a map of your community showing the location of the various schools and the distribution of students within those schools. Find out what factors determine who goes to which school.

5. If you are attending a public school, conduct research on the financing of your school district. Find out where the money comes from (local, state, federal government), how much it costs per student per year, and how the money is spent (the school budget). What problems in financing does the school district face? How much has the budget increased recently? What solutions would you recommend?

6. If you attend a private or parochial school, study the finances of your school to find out where the money comes from. What financial problems are faced by your school? What solutions can you offer?

7. Investigate suggestions of various courts, especially in California and New Jersey, concerning new ways of funding education. Then talk to an official of your local school board about changing methods of school financing. Is your school being affected by any of these changing methods?

8. Choose a particular extracurricular activity in which you have participated. Construct a poster or bulletin board that illustrates the educational function which this extracurricular activity provides.

9. Obtain catalogs for the various kinds of institutions of higher education. How do they differ in programs, cost, objectives, and so on?

TOPICS FOR INQUIRY

1. Has your own education up to this point provided for the seven aspects of socialization stated in the chapter? Which primary functions do you feel are the most important? Which functions do you think have been accomplished most successfully by your schools?

2. Discuss the secondary functions of education. Do some of these functions hinder innovations in the educational program of the schools? How important is each secondary function to you? To society?

3. Describe your view of the ideal high school.

4. Debate: Most of the knowledge taught in the high schools has little practical value for the individual student.

5. Obtain the most recent edition of the U.S. Bureau of the Census, *Statistical Abstract of the United States* and compare current statistics with the statistics given in the chapter. What are the current trends in education?

6. Speculate about the effects of decreasing school enrollments on the community, the teaching profession, and on job opportunities for graduates.

7. Discuss the consequences of the increased proportion of high school graduates going on to college.

8. Debate: Our society places too much emphasis on a college education.

9. Discuss the advantages and disadvantages of private and public schools for elementary, secondary, and college education.

SUGGESTIONS FOR READING

NONFICTION

DAWSON, Helaine S., *On the Outskirts of Hope: Educating Youth from Poverty Areas.* McGraw-Hill, 1968 (and pap.). First-person accounts of ghetto youth in school settings.

DECKER, Sunny, *An Empty Spoon.* Harper & Row, 1969 (and pap.). A young white girl's story of two years of teaching English in a high school in Philadelphia's black ghetto.

HERNDON, James, *How to Survive in Your Native Land.* Simon & Schuster, 1971. A witty, personal description of teaching in a public school.

————, *The Way It Spozed to Be.* Simon & Schuster, 1968 or Bantam (pap.). This is a sad, funny story of life in a ghetto school and of an ill-fated, sometimes hilarious, attempt to beat the educational system.

LINDQUIST, Harry M. (ed.), *Education: Readings in the Processes of Cultural Transmission.* Houghton-Mifflin. 1970 (and pap.). A book of readings dealing with comparisons in education between the developed and the developing nations.

MEAD, Margaret, *Growing Up in New Guinea: A Comparative Study of Primitive Education.* Apollo, 1962 or Dell (pap.). A classic study of education and adolescence in the Manus society.

RIST, Ray C., *The Urban School: A Factory for Failure.* MIT Press, 1973. A firsthand, day-by-day study of the educational process at a St. Louis ghetto school.

SILBERMAN, Charles E., *Crisis in the Classroom.* Random House, 1970 (and pap.). A comprehensive view of the problems found in our American schools today.

FICTION

DAHLIN, Doris, *The Sit-in Game.* Translated from the Swedish by Joan Tate. Viking. Failing to find understanding from their teachers, a group of high school students stage a sit-in.

HUNTER, Evan. *The Blackboard Jungle.* Bentley. A realistic novel of a creative teacher attempting to communicate with his ghetto students.

KAUFMAN, Bel, *Up the Down Staircase.* Prentice-Hall. A humorous and heartwarming novel about a novice English teacher's experiences during her first few months with high school students.

MCLEOD, Ruth, *Buenos Dias, Teacher.* Messner. Set in a large city in California, the novel tells of the trials of a first-year teacher among students of an ethnic minority.

SKINNER, B. F., *Walden Two.* Macmillan (pap.). A fictional novel about life in an utopian society, where all learning is achieved through a reward system.

Highlight

How does education affect other social institutions?

A striking feature of modern society is the way its various parts fit together. Let's look at the interdependence of the institution of education and other social institutions. There is, for instance, a strong connection between schools and the political institution. Schools are often related directly to municipal, county, or state governments. Most public school districts are created by a municipal government. Other public school districts fall under the direct authority of the county or state. A school may also fall within the jurisdiction of a religious governing body, such as the Roman Catholic Church. Still other schools are established under law as private organizations.

Thus schools are closely related to their legal and political connections. Think about the implications for curriculum, teaching staff, and attendance requirements stemming from these connections. Imagine how schools would be different if they stood alone. How do the differences between public, private, and parochial schools reflect their different legal and political connections?

Another link is the interdependence of schools and the economic institution. Most schools are not profit-making organizations. In fact, unlike most businesses, the more "customers" they get, the more money it costs them. Public schools are funded through tax revenues. Often local taxing authorities must provide the bulk of the funds. What differences might result when financial backing is from religious organizations? How might schools be different if their financial support came mostly from students' tuition?

This interdependence of the educational and economic institutions means also that the economy is affected by schools. The labor market would be tremendously affected if there were no high schools or colleges. Would all those teen-agers be able to find jobs? We might have to encourage retirement at age fifty to open more job opportunities. And could business and industry train its own skilled labor force without the schools?

Finally, what about the interdependence of education and the institution of marriage and the family? What mutual influences exist between the school and the home? Do you think marriage patterns would be changed if there were no coeducational secondary schools or colleges?

At this point you might make a list of ways in which education influences and is influenced by some other social institutions. What relationships exist, for instance, between the school and religion?

Because of such factors as a lower birth rate, it appears that the school-age and college-age population of the United States may be smaller during the next twenty years than it has been in the last twenty. As a result, fewer schools may need to be built. There may be a decreased need for new teachers. Perhaps fewer school buildings will be in use. There may be an opportunity to cut school budgets—or to increase the quality of instruction.

How do you think schools could adapt to this situation? Consider specific ways in which the schools might be different from today. How do you think this projected change in the institution of education might affect other institutions?

15 Religion

▶ What is the difference between religion and a church?

▶ What are some religious roles?

▶ How do religion and culture influence each other?

SECTION 1:
Religious Structures and Functions

People in every society throughout the ages have pondered questions dealing with such matters as existence, purpose, and divinity. To help explain the unexplainable, provide a sense of purpose in life, and make the unknown future less threatening, every society has developed the institution of religion. All societies have developed values, norms, and roles related to religious beliefs.

Religion means many things to many people. However, we will define RELIGION as *a system of beliefs and practices by which people recognize the apparent existence of one or more supernatural beings and attempt to either control these beings or live in harmony with them.* The two important aspects of reli-

gion are belief and practices. Religion involves faith, which is belief unsupported by empirical evidence. These religious beliefs cause people to carry out specific practices, or behaviors, such as meditation, prayer, and religious ceremonies.

How Does the Sociologist Study Religion?

The content of religion is beyond the reach of everyday observation, and is regarded as sacred or holy. Therefore it is particularly difficult to study. One of the biggest problems for the sociologist is that the strongly held, often emotional beliefs associated with any particular religion make objectivity hard to achieve. As a scientist, however, the sociologist must follow the same guidelines of scientific research that would be used in studying any phenomena.

The sociologist cannot enter into the debate of whether or not there is a God. For this

269

Sociologists study how the teachings of a religion affect the behavior of its believers.

Sociologists also look for similarities in different events. They often are more concerned with the similarities among different religious beliefs than with their differences. For example, the theme of love is found in many of the world's great religions. Confucius said, "A heart set on love can do no wrong." Buddha said, "Hatred is not diminished by hatred at any time. Hatred is diminished by love—this is the eternal law." The Hebrew Scriptures of Judaism say, "Hatred stirs up strife, but love covers all sins." And Jesus Christ established the commandment, "You shall love your neighbor as yourself." Many such recurring themes are found in the world's various religions. These similarities are of interest to sociologists.

The sociological approach also examines how a specific religious perspective helps pattern human societies, and thereby affects the shape of history. It examines how individuals place themselves in the society by occupying or not occupying a religious role. Finally, the sociology of religion seeks to do what any other area of sociology does—it seeks to discover general laws of human behavior that will apply anywhere, at any time, for any population.

The Organization of Religion

From a sociologist's point of view, the organization of religion is similar to the organization of any other institution. Within the institution there are a number of large associations, many more smaller associations, still other small formal groups, and countless informal social groups. Some of these are relatively long in duration and others quite short-lived. Also involved in the organization of an institution are a great many social roles, which are attached to as many statuses or social positions.

As we begin to look more closely at religious structures, bear in mind the basic organizational similarity of the structures of

cannot be tested objectively, empirically, or logically. Neither can the sociologist make statements about whether such great religious leaders as Buddha, Mohammed, or Jesus Christ existed as real persons. The main concern of the sociologist is the effect that the belief in God or the teachings of religious leaders has on the social relationships of the believers. Every religion provides some kind of an ethical system that gives guidelines for human behavior. Sociologists study how believers in a particular religion actually do behave in their human relationships.

all institutions. Notice also the ways in which specific institutions differ in scope and purpose.

Informal Religious Structures

Many nontechnological societies make little distinction between the natural and supernatural. They explain most phenomena in terms of gods or a god. This fusion of the natural and supernatural is found in Greek mythology, where every event that takes place is related to one of the many gods. In such societies the people fear the supernatural. They therefore attempt to exert some sort of control over the gods to prevent the supernatural from harming them. Often fetishism develops. FETISHISM *is the belief that some object, either animate or inanimate, is possessed by indwelling spirits.* For example, some African tribes believe that the crocodile is the home of the spirits, and that when people die their souls go into the crocodile. The crocodile becomes a fetish. Members of these tribes make sacrifices of chickens to keep the spirits from harming them.

Formal Religious Structures

As societies become more complex, a distinction between the natural and the supernatural evolves. In tribal societies, religion is an integral part of people's lives. In more complex societies, religion becomes a separate aspect of life. When this happens, separate formal religious structures develop. FORMAL RELIGIOUS STRUCTURES *are secondary groups, organizations, and associations related to the beliefs and practices of religion.* Churches, denominations, sects, and cults are examples of formal religious structures.

Churches. A CHURCH *is a number of people organized for religious purposes, with a hierarchy of officials and a set of doctrines that provide some unity of belief and practice.* In our society the word "church" is used in several ways. We may refer to the church in the largest sense, meaning a whole body of doctrine, such as the Christian Church or the Buddhist Church. We also use the word "church" to refer to a building in which religious worship is conducted. The word "church" may refer to a local congregation,

The early Greeks explained many events of nature in terms of the gods. For example, in Greek mythology the movement of the sun is explained as the god Apollo riding in the sun chariot across the sky each day.

such as St. Mark's Community Church. We also speak of the Baptist Church, United Methodist Church, or Lutheran Church, although actually they are denominations.

Denominations. *A* DENOMINATION *is an association of people within the larger church.* The Baptists, Methodists, and Lutherans are separate denominations of the Christian Church. A denomination may include a number of congregations and places of worship. St. Mark's Community Church may be a local congregation of the Lutheran denomination, for example.

Sects. *A* SECT *is a small body of individuals who separate from a larger church or denomination.* A sect is usually characterized by a very strong "in-group" feeling, emphasis on purity of belief, and a hostility toward the secular world, which is viewed as "evil." As sects grow, they tend to lose these characteristics. They may eventually become denominations. A great number of Protestant denominations began as sects, since they originated as reform movements within the larger church that they broke away from. As these Protestant sects grew in size and adapted to the secular world, they became denominations.

Cults. *A* CULT *is a small local religious group characterized by one doctrine that stands out, an emotional attachment to the leaders, and displays of great devotion by the followers.* Often these cults engage in distinctive acts. One such cult, in West Virginia, centers around the handling of poisonous snakes. The followers of the cult do not worship the snakes. They use them to give testimony of their faith. The cult is based on the words of Jesus: "They shall take up serpents; and if they drink any deadly thing, it shall not hurt them; they shall lay hands on the sick, and they shall recover" (Mark 16:18). Since the follower is seldom bitten by the snakes, or, if bitten, usually recovers, the handling of the snakes provides evidence of the individual's faith and his or her claim to holiness.

Religious Roles

The social institution of religion provides a large number of specific roles that individuals play as they participate in religious activities. The following are some of the more common roles associated with religious structures.

The clergy. The title of clergy is applied to those persons who have special training in religion and theology and have been ordained or commissioned to carry out the work of the church. The three most familiar types of clergy in the United States are the priest, the minister, and the rabbi.

A *priest* is a person who is authorized to perform the sacred rites of the religion and serves as a mediator between the people and God. Usually it is the priest who offers sacrifices to God. For example, the priest in the Roman Catholic Church offers the sacrifice of the Mass.

A *minister* is an individual who is authorized to preach the gospel and administer the sacraments or ordinances of the church. The basic difference between a priest and a minister is that the minister does not offer sacrifices or serve as mediator between the people and God. In the Protestant churches, for example, ministers may provide counseling and offer guidance to people. But they do not serve as mediators between them and God. When ministers have a church or congregation under their charge they may also be referred to as pastors.

A *rabbi* is a person who is recognized as a learned scholar and teacher of Jewish law or as an appointed spiritual head of a Jewish community. The term "rabbi" means "master" or "teacher."

Laity. The laity are people of a religious faith who are not specially trained in religion or theology. They may be members of the church and may perform many roles, such as those of Sunday school teacher, board member, or lay reader.

Religious leader. A religious leader is a philosopher, or founder, who starts a new religion. In this role would be such persons as Prince Siddhartha (the Buddha), Ch'in K'ung (Confucius), Jesus Christ (the Messiah), or Ubu'l Kassim (Mohammed).

Missionary. A missionary is a person who takes the faith to nonbelievers. Missionaries carry out all kinds of activities. They may be members of the clergy, nurses, teachers, social workers, physicians, dentists, dietitians, engineers, agricultural specialists, or technicians. They may work on the other side of town or the other side of the world. The three religions most noted for using missionaries to win new converts to the faith are the Buddhist, Christian, and Moslem religions.

Evangelist. An evangelist is an itinerant preacher or revivalist. Since the word "evangel" refers to the message of redemption and salvation through Jesus Christ, an evangelist is someone who preaches this message.

Mystic. A mystic is an individual who has direct communication with the supernatural through dreams, visions, or other subjective experiences. Mystics are found in a great many religions, including the Christian faith.

In addition to those just mentioned there are many other religious roles, such as those of bishop, archbishop, monsignor, cardinal, pope, patriarch, deacon, elder, parish visitor, choir director, organist, cantor (singer in a synagogue), monk, and nun.

Religious Functions

Many of the functions of religion center around the individual, and therefore more

The man on the right is performing the religious role of an evangelist. He travels from place to place, preaching the gospel and attempting to revive people's religious faith.

properly fall within the sphere of psychology. These functions of religion for the individual believer would include providing him or her with a sense of purpose, making the inevitable reality of death more tolerable, providing a sense of security and a release from guilt coming from human errors, supplying a basis for personal values, establishing guidelines for daily living, and, in general, helping people adjust to times of stress, hardship, and crisis.

Although the functions of religion for the individual are important, the basic concern of sociology is with the causes and consequences of human relationships. Therefore we will consider the functions of religion that affect human relationships. How are people's relationships in groups and how is their behavior in the society as a whole influenced by religion?

Some of the social functions of religion are primary functions (those that are intended, or done on purpose). Some are secondary (those consequences that are unintended, although often very important). As you examine the following list, consider which of the functions are primary, and which are secondary.

1. Religion creates unity in the society because it gives people a common sense of purpose. In spite of the great number of denominations found within the United States, the overall effect of the Judeo-Christian ethic provides a unifying theme.

2. Religion gives stability to the society because it instills a common set of values and norms. The opposite is also true. A society that is deeply split on religion and has conflicting sets of values and norms is likely to be unstable.

3. Religious organizations provide many humanitarian and welfare services to the society. Religious organizations operate hospitals, children's homes, homes for the aged, schools, colleges, and relief agencies. They often help the needy in times of crisis.

4. Religion brings about the formation of many secondary groups that involve individuals in particular kinds of social relationships. The list of secondary groups and the resulting roles related to religion is almost endless, including such groups as Sunday school classes, women's and men's clubs, youth organizations, and prayer groups.

5. Religion guides people in their social relationships. Since most religions stress the way an individual should interact with others, religion exerts a strong influence on social control. In other words, religion provides a set of behavioral norms.

6. Religion may bring about serious conflicts among groups of persons who have differing religious beliefs. History books are filled with descriptions of religious wars, such as the Crusades between the Christians and Moslems, the Arab-Israeli conflict, and the conflict between the Hindus and Moslems in India and Pakistan. Another example is the great amount of anti-Semitism found in many parts of the world in recent times.

SECTION REVIEW

1. What is the sociological approach to studying religion?
2. How are formal religious structures organized?
3. Describe some religious roles, including several not mentioned in the text.
4. What are the social functions of religion?

KEY TERMS

Explain each term and give an example of each.

church	informal religious
clergy	structure
cult	laity
denomination	missionary
evangelist	mystic
fetishism	religion
formal religious	religious leader
structure	sect

Religion has played a very important part in the history of Northern Ireland. Scenes of violence between Catholics and Protestants occurred many times during the 1970's.

SECTION 2:
Religion and Culture

One very important aspect of religion that sociologists study is the interaction between religion and culture. As you know, culture is extremely influential in shaping our lives. It directly determines the way in which we see and define all our experiences. Perhaps the most important aspect of culture is its ability to define situations that might otherwise be chaotic. Imagine, for instance, trying to understand a baseball game or a religious service without the benefit of the cultural definitions attached to it.

A major factor in defining any situation is a system of values—a set of priorities on what is good and bad, right and wrong, proper and improper. In every society it is the religion, or the religious orientation, that provides this core of values. Religion shapes the cultural values of the society. And at the same time the cultural values shape religion. How does religion both influence, and become influenced by, culture?

Some Characteristics of Religion and Culture

One characteristic that is common to both culture and religion is a wide range of variation and diversity. All societies have religion. But the particular religious expression is

A number of people rely on good luck charms during times of stress or uncertainty, believing that such objects will help protect them from misfortune.

rarely the same from society to society. The extent of religious diversity in organization, forms, and belief is enormous. Just consider the wide range of societies studied by anthropologists—from the simplest to the most complex. Virtually any object or happening has had religious significance in some society.

A second characteristic is that, although there is a great deal of religious variation, nevertheless people tend to be quite ethnocentric about their religion. That is, with a few notable exceptions, people everywhere tend to see their own religion as the true expression of divine providence. At the same time, they regard the religions of others as being in error. The concept of sending missionaries out to the "savages" is an expression of this ethnocentrism.

A third characteristic is that religious beliefs and practices, and magic, tend to be relied on during ventures of great importance, when the outcome is uncertain. For example, in a well-known study of the Trobriand Islanders in the South Pacific, the anthropologist Bronislaw Malinowski found that no magic was applied to villagers fishing in the inner lagoon, where everything was safe. But when fishing boats went out into the open sea, where there was danger, an extensive magic ritual was performed to insure their safety. The same general principle can be applied to our own society. Religious beliefs and practices are commonly found at such important and uncertain events as birth, sickness, and death.

A fourth characteristic of the relationship between religion and culture is related to the complexity of the society. As societies become more complex, all of the institutions become more varied and more easily separated from one another. The result is that religion becomes increasingly detached from everyday life. Eventually what we call a secular society emerges. A secular society is one that is officially neutral with regard to religion. Our own Constitution, in the First Amendment, reflects this secularization by separating the functions of church and state.

The Meaning of Religion

What does religion mean, in terms of culture? Perhaps the core of religion is the concept of the *sacred*. Those things are sacred that are set apart from the other elements of a culture. They are, in a sense, forbidden. Furthermore, sacred things involve or require worship, and involve faith and moral commitment. To illustrate the concept of the sacred, we can refer again to Malinowski and his study of the Trobrianders. Malinowski distinguishes between religion and magic on the basis of the sacred and its meaning in social relationships. Religion, to Malinowski, involves those sacred things in a society that are part of a cultural situation. That is, they are called into use as a matter of course, rather than to achieve a specific goal. Sacred rites involving marriage, for example, are religious in nature. They are performed primarily because the god or gods want them to be performed, rather than because they will insure a healthy, happy marriage.

On the other hand, magic, to Malinowski, has a practical or utilitarian meaning. Magic is performed in order to get something done. People fishing out in the open sea needed a magical ceremony to insure their safe return. Magic is also used to get yams to grow, or to insure that enemies have bad fortune.

The same distinction between religion and magic exists in our own society. Religion in-

volves sacred things as a matter of course. People go to church on Sunday not to insure that they will have good fortune through the following week, but because God requires it. Similarly we baptize, confirm, marry, and bury people at various intervals for religious reasons. On the other hand, we also practice magic. We carry rabbits' feet, avoid walking under ladders, and follow a variety of other superstitions. Furthermore we, like the Trobriander, are hesitant to admit that these practices are magic.

Religion and Cultural Change

Another aspect of religion and culture is the relationship between religion and social and cultural change. Perhaps the most famous sociological study on the relationship of religion and the development of modern society is Max Weber's *The Protestant Ethic and the Spirit of Capitalism*, first published in 1904. Weber's concern was with "modern society"—the world of modern capitalism characterized by efficiency, rationality, and the drive for profit. Modern society seemed to him to be fundamentally different from the kinds of societies that preceded it. And he wanted to know how it had come about. Why did modern society develop when it did, and where it did?

Weber noted a parallel between the changes that were taking place in society and in religion. He saw a connection between the development of modern capitalism and the rise of Protestantism, especially Calvinism, in the 1500's. Weber maintained that the Protestant was affected by Martin Luther's and John Calvin's concept of the "calling." This Protestant concept required individuals to make positive efforts at mastering the world instead of simply following traditional practices, as was more characteristic of the Catholic world. It encouraged people to seek out an identity in the world, particularly the business world, as opposed to relying on religious vocations.

Weber argued, further, that John Calvin's doctrine of predestination contributed to the relationship between capitalism and Protestantism. Predestination means that a person is destined from the beginning of time to be either saved or damned. Calvin held that the individual was predestined from the beginning, and could do nothing to change the situation. Nevertheless, there were signs that indicated whether the person was saved or damned. The main sign, according to Calvin, was success at worldly undertakings. It seemed to Weber that this religious doctrine contributed to the growth of capitalism. Weber argued that Protestants, unsure of their position but eager for signs indicating

Andrew Carnegie, the famous industrialist, followed the Protestant Ethic. A poor Scottish immigrant, he became one of the richest men in the world through hard work and individual effort.

that they were saved, tried all the harder to achieve business success to prove that they were among the "elect."

Also, Weber found that the Protestant notion of thrift and frugality influenced society. This notion requires that the individual make a lot of money, but at the same time not spend too much of it. The money should be put back into the business. And the individual must avoid indulging in material excesses. Weber quoted Benjamin Franklin's maxims, such as "A penny saved is a penny earned," as representative of Protestant thinking on the subject. This Protestant view encouraged the reinvestment of profits and the resulting increase in business successes.

Weber then contrasted the influence of the Protestant concepts with Roman Catholic values. He noted the Protestant influence of the calling, predestination, and emphasis on thrift and frugality. He then noted the Roman Catholic stress on tradition, on eternal salvation achieved through the sacraments of the church, on "otherworldliness," and on the prohibition of usury, or the lending of funds for profit.

Weber's purpose was not, of course, to claim that the Protestant religion was better, or worse, than the Roman Catholic religion. Neither did he intend to indicate that Protestantism *caused* the rise of modern capitalism. Rather, the two were related culturally to each other. The conditions responsible for one also helped the development of the other. Weber wanted to indicate the relationship between religious values and other cultural elements. He showed that religion and culture do not exist in a vacuum, independent from each other. They are part of a system, influencing each other. Weber referred to the relationship between the values of Calvinism and the rise of capitalism as the *Protestant Ethic*.

Actually, in the Western world, and especially in the United States, the Protestant

Success through hard work is a value that many people in our society still hold in high regard today.

Ethic has jumped across religious lines. Catholics, Jews, and nonreligious individuals, as well as Protestants, have come under the influence of the Protestant Ethic. This does not mean that people are worrying about predestination and whether or not they will be saved. It means that the values of the Protestant Ethic—hard work, thrift, and individual effort—have become the traditional values of American society.

There are numerous examples today of the link between religion and culture in our society. For instance, studies have related religious affiliation to social class, voting behavior, attitudes and values, and family relations. One authority on the sociology of religion has stated that the religious factor is as important as any other single factor in determining social and cultural behavior.

SECTION REVIEW

1. What are some characteristics of religion?
2. What is the concept of the sacred?
3. How do religion and magic differ?
4. What is Weber's theory on the relationship between Protestantism and capitalism? Do you agree with his theory? Why or why not?

KEY TERMS

Define each of the following terms.

magic   sacred
Protestant Ethic

PROJECTS AND ACTIVITIES

1. Study a religion or denomination using the sociological approach.

2. Choose one of the Eastern religions (such as Taoism, Confucianism, Hinduism, or Buddhism) and one of the Western religions (such as Judaism, Christianity, or Islam). Make a list of similarities and differences in the beliefs and practices of the two religions.

3. Construct a collage showing the various ways people all over the world worship.

4. Study the church page in your local newspaper (usually in Saturday's edition) to determine the sermon topics, programs, and activities being carried on in the churches in your community. Evaluate these in terms of whether they relate to current topics and problems in the community.

5. Do research to discover the various types of activities carried out by missionaries in the new type of evangelism engaged in by churches today.

6. Visit a church, synagogue, or temple of some religion other than your own in order to gain insight into the religious beliefs and practices of others.

7. Do research on wars in the past that have involved religious conflicts.

8. Examine the statistics for membership of the major religions in the United States over the past fifteen years. What trends do you see? Is membership increasing or decreasing? How is the proportionate membership of the religions changing?

9. All religions give guidelines for people to follow in their relationships with others. Do research on the major religions of the world to determine the similarities and differences in their guidelines for human relationships. Try to determine how each of the various religions has affected the interactions of the people who practice its specific teachings.

10. Write a newspaper article on "The Importance of Religion in the American Culture."

11. Read Nathaniel Hawthorne's nineteenth century American novel, *The Scarlet Letter*. Evaluate the effect that religion had on the life of the individuals in the story.

TOPICS FOR INQUIRY

1. Discuss what you consider to be positive aspects of religions. Does religion sometimes involve what some people might consider to be negative aspects? Explain.

2. What are the differences between denominations, sects, and cults? Give examples for each. Did some denominations originate as sects or cults?

3. Compare the roles of the clergy and lay members in some church, denomination, sect, or cult. How are these roles similar and in what ways do they differ?

4. Discuss: If the people of the world followed the basic teachings of the world's great religions, the world would be a better place in which to live.

5. Debate: America is a secular society.

6. Which of the religious functions would you consider to be primary and which secondary? Why?

7. What do you feel is the single most important function of religion in our society today? Explain.

8. Debate: Churches should not engage in controversial issues such as poverty, civil rights, war, and international relations but should devote their energies to bringing people to God.

9. What influence do you think culture has had on your religious beliefs?

SUGGESTIONS FOR READING

NONFICTION

DUBOS, René, *A God Within*. Scribner, 1972 (and pap.). A famous biologist gives a positive philosophy for a more complete fulfillment of human potentiality.

FREUND, Julien, *The Sociology of Max Weber*. Translated by Mary Ilford. Pantheon, 1968. A study of the sociological ideas, concepts, and methodologies of Max Weber.

GAER, Joseph, *What the Great Religions Believe*. Dodd, 1963 or New American Library (pap.). A very readable discussion of the beliefs and practices of the followers of the world's great religions.

MALINOWSKI, Bronislaw, *Magic, Science, and Religion, and Other Essays*. Doubleday, 1954 (pap.). A series of essays, including Malinowski's understanding of the sacred and his studies of magic and religious beliefs and practices.

NOSS, John B., *Man's Religions*. Fifth ed., Macmillan, 1974. A complete guide to the religions of the world.

OURSLER, Will, *Religion: Out or Way Out*. Stackpole, 1968. The author explores the many new forces affecting churches and religious life in America. A look at what's happening in and around churches today.

ROSTEN, Leo (ed.), *Religions of America*. Simon & Schuster, 1975. An almanac of religion in America. Contains many articles discussing the beliefs of the many religions, statistics on membership, changes in churches, and so on.

FICTION

BALL, John, *The Fourteenth Point*. Little, Brown. A minister and a millionaire decide the whole world should have one religion.

BARRETT, William E., *Lilies of the Field*. Doubleday (and pap.). An easygoing black man is trapped by the Mother Superior of a newly established convent in the Southwest into building a chapel because she thinks God sent him to do the job.

COZZENS, James Gould, *Men and Brethren*. Harcourt Brace Jovanovich. The problems facing a large urban church in New York City.

GOLDING, William, *The Spire*. Harcourt Brace Jovanovich (pap.). Through the use of symbolism, the author shows a man of the cloth tormented by his lack of faith in himself and his religion.

GREENE, Graham, *The Power and the Glory*. Bantam (pap.). The struggles of a priest who continues to administer to his parishioners during the suppression of the church in Mexico.

HAWTHORNE, Nathaniel, *The Scarlet Letter*. Holt, Rinehart & Winston or Dell or Dutton (pap.). A classic American novel about New England Puritanism and its psychological effects.

LEWIS, Sinclair, *Elmer Gantry*. New American Library (pap.). This novel dramatically portrays the hypocrisy of a minister and his inner rage.

MALAMUD, Bernard, *The Fixer*. Dell (pap.). Yakov Bov, a simple Russian-Jewish peasant, is accused and convicted of murdering a boy in anti-Semitic tsarist Russia.

MICHENER, James A., *The Source*. Random House or Fawcett World (pap.). A fictional tracing of the beginnings of religion with an emphasis on the development of Judaism, built around a saga of the current Arab-Israeli situation.

16 The Economy and Government

► How is an economic system organized?

► What are the functions of government?

► In what ways are the economy and government interrelated?

SECTION 1:
Economic Structures and Functions

We can't have everything we want. There is a limit to the amount of resources available to us. All societies are faced with this situation—in which the wants of the people are greater than the availability of resources. The economic structure provides a basis for allocating and distributing the available resources. It also helps to regulate what people want beyond what they have. *The* ECONOMIC INSTITUTION *is the system of norms, values, and roles through which the patterned and orderly distribution of the limited resources is achieved.*

Suppose there were no economic structure to regulate the distribution of resources. Competition for the limited resources would

become intense. Individuals would feel unsure in possessing and using whatever resources they had. Chaos would result. No one can be secure in the present or plan for the future if there are no rules regulating competition, no predictability in behavior. The economic structure permits people to gain access to economic resources in an orderly way.

Societies vary widely in their economic institutions. The more advanced a society is technologically, and the more specialized and elaborate its division of labor, the more complex will be its system for the production and distribution of resources. Thus industrialized societies have very complex economic systems and must develop many formal economic structures.

Formal Economic Structures

There are certain essential parts of a formal economic structure. These parts include a system for the production of goods,

A production system changes resources, such as trees, from their natural state into goods.

a system for providing services, some system of distribution to make these goods and services available to people, consumers to purchase the goods and services, and a system of exchange.

Production systems. The function of a production system is to produce goods for the society. To carry out this function, a production system must have the following three basic ingredients. First, it must have *raw materials* or natural resources from which to make the goods. These raw materials may consist of fertile land, minerals, forests, animals, fish, birds, or water resources. A second necessary ingredient is *capital.* Capital may be defined as wealth devoted to the production and distribution of goods or services. It can be in the form of money or goods. If money, it might be cash on hand, bank deposits, or stocks and bonds. If in the form of capital goods, it might be raw materials, livestock, crops, tools, machinery, and other goods that can be used to produce more goods. The third necessary ingredient is *labor.* Raw materials and capital cannot produce goods without a labor force to run the machines and convert raw materials into finished products. Many roles are involved in the labor force, such as those of managers, scientists, technicians, machinery operators, and farmers.

Worker roles are essential in production and are interdependent. The workers, however, can do nothing without raw materials and capital. A production system must have all three basic ingredients—raw materials, capital, and labor.

Service systems. Not only do the members of the society need certain material goods, but they also require certain services from others. For example, people often become ill and need the services of a doctor. They might become involved in some legal problem and need the services of a lawyer. A person may wish to build a house and desire the services of an architect. Managers of business and industry find that they don't have time to keep the records of the company. They require the services of accountants, auditors, and clerical personnel. The services of teachers are needed for the education of children. Religious organizations must have specially trained clergy to carry out the programs and services of the church, synagogue, or mosque. With all the complex consumer goods now available, individuals are often in need of people who are specially trained to fix their cars, home appliances, or television sets. Communities require the services of police officers and firefighters, of restaurants and public transportation.

As a society becomes more complex, the number of services that people want increases. Therefore, one of the characteristics of a modern society is the expansion of the service sector. In fact, in the United States the service system now occupies a greater part of the economic order than in the past. It is growing faster than the economy as a whole.

Distribution systems. Neither the production system nor the service system can operate without a system of distribution. The goods and services must be made available to consumers, if these two systems are to be adequate. In the case of the production system, for instance, manufacturers must distribute their finished products and receive payment so that they can purchase

materials and labor to produce more goods.

For a distribution system to work, three elements are necessary. The first is the product or service. The second is capital to provide for the buildings, such as warehouses, retail stores, medical clinics, and barber shops, and for the personnel needed in distribution. The third element is the labor force required for the distribution of goods and services. Many different types of laborers, such as warehouse and dock workers, truck drivers, railroad engineers, managers, accountants, wholesale and retail salespeople, and clerical workers, are needed in distribution.

The distribution system may be quite simple or very complex. A small plant may produce a product that is sold at the plant itself. On the other hand, a large plant may produce a product that is shipped to wholesalers all over the country, who store it in huge warehouses. By keeping large supplies

Labor is an essential part of the distribution system. Through the efforts of workers such as this one, crates of goods are unloaded from trucks and distributed to the consumer.

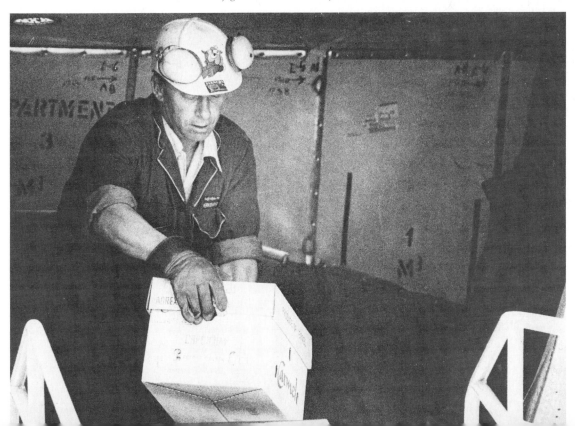

of the product in warehouses, they can meet the rise and fall of consumer demand for the product. The wholesalers then sell the product to retail outlets, which, in turn, sell it to the general public.

Distribution systems for manufactured products are usually more complex than distribution systems for services. For example, television sets produced by a manufacturer are shipped to regional warehouses owned by the manufacturer. Then the manufacturer's sales force sells the sets to distributors (wholesalers), who move them to their own warehouses. Next, representatives of the distributors sell the sets to retail outlets, where they are again stored until sold. When sold by the retail salespeople, the sets are delivered to the homes of purchasers and adjusted for proper reception by an installer.

In the case of services, the distribution is often much simpler. For instance, lawyers have a service to offer the public. To make this service available, a lawyer may simply rent an office and hire a secretary-receptionist to set up appointments and greet the people when they come into the office. Or lawyers may join a law firm that provides for the distribution of their services.

Some distribution organizations handle both goods and services. For example, the retail store that sold the television sets is likely to have a service department that repairs defective sets for the public. Also, most automobile dealers offer services as well as sales.

Consumers. In many ways the consumer is the most important person in the economic system. Without the consumer there would be no need for production, service, and distribution systems. Usually people who play the role of consumers also play some role in the labor force. The individual consumer must have income with which to purchase the products and services provided by the systems of distribution. Not every consumer is employed in the labor force. But some member of the family must be employed or have sufficient capital if the family is to be a consuming family.

A system of exchange. There must be some system of exchange to pay for goods and services. Many simple societies have used the *barter system,* in which goods are traded for other goods. However, a complex society must develop a *monetary system* in which some symbol of value is used as a medium of exchange. It is impossible for the automobile dealer to accept the farmer's cows, the miner's coal, or the lawyer's advice in return for an automobile. Therefore governments print and coin money that is backed by some goods of value, such as gold or silver, or, ultimately, by confidence in the government. A very complex system of exchange allows people to use credit cards and checkbook money—personal checks, rather than currency—to pay debts. Complex exchange systems also include a system of credit, whereby individuals or firms may purchase goods and services that will be paid for at some later date. A complete monetary system would involve systems of bank loans and deposits, insurance, exchange of stocks and bonds, the buying and selling of real estate, and some regulation of money and banking.

Economic Functions

These, then, are the major parts of the economic system. Consider now five of its major functions. The first function is primary. The other four are secondary. Perhaps you will think of a number of other secondary functions. The economic system:

1. Determines the production, distribution, and consumption of goods and services.

2. Causes some socialization through on-the-job training, consumer experiences, advertising, and the mass media.

3. Brings about a distribution of power.

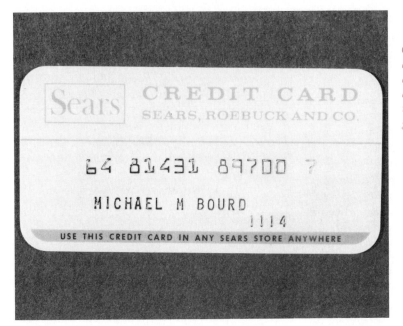

Credit cards have been a rapidly expanding part of our system of exchange. What are some advantages and disadvantages of using credit cards to pay for goods and services?

The economic system sets up many levels of power, such as management and organized labor. In addition, people's economic position affects the distribution of political power, since their economic position influences how they will vote in local, state, and national elections. There is a relationship between people's economic status and their political affiliation in the United States.

4. Influences both the material and nonmaterial aspects of the culture. The economic system changes the material culture by introducing new products, which become an important part of the "way of life" of the people in a society. The economic system changes the nonmaterial culture by influencing the values and norms that govern human relationships.

5. Affects the stratification of the population. By giving various levels of status and income to the members of the population, the economic system plays a very important part in social stratification. The economic roles that individuals assume largely determine their status in the social system.

SECTION REVIEW

1. Why is the economic institution necessary to a society?
2. What are the essential components of a formal economic structure and how are they related to one another?
3. What three basic ingredients are necessary to a production system? What three elements are needed for a distribution system to work?
4. How does the barter system differ from a monetary system? What is involved in a complex system of exchange?
5. Name some primary and secondary functions of an economic system.

KEY TERMS

Define or explain each term.

barter system	labor
capital	monetary system
consumer	production system
distribution system	raw materials
economic institution	service system

289

SECTION 2:
Governmental Structures, Characteristics, and Functions

Societies have norms to regulate the material needs and wants of people. They also have norms to define and locate authority over human relationships so that individuals will act in an orderly, predictable way with others. A system of formal and informal norms is needed to protect and preserve the social order. *The* POLITICAL INSTITUTION *is that system of norms, values, and roles which*

In most large complex societies the political institution includes an army, which serves to protect the society against outside attacks.

defines and locates the ultimate authority in a society and the agencies through which that authority is established. Many norms that are backed by limited authority, such as those of schools or places of work, are not within the political institution largely because their authority is not ultimate. If we feel that we've been treated unjustly under those norms we may appeal to the ultimate authority, the law, which is enacted through the political institution.

Political institutions are necessary for the individual, whose survival and socialization require norms that are publicly supported and enforced. Political institutions are also necessary for the welfare of the society as a whole. There must be a means of settling disputes, of maintaining a common justice and righting the wrongs that people commit. There must be a way to apply sanctions concerning serious forms of deviant behavior. There must be an authoritative way to balance the activities of different persons, groups, and organizations and thus preserve the social order. Finally, there must be some organized way of dealing with problems arising from relationships with other societies. These require some form of organization that can speak and act for the society and marshal its resources effectively in intersocial relations.

Political Structures

Most small, tribal societies have informal political structures, in which the functions of government are carried out by the family and clan. In many such societies authoritative social control is exercised through lineage based on extended family relationships. In other tribal societies the village or band rather than lineage is the basic unit in organization. The village council of elders or a leader may possess considerable informal influence. There is a high degree of agreement concerning social norms in these small societies. Any violations usually bring forth similar attitudes of disapproval and use of sanctions.

When the populations of societies number in the many thousands, however, and become split into many different kinds of interest groups and organizations, informal and custom-dominated methods of solving political problems no longer work. In such societies the body of norms becomes very large. Role specialization increases. The priority among norms becomes more controversial, and competition among different interests and goals increases. At this stage a society must develop more formal governmental machinery or it will disintegrate, or break up into smaller units, or perhaps be taken over by some other society that does have governmental organization.

Characteristics of Government

The fully developed governing organization of a society displays certain basic characteristics. These characteristics can be found in the modern industrial societies of today.

The government acts as the agent of the society as a whole. This applies to both the internal affairs of the society and its external affairs—its relationships with other societies. Since the government is the agent of the society as a whole, the actions of the government should be guided by requirements of the society's welfare rather than by the special interests of particular groups or organizations in the country. However, the distinction between private or local interests and the society's interests is not always easy to draw. For example, consider the problem of determining national defense expenditures in the United States. Money spent for national defense serves the economic interests of the companies that

obtain defense contracts. It also helps those localities in the country in which defense expenditures provide large numbers of jobs. Faced by pressures from companies and localities, the government has to determine just what size the military budget should be. It must somehow distinguish between necessary military expenses and those which are unnecessary but profitable to contractors or localities. But whatever the difficulty of such problems, the government's actions are on behalf of the nation as a whole, even if private interests influence that action.

Government claims a monopoly on the legitimate use of force. The government reserves to itself and insists on the right to use physical force when necessary to fulfill its functions. All use of force or the agents of force, such as police organizations, by nongovernmental interests must be under the sanction of the government. Also, such uses must be according to governmental rules and restrictions. The governments of modern nations permit no private military forces at all.

Government has jurisdiction over a specific territory. Many associations, such as labor unions, professional associations, and places of work, have authority over their members. But they do not have ultimate authority over a territory. The authority that associations may have within the bounds of their property should not be confused with the territorial jurisdiction of the state, which is a political body. The Roman Catholic Church has worldwide religious authority over its members. But the individual church member is under the civil authority of the government of that country in which he or she resides. It is a characteristic of governments that they exercise their jurisdiction within a specific territory.

Government exists everywhere on earth. None of us can avoid national jurisdiction.

True, governments may permit individuals to change citizenship. But this is up to the governments, and must be done according to the provisions established for that purpose. Many persons became stateless (without a nationality) as a result of the upheavals accompanying World War II. Such persons are, however, under the jurisdiction of whichever state they now live in. All populated areas of the world fall under the political dominion of some state. Even unpopulated land areas not claimed by a particular state, such as Antarctica, fall under international agreements. Such agreements have authority over individuals who enter these areas.

Government has sovereignty in international relations. That is, the state is an independent entity in its relationships with other states. The total effect of the preceding characteristics of central political organization is to give government supreme power in the area of international relations.

Can you think of any other basic characteristics of government?

Functions of Government

We might consider five basic functions of political structures: formalizing norms, administering sanctions, settling conflicts, providing services, and protecting the society and its citizens in international relations.

Formalizing the norms of the society. One of the functions that governments perform is to take some of the various informal norms of the society and formalize them into laws. These laws can be divided into three types, based on their origin. *Constitutional laws* are those formalized norms that appear in the consitution of the state. Usually constitutional laws describe the broad duties of the state to the individual citizen and the duties of the citizen to the state. *Statutory laws* are the laws that have been enacted by a legisla-

tive body of the state, such as the acts of Congress, state legislatures, or city councils. *Common laws* are a body of unwritten laws built over the centuries on local custom and precedent, and further developed by judicial decisions. They originate from the judicial branch of government rather than the legislative branch. When a judge is required to make a decision and no specific laws exist, he or she is guided by the past rulings of other judges in similar cases. Common laws become "common," or part of the tradition of a country. They are not permanent. They change as new judicial interpretations are made, although they do maintain a high degree of continuity.

We can also classify laws according to their function. Some laws are *prohibitive laws,* in that they state what an individual or group cannot do. These are the taboos of the society that have been formalized into law. They relate to such activities as murder, theft, and destruction of property. Other laws are *regulatory,* in that they regulate the behavior of the citizens of the state. Some people feel that these laws restrict their freedom. Yet by regulating certain activities these laws sometimes provide greater freedom for everyone. For example, there are laws that regulate our movement on the streets and sidewalks of our communities. Laws tell us which way we can drive on the street, what speed is allowed, and when we must stop and give the right-of-way to others. Regulatory laws enable the citizens to go about their activities in an effective and orderly way. Other regulatory laws apply to such areas as the value of currency, the use of natural resources, imports and exports, marriage and divorce, wages, hours, and working conditions, and the educational system.

Administering sanctions to those who violate the law. The state has the final authority and power to administer sanctions to those who violate the norms of the society. The government, which formalizes most of the important mores and taboos of the society, also performs the function of applying sanctions to enforce these laws. The enforcement of the laws is in the hands of the executive branch of government. The specific sanctions that will be applied are determined by the judicial branch. These sanctions may take the form of fines, imprisonment, or the death penalty.

Settling conflicts within the society. In any society conflicts will develop between individuals and groups. In modern societies these conflicts may involve such areas as property rights, inheritances, divorce, personal liability, bankruptcy, and payment of debts. Some provision must be made for settling these disputes. The state has the final authority to settle these conflicts through its system of courts.

Providing services for the members of the society. A modern complex society requires many services that private organizations cannot effectively supply. Therefore the government performs the function of providing a great number of services for its citizens. Some of these are roads, schools, libraries, parks and playgrounds, the development of natural resources, and welfare programs.

Protecting the society and its members in international relations. Individuals in a society have few means with which to protect themselves in case of invasion by other societies. Therefore the state provides protection for its members and itself. Governments protect their citizens by using diplomacy, international agreements and treaties, or by going to war. The United States government, for example, provides a number of persons who serve as ambassadors, consuls, and representatives to other states and to the United Nations. The federal government also provides an army, navy, and air force to protect the citizens and the

Laws against trespassing are regulatory laws. They regulate people's behavior partly by applying sanctions to those who disobey.

interests of the society against other societies. To perform this function governments must tax their citizens adequately to pay for the diplomatic corps and the military forces. At the same time the state must arrange for some of its citizens to serve in the military, whether by conscription or some voluntary means.

1. Why is the political institution necessary to a society?
2. How do informal political structures differ from formal political structures?
3. What are some basic characteristics of government?
4. Name five basic functions of political structures. Can you think of other functions?

KEY TERMS

Explain and give an example of each term.

common law
constitutional law
political institution

prohibitive law
regulatory law
statutory law

SECTION 3:
The Relationship of Government to Economy

Now that we've discussed both economic and governmental structures and functions, we may look at the relationships. The economic and political institutions are closely related in many ways. One example is the establishment of laws requiring people to meet their contracted financial obligations. Imagine what the effects on the economic institution would be if individuals or organizations ignored their financial obligations whenever they wished. Without laws these obligations could not even be uniformly defined, much less enforced. The economic institutions of all complex societies would quickly crumble.

Another aspect of the relationship of the two institutions is the development of gov-

ernment control in the economic realm. The growth of technology, the vastly increased size of economic enterprises, such as giant corporations, and the development of national and world markets have brought changes and problems. These changes and problems have led to increased governmental regulations of economic activity. Times of national crisis, such as depressions and wars, have been marked by sharp increases in the use of governmental power and authority to regulate the economy. Some governments have assumed extensive control over the economic institutions of their societies on ideological grounds, as in totalitarian (authoritarian) states.

Politico-Economic Systems

The modes of relationship of government to the economy have been so varied in modern societies that political scientists have developed a number of types of such relationships. Through observations of general practices in many societies, they have found four types: capitalism, communism, fascism, and socialism. Although a society may exhibit some features of more than one type, most nations fall within one of these categories.

Capitalism. A capitalistic politico-economic system is characterized by private ownership and management of economic resources. Private enterprise does, however, have some limits. The government usually reserves ultimate rights to protect the public interest. For example, there is government operation and regulation in the United States in those areas where competition among private owners is very inefficient or where monopolies develop in conflict with the public interest, such as with highways, waterways, and public utilities. Despite government operation and regulation in these and many other areas, however, our economy is still basically capitalist because

Communism practices collective ownership and state regulation of production. These workers are preparing the soil for planting on a collective farm in the Soviet Union.

ownership is overwhelmingly private. The profit motive is still the main stimulus to production and participation in business.

Communism. The politico-economic system that contrasts most sharply with capitalism is communism. Communist theory maintains that there should be no private property beyond strictly private possessions. It rests on two basic assumptions. One assumption if that the first and most fundamental effort of human beings is economic. This effort is to provide the basic needs of survival—food, clothing, and shelter. All other institutional forms—familial, educational, religious, political—are determined by the type of economic organization.

A second major assumption in communist theory is that all value in economic goods is produced by the labor that people put forth to transform raw materials into desired products. Since the value of products comes from the efforts of workers, profits resulting from private ownership of the means of production are seen as exploiting the workers. Instead, all such value should be reserved for or returned to the people as a whole through collective ownership.

From a practical point of view perhaps the

greatest problem confronting communism in modern complex societies is how to prevent collective ownership, which is really government ownership, from developing into totalitarianism. This development occurs because of the great concentration of political and economic power in the state as communism is being established. The problem of how to return this power to the people has not yet been solved.

Fascism. The fundamental principle of fascism is "state absolutism." According to this principle, the state has meaning and interests that go beyond the welfare of its citizens. The rulers of the state see themselves as invested with the power and responsibility of governing to promote these overriding interests. Fascist regimes are militaristic. They view all social institutions as existing primarily to serve the state in its military adventures. There is, therefore, rigid state control of the economy. Fascist regimes are totalitarian. Any democratic process for the selection of rulers would be dangerous to the state's interests (which are defined by the rulers).

Socialism. Socialism is a politico-economic system in which the major economic enterprises, including both industries and public utilities, are owned and regulated by the government. Many different patterns of distribution of government and private ownership are possible. Considerable private ownership and operation of smaller economic enterprises may coexist with large-scale government ownership and operation. Socialism can exist in a democratic or undemocratic framework. Many countries, such as those of Scandinavia, are highly socialized and democratic. In these countries, the people participate in representative government. And the government's operation of basic industries and utilities is devoted to serving the public.

As you can see, each of these four systems includes both economic and political aspects. How does each system meet a fundamental need of the society? How does each achieve a measure of social control?

SECTION REVIEW

1. How are government and the economy related?
2. What are the four basic types of politico-economic systems?
3. What are some advantages and disadvantages of each system?

KEY TERMS

Define and give an example of each term.

capitalism	fascism
communism	socialism

PROJECTS AND ACTIVITIES

1. Visit a large factory and observe the natural resources used, the capital involved, and the labor force. Notice the various roles played by the workers in the division of labor. What is the final product? What is done with it?

296

2. Select a specific product that you would like to buy and carefully investigate the various brands available, including the durability, design, and price of each. You might also consult one of the consumer guide magazines. Then choose the brand that you feel would be the best buy and explain your reasons for deciding on that brand.

3. Do a research study of labor unions. Interview some labor union officials and some representatives of management, if possible. What have labor unions obtained for their workers?

4. Construct a game that is based on the economic factors of our society. You might get some ideas from considering a game such as "Monopoly."

5. Visit a business organization that provides services to the public, such as a law office, bank, engineering firm, or repair shop. Determine how the organization makes the services of the individual specialists available to the public. What are the advantages of the organization over each specialist offering his or her services to the public individually? Is it most advantageous for the specialist or for the possible user of the service?

6. Construct a poster or bulletin board that shows the production of some product and its distribution into the consumer's home.

7. Make a comparative study of the governments of the United States and Canada. In what ways are they very similar? In what ways are they different? What are the advantages and disadvantages of each?

8. Watch a television series that is based on some aspect of government, such as the police, courts, or legislature. Then write your own television drama as one program in the series.

9. Visit a legislative body (such as Congress, a state legislature, or city council) in session and write a report on its activities.

10. Conduct research on the public parks and recreation facilities provided by all levels of government in your area. Are these facilities adequate? How might they be improved?

11. Obtain a copy of the laws of the town, village, city, or county (if an unincorporated area) in which you live. Study these laws. Are most laws prohibitive or regulatory? Are any of the laws outdated? Do you feel any of the laws are unfair and should be changed? Why?

12. Carry out research on the economic and political structures of the People's Republic of China. How are they interrelated?

1. In the free enterprise system of capitalism we tend to assume that competition provides the best quality goods at the lowest possible price. Is this always true, or is it possible that competition may actually produce the opposite—inferior goods at higher prices? Explain your answer.

2. Discuss the importance of the labor force to production, service, and distribution systems. What would happen to these systems if labor was not available?

3. As societies become more complex and technological, service systems tend to become much more important. Why do you think this happens? Do you consider these many services as luxuries or essentials? Why?

4. What role does capital play in the production of goods in a modern industrial society? What forms of capital are involved in the production of, say, textiles?

5. Discuss the advantages and disadvantages of being able to buy almost anything on credit. Would the standard of living in the United States be higher if we had no credit and the consumer was able to spend more money on consumer goods instead of spending money for interest on funds borrowed to pay for credit purchases? Why or why not? What would happen to the economy if credit buying were outlawed?

6. Discuss the functions of political structures. What functions do you believe to be most important in our society today?

7. Imagine a society that has no government. How might the functions of the political structure be fulfilled by other institutions?

8. Obtain a breakdown of the current United States budget. Discuss the various items and determine which ones you think should be cut and which should be increased.

9. What do you think would be the result if many of the services now provided by the United States government for the people were turned over to private business on a competitive basis?

10. Discuss the relative merits of the four different kinds of politico-economic systems in terms of providing for the needs of citizens. What are the advantages of each? The disadvantages? Do any of the systems work the same in practice as they do in theory? Discuss.

SUGGESTIONS FOR READING

NONFICTION

DEMARIS, Ovid, *Dirty Business.* Harper Magazine Press, 1974. An exposé of what the author calls the "corporate-political money power game" in which government and business work together to collect millions of dollars from citizens.

DRUCKER, Peter F., *Concept of the Corporation.* John Day, 1972. A classic study of the General Motors Corporation.

_____, *The Future of Industrial Man.* New American Library, 1965 (pap.). Probes the growth of industry today and asks the question: Can an industrial society be a free society?

GALBRAITH, John Kenneth, *The Affluent Society.* Houghton Mifflin, 1971 (pap.). A stimulating book on the economics of affluence.

_____, *The New Industrial State.* Second and rev. ed., Houghton Mifflin, 1972 (pap.). A discussion of the present characteristics of modern developed nations and emerging industrial countries.

LENS, Sidney, *Unions and What They Do.* Putnam, 1968. A discussion about labor unions in America by a man who has spent his adult life in the labor union movement.

LUNDBERG, Ferdinand, *The Rich and the Super-Rich.* Edited by Eileen Brand. Lyle Stuart, 1968 or Bantam (pap.). A study of the power of money in American society.

PARADIS, Adrian A., *Economics in Action Today.* Messner, 1967. This book projects a visual picture of how economic forces actually work in our society.

POSEY, Rollin Bennett, *American Government.* Eighth ed., Littlefield, 1974 (pap.). A wealth of information on American government at all levels—national, state, and local.

RIBICOFF, Abraham and NEWMAN, Jon O., *Politics: The American Way.* Rev. ed., Allyn and Bacon, 1974 (and pap.). An excellent introduction to the political system of the United States.

'SMITH, Adam' (pseudonym), *Supermoney.* Random House, 1972 or Popular Library (pap.). A best selling book about the economy, the stock market, and the individual.

WHYTE, William H. Jr., *The Organization Man.* Simon & Schuster, 1956 (and pap.). A classic study of the effects of industrialization and large corporations on people.

FICTION

DRURY, Allen, *Advise and Consent*. Doubleday or Avon (pap.). The author describes the selection of a Secretary of State, with all its pressures and personal attacks.

HUXLEY, Aldous, *Brave New World* and *Brave New World Revisited*. Harper & Row (and pap.). Two novels dealing with the future in which the government and all social systems attempt to control behavior.

LEWIS, Sinclair, *Babbitt*. Harcourt Brace Jovanovich or New American Library (pap.). A man tries desperately to shake loose from his economic bonds by asserting his individuality.

ORWELL, George, *Animal Farm*. Harcourt Brace Jovanovich or New American Library (pap.). A symbolic portrayal of a revolt and overthrow of a government.

STEINBECK, John, *The Winter of Our Discontent*. Bantam (pap.). A man with a famous family name but little money struggles with his desire to obtain great wealth through devious means.

WALLACE, Irving, *The Man*. Fawcett World or Bantam (pap.). A black man becomes President of the United States.

WARREN, Robert Penn, *All the King's Men*. Random House. The rise of an insignificant man of the people to the office of governor.

SOCIAL
PROBLEMS

Probably you've listened to and joined in many discussions about social problems, the problems currently facing our society. Some widely discussed problems are the high cost of living, crime, unemployment, the energy crisis, and pollution of the environment. Almost everyone has an opinion about what's wrong and what should be done. But why do you think these are social problems? How do you judge whether or not a particular condition is a social problem? In this unit we will consider what makes a situation a social problem, and we will investigate specific problems in our society today.

17 Sociology and Social Problems

▶ What makes a situation or condition a social problem?

▶ How does a sociologist deal with social problems?

▶ What can you do to help solve social problems?

SECTION 1:
Understanding Social Problems

Undoubtedly you are well aware of many of the problems that face our society. Every day the newspapers print stories about such problems as civil rights and race relations, crime and delinquency, poverty and illness. But do you know what a social problem is from the perspective of sociology?

By now you realize that the word "social" pertains to human relationships. We can define the word "problem" as a knotty question for which we seek an answer. Yet the two words together also suggest undesirability. We see social problems as undesirable. We do not want them. A SOCIAL PROBLEM, *then, is a condition involving human relationships that is considered undesirable by a large number of people.*

Criteria of Social Problems

Our next step is to determine just what makes a particular condition a social problem. We may apply four criteria to any condition to find out whether it falls within our sociological view of a social problem. To be a social problem, a condition must meet all four of the following criteria.

There is a conflict between what people think "should" be and what "is." By this we mean that the existing condition is in conflict with the values and norms of the society. It is considered undesirable according to the values of that society. The condition is likely to cause people to make such comments as: "Isn't it just terrible!" "What is the world coming to?" "Why doesn't somebody do something about it?"

For example, one of the values of the United States is the concept that "all human beings are created equal." If all people are equal, then no one should be discriminated

303

against because of race, religion, nationality, or sex. Yet as we look around our society, we see discrimination taking place. We agree ideologically that equality ought to prevail. But it does not. There is a difference between what "should" be and what "is."

Social problems are related to social values. They exist only within the context of social values. A condition is defined as a social problem because it conflicts with one or more of the values and norms of the society.

The condition affects a substantial number of people. If John Jones is living in poverty, he does not necessarily represent a social problem. His situation is a personal problem for John Jones. If, however, a large part of our population is living in poverty, we have a social problem.

How many people are required to make it a social problem? We cannot answer in terms of a certain number or a particular percentage of the total population. We can only say that it must be a sizable number of peo-

ple, probably in the thousands. When we consider such major social problems as slums, poverty, alienation, crime, discrimination, war, alcoholism, and divorce, we are talking about millions of people. However, the criterion is related less to the actual number of people than to the fact that enough people are involved for the problem to disrupt the normal functioning of the social system in some way. In other words, the problem must be large enough to affect the entire community or society, directly or indirectly.

A substantial number of people define the condition as a problem. For a social problem to exist, a considerable number of people must be aware of a particular condition and believe that it is a social problem. One person believing that a social problem exists does not make it a social problem. For example, you might be required by your teacher to stay after school. This experience causes you to believe that there is a social problem of disciplinary actions by teachers. Actually, however, it is a personal problem for you, not a social problem. For it to become a social problem a sizable number of people would have to be aware of it and regard it as a social problem.

Conditions often exist for many years before they become social problems. This is because people aren't aware that there is a problem. Slavery existed for many years before it was widely considered a social problem. There was little value conflict present. After all, the majority reasoned, if the United States Constitution said that a slave was to be counted as only three fifths of a person, didn't this indicate that a slave was unequal? It was not until public opinion against slavery began to develop, and many people began to regard slavery as unjust and inhumane, that it came to be defined as a social problem.

People feel that something can be done about the problem through collective social action. Two factors are involved. First, people must feel that something can be done. Second, the situation must require collective social action. For example, if a crazed individual shoots and kills ten people in a park, it is not a social problem. It does not require collective action for its solution. It only requires action by the police force and the application of existing laws. When the individual has been confined, the problem of that particular shooting no longer exists. If, however, a lot of individuals go about shooting a great many people over an extended period of time and the police are unable to control the situation, then it becomes a social problem. People can do something about it through collective action. They can campaign for a stronger police force and more street lights. They can organize a legally sanctioned vigilante committee to patrol the streets and parks. They can campaign for the enactment of laws that would control the sale of guns. They can take any number of actions. Their actions might not solve the problem. But if they feel that their collective action will help solve the problem, our criterion has been met.

Usually this belief in the effectiveness of collective social action results in the development of some social movement. Such movements have included the abolition movement, the prohibition movement, the woman's suffrage movement, and the civil rights movement. In each case, the people organized for collective action because they felt that something could be done about the problem.

For a particular condition to be a social problem, then, there must be a conflict between what "ought" to be and what "is." The condition must affect a substantial number of people. A substantial number of people must define the condition as a problem. And people must feel that something can be done about the problem through collective social action.

Fallacies about Social Problems

In addition to knowing the criteria for determining whether or not a particular situation is a social problem, you should be aware of the mistaken beliefs, or fallacies, that exist about social problems. To enable us to look more objectively at social problems, we will consider some of the more important fallacies.

Fallacy: that people agree on what the social problems are. Take poverty, for example. Some people see poverty as a serious social problem that can be eliminated. Others accept poverty as a fact of life that will always exist. Some religious people believe that poverty is good and that only the poor will go to heaven.

Another example is the debate today over whether smoking is a social problem. The

American Cancer Society says that it is a problem and is carrying on an intensive campaign to get people to stop smoking. The tobacco industry, on the other hand, says that none of the findings of research to date have proved absolutely that smoking causes cancer and other health problems. Therefore, the tobacco industry claims, there is no proof that a problem exists.

Fallacy: that everybody wants the social problem solved. Actually, not everyone is in favor of changing the situation. For every recognized social problem, there are usually three basic attitudes. Some persons feel strongly about the problem and work hard to alleviate it. Others are indifferent to the

Some people think that the problem of high beef prices in the market would be solved if ranchers accepted lower prices for their cattle. Yet ranchers point out that the prices they get for their cattle vary widely. Sometimes the prices don't even cover their expenses. Can this problem of high beef prices for the consumer be solved to everyone's satisfaction?

problem because it does not affect them directly. A third category of people are strongly opposed to doing anything about the problem. They like the situation the way it is and say that no real problem exists. Many persons view the existence of slums as a social problem. But for others slums are a profitable business. Returns from rent in the slums are much higher in proportion to the value of the real estate than in other areas. Landlords of slum buildings often violently oppose any proposal for urban renewal.

We might consider war as the greatest of all social problems, and assume that there would be universal opposition to it. However, people are sometimes indifferent to a war that is fought in a distant territory and does not affect them directly. And some governments view wars as ways to unify their people and provide a booming economy.

We might also think that everyone would want to do away with unemployment. But this is not the case. Many employers like to have some unemployment because it gives them a greater selection of workers, makes it easier to obtain workers to do the undesirable jobs, and keeps the workers "on their toes" because of the threat of unemployment.

Fallacy: that all social problems can be solved. Many people think that all problems can be solved and that problems continue to exist only because influential people do not want them solved. In reality, few social problems can be completely solved. At least they cannot be solved without causing other social problems or greatly disrupting the social system. If it could be done at all, solving such problems as poverty, crime, discrimination, alienation, gambling, alcoholism, and divorce would require drastic changes in our social structures and institutions, which the society doesn't want. In a sense, society is like the fat person who wants to lose weight but doesn't want to stop eating. We want the problem solved, but we don't want the solution to affect our customary habits and relationships. As a result, often we don't try very hard to bring about a solution.

Fallacy: that time alone will solve the social problems. There are always some people who believe that the problem will go away if people will just let it alone. They rationalize with such statements as: "The situation is getting better," or "It's not as bad as it used to be." Many people have said that the civil rights problem will work itself out if we just give it time. We hear people say, "Why can't blacks—or Mexican Americans—or American Indians have a little patience, instead of wanting everything now?" Time has not automatically solved the problem over the past three hundred and fifty years, however, and there is little reason to believe that it will in the future.

Fallacy: that social problems are caused by "bad" people. This attitude is a rationalization of the problem, but a normal response for people who have been overexposed to the good-bad extremes. From our nursery tales, novels, movies, television programs, and comics we've learned that problems are always caused by the villain. The solution to the problem is the "good" guy. The "good" guys defeat the "bad" guys, and everybody lives happily ever after. When we find and punish the "bad" guys, we've solved the problem. This approach turns the study of social problems into little more than a detective game in which we put on our Sherlock Holmes cap and, with the help of a magnifying glass, seek out the culprits.

Actually, various social arrangements cause people to act in certain ways. It is frequently the social values, structures, and practices that are at fault. "Bad" people may take advantage of the situation, but they do not cause the problem. In fact, we might say that social problems cause "bad" people.

Fallacy: that social problems are abnormal.

Many people believe that social problems are abnormal. Alcoholism, for example, is considered abnormal. We view the alcoholic, the "drunk," with distaste. Yet in many movies, television programs, and novels we find that our hero is always stopping by the saloon, bar, or club for a shot of whisky or a cocktail. We are constantly exposed to advertisements encouraging us to buy a particular brand of alcohol. Many social functions center around the cocktail hour. Is the social problem of alcoholism abnormal, when viewed in its cultural setting?

We deplore our high rates of crime, mental illness, suicide, and divorce. Yet our society places a very high value on individualism, self-achievement, and the acquisition of material goods. Illegitimacy and venereal disease can hardly be considered abnormal in a society that places such great emphasis on sex and sexual attraction. Social problems, then, are not abnormal. They are normal, logical, explainable consequences of the social values, structures, and practices of the society.

These are some of the most common fallacies about social problems in our society. If we are aware of these fallacies, we may be able to avoid their influence as we attempt to look objectively and realistically at some social problems in the United States.

SECTION REVIEW

1. What are the criteria of a social problem?
2. What are some fallacies about social problems?
3. Why are social problems not considered abnormal?
4. Can social problems be solved?

KEY TERMS

Define and give an example of each.

collective social action   social problem

SECTION 2:
The Sociologist and Social Problems

You now know some of the difficulties and common misunderstandings about social problems. How, then, do sociologists approach social problems? Naturally, they try to avoid the fallacies. They also avoid a moralistic or emotional approach to social problems. Instead, sociologists try to use the same unbiased, empirical, objective approach in studying social problems that they use in studying any other aspect of human relationships. They use, in other words, the scientific method.

The purpose of the sociologist is to seek, through research, an understanding of the problem. Sociologists want to know the causes and consequences of the problem. They want to know how the problem relates to other areas of human relationships. Therefore they collect data and develop theories that attempt to explain the social problem. As they carry out their research, make their analysis of data, and develop their theories, they rely on a number of concepts that are important in the sociological perspective.

The Sociologist's Perspective

To maintain as unbiased an attitude as possible toward the problems they are studying, sociologists constantly remain aware of certain factors. The following concepts and factors are a part of their perspective as they carry out their research on social problems.

The concept of cultural relativity. The concept of cultural relativity involves the belief that any one of a large number of possible cultural practices may satisfy the needs of a particular society. An awareness of this con-

cept helps keep the sociologist from evaluating a problem on the basis of any one set of values. The average citizen tends to evaluate social problems ethnocentrically, on the basis of his or her own values, attitudes, and practices. Sociologists, on the other hand, evaluate problems on the basis of cause and effect. They try to determine the relationship between the cultural practices of a society and the social problem.

All behavior is learned. Human behavior is not regulated by instinct. Humans behave in a particular way, both when they're alone and in a group, because they have learned to behave that way. People learn to break the law, carry out deviant behavior, hate, or discriminate. People differ in their attitudes and in their treatment of others, but they have all learned these attitudes and behaviors. Sociologists can study people's attitudes and behavior with detachment because sociologists realize that behavior is learned and that individuals act the way they are taught.

Society changes constantly. Sociologists know that change occurs continually in every society, and that any social problem is closely related to the changes taking place. They know that because of this constant change, there is always a certain amount of disorganization in the society. If the change is more rapid, there is a greater amount of disorganization and, as a result, a greater number of social problems.

Social problems can only be solved by changing basic social institutions. Social problems are normal, logical, explainable consequences of the social values, structures, and practices of the society. Therefore they can only be solved by changing these values, structures, and practices. However, as we mentioned earlier in the chapter, a change that will solve one problem is also likely to cause one or more other problems. The sociologist approaches social problems with an awareness of the difficulties involved in finding solutions.

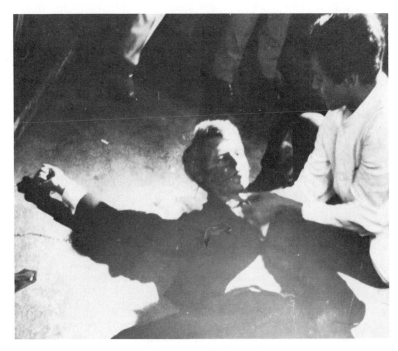

One of the social problems examined by sociologists is that of violence. An example of violence in our society is the assassination of a political figure, such as the shooting of Senator Robert F. Kennedy in 1968.

The concept of multiple causation. Behind this concept is the belief that there is no single cause of a particular problem. Instead, there are many causes, some of which cannot even be identified. Social problems are very complex social phenomena that cannot be explained by any one earlier event. In attempting to determine the causes of a social problem, sociologists remember that human relationships are affected by a number of factors. In determining the causes, they consider such factors as the physical environment, the cultural environment, biological factors, psychological factors, and social factors.

The *physical environment*—geography, climate, and the topography of the land—certainly exerts an influence on human behavior. Rural environments have a different effect on the individual than do urban environments. The artificial environment, built by humans, is also important. People are influenced by whether they live in a well-kept home and community or a run-down slum.

The *cultural environment* also plays an important part in human behavior. The cultural traits—the tools, acts, and beliefs—are significant factors in determining the behavior of people. People learn to behave in a way that is acceptable to their culture or subculture.

Biological factors affect human behavior, too. People's physical characteristics (such as sex, race, health, and possible physical defects), their temperament, and their aptitudes (such as manual dexterity and intelligence) all exert an influence on how they behave. These biological factors don't operate alone. They're related to the way in which others react to the individual.

Both individual and social behavior are closely related to *psychological factors*—to the motivations, emotions, anxieties, and self-concepts of individuals. The psychological aspects of an individual's personality develop through the socialization process. Traumatic experiences, lack of affection by parents, or rejection by others may be re-

309

sponsible for the development of a negative self-image or a maladjusted personality. The individual's self-concept, or ego, is extremely important in determining behavior. It has been said that a person's most lavishly indulged and jealously guarded possession is his or her own ego.

Social factors also exert a strong influence on both individual and group behavior. People's attitudes, beliefs, and behavior are the result of their interactions with others. Through their experiences in primary groups, secondary groups, and associations, they develop a unique personality. Social factors can also cause people to change their usual behavior. The influence of emotional contagion can change a peaceful crowd into a raging mob.

When they study a social problem, sociologists take all of these factors into account. They realize that no one of them caused the problem. Instead, social problems result from the relationships of many factors.

The Sociologist's Role in Solving Social Problems

In dealing with social problems, sociologists have the advantage of knowing what fallacies and approaches to avoid as well as the concepts and scientific techniques to apply. But how do the research activities of the sociologist help solve social problems? As you know, social problems involve a great number of people and must be solved through community action. What part can the sociologist play in this process? Actually, the sociologist can perform two basic functions that can contribute to the eventual solution of a social problem.

Sociologists can provide facts about the problem. Since there are a number of different attitudes about the problem, there are often a variety of unsupported statements about it. Many different stories usually circulate—some truths, some half truths, and some lies. Here the sociologist can perform a

A problem such as alcoholism has not just one cause—it has many causes. Alcoholism is influenced by biological factors, psychological elements, and social interactions.

very important function. He or she can carry out research to determine the facts. When the facts are revealed, the people can separate fact from fiction and better determine what course of action should be taken.

Quite often the facts reveal that the problem is more complex than people believed. In one city, for example, a black organization was protesting that black members of the police force were discriminated against because they weren't given promotions. The records of the police department were checked to determine if the charge was true. It was found that black members of the police force had received promotions at a higher rate than white people. However, the records also showed that black police officers made up only 2 percent of the department, whereas Black Americans comprised 10 percent of the city's population. As a result, the black organization began a campaign to increase the number of black police officers on the force.

Sociologists can suggest possible courses of action. When sociologists have determined the causes and consequences of the problem, they can suggest alternatives. By relating the problem to the normal social structure, they can recommend possible courses of action that the community might take. They can also determine what consequences might result from a particular action. With this information the community can decide on a course of action that would be the least disrupting to the social structure. Without this information, the community might pursue a course of action that would result in even greater problems.

It is important to remember that sociologists don't solve the social problem. They only provide a body of knowledge about the problem. They make this body of knowledge available to groups working on the problem. These groups are then better able to bring about the desired results.

Sociologists are constantly carrying out research on a great number of social problems.

By analyzing their research and reporting their findings in meetings and professional journals, sociologists make facts about social problems readily available to public officials and concerned citizens.

Why We Study Social Problems

Before beginning to examine specific social problems, you may want to know what you can gain from a study of social problems. What will we attempt to accomplish? If we have no goals, our study cannot be a purposeful activity. The following are some goals and reasons for studying social problems.

To develop an awareness of social problems. We must live as citizens of a society. Any society that we live in will have social problems. As citizens we should be aware of the social problems of our society.

By studying social problems you will develop a background knowledge and an awareness that will continue to grow. Any mention of a social problem in the mass media or in public conversation will quickly catch your attention. You will find that reading the newspaper or watching a news broadcast on television will become a more important and meaningful experience. As your awareness of the problems of the society continues to grow, you will become a better citizen of the community.

To gain factual knowledge of social problems. An intelligent discussion of any topic is dependent on facts. We cannot accomplish anything by a discussion of social problems unless we know the facts. Discussions based on half truths and untruths confuse the issue and help create obstacles to the eventual solution of the problem. We must be aware of the facts if we are to make an intelligent analysis of the problem.

To develop a sociological perspective toward social problems. If people can view social problems through a sociological frame

Doing research to gain facts about a specific social problem helps us understand the problem better. How would you go about obtaining facts about a particular social problem?

of reference, they are not easily swayed by the personal biases and exaggerated charges of persons who are less informed. This doesn't mean that they will ignore personal biases and values. Rather, they will take them into account as they make an enlightened evaluation of the problem.

Many people tend to panic when they become aware of a new social problem. They panic because they see each new problem in social relationships as a threat to the society. The informed person with a sociological perspective will be able to keep calm and view the situation comprehensively, knowing that throughout history human beings have always been plagued with social problems. No civilization has ever escaped them and probably no society ever will. Societies are constantly changing. When one problem is taken care of, another usually appears. Enlightened persons take social problems in stride and do what they can to improve the situation.

To understand the role of the social scientist. Many people distrust experts, especially social scientists. Some think, mistakenly, that social scientists want to control the society. Others believe that social scientists have no values or morals. These people do not understand that though scientists are devoted to

finding the truth in an objective, unbiased way, as citizens they live their personal lives on the basis of their own values and morals. Some believe that social scientists attempt to tell people what they should want. Actually, however, the role of the scientist is to tell people how they might best obtain what they want. Individuals who come to understand the true role of social scientists no longer see them as a threat to society.

To develop a personal orientation toward social problems. Each of us needs to ask, "What is my relationship to the problem? How do I feel about it? What must be done? What can I do?" You may think that the individual is helpless in such situations, where great numbers of people are involved. Yet history assures us that the individual is extremely important in bringing about social changes. For example, improvements in the conditions of American jails and poorhouses were made in the 1840's largely through the efforts of one woman, Dorothea Dix. She began her campaign by visiting jails and poorhouses throughout Massachusetts. She then presented the Massachusetts legislature with documented proof of the horrifying conditions she found. As a result, the legislators passed laws to change those conditions.

The individual can discuss, campaign, vote, and act. When joined with others in the same cause, the individual citizen usually obtains results. Each individual has a part to play in social affairs. What part will you play?

SECTION REVIEW

1. What concepts are a part of the sociologist's perspective in dealing with social problems?

2. Explain the concept of multiple causation.
3. What role does the sociologist play in solving social problems?
4. What are some reasons for studying social problems?

KEY TERMS

Define and give an example of each concept in relation to some social problem.

cultural relativity   multiple causation

PROJECTS AND ACTIVITIES

1. Do historical research to determine what social problems have existed in the past in our society. Which of these problems were solved or greatly alleviated and which have continued until the present time?

2. Pick a social problem that is important to you, and write a newspaper editorial or persuasive speech in which you attempt to gain public support for doing something about the problem.

3. Obtain a copy of the journal *Social Problems* or a similar journal. List the problems studied by the sociologists writing in the journal. Evaluate the sociologists' contributions toward solving each problem.

4. Study the lyrics of a number of songs for references to social problems. Prepare a bulletin board or poster to display what you've found out.

5. Watch a television program that deals with some aspect of a current social problem, and note the attitudes toward the problem that are presented. Do any of the attitudes involve fallacies about the problem?

6. Test the fallacy that "everybody wants a social problem solved" by writing down several social problems and interviewing people about their attitudes and feelings of responsibility toward solving the problem.

7. Obtain permission to sit in on a court session. What can you discover is being done by the courts to lessen social problems?

8. Conduct a survey of your community to determine the conditions and situations that people consider to be social problems.

9. Clip various articles from a newspaper and put them into a notebook. Show the notebook to a number of people, asking them which articles refer to social problems. Then make your own analysis according to the material discussed in the chapter. Complete the project by stating what you discovered about what people *think* are social problems.

10. Part of the sociologist's perspective is his or her awareness that much behavior is learned. Write a short report on your own behavior toward a specific social problem and how you learned to behave in that fashion.

11. Compose a song or write a poem that portrays some social problem in American society.

12. Do a content analysis of the mass media to determine which social problems are discussed most often.

TOPICS FOR INQUIRY

1. Make a list of some situations and conditions that you consider to be social problems. Then apply the four criteria to each. What are some fallacies related to these social problems?

2. If social problems are normal, logical, explainable consequences of the social values, structures, and practices of the society, then is it possible to have a society without social problems? What kind of society might have the fewest social problems?

3. Discuss a particular social problem in terms of whether everyone wants to see it solved. What are the major existing attitudes toward finding a solution to the problem? What is your attitude?

4. Do you agree with the statement that social problems can only be solved by changing basic social institutions? Discuss this statement in terms of specific social problems, including how willing the society is to accept or allow these changes. Does this statement help explain why many social problems have existed for years?

5. What differences, if any, are there between using the scientific method to study social relationships and using the scientific method to study social problems?

6. Analyze the collective social action involved in some specific social problem. Do people feel that something can be done? What collective action is taking place to help solve the problem? What action would you recommend?

7. In what ways do you think that you might benefit from the study of the social problems of your society?

SUGGESTIONS FOR READING

NONFICTION

CARNOY, Judy and WEISS, Marc (eds.), *A House Divided: Radical Perspectives on Social Problems*. Little, Brown, 1973 (pap.). A book of readings emphasizing individual participation and unorthodox solutions to social problems.

CARVELL, Fred and TADLOCK, Max (eds.), *It's Not Too Late*. Glencoe, 1971 (pap.). Readings that stress the relationship between ecology and social problems.

CRM BOOKS, *Social Problems*. Random House, 1975. A college textbook that emphasizes a wide range of social issues and problems.

MCNALL, Scott G., *Social Problems Today*. Little, Brown, 1975 (pap.). A brief but comprehensive survey of social problems with recommended solutions.

MERTON, Robert K. and NISBET, Robert A. (eds.), *Contemporary Social Problems*. Fourth ed., Harcourt Brace Jovanovich, 1976. Contains fifteen chapters on various aspects of deviant behavior and social disorganization. Each chapter is written by an outstanding sociologist.

SKOLNICK, Jerome H. and CURRIE, Elliott, *Crisis in American Institutions*. Second ed., Little, Brown, 1973 (pap.). Readings stressing the institutional basis for social problems.

FICTION

DICKENS, Charles, *Bleak House*. Crowell (pap.). A social criticism of life in nineteenth-century England, focusing on the injustices in the legal and political structures of society.

HUGO, Victor, *Les Miserables*. Dutton (pap.). A powerful novel that depicts the injustice of society toward the poor and defenseless through the story of Jean Valjean, a man forced to suffer a lifetime of persecution for stealing a loaf of bread.

SINCLAIR, Upton, *The Jungle*. New American Library (pap.). A novel depicting the deplorable working conditions facing the immigrants who found jobs in the stockyards of Chicago.

Highlight

How should sociologists approach social problems?

One of the most difficult issues now facing sociologists is how to deal with social problems. The world seems to be in a state of increasing turmoil, disorder, and distress. The problems are so numerous that just to try and list them all is a huge task. In our society alone, where would you begin? Illness? The environmental crisis? Poverty? Alienation? The quality of urban life? Drug abuse? Crime and delinquency? Care of the elderly? Governmental corruption? The high cost of living?

Suppose we look briefly at one problem facing sociologists: the very high unemployment rates of urban minority youth. At first glance, the problem seems to have an obvious solution — find jobs for these young people. But the question of how to do this presents the sociologist with a number of difficulties.

Job opportunities for urban minority youth are influenced by many factors. One factor is the location and types of jobs available. Another is the training and skills required of the applicants. A third is the motivation of the applicants. Other factors include the number of other people competing for the jobs, the ability of the applicants to move to available jobs, the amount and kind of bias among the employers, and governmental policies regarding hiring practices.

Think about what is involved in recommending and making changes in any of the factors just mentioned. The location of job opportunities, for example, is related to the general condition of our cities. Maintaining industry in the cities requires keeping the cities themselves economically healthy. That, in turn, may require changes in the tax structure, changes in government subsidies, and the movement of much of the middle class back to the cities. And these changes may have undesirable effects on suburban development. They may possibly produce a new kind of blight and economic inequality.

Thus even when the solution to a social problem is widely agreed on, the means to achieve it are likely to bring about other difficulties. When the solution is not obvious, as is more often the case, the difficulties are far greater. What position do you think sociology should take on all these social problems? Where do you stand as a sociologically informed person?

Max Weber, a German sociologist, established the guidelines that relate sociology to social problems. He called for a sociology that is both objective and value free. An objective sociology means one that doesn't take sides. It doesn't start with a position on how a question should come out. It isn't influenced by the personal opinions of the sociologist, regardless of his or her political, religious, racial, or sexual views. In other words, there can't be a democratic or a totalitarian sociology. There can't be a Catholic sociology, or a Protestant or a Jewish one. Nor can there be a black sociology, or a white one — or a male or a female sociology.

A value-free sociology means one that does not establish a set of values as being true or correct. According to Weber, sociological analysis can only deal with facts, because value decisions lie outside the realm or framework of science. Of course, sociology must deal with values, but only as they are facts. Sociology must consider the value orientations of a society in understanding that society. But it can't determine the ultimate worth of these values.

Most sociologists have accepted these two standards of objectivity. They value objectivity as the appropriate approach to social problems. Lately, however, some sociologists have been challenging these guidelines, asking questions about them. For instance, why should the sociologist remain objective? Is a doctor objective when he or she must decide about whether or not to save a life? Why should the sociologist, who is an expert in the area of social relationships, not be allowed to take a stand on such matters?

Others have asked the more basic question: *Can* the sociologist be objective? Can sociologists remove themselves from the prejudiced notions that we all have, as a normal part of becoming socialized? The very task of selecting a problem to study forces the sociologist to show a preference. His or her choice of method, selection of important variables, and rejection of other variables as not meaningful, all involve subjective factors that can't be made entirely objective. All of these include value choices. Just choosing one scientific framework over some other involves a value decision.

Is it possible, then, for sociology to investigate social problems in an objective and value-free way? And, if it can, should it? On the one side is Weber's position, which says that it can, and must. Weber never said that *sociologists* must be com-

pletely objective, or that they could be value free. But he did say that *sociology* must be so. Otherwise, if sociology examines political problems, for instance, its findings will be no more accurate than those of a business executive or of political propaganda. This side claims, moreover, that sociology can't provide ultimate solutions to social problems. These solutions must be political. Such solutions don't come from the scientific method.

On the other side are other sociologists, graduate students, and sociologists dedicated to social or political commitments who believe that sociology should participate in the easing of social problems. This side claims that you can't separate facts from values. Facts are based on your perception. And the way you perceive things depends on your values. Therefore, there are no separate facts. There are only degrees of objectively founded value judgments.

Furthermore, this side claims that by merely investigating major social problems, sociology begins to make people more aware of their own social situations. As people develop a broader perspective and see the world in a more accurate way, they begin to change society. Sociology, then, can't help but affect the world. The question that these sociologists ask is: What effect should it have?

As you read about and investigate social problems, consider the above points of view. Where do you stand on these issues? What is your point of view?

18 Equal Rights

► How have minorities been deprived of their civil rights?

► What efforts are being made to insure equal rights for everyone?

► What are some causes of the problem?

SECTION 1:
The Issue of Civil Rights

Civil rights are the rights of individual citizens to vote, seek public office, serve on juries, own property, receive a fair trial under law, have freedom to live and travel where they wish, and be free from discrimination due to race, sex, religion, or national origin. The basis of civil rights in the United States is stated in the Declaration of Independence: "We hold these truths to be self-evident: that all men are created equal, that they are endowed by their Creator with certain unalienable rights, that among these are life, liberty, and the pursuit of happiness." Behind American democracy is the concept of equal rights for all citizens.

However, there have been considerable differences between the concept of equal rights and the practice of them. Many people have been, and continue to be, denied some measure of equality. The problem, then, is this: not all people in our society enjoy full civil rights. It is a social problem, as it meets our four criteria (discussed in the last chapter). There is a difference between what should be and what is. The problem affects a substantial number of people. Large numbers of people are aware of it. And people feel that something can be done about it through collective social action. Before considering what can be done, though, let's look at some of the groups of people who have been particularly affected by this problem.

Black Americans

Blacks have been in America since the early days of its settlement by Europeans. In fact, the first blacks came to what is now the United States in 1619, a year before the Pilgrims landed in Plymouth! Yet they have almost always been denied full equality. By 1661 one state had made all newly arriving Africans, and the children born to them, slaves forever. The institution of slavery puts the problem of black civil rights in a special category. Few people coming to these shores have suffered the kind and degree of deprivation that blacks have.

After the Civil War and the end of slavery, there remained a pattern of enforced segregation between white southerners and black people. This pattern was legalized in 1896 by the Supreme Court decision of *Plessy v. Ferguson,* which permitted "separate but equal" facilities for Black Americans.

The situation today. It was in the 1950's that the struggle for legal equality began to bring about important changes. A major advance was the 1954 Supreme Court decision in the case of *Brown v. Board of Education of Topeka,* which outlawed segregation in public schools. Ten years later, the Civil Rights Acts of 1964 and 1965 ended legal discrimination in public facilities, public schools and colleges, employment, and voting rights.

Legal equality was becoming a reality, though it was not enough. Some discrimination and inequalities still existed. Also, years of slavery followed by years of legal and economic discrimination had affected the development of a positive self-awareness and strong self-consciousness. Achieving full legal equality for black people in America merely served as a beginning for a new and equally important struggle—the quest for black consciousness and self-identity.

As black consciousness developed, it became clear that black people were not the only ones who were denied a full share in the promise of equal rights. Other groups joined in the civil rights movement and became actively involved in developing their own self-identity. Among these groups were Spanish-speaking or Hispanic Americans, women, "white ethnics," and American Indians.

Hispanic Americans

Hispanic Americans are persons of Spanish descent. The Spanish have been influencing American culture for hundreds of years. In fact, the Spanish settled at St. Augustine, Florida, well before the first English settlers arrived at Jamestown, Virginia, or Massachusetts Bay. The bulk of the Spanish influence came from the large portions of the southwestern United States that were originally part of Mexico. This area includes California, Nevada, Arizona, New Mexico, Colorado, and Texas. Like Mexico, this area was settled by the Spanish or brought under Spanish cultural influence. Both the language and life style were Spanish.

Unlike the English, the Spanish intermarried with the Indians. They tended to bring the Indians under their cultural control, converting them to Catholicism and to the Spanish language. Unlike the descendants of the British settlers, the descendants of the Spanish settlers are usually of mixed Spanish and Indian ancestry.

By the 1900's, the British culture dominated in the once Spanish lands. Spanish-speaking people (with few exceptions, such as in New Mexico) were assigned to the lower rungs of the economic and prestige ladder. Migrant farm labor was a typical occupation among Mexican Americans. They were paid substandard wages for picking grapes and lettuce and they lived in squalid conditions. By looking the other way, some authorities encouraged illegal Mexican aliens to move across the border into the Southwest and work on the farms. These Mexicans,

321

coming in search of a better life, frequently found only more misery, a low standard of living, and low social status.

Puerto Ricans. In a separate development, and much later in time, a Hispanic influence appeared in the eastern part of the United States. As a result of the Spanish-American War, the island of Puerto Rico became an American Commonwealth at the turn of the 1900's. Its residents were, therefore, American citizens who enjoyed the right to migrate to the United States mainland without any immigration restrictions.

After World War I, increasing numbers of Puerto Ricans took advantage of their citizenship and did come north. They settled mainly in the large cities of the Northeast and Middle Atlantic states. There they often fared even less well than blacks, as they competed for rundown housing and low-paying jobs.

Today in neighborhoods such as East Harlem in New York City, Spanish is the language that is used most often. There are Spanish-language radio and TV stations, Spanish-language newspapers, and Spanish-language shops and stores.

Neither Mexican Americans nor Puerto Ricans have yet enjoyed a full share of American rights and opportunities. But there is now a growing awareness of the problem, and a heightened sense of self-identity among them.

Women

A few years ago, the idea of "women's liberation" was only beginning to be taken seriously. But now we generally recognize that sexual discrimination has been widespread and completely taken for granted. It has been an accepted part of everyday life—accepted by both men and women.

The fact remains that women have been underrepresented in most of the professions. They have tended to be paid less than men for the same work. And they have been hired for work at a level below their aptitudes. Employers often ask female college graduates if they can type, for example, while males are hardly ever asked that question.

We know now that differences in male and female behavior are the result of far more than physical differences alone. Traditionally, from their earliest socialization experiences, boys and girls are treated differently. Usually boys are taught to be aggressive, competitive, and dominant. They are encouraged

to adopt traits closely linked with success in, say, the business world. Girls are taught to be docile, cooperative, and submissive—traits linked with homemaking. Along with different socialization experiences, there are different cultural expectations of a woman's role as opposed to a man's role in society. The result is almost certain to produce a denial of rights and recognition of women as contrasted to men.

In some instances this situation works to the disadvantage of men as well. Sexism denies men the right to display certain traits traditionally associated with women, such as sensitivity and artistic inclination. Actually, such traits are neither feminine nor masculine. They are human. To deny them to one sex is to deny members of that sex a portion of their humanity.

White Ethnics

When you think of an American, what sort of person do you picture? For much of our history as a nation, the term "American" has usually brought forth an image of a person of British or northwestern European ancestry, with fair skin and hair, and of Protestant religious heritage. And the white Anglo-Saxon Protestant, or WASP, became the measuring rod by which other Americans were judged. An English surname was most desirable. A Dutch, German, or Scandinavian name, if properly anglicized, was acceptable (Johnson, not Johannsson; or Van Dyke, not Van Dijk). An Irish name might be okay—if the bearer was Protestant. Similarly, blond hair was considered better than black, and fair skin better than dark.

323

But, of course, the WASP image leaves out a lot of people—and they are not all black, Spanish-speaking, or Oriental. There are many Americans who are not Protestant, not particularly fair-haired, and not Anglo-Saxon in ancestry. The term "white ethnic" is applied here to those Americans who are of southern or eastern European ancestry and usually Catholic in religion. Italian Americans, Polish Americans, Greek Americans, Slavic Americans, and others fall into this category.

For the large part, white ethnics have been by-passed by the American middle-class dream. While there are Catholics of southern and eastern European ancestry in all walks of American life, and at all economic levels, they tend to be mainly at the blue-collar, working-class, economic status. They may be employed in mines, steel mills, and automobile assembly lines.

Their ancestors came to America with the expectations of bettering the peasant conditions they left behind in Europe. They made up the great wave of immigration that occurred during the last decades of the 1800's and the first two decades of the 1900's. Most were successful, when measured against their European ancestors. But when measured against the WASP American image, they haven't always fared so well. Many white ethnics have not obtained their fair share of rights and recognition. In general, immigrants have accepted the WASP yardstick as the cultural ideal in America. It appears that white ethnics now may be developing some resistance to striving toward this ideal.

American Indians

A prime example of people who have been denied their full civil rights are the original inhabitants of the Americas—the people Columbus misnamed "Indians." The Indians were exploited, mistreated, and distrusted by the European explorers. Indians were kidnapped to Europe and sold there as slaves. As the number of colonists increased, the settlers took more and more land from the Indians.

After the Revolution, the federal government signed treaties with each Indian group, taking some land from them and setting aside other land for Indian use only. Indian treaties were constantly broken and renegotiated, however, as settlers kept occupying Indian land. Wars with the Plains Indians in the 1860's ended in establishing reservations for Indian groups and made them subjects of the United States. But American Indians were not granted citizenship until 1924.

The Indians have made contributions to American society in agricultural development, technology, food habits, language, and philosophy. They fought a losing battle from the beginning to maintain their own identity and self-consciousness. It is only fitting that as others have become conscious of their own potential for self-development, so have American Indians. It is not surprising that many American Indians themselves now see their struggle as one of recapturing and preserving their original heritage.

The Problem Today

The main social problem concerning civil rights is no longer one of legal equality. We have no laws that discriminate against Black Americans. There are no laws keeping Puerto Ricans in barrios or American Indians on reservations. Neither are there laws keeping women in the home.

The problem has become one of self-awareness. The struggle now involves building a new sense of identity—a new direction. Today the problem of civil rights is perhaps one of cultural rights. Having overcome un-

This Pueblo Indian family is picnicking in a national park in New Mexico. There has been a greater awareness recently of the struggle by American Indians for equal rights.

equal legal treatment, many minorities find that they are up against cultural conditions that produce prejudicial treatment. Many minority members find that they must overcome their own background. For their background included these same cultural traditions that discriminate against them.

What is the solution?

SECTION REVIEW

1. Why is civil rights a social problem?
2. In what ways are Black Americans denied their full civil rights?
3. What evidence is there that Hispanic Americans have not enjoyed equal rights?
4. To what extent have women, white ethnics, and American Indians been deprived of equal rights?
5. What is the situation today?

KEY TERMS

Explain the meaning of the following terms.

Brown v. Board of
   Education of Topeka
civil rights

Plessy v. Ferguson
white ethnics

SECTION 2:
The Response

What should a person do? Should one remain quiet and accept the dominant cultural assumptions, even when they limit one's civil rights? Or should a person rise up and fight against them? The answer for many Americans in recent years has been to stand up and fight. They have fought not so much with fists or guns as with a new sense of self-worth and, even, with new feelings of separateness.

Black Power

During the 1950's and early 1960's, the focus of organizations such as the National Association for the Advancement of Colored People (NAACP) and Dr. Martin Luther King, Jr.'s Southern Christian Leadership Conference (SCLC) was primarily on attaining equal legal rights and equal economic opportunity for Black Americans. There was a feeling that once legal equality became a fact, meaningful differences between blacks and whites in the United States would no longer exist.

That did not happen. Legal equality did not end cultural discrimination. Blacks were still regarded as different, and therefore unequal, by many whites. Some features of racial discrimination were still part of the institutional structure of American society. Blacks still lived mainly with other blacks, and so went to school mainly with other blacks. Blacks still had a lower per capita income, a lower average level of education, a higher infant mortality rate, and so on.

At the same time Black Americans found that they, too, regarded themselves as different. At an earlier stage, black people had tried to be more acceptable by emphasizing

"white" qualities. Lightness of skin color was considered desirable. Popular magazines for black readers advertised products such as skin-lightening creams and hair-straightener lotions. A popular expression in some black circles went something like:

> If you're black, step back
> If you're brown, hang around
> If you're white, you're right!

Yet no amount of "whiteness" on the part of Black Americans brought them acceptance by the white population.

Then gradually, during the 1960's, being black took on its own importance. Black was indeed beautiful! A new consciousness developed.

When did it start? It isn't possible to pinpoint the exact birth of the idea of black power. Its roots go back at least to the 1800's. However, a speech by Stokely Carmichael in 1964 brought the concept to the attention of millions of Americans, both black and white. Carmichael said that black people could expect no real change in their condition by waiting for action from the white society and its institutions. Rather, Black Americans would have to organize their own forces and help themselves. Black power would include black political power and black economic power. Black people would have to control their own political fortunes by electing blacks to office. They would have to take economic control of their affairs by owning their own businesses and residences, rather than depending on whites for such services. They would have to recognize that blackness was an asset, not a stigma.

Stokely Carmichael's vision of black power was interpreted in different ways. Many whites saw it as a threat to their own security. They envisioned blacks using anger and violence to achieve equal rights. Many blacks saw it along similar lines. Some interpreted it as a call for black separatism or even black nationalism.

The use of force. In fact, the early development of the black power movement did occur during a period of urban civil disorders. By 1966 domestic turmoil appeared to be a regular part of the American scene. A total of forty-three disorders and riots took place. Often they began as minor incidents, which quickly spread, fanned by antagonism between the black population and the police. Such situations widened the gap between blacks and whites. Sometimes whites engaged in acts of violence against the black community in a kind of "backlash" manner.

The year 1967 saw disorders take place on a number of college campuses as well as in the cities of Houston, Tampa, Cincinnati, Atlanta, Newark, Plainfield and New Brunswick, N.J., and Detroit. The Detroit riot was the worst in the nation's history. It took on the nature of a small war as snipers, police officers, and troops exchanged gunfire. Block after block was burned. More than 7,200 persons were arrested. The number of dead reached at least forty-three people—thirty-three blacks and ten whites.

The largest number of civil disorders took place in 1967, although some riots continued to occur in the years that followed. Student groups on campuses also began to demonstrate for black studies programs and new admissions policies.

Yet the importance of black power—or the black revolution—cannot be measured by the number of demonstrations and disorders that took place. Its importance lies in the refocusing of attention and priorities. Black Americans have made considerable gains—in voting rights, education, employment, and housing. And black power has enabled blacks to see themselves as worthy on their own terms, in their own color.

By the 1970's, the black revolution was completed. It was completed in that a whole generation of black people came of age aware and proud of their heritage.

To be sure, there is still much to do. Eco-

During the 1960's, Black Americans became increasingly aware of their own identity, importance, and self-worth.

nomic inequality, for example, remains a fact. The recession of the mid-1970's affected blacks to a greater degree than whites, as economic downturns always have. Cities still contain large numbers of black people crowded into ghettos. Urban education systems are underfinanced.

Yet the old racism cannot easily recur. Blacks themselves will no longer allow it.

Other Responses

Revolutionary fervor is often catching. The problems of Spanish-speaking people, women, and American Indians are not identical with those of blacks. Yet changes in the self-concepts of these people no doubt occurred partly as a result of the black revolu-

327

tionary movement that was sweeping the country.

Hispanic Americans. Mexican American farm workers organized in the 1960's under the leadership of Cesar Chavez. They conducted boycotts first against grapes and later against lettuce. The purpose was to improve the situation for grape pickers and lettuce pickers (largely Mexican Americans) who were paid substandard wages and worked under less than ideal conditions.

A distinctive consciousness emerged among younger Mexican Americans, who call themselves *Chicanos.* The Chicano movement embraced a philosophy similar to that of the black power movement. Chicanos stressed self-help measures, Hispanic identity, and Spanish-language recognition. Similarly, among Puerto Ricans, self-help programs and bilingualism are being stressed.

Women. The women's liberation movement parallels the black liberation movement in an interesting way. Even more than blacks, women have traditionally accepted their status. Differences in male and female behavior were accepted as the "natural" result of sex differences. And who could argue with *Mother* Nature? Both men and women tended to accept their different roles, and even to argue in favor of them.

Like the black movement, the women's movement stressed both legal equality and separate consciousness. To achieve legal equality, they supported an Equal Rights Amendment to the United States Constitution. They have worked toward cultural equality, but it has yet to happen. We only need look at the society's professional, political, and business leaders to see that it is still very largely a man's world. Yet for many

Here a Mexican American family is standing in front of the new house that they built in California through a "self-help" housing program.

This Affirmative Action program, which is sponsored by a large corporation, gives minority individuals an opportunity to develop their skills in a chemical lab.

women, especially (but not only) younger ones, the change of consciousness has occurred. No longer are they content to believe that females have limited fields of interest or capability. Women now have more choice in the roles they wish to pursue. That is a revolutionary change.

Affirmative Action

Our society has responded to the problem of unequal rights with legal and Constitutional requirements of equal opportunity. It has also responded with the policy of "Affirmative Action." This policy involves making special efforts in the hiring and promoting practices of corporate, educational, and governmental institutions to be fair to minor-

ities and women. Minorities are usually defined as Black Americans, Hispanic Americans, and American Indians, although the term may include others, such as Orientals. Generally it does not include any category of white males.

The reasoning behind the policy of Affirmative Action is that most minority members and women have been denied access to these institutions in the past. As a result, they are not always in a position to compete equally. Suppose, for example, a woman has spent the last ten years being a homemaker and mother. She therefore lacks the kinds of experiences that would make her as attractive a candidate for a professional job as a man who pursued his career without the time requirements of motherhood. Yet that woman

This rally by white ethnics occurred in New York City in May 1970. It was a display of unity to support their belief in America's basic values and ideals.

may be every bit as capable of doing the job. Affirmative Action would require that such a woman be treated on an equal basis with the male candidate (assuming her other professional qualifications are similar).

There is another aspect to Affirmative Action. Because women and minorities have been underrepresented in certain professional occupations, there have not been many role models for women and minority members to follow. Black college students, for example, have not typically encountered very many black professors. Their education therefore lacks the chance to learn from, and model themselves after, a black professor. White professors cannot completely communicate the "black experience." Thus Affirmative Action policies try to make education more meaningful to minorities and women by bringing more minority members and women into professional categories.

Reactions of the White Ethnics

The forces that produced the changes in minority and women's consciousness did not affect the working-class ethnics in quite the same way. Nor were the responses of society at all similar. As blacks and others steadily increased their civil rights, the millions of Polish Americans, Italian Americans, Greek Americans, and Slavic Americans felt threatened, and even left behind. They continued to be discriminated against. There were no programs designed to help them. They saw themselves as too poor to enjoy the fruits of the middle class, yet too rich to qualify for welfare programs. They resented Affirmative Action policies as making their situation worse.

Many white ethnic Americans felt that they were the objects of middle-class bigotry. As nonwhites continued to gain in respectability, Polish Americans were seen as characters in Polish jokes and Italian Americans were pictured as spaghetti-eating gangsters. As a result, ethnic self-consciousness has increased. So far, it has shown itself mainly in resistance to such things as welfare programs, school integration, and Affirmative Action policies. Full recognition of Americans of white, non-Anglo-Saxon and non-Protestant background lies in the future.

SECTION REVIEW

1. How has the black power movement affected the problem of civil rights?
2. What are some reactions of Hispanic Americans, women, and white ethnics to the civil rights problem?
3. What is the policy of Affirmative Action? How effective do you think it might be?

KEY TERMS

Explain and give an example of each term.

Affirmative Action   black power

SECTION 3:
Causes of the Problem

We've considered briefly some historical and cultural aspects of the civil rights problem in the United States, and some attempts to deal with the problem. Our next step is to look at some possible causes. What causes the prejudice and discrimination that have produced the problem? Why have many members of the white majority discriminated against minorities and women, not permitting them to exercise equal rights?

Four Theories

The list of causes that follows is offered to you for analysis and discussion rather than as demonstrated fact. Consider these theories as possible causes of prejudice and discrimination leading to the civil rights problem.

Economic competition and conflict. This theory states that when groups compete, hostilities and prejudices often arise. If the two conflicting groups can be easily identified, the conflict is more likely to continue. For example, the Irish, once seen as a serious threat, were eventually assimilated into the American society. Black Americans, who are easier to identify than the Irish, have not been.

Research tends to indicate that people are most prejudiced against those people who pose the greatest threat to their jobs. For example, lower-class whites tend to be much more prejudiced against blacks than are white people in higher classes. In the past, blacks have posed a real threat to the lower-class person with little formal education and a nonskilled job. They have not posed a great threat to the white-collar worker or the blue-collar specialist. Prejudice against Jews, on the other hand, tends to be greatest among middle-class persons. Since Jews usually are well educated, they pose the greatest threat to persons in white-collar or skilled jobs. They offer little threat to the nonskilled laborer.

Another aspect of this theory is economic exploitation. If a person believes that Black Americans, for example, are incapable of competing effectively on the labor market, he or she can rationalize hiring them to work cheaply. Because of this view blacks, Puerto Ricans, Mexican Americans, and other minorities have been forced to work for lower wages than those given to members of the majority category for the same task. This view has, as we noted, also been applied to sex, and for years many women have been

Here is an illustration of the scapegoat. On the Day of Atonement, the sins of the ancient Jews were confessed over the head of a scapegoat. The goat was then driven into the desert.

paid less than men for doing the same job.

The frustration-aggression theory. Some research has shown that when people are frustrated, they become aggressive. When they feel aggressive, they search for some object or group to vent their aggression on. Often they find a *scapegoat* to blame. The term "scapegoat" comes from the ancient Hebrew custom of identifying the sins of the people with a goat and then driving the goat into the wilderness. Actually, the practice of placing the blame for our troubles on something or someone besides ourselves is common to most cultures.

Scapegoating can take many forms. If workers are frustrated because they are unemployed, they may blame immigrants or some other minority members for their unemployment. If business managers are not doing well, some may try to place the blame on the Jews, who, they claim, have a monopoly on business. In many cases there is no real relationship between the problem and the scapegoat chosen. For example, research has shown that the lynching of blacks in the South was related to the price of cotton. As the price of cotton went down, the number of lynchings went up. Yet blacks had nothing to do with the price of cotton. They were simply a readily available scapegoat.

This example points out a difficulty with the theory. In some cases there is no perceived connection between what went wrong and the prejudice, as with the low price of cotton and lynchings. We then must apply the theory by assuming the subconscious or unconscious motivations of the people showing prejudice. This presents the problem of proving the accuracy of assumptions about unperceived motivations.

The personality of the prejudiced individual. Another theory bases an explanation of prejudice on the personality of the prejudiced person, rather than on the character of the group that the prejudice is directed against. A number of studies have shown a significant difference between the personalities of prejudiced and unpreju-

332

diced persons. The prejudiced person tends to be authoritarian, a compulsive conformist, superstitious, a rigid follower of middle-class values and norms, egocentric, and emotional rather than rational.

Cultural factors. We've mentioned that there are certain widely held beliefs in American society that work against some portion of the population. Racism and sexism are two of the most important of these culturally sanctioned beliefs. RACISM *is the belief in the superiority of a group of people on the basis of race (or other ethnic factors).* Since racism is related to the desire to maintain racial purity, racists stress the separation of the races. SEXISM *is the belief in the superiority of the members of one sex over members of the other.* Sexists encourage separation of sex roles. They may limit women to mother and homemaker roles, or to low-status work tasks. They may limit men to the roles of provider and protector.

Both racism and sexism are deeply ingrained in our culture. Certainly some individuals are more racist or sexist than others.

But it would be inaccurate to blame either belief on individuals. We all learn racist and sexist attitudes in the course of growing up.

Racism and sexism are usually accompanied by two phenomena: stereotyping and the self-fulfilling prophecy. The term "stereotype" refers to a plate used in printing. The plate produces a number of copies that are all exactly alike. SOCIAL STEREOTYPING *is a process by which we view all persons in a particular social category as being alike.* In other words, we judge persons on the basis of their social category rather than their individual character and personality. We see a black person first as a black person, or a white person first as a white person, regardless of his or her individual behavior. Stereotyping occurs to a limited extent in all social situations. In racist or sexist stereotyping, however, a negative stereotype is usually applied.

Closely related to stereotyping is the SELF-FULFILLING PROPHECY, *which consists of situations in which people, by believing in a stereotype or other myth, help to make it come true.*

A number of politicians have taken a strong stand against sexism and racism. One of these is Bella Abzug, a Democratic Congresswoman from New York.

If people really believe a stereotype, and they act on it, they help make it a reality. Suppose, for example, you are convinced that you are no good at mathematics. Every time you start to do your math homework, your mind just seems to go "blank." Because you are anxious about your ability in math, you may overlook a part of the math problem or forget an important concept. As a result, you have difficulty in doing the homework. And you become more sure than ever that you can't do math.

Another aspect of the self-fulfilling prophecy is its impact on the people who are the object of the stereotype. For example, if women are believed to be less able than men at, say, mechanical tasks, they themselves will tend to shy away from such tasks. As a result women, because they have less experience at mechanical tasks, may in fact become less good at them.

These, then, are some of the theories that have been suggested as the cause of prejudice and discrimination, and therefore the problem of unequal rights. Which theory, or combination of theories, do you think best explains the problem? Why? What theories of your own would you suggest to explain the cause of this problem in America?

SECTION REVIEW

1. What are the four theories offered to explain the civil rights problem and what is the essence of each theory?
2. What is the difference between racism and sexism?
3. Explain social stereotyping.
4. Describe how the self-fulfilling prophecy works.

KEY TERMS

Define and give an example of each term.

racism
scapegoat
self-fulfilling prophecy

sexism
social stereotyping

PROJECTS AND ACTIVITIES

1. Do research to find out what specific contributions were made by various Presidents of the United States in helping to bring about equal rights for all citizens.

2. Find a book of songs, stories, or poetry relating to the treatment of blacks, women, or some other minority in this country. Study the content and write a short report on what is said about unequal rights.

3. See a movie that deals with some aspect of the civil rights problem, such as race relations, the economic inequality of a minority, or social discrimination against a specific minority. Take note of the methods used to deprive the individuals of their civil rights.

4. In a novel or short story that you've read, find an example of social stereotyping. Bring it to class, and discuss.

5. Draw a cartoon or comic strip sequence to illustrate the self-fulfilling prophecy.

6. Interview members of different minority categories to obtain their views on equal rights. Are their views of civil rights the same or different?

7. Interview several women regarding their views on women's consciousness and women's liberation. Compare the views you receive.

8. Find a book or short story depicting equal rights and then re-write the story into a play for the class to perform.

TOPICS FOR INQUIRY

1. Discuss the position of various minorities in society today, such as blacks, Mexican Americans, women, Jews, American Indians, Orientals, white ethnics, and the foreign born.

2. Compare the rise of black consciousness to the development of women's awareness. How might each learn from the other?

3. In what ways do the needs and aspirations of white ethnics parallel those of blacks and other racial minorities? To what extent are their needs different?

4. Discuss what you think happened to cause a nation founded by people seeking freedom and equality to become a nation in which many people are denied their civil rights.

5. What do you think can and should be done to help alleviate the civil rights problem? What should be done by (1) government, (2) industry, (3) labor unions, (4) schools, (5) religious organizations, (6) civic organizations and clubs, and (7) you as an individual?

6. Debate the pros and cons of the Affirmative Action program as a means of solving the problem of equal rights.

7. How has the civil rights problem affected your life? Have you ever been involved in any civil rights activities? Have you ever felt that you were denied your civil rights?

8. Discuss the pros and cons of the four theories presented to explain the causes of the civil rights problem. Which theory do you think best explains the causes of the problem? Why? What other theories can you suggest that explain the problem?

NONFICTION

BANKS, J. A. and GRAMBS, J. D. (eds.), *Black Self-Concept*. McGraw-Hill, 1972 (and pap.). A series of readings exploring the rise of a new black self-consciousness.

BROWN, Claude, *Manchild in the Promised Land*. Macmillan, 1965 or New American Library (pap.). An autobiographical study of a black boy growing up in Harlem.

CARMICHAEL, Stokely and HAMILTON, Charles V., *Black Power: The Politics of Liberation in America*. Random House, 1968 (and pap.). A discussion of the political framework and ideology of black power, which the authors feel represents the last opportunity for our society to work out its racial problems, short of destructive guerrilla warfare.

COHEN, Tom, *Three Who Dared*. Doubleday, 1969 or Avon (pap.). The true stories of three young men—two white, one black—who went South to help in the civil rights movement.

JANEWAY, Elizabeth, *Between Myth and Mornings: Women Awakening*. Morrow, 1974. A first-person analysis of the changed women's role.

KRONUS, Sidney, *The Black Middle Class*. Merrill, 1971 (pap.). A statistical and comparative analysis of black middle-class life. Case histories are included.

NOVAK, Michael, *The Rise of the Unmeltable Ethnics*. Macmillan, 1972. A hard-hitting account of the minority status of Poles, Italians, Greeks, and Slavs in America.

SALPER, Roberta L. (ed.), *Female Liberation: History and Current Politics*. Knopf, 1971 (pap.). A series of readings on women's liberation that includes a comprehensive historical background.

SOCHEN, June (ed.), *The New Feminism in Twentieth Century America*. Heath, 1971 (pap.). Readings on the developing female consciousness.

STODDARD, Ellwyn R., *Mexican Americans*. Random House, 1973 (pap.). A sociological analysis of Mexican Americans, with an emphasis on changes in law and consciousness.

FICTION

BORLAND, Hal G., *When the Legends Die*. Lippincott or Bantam (pap.). A Ute Indian boy is "civilized" against his will, rejected by his peers, and turns to the white people's world of rodeo.

CRICHTON, Michael, *The Terminal Man*. Knopf or Bantam (pap.). An exciting science fiction novel in which one of the characters is a female physician who must cope with the insecurities of being a woman in a male-dominated world.

HERSEY, John R., *White Lotus*. Knopf or Bantam (pap.). All Americans become slaves in this futuristic novel of conquest by China. It suggests the universal elements of slavery within all cultures.

19 Ecology

▶ Does the earth have a balanced environment?

▶ Are the problems of pollution, decreasing natural resources, and population growth getting worse?

▶ How do ecological problems affect your life?

SECTION 1:
The Interaction of People and Their Environment

Living organisms don't exist alone. All populations of living organisms interact with other populations. Every population also interacts with its environment. It doesn't matter what kind of population we are considering—ants, rabbits, deer, fish, or humans. All organisms live within an environment. This environment is the sum of all substances, conditions, and forces acting together to affect the living conditions of every organism.

Ecology has been defined as the study of the relationships between organisms and their environments. Ecologists, however, prefer to think of ecology as the study of structure and function in ecosystems. *An* ECOSYSTEM *is a unit of biological organization composed of all the populations of plants, animals, and humans interacting with one another in a physical environment.*

Kinds of Environments

Human ecology is concerned primarily with humans and how they relate to other organisms and their environment. It is concerned with the part humans play in the ecosystem.

In human ecology we can consider three kinds of environments. The first is the physical environment—such as soil, air, water, and sunlight. The physical environment is essential for all life. The second is our biological environment. It consists of all species of plants and animals that influence our lives in any way. The third is our cultural environment. This refers to the particular behavioral characteristics that we share as members of a society. Also included in our cultural environment are our attitudes, beliefs, and ideas — the way we look at ourselves and our physical and biological environments.

Our cultural values are very important in determining how we as humans relate to the total ecosystem. For example, in the Western world humans have considered themselves superior to nature. We have viewed nature as an opponent to be conquered. In parts of the Eastern world, on the other hand, people have viewed themselves as a part of nature and tried to live in harmony with nature.

Balance in the Environment

Ecologists are concerned with the influence of industry and technology on the delicate balance of the earth's environment. As more and more nations of the world become technologically developed, the problems will multiply. Recent ecological research shows that the balance of nature is being disturbed.

What is a balanced ecosystem? To answer this question, we need to know something about how an ecosystem functions. It includes three kinds of organisms, which perform three different functions. These are the living parts of the ecosystem.

First, there are the *producers*. These are the green plants that take in substances such as nitrogen, phosphorus, carbon dioxide, and water. With energy from the sun, they convert these substances into foods needed by all forms of life.

Second, there are the *consumers*. Some consumers are herbivores, or plant eaters. Others are carnivores, which eat the flesh of animals. Still others are omnivores, which eat both plants and flesh.

Third, there are the *decomposers*. These are mostly bacteria and fungi, which reduce the bodies of the producers and consumers back to inorganic (nonliving) substances — which are returned to water, air, and soil. The cycling of matter from inorganic to organic and back again is essential to life.

We can also see how the physical part of an ecosystem functions. Energy follows a one-way path through the system (see page 341). The constant energy of the sun makes it all possible. The sun is part of the process by which green plants provide food energy for the consumers and at the same time also release oxygen into the air. Almost all forms of life depend on this process. Therefore any environmental condition that is damaging to plants can be dangerous to all life.

A balance must be maintained among all parts of the ecosystem. The producers, consumers, and decomposers; air, water, and soil; and solar energy all must be present for the process to work. An ecosystem can adjust to many changes. However, with advanced technology we may be making changes much faster than the ecosystem earth can make adjustments.

"Laws" of Ecology

Ecologist Dr. Barry Commoner says that ecology has not yet developed specific laws, as has physics. But he suggests four generalizations that have resulted from ecological research on ecosystems. These might be considered as an informal set of laws of ecology.

Everything is connected to everything else. Everything plays a part in the endless cycles of ecosystems. Too much stress at any one point in the ecosystem may lead to a collapse of the entire ecosystem. For example, suppose a large amount of sewage is dumped into a river. The bacteria use up all of the available supplies of oxygen in the water as they decompose the masses of sewage. As the oxygen level of the water falls, most forms of life in the river begin to die. In time the river is a smelly sewer.

Everything must go somewhere. This is one of the basic laws of physics — that matter

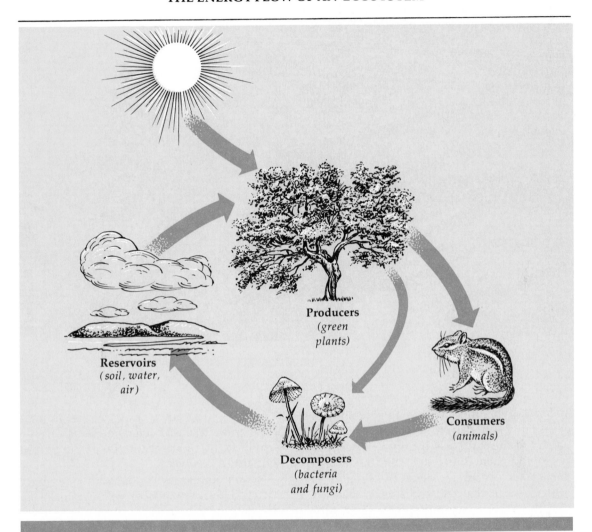

Producers
(green plants)

Reservoirs
(soil, water, air)

Consumers
(animals)

Decomposers
(bacteria and fungi)

is indestructible. In ecology, it means that there is no such thing as waste in nature. What is given off by one organism as "waste" is taken up by another organism as food. For example, animals give off carbon dioxide as respiratory waste. Carbon dioxide is essential in the food-making process in green plants. Plants give off oxygen, which is essential for all animals. Animal organic wastes feed the bacteria of decay. Bacterial wastes—such as nitrites, phosphates and carbon dioxide—become part of the food-making process for algae. And so the cycle goes in nature.

But what happens when people come along and create new substances from the

341

People have thrown nature off balance by introducing substances into the ecosystem that nature can't break down, such as cars. What do you think should be done with old cars?

materials of nature? Take a simple item we all use — a dry-cell battery. We buy a dry-cell battery at the store, use it until its energy is gone, and then throw it in the trash. It is then taken to an incinerator. When it is heated, the mercury it contains is released into the air as mercury vapor, a toxic substance. This mercury vapor is carried by the wind. When brought to earth by rain or snow, it eventually finds its way to a mountain lake. There it is acted upon by bacteria and converted to methyl mercury, which is absorbed by the fish in the lake. The mercury gathers in the organs and flesh of the fish. When the fish is caught and eaten by humans, the mercury becomes deposited in the humans' organs. In sufficient quantities mercury can be extremely harmful.

Nothing just goes away. It always goes somewhere. It may even come back, directly or indirectly, to affect the life of the person who threw it away.

Nature knows best. Many changes have occurred over billions of years to make up the delicately balanced ecosystem that we have today. For every organic substance produced by a living organism, nature has provided an enzyme capable of breaking down that substance. Nature takes care of all natural materials, both organic and inorganic.

What happens to this balance when people introduce new substances not found in nature? Take, for example, a simple thing like a shirt. When a shirt made of a natural material, such as cotton, is thrown away, it will soon rot and become a part of the earth. A synthetic shirt, however, does not rot or become a part of the soil. The most effective way to get rid of it is to burn it. And this pollutes the air. Otherwise this discarded shirt must occupy space somewhere.

Synthetics are not the only nonnatural materials that we've introduced into the ecosystem. Consider the tremendous quantities of detergents and insecticides we use every year. Nature cannot break most of them down. The problems that result suggest very strongly that nature does know best.

There is no such thing as "a free lunch." All life in nature lives at the expense of some other life. Every gain is won at some cost. Nothing is free. It is wonderful that we have polyester shirts that need no ironing. But sooner or later we must pay the price for this convenience.

SECTION REVIEW

1. What is an ecosystem?
2. Why should the environment be balanced? What happens if it is not?
3. What are the four "laws" of ecology described in this section? Do you agree with each one?

KEY TERMS

Describe both of these terms.

ecology   ecosystem

SECTION 2:
The Ecological Crisis

Ecologists are concerned that our environment, the earth, will become unable to support us at some time in the future. Three factors are contributing to this situation: the pollution of our environment, the using up of our natural resources, and the tremendous growth of human populations. These three factors are operating together to produce an ecological crisis.

Pollution of the Environment

POLLUTION *consists of adding any substance or form of energy to the environment at a rate faster than the environment can deal with it.* Pollution is a social problem. The end result of this problem is the subject of great debates by ecologists, conservationists, developers, business people, and citizens.

Air pollution. Have you ever approached a major city and been aware of great clouds of smog (smoke and fog) hanging over it? This smog is particularly noticeable on days when there is little wind. Even on days when no pollution is evident, however, the problem still exists. The pollution is being carried away from that city. But it is still going somewhere—out over farmland, or desert, or into the atmosphere.

Scientists estimate that about 80 percent of the pollutants in the air come from the burning of fossil fuels, such as coal and gas. Oxides of nitrogen, sulfur dioxide, carbon monoxide, hydrocarbons, ash, soot, and other particles are released into the atmosphere. In the early 1970's, we were discharging more than 200 million tons (181 million metric tons) of pollutants into the air annually. This amounts to a ton each for every man, woman, and child in the United States. Coal-burning electric generating plants were pumping 20 million tons (18 million metric tons) of sulfur into the air each year. With the production of electricity expected to triple by 1990, the situation will probably become worse in future years.

Even more pollution comes from motor vehicles than from the burning of coal. The

Environmental Protection Agency's Office of Air Programs estimates that an average of approximately 60 percent of all air pollutants by weight are produced by transportation—mainly cars. In many urban areas they found the average to be as high as 80 percent. We now have one car for every two people in the United States, and the number of cars has been increasing twice as fast as the population.

Other sources of air pollution are dusts from mining and industry, various chemicals from agricultural spraying, and radioactive particles released from various atomic installations. Even though these installations do follow extreme safety precautions, accidents can and do happen. One example is the fire at the Rocky Flats Atomic Energy Plant near Denver, Colorado, in 1969. The fire released plutonium—a substance known to cause cancer—into the atmosphere. Any use of atomic energy for power generation produces some waste materials that are highly radioactive and extremely dangerous. The real problem is how to dispose of these wastes without harm to the environment. As we turn more and more to atomic fission for power to replace coal, we will have more and more of these radioactive wastes to contend with.

What are some of the effects of air pollution on our lives? Pollution works continuously and silently. It affects the health and respiration of many people. It causes oxidation of paint, brick, and stone, requiring more maintenance of our buildings. It makes our clean laundry hanging on the line dirty again. It also affects plant and animal life in the ecosystem. More and more we are finding that fields of crops growing near large metropolitan areas are turning yellow and dying from the effects of pollution. Millions of pine trees in the forests east of Los Angeles have died. The combined effects of pollution and environmental destruction threaten the existence of no fewer than 280 mammal, 350 bird, and 20,000 plant species around the world. Such losses would be a tremendous shock to the total ecosystem, on which humans depend for life.

Water pollution. Pioneers in America often settled near a river, because they could use it both as a water supply and as a sewer to carry away their wastes. Suppose, however, you live in a community that is down-river of such a settlement. We now have chains of cities located along rivers, with each city using the river both for its water supply and as a sewer. Therefore cities must spend millions of dollars on large water filtration systems and add vast amounts of chlorine to make the water safe to drink.

But human wastes don't cause the greatest problem. Nature provides bacteria that will destroy reasonable amounts of human wastes. A greater problem is the industrial wastes that are dumped into our rivers. These wastes contain elements that a river's natural ecosystem can't break down. Some elements, such as mercury and lead, are very toxic and continue to build up over the years. Chemical pesticides and fertilizers are washed off the fields and into the rivers by rains. Detergents also collect in the rivers since they cannot (unless they are biodegradable—able to be broken down by nature) be destroyed by a river's ecosystem. Petroleum and other substances find their way through the storm sewers into the rivers and streams. One river in America actually became so polluted with petroleum that it caught on fire!

The waters in these rivers find their way into lakes and eventually into the ocean. It is estimated that 25 percent of all DDT ever produced by humans is now in the oceans. For years large amounts of garbage and urban sewage have been dumped into the oceans. As a result, the oceans of the world are becoming extremely polluted, especially along the shores. And most of the sea life that we harvest for food comes from along the shores. Some fish that are caught have such high concentrations of mercury or DDT that they cause illness and even death to anyone eating them.

This is what a polluted lake looks like. Such materials as tin cans, scum, and dead fish float on the surface. What measures might we take to prevent water pollution?

Solid wastes. Solid wastes consist of anything from papers, plastics, bottles, furniture, and garbage to junked cars. In 1970 the average household in the United States was producing 5.3 pounds (2.4 kilograms) of solid wastes per day. It is estimated that this will increase to 8 pounds (3.6 kilograms) per day by 1980. If we add to this figure the industrial wastes from mining and manufacturing, we arrive at about 50 pounds (22.7 kilograms) per day for each person.

What is being done with solid wastes? It is possible to recycle some wastes, such as paper and bottles, so that they can be used again in another form. But most non-industrial wastes end up in the community dump — often as land-fill. Nonnatural materials create the greatest problem because they cannot be destroyed. Things made from the materials of nature, such as metals, wood, cotton, or wool, will eventually decompose and become a part of the soil. Plastics, however, will never decompose but simply build up as solid waste.

A great amount of solid waste comes from mining. Mining produces waste called "tailings." Half of the material taken out in mining is left behind after the desired minerals are removed. As the need for more minerals grows, we are turning more and more to strip mining, or mining the land's surface. Over 3 million acres (over 1 million hectares) of land in the United States have been stripped. Only a third received any repairing of the surface at all. What we do with our solid wastes has a sizable effect on our ecosystem.

Noise pollution. Cities are noisy. The more people we concentrate into one area, the more noise we have. We have the sounds of airplanes, cars, trucks, motorcycles, trains, construction equipment, and buses, including horns and sirens. We have the noises of our neighbors' voices, radios, or tapes. The noise level is greatest in the central city. But suburban dwellers do not always escape. They may live near a highway, or find construction machinery working all around them. Or their homes may be in the flight pattern of the city airport.

Noise pollution may not seem to be a serious problem. It certainly doesn't have the consequences of other forms of pollution. We need to consider, though, what the effects of noise might be on human beings. Could it make them more irritable, aggressive, and unfriendly? Could it make them deaf? Could human relationships be affected? Some social scientists think so.

What's being done? These are some of the problems of pollution. But the situation is not all negative. Some progress is being made. Many factories are installing filters on their smoke stacks. New cars are meeting stricter emission standards. Some rivers are being cleaned up, and fish are coming back. Some cities have developed trash incinerators that produce heat for municipal buildings.

The real question is whether we are doing enough to avoid disaster in the near future. Is it a case of "too little and too late"? Some ecologists believe that we've done so much damage to the fragile ecosystem that it is too late to reverse the destruction. What do you think? What is being done in your area to alleviate the problems of pollution? How can you help?

Using Up Natural Resources

As we become more industrialized and technology increases, we are using greater amounts of the world's nonrenewable resources. Compare the demands of a child born in the United States with the demands of a child born in India. The American child will consume about one million calories of food and use the energy equivalent of 13 tons (12 metric tons) of coal for each of the sixty-five years he or she lives. The Indian child will consume only about half a million calories and almost no energy other than his or her own for each of the fifty years the child spends on earth. This means that the American will use up the ecosystem's available supplies hundreds of times faster than the Indian.

The United States, with only 6 percent of the world's population, is now using over 30 percent of the world's total natural resources. Suppose the rest of the world raised its level of consumption to the level of ours. Could the ecosystem provide for the needs of the world at this high level of consumption?

These students are analyzing a sample from a nearby river for possible water pollution. One approach to the problem of pollution is to examine its causes and consequences.

How long will the natural resources of the earth last? This is hard to determine. The rates of use are constantly changing as the technological development of the world increases. If we use the average rate increase since 1960 as a basis, we find that the known reserves of sixteen major metals will be exhausted within fifty years. If we consider fossil fuels at the same increasing rate from 1960 to the present, we find that our known reserves of natural gas will last for fourteen years, petroleum for twenty years, and coal for three hundred years. Our underground water supplies are also being used at a much faster rate than they are being refilled. Since all life requires water for survival, this shortage could become very serious at some time in the future.

Predicting how long our resources will last is difficult for another reason. We do not know what reserves there are of un-known resources. What kinds of resources are there that we have not yet discovered? Which resources now considered of little value may later become very valuable with new technology? We might learn how to make more effective use of the sun, the wind, or the tides as a source of power in the future. Even now, some houses are being built with solar heating. Another possibility is that we may decrease our use of certain resources as they become more and more expensive. For example, would you drive a car less if you had to pay several dollars per gallon for gasoline?

And what about our relationships with the developing nations? Will our ecosystem earth allow them to come up to our level of living? Or must we lower our level to make it possible for them to raise theirs? For example, fertilizer is in short supply around the world. The amount of fertilizer used to keep our lawns, cemeteries, and golf courses green would produce 100 million tons (91 million metric tons) of food to feed starving people in other countries. We also spend 1.5 billion dollars per year on food for our pets. How many hungry people would this feed? The United States has been acquiring non-renewable resources from all over the world. Many nations may find their reserves exhausted by the time they are ready to use them. Is it fair to buy and use up their resources, when they themselves may need them to raise their standard of living in the future? What do you think?

We depend on oil for energy. Therefore, we are constantly searching for new sources of oil. Here we are drilling for oil in Alaska.

Is there a solution? Some people say that science will find solutions to the problem of decreasing resources. Others say there is only one solution. We must change our style of life. They suggest that we must use less energy, waste less, pollute less, and live in harmony with the ecosystem. What is your view? What changes would you be willing to make in your lifestyle?

Population Growth

A quick look at population growth in the world is rather startling. Around the year 1 A.D. the world's population was 250 million (just a little more than the population of the United States today). By 1600 it had grown to 500 million. By 1900 it was 1.5 billion. Seventy years later, in 1970, it had more than doubled to 3.5 billion. Present projections are for almost 7 billion people by the year 2000. If the present growth rate continues, it is estimated that by the year 2100 there will be over 50 billion people on the earth. That would mean 1,000 persons for every square mile (2.6 square kilometers) on earth, including all mountains, deserts, and both polar icecaps!

The "population explosion" is not a simple phenomenon. Growth rates are not the same throughout the world. There is a difference between the growth rates of the industrially and technologically developed nations and those nations that are just beginning to develop technology and industry. The developed nations in North America and Europe, plus the U.S.S.R., Japan, and Australia, have a little more than one fourth of the world's population. Their populations are increasing at an average rate of just under 1 percent per year. The developing nations have an average population increase of 2.5 percent, with some as high as 3.4 percent. The average for the world as a whole is 2 percent. This means that the world's population will double in thirty-five years.

Population control. Can population be controlled so human beings can avoid the disasters accompanying unchecked population growth? Let's first consider the effects of population control. Suppose each couple in the United States had an average of three children. The resulting population would be 300 million by 1989, 400 million by 2014, and 1,000 million by the year 2070. If each couple had only an average of two children, though, the population would stabilize somewhere between 370 and 400 million by about the year 2090.

Culture plays a very important part in birth rate. Nothing can be done until people *want* to control population. In the United States today, for instance, many couples don't want more than two children. The present birth rate is very low. In the Philippines, on the other hand, women tend to want more than six children.

The food supply. Given the present rate of population growth, it would seem that we must double the world's food supply in thirty-five years. This, however, would mean that we would only continue at the present level of food consumption. Probably two thirds of the world's population today are living just above the starvation level. Doubling the food supply in thirty-five years would still keep them just a little above starvation. As nations industrialize, their people tend to eat more food and better quality food, including more meat. This increases the burden on the land, since it takes much more land to produce meat than it does to produce grains and vegetables.

What are the chances that we could even double the production of food in thirty-five years? At the present time about 3.6 billion acres (1.5 billion hectares) of land, or 11 percent of the earth, are under cultivation.

This may not seem like much. But remember that a great proportion of the earth's surface is difficult or impossible to farm, such as mountains, deserts, or water. Some scientists who have studied the situation believe that very little more land can be successfully cultivated.

One problem is that any increase in the amount of land under cultivation would require tremendous amounts of fertilizer, pesticides, farm machinery, energy to power the machinery, and irrigation. A great deal of capital would be needed to provide this. And most of the developing nations simply do not have enough capital available. Another problem is that most of these needs involve large amounts of petroleum, which is already in short supply.

What about the possibility of increasing production on land currently cultivated? Such gains in yield come at great cost. Over a twenty-year period the United States increased its per acre yield by 11 percent. The cost of this increase, however, was a 648-percent increase in the use of nitrogen fertilizer and a 267-percent increase in the use of pesticides. Britain obtained a 35-percent increase in yield, but at the cost of an increase of 800 percent in the use of nitrogen fertilizer.

An important problem with fertilizers and pesticides is that amounts needed tend to increase with use. Take pesticides, for example. They kill not only the pests but other forms of life that previously destroyed the pests. We then have to rely on pesticides to do the entire job. At the same time we never kill all of the pests. There are always some that are not affected by the pesticides. We now have some 250 species that are resistant to various pesticides. The result is that we continue to develop pesticides that are more and more powerful, and more damaging to the ecosystem.

What are the solutions? Again, the picture we have presented is negative. Can the ecosystem earth meet the tremendous demands placed on it? Some ecologists believe

There was a scarcity of fertilizer in the early 1970's. As a result, the price of fertilizer on the world market rose very high. This affected the food supply of nations that had planned to use fertilizer to increase the amount of food they produced.

that the ecosystem earth will break down during the lifetime of children already born. Other experts feel that it may be possible to balance the ecosystem by increasing food production and reducing population growth. What do you think? What could be done around the world to alleviate the pressures on our ecosystem? What could you do as an individual?

SECTION REVIEW

1. Describe the various types of pollution that are affecting our environment. What measures can be taken to reduce each type?
2. What is happening to the natural resources on our earth? What can we do to improve the situation?
3. What are some problems involved in the population explosion? Do you think that the world's population growth can be slowed down?

KEY TERMS

Define and give some examples of this term.

pollution

SECTION 3:
What Can Be Done?

The continuing pollution of our environment, the declining reserves of natural resources, and the booming population explosion give us a very gloomy picture of what the future might hold for us. You may ask, "Why doesn't somebody do something?" Many things are being done. But the question is whether we are doing enough soon enough. An important aspect of the problem is whether we are willing to spend enough money to resolve the ecological crisis. For solutions will not come cheap. And a simple solution won't work. Many factors are involved. Let's look at some of these factors.

Personal Freedom

Americans have always placed a great value on personal freedom. We want to do what we want, when we want to do it. How will the ecological crisis affect this personal freedom that we have come to take for granted? Will we be able to drive our cars whenever we wish? Or might we have to give up driving large cars? Or even give up cars completely and rely on public transportation? Will we have a large selection of foods to choose from, or will we be glad to eat anything we are fortunate enough to obtain? How might our recreational activities and travel plans change? And what about our freedom to have as many children as we want? Can we allow people to have more children than our ecosystem can support?

These are deep and troubling questions. But could they become possibilities if the pressures on the ecosystem become extremely great? Which freedoms would you be willing to give up for the benefit of the entire society?

Land Use

When our nation was predominantly rural, we believed that people had the right to do whatever they wanted with their property. We found, however, that as more and more people moved into smaller spaces, some regulation was needed. We couldn't allow someone to put a hog farm in the middle of a residential area just because that person owned the land.

America has some beautiful wilderness areas. What can be done to protect such areas?

Recently state legislatures all over the nation have been working on legislation to control the use of land. They are concerned with ways to control strip mining to protect ecological balance as well as the beauty of the environment. They are also concerned with the commerical development of scenic areas, of mountains and shorelines. How do you feel about land use? Should strip mining be allowed to damage the environment so you can have electricity? Should some land be saved for open space, parks, and wilderness areas? Should we stop building single-family residences and instead build town houses and high-rise apartments, since they take up less space? How should we regulate the use of all our land—in the cities, the suburbs, the rural, and the undeveloped areas?

Economic Considerations

In recent years we've seen battles among environmentalists and developers. Environmentalists have prevented the construction of new power plants, which would pollute rivers. They also successfully held up the construction of the Alaska pipeline, until the oil embargo of 1973–74. On the other hand, we continue to give permits to municipal power plants, allowing them to pollute the city's air. We would rather have some pollution and electricity than no pollution and no electricity. Can our country afford to pay the added costs of using nonpolluting forms of energy? Can we afford *not* to? What economic factors are involved?

We believe in the free enterprise system, in which companies compete to sell their products. It is usually cheaper to pollute than not to pollute. Also, it is usually less expensive to use new natural resources than to recycle old materials. Competition and mass production methods have made it possible to sell material goods at very low prices. In fact, it is often cheaper to buy a new small appliance than it is to repair the old one. The cost of labor is high. Labor can more efficiently build new appliances on the assembly line than they can repair old ones.

The concept of waste is a part of our economic system. As long as people continue to buy new goods instead of repairing the old ones, employment is kept at a high rate. The profits made by those companies are used to expand. This expansion gives jobs to thousands of workers building and operating the new facilities. If we stop waste and don't buy new goods then sales go down, profits go down, expansion programs are stopped, and unemployment goes up.

Which is most important—clean air and water, or jobs? Resolving the ecological crisis will demand some real changes in our economic system. It can be done. But it won't be easy. It would affect the jobs and pocketbooks of many people. What proposals can you come up with to lessen the pressure on the ecosystem and at the same time not bring about the collapse of our economic system?

World Trade and International Relations

The environmental crisis is not an American phenomenon. It is world-wide. The problem of air pollution is so bad in Tokyo, Japan, for example, that police officers occasionally have to use oxygen masks so they can continue to direct traffic. Furthermore, every nation is affected by diminishing natural resources. For the natural resources of the world are not equally distributed. South Africa, for example, has almost all of the world's gold supply. And the Arab states of the Middle East have over half of the total known supplies of crude oil. Nations trade with one another, selling the resources they have (or goods produced from them) and buying the goods they lack.

If a nation is to stay economically sound in world trading, over a period of time it must sell more abroad than it buys. This is known as a favorable balance of trade. The Arab states increased the cost of a barrel of oil from less than $2 a barrel in 1970 to over $11 a barrel in 1975. The increased cost of oil put most developed countries in a position where they then had a negative balance of trade. A negative balance of trade places a severe strain on a nation's economy and eventually leads to unemployment. At the same time, the Arab states gained great monetary power because of their tremendous cash reserves from the oil sales. They also

Trade among nations is necessary because no nation has all the natural resources it needs. Many nations, for instance, rely on the United States for their supply of salt.

had power over countries, such as Japan, whose economy was dependent on oil from the Arab states.

International relations are affected. The United States has given a great deal of aid to other countries since World War II. We shared our large surpluses of grain with hungry people the world over. Now more and more people are starving. But the United States doesn't have a significant surplus of grain to share. Suppose we fail to share with nations whose citizens are starving, yet continue to live at our present high standard of living. Will the developing nations tolerate our living in luxury? How might our relations with other countries of the world be affected? Should we give up our present standard of living to share what we have with others?

These, then, are some of the many factors involved in a consideration of the ecological crisis and what can be done. The ecological crisis is a very complex problem. And aspects of the problem are changing constantly. What do you think should be done to deal with this problem?

SECTION REVIEW

1. What are some ways in which our personal freedom may be affected by the ecological crisis?
2. How should we change our use of land to ease the ecological crisis? What problems would such changes in land use create?
3. Name some problems for our economic system that the ecological crisis raises.
4. How do problems of decreasing natural resources affect world trade and international relations?

PROJECTS AND ACTIVITIES

1. Do research to find out more about the earth as an ecosystem.

2. Interview community leaders such as business executives, city officials, teachers, social workers, and union officials to find out what ecological problems exist in your own community.

3. Compare the environmental problems of a developing nation with those of the United States. How do the problems of the two nations differ?

4. Look in current newspapers and news magazines to determine what steps are presently being taken to help solve some of the world's ecological problems.

5. Conduct research and develop a plan that you think would be successful at alleviating some aspect of the ecological crisis.

6. Write a persuasive speech presenting your proposal for alleviating a waste disposal or pollution problem in your community.

7. Construct a collage, bulletin board, or poster that shows how overpopulation causes problems in your community, your nation, and the world.

354

8. Do research on Mexico, India, Sweden, or Japan to find out what some of their population problems are and how these problems are being handled.

9. Write an editorial on the topic "Why the World Must Lower Its Birth Rate."

10. Do research on scientific experimentation aimed at increasing the world's food supply.

11. Conduct research to determine how international relations, balance of power in the world, and world trade are affected by the environmental crisis.

TOPICS FOR INQUIRY

1. Debate: Human beings can survive only by realizing that they are not outside of and above nature but are a part of nature and must live in harmony with nature.

2. Many species of animals are now extinct and many more are on the endangered list (in danger of becoming extinct). It has been said that humans are the real endangered species because we cannot live without animals. Why might this be true? What do you think?

3. What changes would need to be made in our technology if we applied Dr. Commoner's "laws" of ecology to all aspects of life? Do you think we should? Why or why not?

4. Debate: The problem of pollution is not a technical problem but rather a political, economic, and social problem. The real questions are: Can I get reelected if I support that bill? Do we really want to spend all that money on ecology? and, How would it affect my standard of living?

5. People have been aware of the ecological crisis for many years. (For example, a government study of energy completed in 1952 recommended that immediate action be taken to avoid a serious energy shortage.) Yet seemingly very little has been done about it. How would you explain this lack of action? Who is at fault, in your opinion?

6. The conflict over ecology is often presented as "the economy" vs. "the environment." Is this the real conflict, or is it much more complicated and involved? Explain.

7. What can be done by (1) government, (2) industry and business, (3) your school, and (4) you as an individual, to help alleviate the environmental crisis?

8. Discuss the kinds of noise pollution that are most offensive to you. How much agreement is there among members of the class? What do you think could be done to lessen noise pollution?

9. Debate: We could cut our consumption of natural resources in half just by eliminating the waste and misuse of these resources.

10. What changes would you be willing to make in your lifestyle to help bring the ecosystem earth back into balance?

SUGGESTIONS FOR READING

COMMONER, Barry, *The Closing Circle*. Knopf, 1971 and Bantam (pap.). Considered one of the most knowledgeable books on environmental issues.

DASMANN, Raymond F., *A Different Kind of Country*. Macmillan, 1968 (and pap.). A discussion about the human environment and what we must do to keep it fit for people to live in, written by a distinguished ecologist and conservationist.

EHRLICH, Paul R. and EHRLICH, Anne H., *The End of Affluence: A Blueprint for Your Future*. Ballantine, 1974. Contains a broad range of money-saving options that will help us adapt to the era of limited resources.

———— and ————, *Population, Resources, Environment: Issues in Human Ecology*. Freeman, 1972. Suggests ways of dealing with overpopulation and a decline in natural resources.

ESPOSITO, John C., *Vanishing Air: The Report on Air Pollution*. Grossman, 1970 (pap.). A Ralph Nader study group report on air pollution.

HODSON, H. V., *The Diseconomics of Growth*. Ballantine, 1972 (pap.). An analysis of economic values in the areas of population, urban growth, and conservation.

LEINWAND, Gerald, *Air and Water Pollution*. Pocket Books, 1969 (pap.). One of a series of books by Leinwand on social problems in America.

MURPHY, Earl F., *Governing Nature*. Watts, 1970 (pap.). A discussion of the state of air, water, and forests around us as well as the costs, conflicts, and choices we face in creating an attractive environment.

NATIONAL GEOGRAPHIC SOCIETY, *As We Live and Breathe: The Challenge of Our Environment*. National Geographic Society, 1971. A pictorial presentation of the crisis of the environment.

PAPANEK, Victor, *Design for the Real World*. Bantam, 1973 (pap.). A revolutionary book about what the world needs now, why we have so much waste today, and why things don't work.

PIRAGES, Dennis C. and EHRLICH, Paul R., *Ark Two: Social Response to Environmental Imperatives*. Freeman, 1974 (pap.). A collaboration by a social scientist and a biologist emphasizing the interrelatedness of social and environmental concerns.

TOFFLER, Alvin, *The Eco-Spasm Report*. Bantam, 1975. A compact overview of our economic crisis—the breakdown of industrial civilization.

WARD, Barbara and DUBOS, René, *Only One Earth: The Care and Maintenance of a Small Planet*. Norton, 1972. A book based on environmental research carried out by many countries through the United Nations.

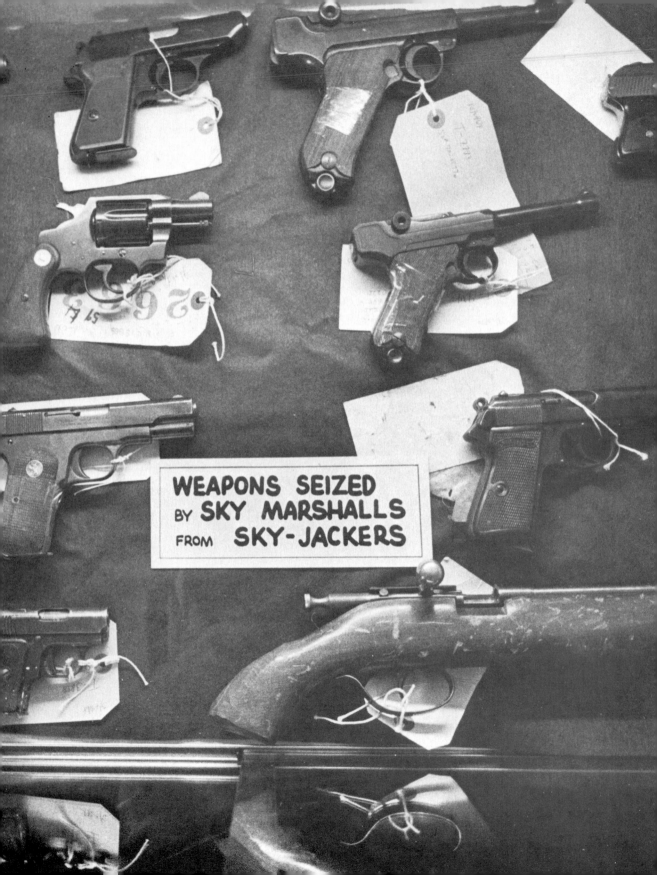

WEAPONS SEIZED
BY SKY MARSHALLS
FROM SKY-JACKERS

20 Crime

▶ Who is a criminal?

▶ How much crime is there in the United States?

▶ What roles do the police, the courts, and the prisons play in dealing with crime?

SECTION 1:
Crime, Criminals, and Delinquents

All Americans are affected by crime. Some are victims, some are criminals. Some, even, are both! The majority, however, are affected as bystanders. We get a daily dosage of crime from newspapers, radio, television, and the movies. As a result of our experiences and exposure through the mass media, most of us are concerned about the problem of crime.

The Sociological View of Crime

Emile Durkheim, the great French sociologist, pointed out around the turn of the century that crime is "normal" in all societies. It is normal because it is inevitable—it occurs regularly in all societies. And it is normal because it is necessary. It tells us what behavior to avoid. By identifying crime and punishing criminals, we know what noncriminal behavior consists of.

Pointing out crime and criminals also lends moral support to noncriminal behavior. For example, suppose a public officeholder enriches his or her own pocket at the public's expense. The person is found out and punished. It then becomes clear that such behavior is inappropriate—that politicians must separate their own finances from public finances. Identifying and punishing this behavior also encourages other politicians to separate their finances. Suppose, on the other hand, this same officeholder was found out and no action was taken. Everyone just yawned and said, "Well, that's what politicians do." The moral authority backing up honest behavior in politics would be weakened. Eventually it would no longer seem wrong for politicians to use public funds for their personal affairs. The existence of crime, then, helps define law-abiding behavior.

Why is crime a social problem? One reason is that crime provides a risk to the individual citizen. When the crime rate increases, each individual has a greater chance of being a victim. And no one wants to be a victim—even if victims may be helping to support society's moral authority! Although there will always be crime, the amount and kind of crime can be changed. A second reason is that crime endangers the well-being of society. If large numbers of people violate the laws of the society, the very stability of the society is threatened. Finally, crime is a social problem because it fits our definition of one. A social problem is a condition of human relationships that is considered undesirable by a substantial number of people, who feel that something can be done through collective social action. Our mass media indicate that vast numbers of people in the United States view crime as undesirable, and believe that something can be done about it.

Exactly what is crime? *A* CRIME *is any act that is defined as such, prohibited by law, and punishable by the state.* Thus a crime is any violation of the criminal law. A champion swimmer who stands and watches a friend drown instead of attempting to rescue the person may have violated a moral code. But in most states the swimmer hasn't violated a law and therefore has not committed a crime. Disobeying traffic laws or civil laws (laws relating to private matters) is ordinarily not considered a crime either, since these are not criminal laws.

The Classification of Crimes

To find out what acts are prohibited by criminal law, we can look at the classification of crimes used by the Federal Bureau of Investigation (FBI). For their uniform national crime reporting system, the FBI classifies offenses into the following twenty-nine categories. The categories are divided into two parts, depending on the seriousness of the offense.

Part I Offenses

(1) CRIMINAL HOMICIDE—All willful killing (also called murder and nonnegligent manslaughter).

(2) FORCIBLE RAPE—Sexual violation of a person by force and against the person's will.

(3) ROBBERY—Taking anything of value from a person by using force or threat of force.

(4) AGGRAVATED ASSAULT—An unlawful attack by one person on another for the purpose of inflicting severe bodily injury.

(5) BURGLARY (breaking or entering)—An attempt at or unlawful entry of a structure to commit a felony or theft.

(6) LARCENY (theft, except auto)—The unlawful taking or stealing of property or articles without the use of force, violence, or fraud. Examples include shoplifting, pickpocketing, and bicycle thefts.

(7) AUTO THEFT—The unlawful stealing or driving away and abandoning of a motor vehicle.

Part II Offenses

(8) OTHER ASSAULTS—Attacks of a less serious nature than aggravated assaults.

(9) ARSON—Willful or spiteful burning, including attempts at such acts.

(10) FORGERY AND COUNTERFEITING—Attempting to or making, altering, or possessing anything false that is intentionally made to appear true in order to deceive.

(11) FRAUD—Deceitful obtaining of money or property by false pretenses.

(12) EMBEZZLEMENT—Misappropriation or misapplication of money or property entrusted to the individual's care, custody, or control.

(13) STOLEN PROPERTY—Attempting to or buying, receiving, and possessing stolen property.

(14) VANDALISM—Willful or vicious destruction, injury, disfigurement, or defacement of property.

(15) WEAPONS—All violations of regulations relating to manufacturing, carrying, possessing, or using firearms.

(16) PROSTITUTION AND COMMERCIALIZED VICE—Sex offenses of a commercialized nature.

(17) SEX OFFENSES—Includes such charges as statutory rape (in which the girl consents but is under age) and offenses against common decency, morals, and chastity, or attempts at these offenses.

(18) VIOLATING NARCOTIC DRUG LAWS—The unlawful possession, sale, or use of narcotics.

(19) GAMBLING—Promoting, permitting, or engaging in gambling.

(20) OFFENSES AGAINST FAMILY AND CHILDREN—Nonsupport, neglect, desertion, or abuse of family and children.

(21) DRIVING UNDER THE INFLUENCE—Driving or operating any motor vehicle while under the influence of liquor or narcotics.

(22) VIOLATING LIQUOR LAWS—Violations of state or local liquor laws.

(23) DRUNKENNESS—Intoxication.

(24) DISORDERLY CONDUCT—Breach of the peace.

(25) VAGRANCY—Includes vagabondage, begging, and loitering.

(26) SUSPICION—Arrests for no specific offense, followed by release without placing charges.

(27) CURFEW AND LOITERING LAWS (JUVENILES)—Violations of local curfew and loitering laws, where such laws exist.

(28) RUNAWAYS (JUVENILES)—Limited to juveniles taken into custody under local statutes as runaways.

(29) ALL OTHER OFFENSES—All violations of state and local laws except traffic laws and those listed here.

The crimes listed here are classified in three ways. First, they are classified as either "Part I offenses" or "Part II offenses," based on their seriousness. Part I offenses are often used to obtain an overview of crime in the United States, because of their frequency of occurrence and likelihood of being reported.

Second, crimes are classified as "crimes against the person," "crimes against property," or "crimes against the public safety and morals." Crimes against the person involve personal contact with people, such

The crime of shoplifting can be classified in three ways. These ways are described above and on page 362. What are the three ways in which you would classify the crime of shoplifting?

as criminal homicide, rape, robbery, and assault. Crimes against property involve crimes in which there is no personal contact with the victim, such as burglary, larceny, auto theft, arson, and vandalism. The basic difference between robbery and burglary is that a robber takes articles from the person by force or threat, whereas a burglar takes something of value from the person's home or office. Crimes against the public safety and morals include such crimes as gambling, prostitution, narcotics violations, public frauds, or drunkennesss.

Third, crimes are classified according to the penalty that may be given. FELONIES *are major crimes that are punishable by imprisonment for longer than one year.* MISDEMEANORS *are minor crimes that are punishable by imprisonment for less than one year.* Felonies and misdemeanors vary to some degree from state to state, depending on the penalties provided for the various crimes. All serious crimes (categories one through seven) are felonies. In some cases of larceny the value of the money or goods stolen determines whether it is a felony or a misdemeanor. Auto theft is a felony, but joyriding is a misdemeanor. The difference between the two is that in auto theft it is assumed that the person will later sell the car or remove it from the community. In joyriding the person simply "borrows" the car for a while and then returns it. Both, of course, are criminal offenses.

The Classification of Criminals

Now that we have classified crimes, we might look more closely at the persons who violate the laws and earn the label "criminal."

Members of organized crime syndicates. One major difference in criminals is between those who engage in crime on an individual basis and those who are a part of organized crime syndicates (sometimes called "families"). Such organizations pursue crime as a big business, whereas individuals operate alone or in small groups. Crime syndicates are large-scale organizations of professional criminals that control some vice or business through violence or the threat of violence. These syndicates operate in all areas of business, many of them legal. But they are best organized in the areas of gambling, narcotics, and prostitution. Through such methods as loansharking (using unprincipled means to lend money at high interest rates), unfair labor practices, hijacking merchandise, and cheating on income tax, organized crime obtains a high profit rate.

Many of the crime syndicates carry out their operations through some legitimate organization, which serves as a "front" for the criminal activities. This enables them to make contacts with legitimate businesses and reinvest their profits from illegal sources. To insure their operations, crime syndicates usually seek some protection from city and police officials. They may make payments to the officials, who then notify the syndicate whenever they plan to make a raid on one of the organization's establishments. The syndicate thus has time to destroy the evidence and allow all important members to escape. In turn, by carrying out periodic "raids," the city officials can appear to be doing their jobs.

Recently, however, law enforcement agencies have been able to use eavesdropping and wiretapping devices to convict members of crime syndicates. In 1968 the Supreme Court ruled that people under investigation do not have to be notified before their phones are tapped. Also, wiretapping devices can be used to convict individuals as long as the person bringing suit obtains a warrant before using the devices. The Organized Crime Control Act of 1970 gave the federal courts increased powers to prosecute crime syndicates and established federal jurisdiction over large-scale gambling operations.

362

"Miss Dugan, will you send someone in here who can distinguish right from wrong?"

Corporations. Another source of crime are certain corporations. The laws of incorporation state that for certain purposes corporations are considered as "legal persons." They then become subject to the same laws as other people. One famous study found that over a period of forty years, the 100 largest corporations in the United States had been convicted of more than 1,500 criminal offenses. These crimes included unfair labor practices, dishonest advertising, restraint of trade, and food and drug violations. That is an average of about fifteen convictions for each corporation!

"White-collar" criminals. These are individuals who, in working for a corporation, or in any business operation, violate the law. Misrepresentation, fraud, and embezzlement are examples of white-collar crime. White-collar criminals are almost always from the middle and upper classes. And their violations tend to be played down by the press and the public. People get more excited over street crimes.

A variation on white-collar crime is governmental or political crime. One example are the "Watergate" criminals, who burglarized the Democratic National Committee offices in the Watergate Apartments complex during the 1972 presidential election campaign. Another example are the politicians who take bribes. The city officials who accept payoffs from syndicates are committing such crimes. And there are the politicians who, for a price, promise to use their influence to obtain special interest legislation. Political crimes may also involve violating a person's liberties through illegal eavesdropping, opening of mail, breaking and entering, and the like.

Criminals by predicament or habit. These are the occasional offenders who engage in violent, disorderly, "immoral," or other criminal violations as a result of particular circumstances or of habits that are considered illegal by the society. They violate the laws relating to gambling, intoxication, narcotics, vagrancy, and so on. They do not engage in crime as a primary means of support. Situational or habitual criminals make up the bulk of all those arrested. And they constitute the largest portion of the prison population.

Professional criminals. These persons make crime their life's work. Some are involved in organized crime. Others work in groups of three or four. A pickpocket "mob," for example, may consist of someone to divert the victim's attention, someone to actually pick the pocket, and someone to make sure the theft goes unnoticed by the crowd. Similar groups are engaged in shoplifting and confidence (swindling) operations. Professional criminals are more experienced than the occasional offenders. Therefore they are generally more skilled at staying clear of the law. Nevertheless, they are frequently arrested, and must consider jail terms as part of the cost of doing business!

Juvenile delinquents. One of the largest categories of criminals in the United States today is the juvenile offender. Traditionally, we've treated juvenile delinquency differently from adult crime. Each criminal law for adults refers to precisely defined offenses, carries specific punishments, and applies equally to all offenders. The laws pertaining to juvenile offenses have been much less specific or uniform. They've contained vague provisions about, for example, "incorrigible, ungovernable" children, who associate with "immoral or vicious persons." And the sen-

In our society, juvenile delinquents and adult criminals are given different treatment. These girls live at a Youth Guidance Center—a boarding school for delinquents.

tences have not been uniform. Consequently, a juvenile (a person under eighteen) could, and sometimes did, remain in custody for a longer time than an adult convicted of the same misdeed.

The rationale for separate regulation was that juvenile offenders, because of their age, were not as responsible as adults. Therefore they needed a special, more considerate, kind of treatment. Sometimes, however, the result was to deny juveniles equal protection under the law, without providing the special care and attention intended by the juvenile court.

To guard against this, the courts now must guarantee juvenile defendants the same legal rights and privileges that are granted to adult defendants. At the same time, juvenile delinquents are still regarded as special kinds of offenders. Juvenile courts try, officially at least, to provide many more services than the regular adult criminal court system.

SECTION REVIEW

1. What is a crime, and what are the three ways that crimes are classified?
2. Describe the various kinds of criminals and the basic characteristics of each.
3. What kinds of criminals can you think of who have not been included in these classifications?
4. How do you think juvenile delinquents should be treated by the law?

KEY TERMS

Define and give an example of each term.

aggravated assault	forgery
arson	fraud
burglary	larceny
crime	misdemeanor
criminal homicide	robbery
embezzlement	vagrancy
felony	vandalism
forcible rape	

SECTION 2:
Patterns of Crime

Part of the difficulty in dealing with the social problem of crime is in obtaining exact figures. It's harder to work toward a solution when we don't know the specific dimensions of the problem. Yet nobody really knows how much crime there is in the United States.

Statistics on Crime

The basic problem is that the available statistics on crime are not an accurate indication of the amount of crime that takes place. Consider the difficulties in obtaining accurate data on crime.

Much crime is not reported. A great deal of shoplifting is not reported and does not appear in statistics on crime. The murder that is accepted as an accident or natural death fails to make the crime statistics. Sex crimes are often unreported because the victim doesn't want publicity and fails to prosecute. Other persons who are victims of crime fail to report the crime because they don't want to risk a police investigation. Thus a great deal of crime never gets reported.

Many offenses are committed by average citizens who don't get reported or caught. One study attempted to find just how much crime the average citizen commits. A total of 1,020 men and 678 women were asked to check off which of some forty-nine listed offenses they had ever committed. The results showed that the men had committed an average of eighteen offenses each, and the women eleven. Sixty-four percent of the men and 27 percent of the women admitted committing at least one felony, an offense for which they could have been imprisoned for over one year.

Jurisdictions vary in how they report their crimes. Although the FBI has a standard listing of crimes to be reported, no police department or sheriff's office is required to report their crime statistics. All the data that jurisdictions provide is voluntary, and may be far from accurate.

Some rural communities solve crimes informally and do not consider them as crimes. Some cities don't report all of their known offenses because they think that a high crime rate might hurt the city's tourist trade or some other aspect of the local economy. Other cities are very complete in their reporting.

Another factor that causes variations in the crime statistics reported is the efficiency of the police department. If the police department is inefficient, the city is apt to have a low crime rate, because most of the crimes go undetected. If the city has an excellent police department, on the other hand, the city may show a very high crime rate, because the department knows about almost every violation of the law.

Also, increases in the crime rate may not mean actual changes in the amount of crime. For example, an increased public awareness of crime may cause law enforcement agencies to become more careful, make more arrests, and thereby create a higher crime rate. Yet the actual amount of crime may not have changed at all. Or the opposite situation may occur. If the public is less concerned about crime, the crime reports of the FBI are apt to show a reduction in the crime rate. Crime may then appear to be less of a problem. But the amount of crime may have remained the same.

The nature of the statistics makes evaluation difficult. We can evaluate the amount of crime on the basis of a number of criteria. We can base our evaluation on the number of offenses known to the police, the number of persons arrested by the police, or the number of convictions obtained for the various crimes. The statistics involved in each of these criteria are very different, and result in different evaluations.

The number of offenses known to the police is probably the best indicator of the actual amount of crime, since it includes all offenses that have been reported to the police. Statistics related to the number of arrests are less good indicators of the amount of crime, because there is a great difference between the number of known offenses and the number of arrests. There are many more known offenses than arrests. Statistics on convictions are often misleading because many persons are convicted of lesser offenses than the original charge. For example, many persons charged with murder are convicted of manslaughter. Many charged with rape are convicted of disorderly conduct. Others charged with armed robbery are convicted of carrying a concealed weapon. The reason for conviction on a lesser charge is that many persons plead guilty to a lesser charge and the court may not have sufficient evidence to convict the person on the original charge.

Because of all these difficulties, the statistics found through the FBI's uniform crime reporting program cannot be used as absolute data in determining the amount of crime. Even the FBI acknowledges that these reports serve only as a rough index of the crime situation in the United States. By comparing data for different years, however, we may be able to tell if the amount of crime is increasing or decreasing. We can also gain some information about the types of crimes being committed. Furthermore, the crime statistics do reveal a number of crime patterns.

Crime Patterns in the United States

The Uniform Crime Reports of the FBI indicate the following general trends.

Crime is increasing. Although, as we have said, a public awareness of crime can cause the crime statistics to rise without any actual

Is the number of arrests an accurate indication of the amount of crime that occurs? Consider that some crimes take place for which no one is arrested. And some people are arrested who are later found to be not guilty. The number of arrests is, however, a useful indication of the amount of police activity that occurs.

increase in crime, nevertheless the reports show a tremendous increase. Between 1960 and 1974 the number of Part I crimes known to the police soared from 2,015,000 to 10,192,000—which is an increase of five times. A more accurate indication of the actual increase is the crime rate. *The* CRIME RATE *is the number of Part I crimes per 100,000 population.* It therefore allows for the increase in population. During the five-year period 1969 to 1974, the crime rate increased by 24 percent. And this trend of an increasing crime rate has continued further into the 1970's.

Most arrests are for Part II crimes. Actually the arrests for Part I crimes (criminal homicide, forcible rape, robbery, aggravated assault, burglary, larceny, and auto theft), amount to less than 25 percent of all arrests. The table on page 368 shows the number of arrests for all twenty-nine crimes. From this table we can see that the greatest number of arrests are for drunkenness. In fact, we find that over one third of all arrests in the United States are related to violations of narcotics and alcohol laws. By adding the number of arrests for violating drug laws, driving while intoxicated, violating liquor laws, and drunkenness, and then dividing by the total number of arrests, we find that these offenses accounted for almost 35 percent of all the arrests made that year.

THE NUMBER OF ARRESTS BY OFFENSE, 1974

OFFENSE CHARGED	NUMBER OF ARRESTS
TOTAL	9,101,630
Criminal Homicide	23,970
Forcible rape	26,380
Robbery	148,720
Aggravated assault	234,060
Burglary — breaking or entering	516,100
Larceny — theft	1,056,300
Auto theft	158,600
Total for Part I crimes	2,164,130
Other assaults	391,100
Arson	16,900
Forgery and counterfeiting	60,600
Fraud	148,600
Embezzlement	13,000
Stolen property	113,200
Vandalism	221,100
Weapons	170,300
Prostitution and commercialized vice	68,400
Sex offenses (except forcible rape and prostitution)	64,600
Narcotic drug laws	642,100
Gambling	61,900
Offenses against family and children	61,000
Driving while intoxicated	843,600
Liquor laws	310,000
Drunkenness	1,332,600
Disorderly conduct	767,600
Vagrancy	44,700
Suspicion	45,900
Curfew and loitering	151,000
Runaways	239,600
All other offenses (except traffic)	1,169,700
Total for Part II crimes	6,937,500

Source: FBI, *Crime in the United States, 1974: Uniform Crime Reports.*

The police recover about one third of all stolen property. In any single year property worth more than two billion dollars is lost as a result of robberies, burglaries, larcenies, and auto thefts. Recoveries by the police reduce this loss by 30 to 40 percent. There is a great difference, however, in the kinds of property recovered. The recovery rate for stolen automobiles is high—often about 70 percent. But the recovery rate for other items, such as money, jewelry, furs, and clothing, tends to be very low—lower than 15 percent, due to the difficulty of tracing stolen goods.

Crime rates are highest in cities and lowest in rural areas. In the year 1974, for example, the rate of arrests for all crimes (per 100,000 people) was 4,821. The rate of arrests for the cities was 5,622. For suburban areas, it was 4,027. In rural areas it was only 1,747. The number of offenses known and the number of arrests is also higher for cities than for suburban or rural areas. However, in recent years the volume of crime has been increasing fastest in the suburbs.

Arrests are highest for males and are increasing fastest for people under eighteen years. The arrests of males tend to outnumber females by five or six to one. During 1974, for example, a total of 5,185,110 males and 994,296 females were arrested. However, the percentage in the change of numbers of females being arrested is higher than it is for males. Perhaps due to recent efforts to treat men and women equally, the percentage of arrests of women as compared to men is now increasing.

Regarding age, the greatest increase in arrests is for persons under the age of eighteen. The arrest rates for the years 1960 to 1974 indicate that the total arrests for all ages increased by 33 percent. The increase for persons under the age of eighteen was 138 percent. The increase for persons eighteen years and over was only 16 percent. But remember that a far greater *number* of those arrested are eighteen and over.

The Causes of Crime

Many different theories have been advocated over the years as to the causes of crime. Some are biological in nature, some psychological, and some sociological. Sociological theories recognize that crime is very complex and cannot be explained by any one cause. The following three basic theories of crime attempt to provide a general framework for the many causes of criminal behavior.

The differential association theory. This theory of the American sociologist Edwin Sutherland states that individuals learn patterns of criminal behavior in the same way they learn patterns of lawful behavior. They learn through their interaction with others, who define the codes of behavior. The differential association refers to the ratio of associations that the individual has with criminal behavior patterns and anticriminal behavior patterns. Persons become criminals because they have a higher number of pro-criminal associations than of pro-law associations. It is possible to obtain pro-criminal experiences from noncriminals who nevertheless present crime in a favorable light. It is also possible to learn anticriminal patterns from criminals who obey most laws.

This theory suggests that the basic learning of criminal behavior occurs in small personal groups. People become criminal or law-abiding the same way they learn how to speak English or Swedish—they have personal relationships with more people who are disposed in that direction.

The culture conflict theory. Proposed by the sociologist and educator Thorsten Sellin, this theory emphasizes the conflicts caused by different rules of conduct. In a complex society the individual belongs to a great number of diverse groups, each with its own specific activities. The norms of one group may permit one response to a particular situation. The norms of another group may permit an opposite response. The individual

You've just read about the differential association theory. This theory states that people learn criminal behavior patterns from their association with pro-criminal behavior. What can our prisons do to reduce criminal patterns? To increase law-abiding behavior?

may have to choose between two conflicting rules of conduct in a particular life situation. If the person follows the norms of a subculture, and this behavior is considered criminal by the culture, the person becomes a criminal. Sellin suggests that the sociologist should not focus on the criminal but should study the conflicts of cultural norms in specific situations.

The anomie theory. Developed by sociologist Robert Merton, this theory sees crime resulting when people learn to value widely held goals in the society, but are denied the means to achieve these goals. You may remember from Chapter 4 that anomie means normlessness. Merton explains crime as a breaking of the social norms in order to obtain certain goals. As we mentioned in Chapter 4, in the United States individuals of every social class learn to value wealth and material success. Yet the means for achieving success are denied many lower-class people. This difference between goals and access to approved means causes some people to develop new and perhaps illegal means to achieve material success.

This theory helps explain why certain categories of people, particularly lower-class minorities, are overrepresented in certain types of crime, such as the rackets. Merton recognized, of course, that most poor people do not resort to illegal ways of gaining wealth. Those categories of people who have done so, he suggested, have either not resided in our society long enough to identify with its norms or else have been denied adequate opportunity to identify with the society.

Each of these theories is tied to the concept that behavior is learned, and that the culture and the group exert a great influence on individual behavior. Yet each of them has a different emphasis. Which theory best explains crime in the United States? What theories of your own would you suggest? How might the problem of crime be reduced? What kinds of programs might bring about lower crime rates?

SECTION REVIEW

1. What are some of the problems involved in obtaining accurate crime statistics?
2. What are some trends in crime patterns in the United States?
3. Describe the three theories advocated by different sociologists to explain the causes of crime.

KEY TERMS

Explain the meaning of each term.

anomie theory
crime rate
culture conflict theory
differential association theory

SECTION 3:
The Criminal Justice System

People respond to the problem of crime in various ways. Some may complain angrily that the crime rate is getting out of hand. An elderly person in a large city may refuse to go outside after dark for fear of being robbed. Newspapers may print editorials exposing one crime or another. Universities may give courses or whole programs in the field of criminal justice. The society, however, has an official response to crime. It is the criminal justice system. This system consists of the police, the courts, and the prisons.

The Police

The police are society's first line of defense. Police officers on the beat must deal immediately with all kinds of irregular behavior, both legal and illegal. They must decide when to ignore a situation, when to lend a helping hand, when to give a stern warning, when to make an arrest, when to call for help, and when to use violence.

The dilemma. On the one hand, the police are expected to maintain law and order, and to use good judgment in doing so. To be effective, they need to be viewed as a positive force in the community. On the other hand, the police are regarded as a negative force by some members of the society. Among the urban poor, especially minorities, and among some segments of the younger population, police officers are often categorized as "the enemy." The riots of the 1960's, involving inner-city blacks as well as college students, sometimes began as confrontations between citizens and the police. One reason was that police officers were largely drawn from the same population that felt threatened by minorities and students, so they themselves felt threatened by the rioters.

Some ways of dealing with the problem. The police are becoming increasingly aware of this problem of convincing all members of the community that they are enforcing the law in a fair and even-handed manner. One way of creating a convincing positive image is to perform at or above the level of community expectations. This requires some expertise. There is now an emphasis on professionalism within the ranks of the police, especially among younger officers and within larger departments. In the New York City Police Department, for example, a substantial number of patrol officers have bachelor's degrees. Some even possess a law degree. In many parts of the country police officers have enrolled in college programs which offer courses in sociology, psychology, urban problems, criminology, and criminal justice. These are in addition to the police science and lab courses that sophisticated police departments have always provided for their members.

Nevertheless, the problem persists. Recent surveys have indicated that the police are still not very highly regarded as a professional group. There is a lingering belief on the part of some people that graft and corruption are widespread among police officers. Today, however, a large number of well paid, professionalized police departments are unwilling to put up with professional misconduct. More effective means of "self-policing" are being developed.

The Court System

The purpose of the courts is to decide on the relative merits of the DEFENDANT's claim of innocence versus the charge of the PLAIN- TIFF—*the person bringing suit*. There are various kinds of courts, such as traffic courts, civil courts, and criminal courts. In the criminal courts, the defendant is an individual or a corporation charged with violating some provision of the criminal law. The plaintiff is a particular state, if a state law may have been violated, or the United States of America, if a federal law is involved.

Normally a case does not come to trial unless a grand jury first hands down an INDICT- MENT—*a statement charging a person or corporation with an offense.* Such an indictment indicates that the grand jury believes the evidence presented by the state deserves further consideration in a criminal trial. The process, which begins with the arrest by a law enforcement official, ends with a verdict by a jury or judge. For a guilty verdict, guilt must be established "beyond a reasonable doubt."

Some problems faced by the courts. One problem is how to determine what is "be-

Today many police departments have classes for their police officers. The departments encourage their members to take special training to increase their ability on the job.

Many aspects of our judicial system come from the British legal system. One of these is the use of a jury. Another is the idea that a person is innocent until proven guilty.

yond a reasonable doubt." It is not the same as "beyond *any* doubt." If a guilty verdict were given only in cases where there was no doubt at all, our legal system would have fallen apart centuries ago!

Another problem is the overcrowded schedules of the courts. Often court calendars are backlogged for months and even years. Recently there was a backlog of over 9,000 felony cases in New York City alone. Defendants awaiting trial on criminal charges in that city are often kept in jail for months.

Because of this heavy caseload, prosecutors (those who begin and carry on legal proceedings against someone) are frequently tempted to use "plea bargaining." PLEA BARGAINING *involves a prior arrangement between the prosecutor and the defendant. The defendant*

agrees to plead guilty to a lesser charge. And the prosecutor agrees not to prosecute on the original, more serious, charge. This has the effect of speeding up the judicial process. But it may also involve a compromise with justice. In some instances a person guilty of a more serious crime merely accepts punishment for a lesser one. But in other cases a person may be persuaded to plead guilty to a crime when he or she is not guilty at all. This is especially possible with less educated people, who are less likely to be fully aware of their rights under the law.

Not everyone in our society looks to the judicial system with equal confidence. Members of the lower socioeconomic levels, and especially minority members, often view the courts as part of the "enemy establishment."

While middle-class people usually see the criminal justice system as serving their interests, some lower-income people view that same system as favoring interests other than their own. This belief then influences what action different members of our social structure take.

Conflicting philosophies. There is also the question of the civil rights of defendants versus the need of society to control crime. How tough on defendants should our legal system be? Do judges coddle criminals by respecting their civil liberties — as some have maintained? Or is our system too harsh — as others have said?

The tendency in recent years has been to increase the rights of defendants. Several Supreme Court decisions have broadened individual rights in criminal trials. *Miranda v. Arizona* (1966) established the necessity of warning defendants of their legal rights. *Escobedo v. Illinois* (1966) strengthened defendants' rights of counsel, as did the case of *Angersinger v. Hamlin* (1972). The case of *Furman v. Georgia* (1972) declared capital punishment unconstitutional, except in a few very carefully defined circumstances.

Yet the pendulum may be starting to swing the other way. The case of *Cady v. Dombrowsky* (1973) took away some of the individual's protection from search and seizure. The Supreme Court held that, under certain conditions, material found in a search held without a warrant could be used as evidence.

At issue is the very delicate balance between society's need to protect its citizens and the freedoms and liberties of the individual. The British jurist William Blackstone concluded in the 1700's: "It is better that ten guilty persons escape than that one innocent suffer."

The Prisons

People who are convicted of criminal offenses in the United States receive relatively long prison sentences compared to people in other parts of the developed world. Yet such imprisonment is not accomplishing all that it might.

The functions of the prison system. Imprisonment is supposed to perform three functions. The first is to keep dangerous people from inflicting more harm. The second is to provide a deterrent effect — to discourage others from committing crimes by showing that criminals are punished. The third is to rehabilitate the offenders — to turn them into law-abiding citizens.

If putting criminals in prison for a long time kept "dangerous" people off the streets, then the crime rate should decrease. The crime rate should also go down if imprisonment deterred people from committing crimes. But our crime rate is not low. Instead, the United States has both long sentences and high crime rates.

Also, a prison sentence does not deter convicted offenders from committing future crimes, since former prisoners are very likely to wind up back in jail. For many prisons in the United States, the rate of people going back to prison is as high as 75 percent. This means that three out of four of those who have been in prison eventually return there. Perhaps they learn more about crime in prison. They may become embittered. Or they may be ill-prepared for anything else. In any case, if so many people who are processed through the American prison system return to it, the prisons are not succeeding in their rehabilitation function.

It appears that the old answer of "lock 'em up and throw away the key" does not work. Rather than rehabilitating them, the "get tough" approach dehumanizes people, narrowing their rights and choices. After spending time in a state or federal prison, a person is usually less able to perform productively in society.

Proposals for change. Many people are

374

Some prisons make an effort to prepare inmates for their future freedom by developing their skills. Here people in a county prison are taking part in a crafts workshop.

aware of the problem and have made suggestions for changing the present system. Some proposals are rather simple and immediate, such as placing first offenders on probation rather than sending them to jail. Others involve creating minimum-security institutions with less harsh atmospheres where the emphasis is on rehabilitation. Still other proposals are more elaborate and far-ranging, involving work or school release time. In Sweden, for example, prisoners are expected to have jobs (or go to school) on the "outside," to return in the evening, and to pay their own upkeep. This system seems to work—at least in Sweden. The rate of people returning to prison there is less than 25 percent, and the overall crime rate is considerably lower than ours.

Perhaps the problem requires a more thoroughgoing examination of what we, as a society, want from our prisons. If what we want is to severely punish those convicted of crime, knowing that most will be back on the street committing the same (or more serious) crimes sooner or later, then we should continue what we are doing. If, on the other hand, we want to come to grips with the problem of crime, we must take a close look at our system of prisons and what it is meant to be doing.

Considering the problems with our criminal justice system, what would you do? Would you make any changes in the police force? The courts? The prison system? If so, what changes would you make? And what steps would you take to accomplish them?

SECTION REVIEW

1. What problems do the police face in combating crime?
2. What are some difficulties confronting our court system?
3. What are the advantages and disadvantages of a prison system?

KEY TERMS

Explain each term.

defendant
indictment

plaintiff
plea bargaining

PROJECTS AND ACTIVITIES

1. Study the crime reports in your daily newspapers for a week and tabulate the kinds of crimes reported.

2. Watch several installments of a television show that is centered around crime and law enforcement. Take notes, keeping in mind the various kinds of criminals and theories of the causes of crime, and write a short report of your findings.

3. Ask several older members of your community about the kind and amount of crime that occurred when they were younger. Compare their responses to the general conditions today in your community.

4. Construct a crime map of your community, on which you locate the amount of crime in specific areas, by consulting the local police and newspapers. Interview residents in high and low crime districts to find out how their awareness of the amount of crime corresponds to that of the authorities.

5. Write a poem or short story about the exploits and fate of an individual who exemplifies one kind of criminal.

6. Do research on organized crime in the United States. In what areas are crime syndicates most successful? What measures are being taken to limit their activities?

7. Visit the local police station to obtain facts about crime and juvenile delinquency in your community.

8. Do a content analysis of the evening news broadcasts on television to determine what percent of the news reports relate to crime and violence. Obtain a sample of five or six broadcasts.

9. Write a newspaper editorial in which you present a solution to the problem of the increasing rates of crime and delinquency.

10. Conduct a survey in which you ask people how they think crime can be alleviated.

11. Interview several police officers and civilians regarding their ideas about the role of the police. How do their views compare?

12. Sit in on a criminal court case to observe courtroom procedures.

13. Do research to find out the current practices regarding criminal probation or parole in your area.

TOPICS FOR INQUIRY

1. Discuss the many ways in which crime affects you as an individual.

2. How do you account for the continuing increase in crime in America?

3. The Omnibus Crime Control Act of 1968 gave the federal government the authority to use electronic eavesdropping devices in criminal investigations. In 1970 the District of Columbia Crime Bill gave federal agents the right to conduct "no-knock" raids (in which the police enter a home unannounced to catch suspected drug supplies before the evidence is destroyed) in the District of Columbia. Do you feel that these provisions are an undesirable invasion of the citizens' privacy or a necessary step to reduce organized crime and illegal drug use? Explain your answer.

4. Which of the three theories do you feel best explains the causes of crime? Why?

5. Discuss examples of how crime is "normal" and "useful" in society. What is meant by the statement that criminal behavior serves to make acceptable behavior clearer?

6. Debate: Police are part of the problem of crime, just as they are part of the solution.

7. Courts must balance the need for society's protection with the need for preserving individual liberties. Can you think of ways to change the court system to help maintain and insure this balance?

8. Discuss whether the Swedish system of work and school release for prisoners would be effective in the United States.

9. Obtain the latest copy of the U.S. Bureau of the Census, *Statistical Abstract of the United States* and look up statistics that correspond with the statistics given in this chapter. What are the latest trends in crime in America? How are they changing?

NONFICTION

BLUMBERG, Abraham, *Current Perspectives on Criminal Behavior.* Knopf, 1974. A book of original essays on criminology, including such areas as underworld crime, violent behavior, sexual criminality, and criminal justice reform.

CLARK, Ramsey, *Crime in America.* Simon & Schuster, 1970 or Pocket Books (pap.). The former Attorney General of the United States examines the problem of crime in American society and makes specific suggestions concerning the prevention and control of crime.

CORTES, Juan and GATTI, Florence M., *Delinquency and Crime: A Bio-psycho-social Approach.* Academic Press, 1972. An interdisciplinary textbook focusing on the empirical, theoretical, and practical aspects of criminal behavior.

GOWAN, Paul, EGLESON, Nick, and HENTOFF, Nat, *State Secrets: Police Surveillance in America.* Holt, Rinehart and Winston, 1974. An investigation that explores corruption in American government by focusing on the Watergate controversy.

HILLS, Stuart L., *Crime, Power, and Morality: The Criminal Law Process in America.* Chandler, 1971 (pap.). A sociological analysis of crime in America, stressing the process of criminal law.

HOOD, Roger and SPARKS, Richard, *Key Issues in Criminology.* McGraw-Hill, 1970 (and pap.). A straightforward presentation of the issues and data of crime in the United States, with emphasis on the sentencing and treatment of criminals.

HUGHES, Helen M. (ed.), *Delinquents and Criminals: Their Social World.* Holbrook, 1972 (pap.). A series of readings by sociologists, rewritten in a nontechnical manner.

PRINS, Herschel, *Criminal Behavior: An Introduction to Its Causes and Treatment.* Beekman, 1974 (and pap.). A criminology textbook dealing with defining and measuring crime, with social, environmental, and constitutional explanations of crime, and with the court system of disposing of criminals.

QUINNEY, Richard (ed.), *Criminal Justice in America: A Critical Understanding.* Little, Brown, 1974 (pap.). A comprehensive book of readings treating virtually all aspects of the criminal justice system.

———, *Criminology: Analysis and Critique of Crime in America.* Little, Brown, 1975. A college textbook in criminology that presents an extended picture of crime and punishment.

378

SCHUR, Edwin M., *Crimes Without Victims—Deviant Behavior and Public Policy.* Prentice-Hall, 1965 (pap.). A discussion of the violations of laws on abortion, homosexuality, and drug addiction.

FICTION

BOULLE, Pierre, *The Virtues of Hell.* Vanguard. A novel about a drug addict who cures himself by totally involving himself in a job he likes.

CHILDRESS, Alice. *A Hero Ain't Nothin' but a Sandwich.* Coward, McCann and Geoghegan or Avon (pap.). Benjie, a thirteen-year-old black, tells what it is like to grow up in the inner city with a drug habit.

DOSTOEVSKY, Feodor, *Crime and Punishment.* Dutton (and pap.). A story of a man who escapes detection after murdering an old pawnbroker but who, after much psychological anguish, is driven to confess.

KAFKA, Franz, *The Trial.* Random House or Schocken (pap.). A story of an honest banker who one day is unexplainably arrested and who must spend the rest of his life fighting charges made against him concerning a crime he did not commit.

Highlight

What is the law?

One way that we know what goes on in a society is through its "official" definitions. We find these official definitions in such places as constitutional texts, holy scripture, and the society's laws and legal system. These definitions don't include the many informal understandings and inter-relationships that exist in every society. Nevertheless, the official definitions do tell us a great deal about a society and how it functions. They tell us, among other things, how its members wish to conduct themselves within the society.

The laws and the legal system are particularly important aspects of society's official organization. We are all, as individuals, under the influence of laws. We all participate, however indirectly, in their creation and operation. Some knowledge of our laws and legal system is essential if we are to understand the workings of our society.

Unlike customs or manners, laws are legislated. That is, laws are created and passed by special lawmaking groups, or legislatures. These legislatures may be the United States Congress, or the various legislatures of the fifty states. Since municipal councils are also a kind of legislature, their ordinances are a type of law. In addition, some federal and state administrative agencies are empowered to set rules and regulations, which often have the force of law.

No other rules are laws. Regulations, such as those made by employers, schools, professional organizations, and the like, are not laws. Violators may not be brought to court—although they may be dismissed, expelled, refused entrance, or punished in some other way by the agency. For example, if you refuse to pay your school library its fines for overdue books, you can't be tried in court. The school might inflict its own controls, such as denying you future library privileges. Nevertheless, no question of law is involved.

There are several kinds of law. It is possible to distinguish between federal and state law, between national and international law, between civilian and military law, and between criminal and civil law. Perhaps the most convenient way for us to distinguish between the various types of law, though, is on the basis of whom or what they are intended to protect.

Criminal Law

The first thing that needs protecting in any society is the society and its members. The criminal law protects the rights of the people, who are represented by the state. Its purpose is to guarantee law and order. Criminal law deals with crimes of violence, crimes against people and property, crimes against the security of the state (such as treason), and offenses against regulatory laws.

A criminal act may cause injury to a private party—either to the person or to property. But a criminal act is first of all an offense against the public order. Because criminal acts are violations of public order, punishment is given in the name of the state, not in the name of the injured party or parties. That is, if a criminal is fined, the money is paid to the state, not to the victim. If the victims of a crime seek payment for damages done to them by the criminal, they must begin a separate civil proceeding (at which the court can grant financial awards).

Thus the system of criminal justice serves to protect the safety of life and property and to provide for the preservation of public order. Yet in doing so, the system of criminal justice takes away some of the personal freedom of individual citizens. Can a criminal justice system both preserve order and maintain liberty? The system must be strong enough to control the professional criminal. Yet it must be flexible enough to allow innocent citizens their freedom.

One form of protection for individuals in our society is the emphasis on providing civil liberties to all citizens. Our civil liberties are guaranteed by our Constitution. They insure that we all receive equal justice under law. They include the right to remain silent when questioned, the right to trial by jury, and the assistance of a lawyer or lawyers. They also include protection against unreasonable searches and seizures, excessive fines, and cruel or unusual punishment.

Civil Law

It is important to protect the state and to provide for law and order. But it is also important to protect the society's general standards and principles. This involves setting up means to insure that justice is done and that individual citizens receive a fair adjustment when they've been wronged. The civil law provides such protection. It protects individuals against unreasonable conditions or acts by any other citizens or by their government. It provides an opportunity to sue for damages, when the damage is the result of an unreasonable action by others.

Civil law rests on the understanding that relationships between individuals ought to be conducted on a reasonable basis. If your injury is a result of my carelessness,

or of my willful action, then you ought to be entitled to collect damages from me. And you are. The civil law upholds the principle that social activity ought to be carried out on a reasonable basis. It upholds this principle by providing the methods by which damages can be determined and payment made. Civil law also can enforce payment of damages, if the wrongdoer refuses to pay.

Contract Law

Still a third kind of law is necessary to protect the right of individuals or groups to make contractual agreements with other individuals or groups. We can call this kind of law contract law, or private law. This type of law allows people to enter privately into understandings that, once agreed upon, are enforced by law.

If one party in a contractual agreement feels that the other party is not maintaining the contract, he or she can start a civil suit. The court may decide that failure to live up to an agreement is unreasonable behavior. Therefore, this type of court decision, forcing a person to obey the terms of a contract, is an example of civil law.

There are many examples of contract law. Agreements concerning transactions of property or goods, terms of employment and payment for personal services, membership in organizations, and arrangements for credit are all everyday examples. Can you think of others? It would be impossible to conduct the business of modern society if these contractual agreements weren't available. Such "private legislation" is necessary to fit the law to specific individuals and to the particular set of facts.

These, then, are three different types of law that exist in our society and help it to function. What might our society be like without these official definitions of the law?

21 Poverty

- What is poverty?

- How much poverty exists in the United States?

- What can be done about the problem of poverty?

SECTION 1:
The Structure of Poverty

The United States has traditionally been recognized as one of the world's wealthiest nations. We have consistently had a high per capita (per person) income. Our cars, our household appliances, the general prosperity of our workers—all are well known, and have caused many nations to envy and imitate us. We have not only helped Europe defend itself in two world wars but have also helped build it up again. We have even put men on the moon.

Yet we have a poverty problem. And it is a more serious one than exists in Europe. Although we have a high per capita income, we rank approximately fifteenth in infant mortality (the death rate among infants up to one year of age), and about nineteenth in male longevity (the length of life for men).

There are a sizable number of Americans for whom prosperity is but a dream, if that. Their living standard is closer to that of people in a developing area of Asia or South America than to the one usually associated with Americans.

What Is Poverty?

How would you define poverty? You might answer that it involves living in a state or situation in which certain essential material goods are lacking. You might give as examples the sharecroppers in the South, the poor residents of Appalachia, the inhabitants of our urban slums, or the starving children of Bangladesh. Both this definition and these examples would be accurate, if you also made certain qualifications.

First of all, poverty is a relative concept. How poor someone must be, and what level of living the person must be at, to be considered in a state of poverty depends on how rich the rest of the people in his or her

These people's per capita income is low, compared to an American's. But are they poor? Poverty is relative to the society in which you live.

society are, and what level of living they enjoy. Persons with a $25,000 a year income will regard themselves as poor in a society of people with $100,000 a year incomes. Similarly, someone having two potatoes in a one-potato world will be considered rich.

Part of this relative concept of poverty is the idea of relative deprivation. RELATIVE DEPRIVATION *refers to determining the poverty*

level by the minimum level of living that the society regards as decent and reasonable. The poverty level is based on what everybody else has. People whose level of living is below that expectation consider themselves poor, and are considered so by others.

The idea of relative deprivation implies that what is considered poverty at one time, in one society, is not necessarily poverty at another time, or in another society. For example, many Americans who are regarded as poverty-stricken by the general public and by official standards would not be considered poor if they were in rural India, or some parts of Latin America, Asia, or Africa.

Relative deprivation also implies that poverty cannot be completely eliminated. The level of poverty has a shifting base. Poverty will continue to exist so long as there is any substantial difference in the distribution of wealth within the society. Those people at or near the bottom will see themselves as deprived, and will be considered as such by others.

Poverty is largely relative. Yet our society is continuing its efforts to solve this social problem. Why? The relativity of poverty does not make its effects any easier to bear. Individuals who are living in a condition of poverty see their lot as unsatisfactory, and want it improved. In fact, improvement may be necessary to achieve social stability. In some cases the presence of poverty goes against the basic beliefs and desires of a society, and can undermine its very existence.

Some conditions of poverty may lead to social revolution. Revolution does not occur if the condition of poverty is stable. It is stable if the people at the bottom see themselves, and are seen by others, as poor, and have no expectations that their situation will improve. They are too busy surviving to focus on social change. But if those at the bottom stop seeing their situation as permanent and begin to expect better conditions, they will get together to attain them. A social revolution is more likely if those at the bottom receive promises of better conditions, but no improvement comes.

In discussing poverty, it is important to distinguish between the relativity of poverty and starvation, which is in no way relative. The human body requires a certain minimum caloric intake. Without it, the body cannot function. Starvation, or the process of dying for want of sufficient food, takes place. Poverty is a social phenomenon. Starvation is a physiological process. The starving children in Bangladesh, for example, are not suffering from relative deprivation alone!

The Data of Poverty

Because poverty is relative, there is no way to determine the exact number of people who are poor. That figure depends on how poverty is defined, and for what purpose. Usually the federal government sets an income standard for a family of four, and places everyone below that level in the poverty class. However, the results are not exact, since we don't know precisely who has what income. Also, in a period of inflation the standard must be raised continually to allow for the decreasing value of the dollar. Finally, in a state of rising affluence, the sense of relative deprivation, the minimum amount that people expect, is constantly moving upward.

Nevertheless, there are various estimates of the number of people living under conditions of poverty. The Census Bureau recently classified some 24.3 million people as poor, based on their yearly income of less than $5,038 for a family of four. In other words, almost 12 percent of the population is living below the official poverty line.

Other estimates have been slightly higher. The Department of Labor, for example, dis-

covered that official statistics, such as those gathered by the Census Bureau, tend to under-count the number of people at the very bottom of our society. Official statistics do not include many Americans who are so marginal that they don't have a permanent address. The Labor Department determined that there are more blacks, more unemployed, and more poor people in the United States than the official figures indicate—although we do not know how many more.

Still other estimates arrive at a much larger figure than the official poverty level by counting the people who are on the borderline of poverty. The Department of Health, Education, and Welfare has estimated that about one fourth of the population are either living in poverty or are only an accident or an illness away from it.

The data of poverty include not only numerical estimates but also the distribution of the poor. First of all, a disproportionate number of the poor are children. This is because those at the bottom of the social order tend to have large families. The President's Council of Economic Advisors estimated several years ago that 15 million children were included as part of the "officially poor." This means that one out of every four children in the nation was living in poverty! Many of these children will receive a substandard education in a world that is increasingly demanding some technical knowledge for everyone. And when they get married, they will probably have more children than the average. This will keep up the high number of children who are poor.

Another characteristic of the distribution of poverty is the disproportionately high number of Black Americans and other minorities. Only about 11 percent of the population is black, while about 30 percent of the poor are black. Furthermore, about one third of the total black population is living below the official poverty level.

Causes of Poverty

In many parts of the world poverty is caused by a scarcity of food and goods. In the United States, however, we have the ability to produce enough food and goods to provide a relatively high standard of living for all persons in the society. For example, government farm programs have kept much of our farmland out of production to prevent large surpluses of food and fiber. Industry, too, has the capacity to produce a far greater quantity of goods than it does now. The real problem is that many people in the society do not have the financial resources to purchase these goods.

One explanation for poverty in America claims that people are poor because they are lazy and don't want to work. However, most people living in poverty do want to work.

But they can't get jobs because of physical disabilities, discrimination in hiring practices, or a lack of adequate training or education. We cannot explain poverty in such simple terms.

From the sociological point of view one of the basic reasons for poverty in our society is INSTITUTIONALIZED INEQUALITY, *or the way in which we establish and practice certain patterns of inequality that then contribute to the continuation of poverty.* Perhaps the best example of institutionalized inequality in America is the stratification system itself. Our society (and all other complex societies) is divided into social classes and statuses. Some people receive a great deal of respect and prestige, and others receive very little. The life style that an individual develops is largely determined by the social class into which he or she is born. The socialization ex-

It isn't true that people are poor in America because they don't want to work. These laborers work hard and yet they are poor.

periences associated with the different social classes help maintain inequality. People at the top of the stratification system are maintaining their positions, which their socialization experiences prepare them to do. On the other hand, many at the bottom are poorly socialized to do anything but remain there. Some people claim that those at the top are there because they work harder than those at the bottom. Actually, if the people at the bottom are to move upward they must work much harder than those at the top, who are just maintaining their positions.

There are many other examples of institutionalized inequality in our society. For instance, many upper- and middle-class people receive subsidies from the government far in excess of anything paid out to the poor in welfare payments, poverty programs, and other forms of assistance. These upper- and middle-class subsidies differ from subsidies granted to the lower class both in amount and in the way they are given. They are not only larger but they are also less obvious. Consider housing, for example. Home owners can deduct both their mortgage interest charges and their property taxes from their income taxed by the federal government. In doing so they realize savings each year that are greater than the amount spent on public housing for the poor. (And many mortgages are guaranteed by the federal government.)

Similarly, the middle class who drive cars to work receive subsidies in the form of tax money invested in highway construction, while urban mass transit decays year by year. Many members of the middle class prefer to use automobiles rather than mass transit. The result is that adequate funds are not made available to help the urban transportation crisis, from which the urban poor suffer most.

Consider, also, the farm support program. Payments to farmers for improving their land are determined by the size of the farm. Thus the large farms and corporation farms re-ceive the biggest payments. The poorer farmers with the smaller farms receive the smallest amounts. Once again, the other classes receive preferential economic advantages.

Another cause of poverty in our society are the economic conditions themselves. Inflation and recession each create more poor people and increase the hardships for those already poor.

Inflation involves a decrease in the value of the currency. It takes more and more money to buy the same items. Prices keep going up. Thus inflation affects mainly those on fixed incomes, since the same amount of money buys less. The elderly poor, and those people living on public assistance, are particularly hard hit. Welfare payments seldom keep up with rising prices during a period of rapid inflation. In addition, people who were "getting by" satisfactorily on their existing income may become poor, if their income doesn't rise as fast as the rate of inflation.

Similarly, recession affects those with the fewest resources—the poor. In a recession the rate of business activity slows down, resulting in fewer jobs, more people laid off, and therefore higher unemployment. When people with few resources can no longer find work, they become poor. It is true that state unemployment insurance helps most people who lose jobs in a recession. But such payments are usually for a specified amount of time. After that, poverty is the fate of many who cannot eventually find employment.

During the middle 1970's, the American economy was troubled by both inflation and recession. This unusual situation increased the problems arising from each economic condition. Many Americans unexpectedly experienced poverty during this period.

To understand the structure of poverty, then, we must examine the structure of society itself. And we must see how that structure affects people in specific social situations. This is the perspective of sociology.

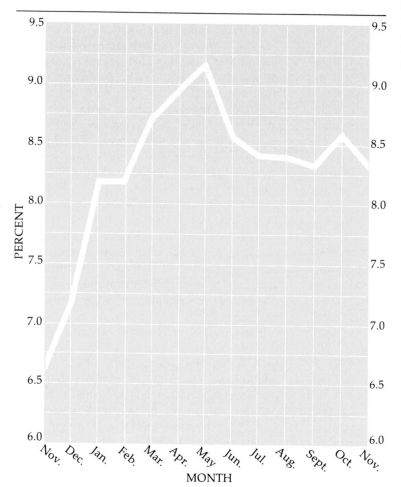

UNEMPLOYMENT RATE

PERCENT

MONTH

Nov. Dec. Jan. Feb. Mar. Apr. May Jun. Jul. Aug. Sept. Oct. Nov.

During the mid-1970's unemployment rose to levels of over 8 and 9 percent in one year. Unemployment is one factor that contributes to poverty.

SECTION REVIEW

1. What is the concept of relative deprivation? Why is it important in discussing poverty?
2. How would you determine how many people in the United States live in poverty? What categories of the population make up more than their share of the poor?
3. What are some of the causes of poverty in America?

KEY TERMS

Define and give an example of each term.

inflation
institutionalized inequality
poverty

recession
relative deprivation

SECTION 2:
The Life of Poverty

So far we've considered the basic questions of what poverty is, who is included in it, and how it is structured into our society. Now let's look more closely at life under poverty. What is it like to be poor? What can be done to lessen the problem of poverty?

The Culture of Poverty

Poverty seems to affect people in a generalized kind of way. Certain similarities of behavior and thought appear among those living under impoverished conditions. Such similarities exist along with cultural or subcultural differences among poor people. These similarities are sometimes called the culture of poverty.

The existence of a culture of poverty is related to the socialization that members of the lower classes receive. As we mentioned briefly in the last section, one of the differences between the upper and middle classes, on the one hand, and the lower classes, on the other, is the ability of each to get by in the world. From the start, the upper classes are socialized into habits and patterns of behavior that lead them to success. Usually, lower-class people don't receive this kind of socialization. This is especially true of people who are at or near the very bottom. Three aspects of the lower-class socialization process help maintain the culture of poverty by making it especially difficult for the poor to "rise." These three factors are trained incapacity, the home environment, and the culture conflict.

Trained incapacity. One of the characteristics of the culture of poverty is a "trained incapacity" to respond in a way that will lead to success. As they grow up, many members of the lower class learn habits and patterns that make it difficult for them to be successful in our society. They are trained by the culture of poverty, which produces an incapacity to break out of poverty and perform in the success-oriented world.

One example of this trained incapacity is language. Some people learn a form of English that, because of its grammatical errors or unusual pronunciation, is not acceptable to the business world. At the same time these individuals may not always understand ordinary English. The effects of this language difference are enormous. Students in lower-class schools fail to learn many things that are necessary for "making it" in the world simply because they and their teachers speak a different language. This sometimes happens in urban schools that have white middle-class teachers and black, Puerto Rican, or Mexican American children.

A second area of trained incapacity is the everyday habits that an individual acquires. People in the lower class often fail to learn the middle-class habits of personal grooming, cleanliness, and punctuality. Such habits are not essential or even possible in the world of poverty. How important some of these habits are in themselves is open to question. Nevertheless, the middle-class majority, and therefore the business world, regards them as important. Personnel offices usually reject the unkempt and unconventionally dressed individual for all but the lowest-paying jobs. Poor habits of punctuality produce similar situations. Knowing what time it is and keeping appointments promptly are essential in the world of work. They are often meaningless in the world of poverty. One of the adjustments for anyone leaving poverty is to develop self-discipline in observing time requirements.

A third example of trained incapacity is the failure to learn the deferred gratification pattern. DEFERRED GRATIFICATION *refers to putting off an immediate satisfaction in favor of some long range goal and future reward.* It is a characteristic of the middle class. It applies to saving money for a "rainy day." But it also applies to an efficient use of time and to many other situations. In contrast, a characteristic of those living in the culture of poverty—because they have so little at any given time—is to enjoy and use what they have now. Since the future is by no means certain, why take a chance at losing what is here now by putting off using it? Instead of deferring gratification, lower-class people tend to choose immediate satisfaction. Examples of the immediate gratification pattern include spending whatever cash is available, or buying goods that the person cannot afford.

Home environment. Another feature of the culture of poverty that puts its members at a disadvantage in getting along in the world is the home conditions found in the lower class. For example, the lower-class family is more

The middle class tends to value time. People are expected to work their full hours.

likely to have just one parent than is either the middle- or upper-class family. When the father is absent, the children must grow up without a male image. This can be psychologically damaging, especially for boys.

Many of the home environment conditions have affected the child before he or she even starts to go to school. The amount of conversation that takes place between lower-class family members is often less than in the middle class, and contains fewer complete sentences and logical constructions. Meanwhile, during this preschool period the middle-class child is learning more words, more concepts, and is given more opportunity to learn how to develop thoughts. Consequently, when lower-class children begin school, they are likely to be at a disadvantage compared to middle-class children. The disadvantage is even greater when we remember that in our society the middle class generally serves as the model for what people ought to be and do.

Culture conflict. An important aspect of the culture of poverty is the phenomenon of culture conflict. The poor as a culture type are in conflict with the rest of society in almost every area. This conflict between culture types quite naturally creates problems. For instance, the school teacher is traditionally a product of the middle class. This makes it difficult for him or her to deal with poor children on their own terms. And similarly, the poor children are even less prepared to deal with the teacher on his or her terms. The differences between their cultures bring about conflicts and misunderstandings.

The culture conflict problem also prevails in dealings between the poor and government officials. It occurs on all levels—between the poor and police officers as well as between the poor and Congress or the President. A number of poor people regard the municipal court not as an agency established to serve them but as an agency that can inflict harm on them. The court can evict them

It is inaccurate to stereotype poor people. There is a variety of life styles and problems among the poor. This family, for instance, has a stable family situation and a low income.

from their apartment, take part of their wages to pay a debt they owe, and harass them in other ways.

Much of the conflict results from the poor person's misunderstanding of the role of government. But, sadly, much of it also results from a social attitude that somehow the poor are poor through their own fault. Whatever the reason, though, the culture conflict that exists serves to hold the poor in their own disadvantaged position.

The poor are not all alike. There are enough similarities in the conditions of the poor to produce a culture of poverty. Yet everyone who is poor is not the same. There is a tendency to stereotype the poor, to see

each person only as part of a mass of poor people. However, the culture of poverty is not uniform. It is possible, for example, to divide the poor according to whether or not they have a steady income, and whether or not they have a stable family situation.

Those who have both a steady income and a stable family situation are relatively well off, by middle-class standards. And actually their life style is quite similar to that of the middle class, except for their lack of material goods. A second category are those who have a stable family but no steady income. These people generally rely on the welfare system. With their stable family situation, they need only a steady source of income to put them in good stead. Others, with a steady income but an unstable family situation, make up still another type. They have a different set of problems, perhaps somewhat harder to remedy. Finally, the most desperate category consists of those with neither a steady income nor a stable family. They may be considered the hard-core poor, because of the overwhelming disadvantages of their situation.

Remember, though, that just as all poor people are not alike, all individuals are not alike. Some individuals can overcome disadvantages that may seem overwhelming to others.

The Welfare System

We can't talk about poverty in America without discussing the welfare system. It is central to the lives of so many of the poor. Its operations affect the lives of those who must deal with it to a greater extent than most people realize.

Before examining what the welfare system is and does, let's consider what it is not. The welfare system is not just a big handout, providing large sums of money to able-bodied people who are too lazy to work. The amounts paid out support only a marginal existence. And very few of the people who receive payments are "able-bodied." For example, in New York City, which is recognized as having liberal welfare provisions, the city itself has estimated that about 95 percent of its recipients are either children, the elderly, mothers with children, the blind, or persons who are incapacitated in some other way. Of the remaining 5 percent, most are without the training or skills needed to get employment.

If we consider what the welfare system is, we find that it is a complex arrangement for providing funds to those who have no other legitimate way of making ends meet. There has been considerable criticism of these arrangements over the years. Welfare programs have been criticized for sapping initiative and for making the receiver dependent on the system.

Welfare programs can sap initiative when they do not permit the receivers to earn money on their own. For instance, suppose a welfare client is receiving $75 per week in benefits, and gets a part-time job that pays $60 per week. The benefits will be reduced to $15 per week because the person is "entitled" to only $75. In other words, receivers get the same amount of money whether they work or not. Under these circumstances, there is little motivation for them to even try to work.

The welfare system can create a dependency situation when the receiver must live up to certain regulations to continue qualifying for benefits. Instead of encouraging welfare clients to become independent, the system can make them live and act according to its regulations. Under these conditions the recipients have fewer rights than other people. This alienates them still further from society. A dependency situation also occurs when there is no economic reason to try to get off welfare, as we discussed above. Two or three generations can grow up in this situation, with little or no hope of becoming freed from the system.

Of course, there have been proposals to improve welfare programs. There have been suggestions, for example, to equalize payments across the nation to discourage movement to the cities, where benefits are greater. The more fundamental suggestions, however, involve some system of guaranteed income or family allotments.

Guaranteed income proposals would provide for a basic minimal income for everyone. There is no need to demonstrate inability to earn, and there are no special demeaning regulations. If individuals want only the minimal income, which would be low, they would not have to work. But if they want more (and most people do), they would not be penalized for working. Since the benefits are on a sliding or flexible scale, the individual always receives more money for working. Once the person earns above a certain sum, benefits cease altogether. Nevertheless, it would always make economic sense to work. On the other hand, those who can't work would be provided for.

Family allotment plans are based on the notion that children are entitled to basic necessities. Under such a plan each child born would receive a certain monthly amount from the government, regardless of the parents' needs. This proposal, like the guaranteed income, would do away with the degrading aspects of welfare.

As you can see, one of the dangers of welfare systems is that they can actually contribute to the continuation of poverty. One of the advantages is that welfare systems can work toward relieving the less desirable effects of poverty. How would you change our present welfare system? What do you think should be done to alleviate the problem of poverty in the United States?

SECTION REVIEW

1. What are some characteristics of living in poverty?
2. How does "trained incapacity" affect the individual's chances of success in the society?
3. How does the welfare system work?
4. What are the advantages of a guaranteed income welfare program?

KEY TERMS

Explain the meaning of each term.

culture of poverty
deferred gratification
family allotment plan
guaranteed income plan
"trained incapacity"

One part of the welfare system in America is the food-stamp program. In 1975, nearly one out of every twelve Americans benefited from food stamps.

FOOD STAMP INTERVIEWING D

PROJECTS AND ACTIVITIES

1. Do research on poverty in a developing or semi-industrialized nation such as India, Pakistan, or certain Latin American countries. Then compare the extent and life of poverty there to poverty in the United States.

2. Basing your information on observation, community officials, and data from the census bureau, draw a map of your community locating those districts where poverty conditions prevail.

3. Do library research on the differences between the urban and rural poor.

4. Write a short story in which the main character rises from an impoverished family background to a middle-class status.

5. Conduct research on poverty among American Indians living on reservations.

6. From the latest edition of the U.S. Bureau of the Census, *Statistical Abstract of the United States* obtain data on the percent distribution of families by income level. What percent might be considered to be living in poverty or near poverty? How does this percent compare for white and nonwhite families?

7. By observation, interviewing, and library research, describe as many life style differences as you can find between the very rich and the very poor.

8. Design a stratification system that you believe would greatly alleviate poverty.

9. Visit your local Department of Welfare and interview a social worker concerning local policies and practices. Also, find out as much as you can about federal programs to alleviate poverty and their effectiveness.

10. Design a welfare system that you think would be best able to break the vicious cycle of poverty and help most people now living in poverty to become self-supporting.

TOPICS FOR INQUIRY

1. Consider some reasons why the United States ranks far down the list in infant mortality and male longevity. Why do you think the United States has not made large increases in male longevity over the last twenty-five years?

2. Economic conditions in the mid-1970's gave some Americans a taste of poverty they might not have had otherwise. Do you think this has had an effect on American attitudes toward the poor?

3. Debate: It would be impossible to have a society with no poverty at all.

4. Consider specific aspects of the culture of poverty. Which features seem most objectionable? Which seem easiest to change?

5. Our society is based on middle-class values. Are there some lower-class values that might be better for American society?

6. Discuss the difficulties and situations faced by an individual born and raised in poverty in attempting to become a member of the middle class. What can an individual do to overcome these difficulties?

7. Despite the antipoverty legislation of the last ten years or so, such as the Economic Opportunity Act, the Education Acts, and the Housing and Urban Development Act, poverty persists in the United States. What legislation would you recommend to deal with the problem of poverty as it exists today?

SUGGESTIONS FOR READING

NONFICTION

BRILL, Naomi, *Working with People: Principles of the Helping Process.* Lippincott, 1973 (and pap.). A manual for social work practice. Contains an interesting analysis of the relationship between individuals and institutions.

CROOK, William H. and THOMAS, Ross, *Warriors for the Poor.* Morrow, 1969. The story of VISTA volunteers. It contains many interesting examples of poverty situations.

FICKER, Victor and GRAVES, Herbert S. (eds.), *Deprivation in America.* Glencoe, 1971 (pap.). Readings and original chapters dealing with economic and social deprivation.

HARRINGTON, Michael, *The Other America: Poverty in the United States.* Macmillan, 1962 or Penguin (pap.). A description of the unskilled worker, the aged, the minorities, and the world of poverty in which they live.

HOUGH, John T., *A Peck of Salt: A Year in the Ghetto*. Little, Brown, 1970 (and pap.). A first-person account of a VISTA volunteer's experiences in the inner city.

LEACOCK, Eleanor B. (ed.), *The Culture of Poverty: A Critique*. Simon & Schuster, 1971 (pap.). A book of readings that is critical of the "culture of poverty" perspective.

LEWIS, Oscar, *Five Families: Mexican Case Studies in the Culture of Poverty*. Basic Books, 1959 or New American Library (pap.). A case study of five families who live in poverty in Mexico.

————, *La Vida: A Puerto Rican Family in the Culture of Poverty, San Juan and New York*. Random House, 1967 (and pap.). A comparative case study which presents first-person biographies of a Puerto Rican mother and her grown children who live in poverty in San Juan and New York.

MORRILL, Richard L. and WOHLENBERG, Ernest H., *The Geography of Poverty in the United States*. McGraw-Hill, 1971 (and pap.). A graphic and statistical account of the location of poverty in the United States.

ROBY, Pamela (ed.), *The Poverty Establishment*. Prentice-Hall, 1974 (and pap.). Readings that focus on those whose business is combating poverty.

FICTION

ARNOW, Harriette S., *The Dollmaker*. Macmillan or Avon (pap.). The story of a strong-willed Kentucky woman and her family who move to the Detroit slums, where they endure loneliness, insults, and squalor.

BALLARD, Martin, *Dockie*. Harper & Row. Forced to quit school and go to work on London's docks, a young man is determined to rise above his family's poverty.

HANSBERRY, Lorraine, *A Raisin in the Sun*. Random House or New American Library (pap.). The struggle by a black family to move out of the poverty of the ghetto and into a white suburban neighborhood.

HERSEY, John, *A Single Pebble*. Knopf. An illiterate man pulls boats up the Yangtze River in China, yet maintains his dignity and internal strength.

ROY, Cal, *The Painter of Miracles*. Farrar, Straus & Giroux. In the early 1900's in Mexico, a poor boy who paints participates in a village revolt against the hacienda owner and loses nearly everything he owns.

STEINBECK, John, *The Grapes of Wrath*. Viking (pap.). The story of the Joad family, who leave their worn-out farm in Oklahoma for the "promised land" of California during the depression of the 1930's.

22 Aging

> ► Is aging mainly a physical or a social process?

> ► What are some problems connected with adolescence, middle age, and old age?

> ► How do people cope with these problems?

SECTION 1:
Age and Society

People everywhere are born, they live, and they die. There is no escaping it. In between they pass through some stages of physical maturation and aging. They grow in physical size. They develop primary and secondary sex characteristics. They reach physical and mental maturity. And they become wrinkled, gray-haired, and, perhaps, enfeebled.

At the same time they pass in and out of various stages of social development, or *age categories*. Although physical development is affected by cultural and social conditions, such as diet, it generally follows a similar pattern for all humans. Age categories, however, are determined mainly by cultural and social conditions. We might say, in fact, that society creates age categories and the meaning given to them. Age categories are a part

of the society's culture. Problems of youth, middle age, and old age, therefore, are related to the society's views of these categories.

Adolescence

One of the most often discussed age categories in our own society is adolescence. Adolescence is the period roughly between the onset of puberty and the attainment of maturity. This includes people ranging from about eleven or twelve years old to perhaps their early twenties.

In our society, adolescence is commonly regarded as a biological phenomenon. Furthermore, we tend to see adolescent behavior and attitudes as biologically fixed, as unavoidable and necessary. If we look at other societies, however, we find that the age at which the individual reaches adulthood varies widely. In some instances—particularly in preliterate societies—a person becomes an adult at the onset of puberty. There is no period of adolescence. Among the Zuñi Indians of New Mexico, for example, a boy becomes a man simply through a ceremonial whipping by his neighbors and relatives, who then reveal to him some of the secrets of the tribe.

Even within our own society, the age at which we become adults varies. Many teenagers are in no real way adolescents. Those in the armed services, for example, or the many who are employed on a full-time basis in the labor force, or those who are married, cannot really be regarded as adolescents.

A number of factors influence the length of adolescence in a society. Societies such as our own require a high degree of learning or technical competence. Because of the extended training required to participate in our society, we have a prolonged period of adolescence. If we consider continuing to go to school full time as a criterion of adolescence, then we have some thirty-year-old adolescents in our society!

Thus the category of adolescence differs from culture to culture, and even within a society. Adolescence has not always existed, and does not now exist in all societies. Therefore we can conclude that the whole concept of adolescence is not rooted in biological development but is created by society. Our society labels certain types of behavior as adolescent behavior. These labels and attitudes regarding adolescents become built into the culture. They are molded by the mass media through advertising, which looks on adolescence as a separate, and profitable, market. And because society comes to expect certain patterns of behavior from adolescents, it structures its institutions to almost insure that these patterns take place. In America we label adolescence as a period of transition and personal adjustment, for instance. Then we structure this assumption into our family life, our schools and colleges, and our religious, economic, and political institutions.

Youth subculture. The phenomenon of adolescence results in the formation of a youth subculture in our society. The behavior of adolescents is distinct and separate enough to be recognized as different. Yet it is similar enough to be seen as part of the same society. While both adolescents and adults use the same language, for example, there are special variations used mainly by adolescents. Similarly, in clothing styles there is a certain youthful way of dressing that is easily recognizable. Yet the styles of the young are not completely separate and distinct from those of adults.

Rather than talk of a single youth subculture, however, it is more accurate to refer to types of youth subculture. For there are different types of adaptations to adolescence. There are differences, for instance, in the behavior, values, and beliefs of Ivy League college students and inner-city ghetto youths. There are differences within a community between, say, adolescents who are planning to go to college and those who are not.

Young adulthood. As we leave the world of school and enter the world of work, we trade in the label of "kid" for that of adult. This isn't done all at once. It takes some time before we gain the kind of experience that produces self-confidence in ourselves and recognition by others as an equal. It may involve, as in the case of skilled craftspeople, several years of menial work as an apprentice, while learning the many aspects of the craft. After that the individual is accepted as an equal. In some instances, such as for doctors, years of graduate training followed by internship, residency, and further specialized training are necessary before acceptance as an adult member occurs.

Middle Age

When does middle age begin? It is difficult to say. To an eighteen-year-old, twenty-five may seem like middle age. To someone who is thirty, no one under thirty-five is middle-aged. And any thirty-five-year-old can tell you that middle age does not begin until well past forty!

There is a strong subjective aspect to the concept of middle age. Nevertheless, we can define middle age as beginning after a person becomes established in his or her occupation. This means that the person has completed whatever training or other requirements are needed, and has a home and probably a family. The end of middle age can be said to coincide with retirement from active participation in the work-a-day world. Middle age, then, is the main period of life between active preparation, such as schooling, and retirement.

Because middle age is such a subjective concept, there is a strong tendency to rely on images and labels as indications. Thus wearing youthful clothing and adopting youthful grooming styles helps put off entering the category of middle age. Similarly, comparisons with older members of an occupational category can prevent the label "middle aged" from being applied. For example, in presidential politics a fifty-year-old candidate may be called young if all the other candidates are in their sixties. A doctor who becomes famous fairly early in his or her career, say by forty, is likely to be viewed as a young doctor.

Perhaps the most obvious distinction regarding the arrival of middle age is the one between the sexes. We characteristically regard women as entering middle age at a younger age than men. Compare, for instance, some magazine advertisements showing men and some showing women. There will be a wider variation in the age of the men. Men will appear in "attractive" poses in their thirties, forties, and fifties. Very few will show women in "attractive" poses any older than in their twenties.

Several years ago a famous men's hat manufacturer showed a man in his fifties—well dressed, gray at the temples, and with a tanned, rugged look—in six different poses. In each photograph he wore a different style hat and had a different young woman in her early twenties leaning on his shoulder, smiling adoringly. How many ads are there in which a fifty-year-old woman is being admired by six different twenty-year-old men? It is unlikely, because we label men and women differently with respect to middle age. For men it is considered a period of great productivity. For women it has been viewed as following the most productive years. As women gain equality in the world of work, however, this concept may change.

As with the concept of adolescence, the category of middle age is socially created and socially maintained. Its meaning varies from time to time, and from society to society. It is not innate or biologically determined.

Old Age

This is also true of the category old age. The age at which the label "old" is applied differs within a society as well as between societies. In our society some people seem old at fifty. Others appear still in their prime in their seventies or eighties.

The amount and kind of involvement in the world has a lot to do with such individual variations. The older person still working at his or her job and associating with persons from a variety of age groups will probably appear younger longer. Those older persons who are less active—by choice or by forced retirement—are likely to assume life patterns associated with older people, and therefore to seem older earlier.

Different societies place different definitions on the concept of old age. In traditional Chinese society, for example, individuals (especially men) continue to gain in relative

status as they get older. The very old are the most respected and revered members of society. They are called upon frequently for suggestions and advice. The process even continues, in a way, after death. Traditionally, the Chinese worship their dead ancestors. It is as if the process of acquiring wisdom and respect doesn't stop with the mere end of life.

The people of Abkhasia, in the Caucasus Mountains of the Soviet Union near the Black Sea, also have a different concept of age. Many of these people live to a remarkably old age—from 100 years up to 130 or so. A number of factors, such as diet, climate, and heredity, help to account for their long life span. A major factor, though, is the society's attitude toward age. Prestige, respect, and even virility continue to a very advanced age.

The Abkhasians have a culture in which all members, at all ages, have a definite role and place. There is a genuine need for people, regardless of age. Contrast this with the American practice of forced retirement from the meaningful participation of work at about age sixty-five.

As you can see, categories of age depend to a large extent on the social meaning that particular societies choose to give them. Age is a matter of labeling.

SECTION REVIEW

1. Name the age categories in our society between infancy and old age.
2. What are some characteristics of adolescence?

3. How do young adulthood and middle age differ?

4. How would you define old age?

KEY TERMS

Explain the meaning of each of these terms.

adolescence	old age
age categories	young adulthood
middle age	youth subculture

SECTION 2:
Problems and Responses

There are some elements that are common to all age categories. For one thing, we all go through each category—if we live long enough! For another thing, we all function within the framework of time. Children and adolescents often have too much of it. Some say, "There's nothing to do," or "I can't wait until I'm old enough to drive." Adults often don't seem to have enough, claiming "There isn't enough time in the day to get all my work done," or "Where did all the time go?"

But there are also areas in which the age categories clash with one another. The generation gap provides evidence of this. Problems can arise both between age categories and for the individuals within a particular category.

Problems of Adolescents

One problem for adolescents is the labels that society attaches to their age category. For example, one of the major assumptions about adolescents is that they are not responsible enough. Parents often don't trust them with cars. They must not use alcoholic beverages. And school officials watch them to prevent them from harming the school building or themselves. The school requires passes of students who are in the hallway during class time—assuming that they must be irresponsible and "up to no good" unless they have a pass. It requires that students ask permission to go to the bathroom, again assuming they are not responsible enough to be allowed to do so on their own. The school generally requires that students be supervised at all times, suggesting that they cannot be trusted to behave without supervision.

Not only the schools but also many other areas of society have images and expectations of the adolescent as irresponsible and immature. For instance, some municipalities have curfew laws, requiring juveniles to be off the streets after a certain hour. The expectation is that if adolescents were given full privileges, they would not conduct themselves properly.

There is another aspect to this process of labeling. As the school, and adult society in general, regards adolescents as irresponsible, they tend to regard themselves in the same way. The label of irresponsible person is applied so well that it is accepted by the student as well as the school. How many times have high school students themselves nodded in agreement to the statement that they were irresponsible, immature, or otherwise incapable of making their own decisions?

We cannot conclude, though, that if adolescents were immediately regarded as fully participating adults, they would act responsibly in every way. The adolescent is now socialized into a pattern of behavior. If, at this point, the school were to suddenly drop all of its regulations concerning hallway activities, attendance, and so on, the result might be chaos. Yet the sociological perspective does suggest that if society no longer labeled adolescents as a special category, but instead established different expectations,

The minimum voting age in federal elections has been lowered to eighteen years. And adolescents have shown themselves to be responsible voters. What other limitations on adolescents do you think should be changed?

the present adolescent patterns of behavior would change.

Problems of Adults

While adults are labeled by a number of factors—ethnic and racial category, sex, and religion, for example—the occupational label is a major one. When two adults meet for the first time, "What do you do?" almost always follows the question, "How do you do?" Before we know how to communicate with a person, we feel we need to know who that person is. This means we need to know what occupational label he or she wears.

But occupational labels frequently create conflict and strain. Many people in our society view their job as a part of their identity. If the occupation is a paying job, there is always the possibility of losing that job. It isn't particularly pleasant and rewarding to be collecting unemployment insurance or welfare payments, either. It can be costly in terms of self-identification, self-worth, and dignity.

Another source of strain related to the world of work has to do with the distribution of relatively important, well-respected, and high-paying jobs as compared to the less important, less well-respected, and lower-paying ones. The problem is that there are many more of the second type. Yet we live in a society that stresses high status, good pay, and the necessity of doing important work. This means that the great majority of adults in our society are left doing work that does not meet the cultural expectations of what work ought to be like. As a result, most middle-aged people have to settle for occupational identities that are less satisfying than they would like them to be. Of course, there remains the hope and possibility of advancement. For some it is realized. When it is not realized—as more often it is not—frustration and anxiety result.

A number of women who are not employed outside the home are also dissatisfied. Traditionally, the socialization process has been somewhat different for boys and girls. Boys learned that work was important and that one day they would do some of it. Girls learned that work was important and that maybe they would do it, or maybe they would be homemakers and someone else would earn money for them. They would be assigned to the unofficial, unpaid job of housework. Or possibly they would get to do

405

Adults have certain expectations about an occupation, such as that of business executive or doctor. Sometimes they must adapt their expectations to the realities of the work.

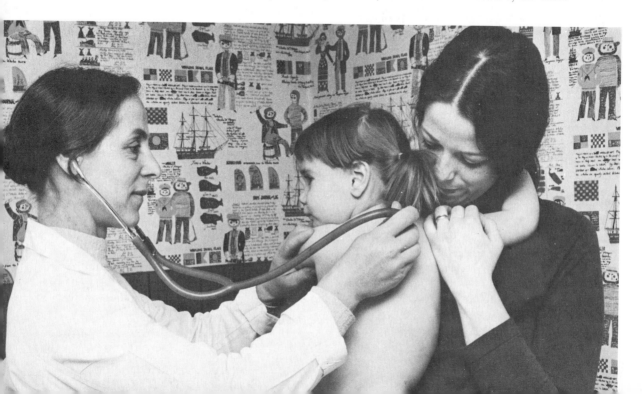

both. Some women have found the situation frustrating.

The adult population deals with such strains in a variety of ways. They learn to reduce the level of their expectations, and thereby reduce frustration and anxiety. They may substitute other—and perhaps more reasonable—bases for their identity, such as family life, sports, travel, and hobbies. It is no wonder that leisure-time activities are such an important part of our culture.

Problems of Old Age

Generally people aged sixty-five and over are no longer considered middle-aged. They are old people, or senior citizens. They make up more than 10 percent of our population.

Old people are freed from the obligation to do productive work. Instead they are expected to pursue a life of leisure, perhaps seeking it in warmer parts of the world. They are expected to finance this life by making use of Social Security payments, their pension (if they have one), and their savings from their working days. Many are able to do just that.

But all too often being a senior citizen means being alone, without much money, in poor health, and with little to do except reflect on the past. Frequently such people are in nursing homes or other homes for the elderly, separated from the rest of society and from their own relatives. Reports of the living conditions in many of these establishments indicate shortcomings in facilities and services.

Senility. One aspect of old age that can create problems is senility. Senility is characterized by a generally enfeebled condition of the body, failure of the memory and other faculties, and a withdrawal from human contact.

We have long regarded senility as a natural condition resulting from excessive age. Yet some people, even at very advanced ages,

seem to escape the condition. Senility is known to have physiological causes, such as hardening of the arteries. Recent studies have also related its occurrence to the number and kind of social contacts a person has. When older people remain in contact with the rest of society—especially with a broad variety of age groups—they are much less likely to show signs of senility. On the other hand, when they withdraw from the world, or are left alone, or associate only with other older people in nursing homes or retirement communities, they are more likely to become senile. Among the Abkhasian people in the Soviet Union, who, as we said, remain active and participating members of society to a very advanced age, senility is virtually unknown.

Certainly there is no easy solution to the problem of age. It is one that affects all of us. Perhaps that is why we don't like to talk about it. What solutions would you suggest? Is our current practice of isolating the elderly, and trying to forget their existence, the best solution? Or is it self-defeating?

Responses

Responses to the problems of adolescence, middle age, and old age are many and varied. The response may take the form of ignoring or denying the problem. Sometimes the response involves hoping or wishing things will get better. In many instances the response results in changed behavior patterns —such as drug use, excessive drinking, or depression and despair.

Drug use. We know that many young people (and also a number of older people) are involved in using narcotics and other drugs. And we know that there are many factors associated with drug use. Perhaps the single most important factor is association with other users. Without that association, an adolescent isn't likely to learn the techniques of using narcotics. Nor is he or she likely to make the contacts necessary to obtain the drugs.

Thus it would be wrong to say that taking drugs is a direct result of any specific problems associated with adolescence. But the fact that a good many adolescents are drug users suggests that adolescent problems are among the contributing factors. The reasons given for taking drugs include to get "kicks" and to "escape" from present conditions. Such reasons can be traced directly to adolescent problems. Yet, sadly, adolescent problems are not improved by the use of drugs. Instead, such problems are more likely to increase. They are also apt to be carried into adulthood.

Alcohol consumption. Alcohol has been used and abused by human beings since before recorded history. Both its benefits and its evils are well documented. It is a common response of many middle-aged persons in this country. During the 1960's, at the height of public concern over drug use, youthful drug users often pointed out that their parents drank alcohol and therefore had

no right to criticize them for smoking marijuana. The parents are still drinking. Now some of their children are joining them.

Young people have vastly increased their consumption of alcohol. This is due partly to the lowering of the drinking age to eighteen in many states. It is due partly to increased fears about drug use. It is no doubt related to the fact that alcohol is less expensive than most drugs. And it is brought about partly by the same search for "kicks" and escape from despair that brings on drug abuse.

Both adolescents and middle-aged persons misuse alcohol for the same kinds of reasons. And their misuse produces the same kinds of results—disastrous. Alcoholism is a far more widespread problem than drug addiction. Yet many of us try to ignore it or treat it as a minor inconvenience.

Retirement communities. Older people are not exempt from drug use or alcoholism. They respond to problems in many of the same ways as other people in the society. The special problem of old age also produces

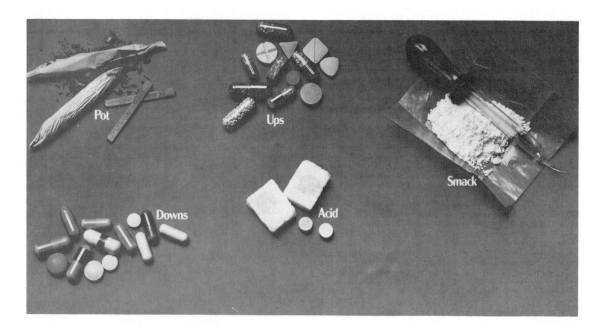

distinctive responses. One growing response to old age is the development of retirement communities inhabited only by older people. The effects of living in such communities remain to be seen. What effects might the limiting of interaction to other older people have? What might be the psychological reaction of the inhabitants to the abnormally high death rates that will occur? Where would you most like to spend your old age?

SECTION REVIEW

1. What are some problems of adolescents? How would you change society to alleviate these problems?
2. What kinds of problems do adults face?
3. What problems can come with old age?
4. Name some responses of adolescents, adults, and older persons to problems of age. What solutions can you suggest?

PROJECTS AND ACTIVITIES

1. Prepare a skit with three or four classmates that includes male and female characters at a variety of ages. Present it to the class, and have class members identify the age of each character by the mannerisms, vocal expressions, and postures used.

2. Interview several people in various age categories, including adolescence, middle age, and old age. Ask them to define the limits of adolescence, middle, and old age. Describe the differences.

3. Do library research on the concept of the different age categories in one or more societies at some other period in history. Compare your findings to present conditions.

4. Make a scrapbook of your life from infancy to old age. Use photographs to portray the past and present. Then make drawings to show yourself as an adult and older person.

5. Conduct a survey of persons in their thirties and forties to determine what their views are about what is wrong with the society. Then ask exactly the same questions in a survey of adolescents and of elderly people, and compare your results. Are the views more similar among people in the same age category, or not? If not, what explanation can you offer?

6. Compare the content and advertising of radio programs on two different radio stations—one that is directed to teen-agers and one that is directed to adults. How do they differ?

7. Do research to determine the extent to which teen-agers are influenced by the older generation. Are there ways in which teen-agers also influence the older generation? Explain.

8. Interview several older people to find out their views of the role of adolescents, middle-aged persons, and old people. How have their views changed over time?

9. Perform a sociodrama depicting role changes associated with each of the various age categories.

10. Visit a retirement community and observe the kinds of interaction that occur. Note how often the residents meet with one another and with nonresidents. Note how many age groups are represented.

TOPICS FOR INQUIRY

1. What proposals would you suggest that would make it possible for different age categories to have a better understanding of each other and better relationships with one another?

2. Discuss the ways in which the society socializes adolescents to be responsible.

3. A poll by *Fortune* magazine, based on a representative sample of eighteen- to twenty-four-year-olds, revealed that over 80 percent of those interviewed thought that their values did not differ greatly from the values of their parents. Do you feel that your values, orientation, and life goals are similar to or very different from those of your parents? In what ways?

4. What are the topics that you find most difficult to discuss with adults (parents, teachers, etc.)? How do you explain this?

5. Discuss how middle age begins. What specific things occur to mark the beginning of that period?

6. Debate: Older people are better off living with other senior citizens in retirement communities than they would be in their own homes.

7. Drinking seems to be on the increase among youth. Do you think this indicates a narrowing of the gap between adolescents and adults? Explain.

SUGGESTIONS FOR READING

NONFICTION

BLAU, Zena S., *Old Age in a Changing Society*. Watts, 1973. A critical analysis of the role of older people in the United States, stressing the lack of opportunities for meaningful participation.

COLEMAN, James S. et al., *Youth: Transition to Adulthood*. University of Chicago Press, 1974 (and pap.). This is the report of the panel on youth of the President's Science Advisory Committee.

COLES, Robert, *The Old Ones of New Mexico*. University of New Mexico Press, 1973. A touching, illustrated book about New Mexico's older people.

FRIEDENBERG, Edgar Z., *Coming of Age in America*. Random House, 1965. The values and ambitions of adolescents and their relationship to American secondary education.

GOSHEN, Charles E., *Drinks, Drugs, and Do-Gooders*. Free Press, 1973. A historical and sociological treatment of drink and drugs that focuses on patterns and solutions.

GUNTHER, John, *Death Be Not Proud*. New ed., Harper & Row, 1971 (and pap.). Author John Gunther records his seventeen-year-old son's heroic battle against a fatal illness.

HARMS, Ernest (ed.), *Drugs and Youth: The Challenge of Today.* Pergamon, 1973. A collection of readings on the effects of drug use and means of drug control.

LE MASTERS, E. E., *Parents in Modern America.* Dorsey, 1974 (and pap.). A sociological analysis of the role of parents in American society, incorporating material on youth counterculture and women's liberation.

LE SHAN, Eda, *The Wonderful Crisis of Middle Age.* McKay, 1973. An optimistic view of life's middle years, stressing communication and openness.

RALSTON, Nancy C. and THOMAS, G. Patience, *The Adolescent: Case Studies for Analysis.* Chandler, 1974 (pap.). Interesting studies of ten adolescents.

SMITH, Bert K., *Aging in America.* Beacon, 1973 (and pap.). An account of the process of aging that emphasizes the possibility of overcoming many of its problems.

FICTION

ARUNDEL, Honor, *The Blanket Word.* Nelson. After the death of her mother from cancer, a young girl realizes that love is a word that can cover many different feelings.

GLOAG, Julian, *Our Mother's House.* Simon & Schuster or Pocket Books (pap.). When their mother dies, seven children build a temple over her private grave and create a religion to keep from being separated.

MILLER, Arthur, *Death of a Salesman.* Viking (pap.). The tragic story of a salesman who, in the later years of his life, looks to his past achievements, only to realize that he is a failure.

NAYLOR, Phyllis R., *Dark Side of the Moon.* Fortress (pap.). A series of situations showing an alcoholic's impact on the family.

WOJCIECHOWSKA, Maja, *Tuned Out.* Dell (pap.). A young teen-ager sees the effects of drugs on his college-age brother.

EPILOGUE

YOU AND SOCIETY

Should you pursue an educational program after high school? What is involved in choosing a vocation? Can the principles of sociology help you develop satisfying relationships? In previous units we've investigated various principles of sociology and we've applied these principles to social problems. Now we will direct our attention to some basic personal questions you may be facing. The presentation of some guidelines may help you in determining your goals and understanding how you might fit best into your society.

23 Developing Your Goals

▶ What should you consider in determining your goals?

▶ How do you select a suitable educational program?

▶ What is important in choosing an appropriate vocation?

SECTION 1:
An Educational and Vocational Self-Analysis

How can sociology help you lead a full life and plan your future goals? First of all, since sociology is the study of human relationships, it should aid you in improving your human relationships. Second, your knowledge of sociology and your understanding of the scientific method should help you develop a more objective way of looking at yourself.

You are nearing the end of your high school career. What will you do after graduation? Will you go to college? Attend a technical, business, vocational, or trade school? Or get a job? Actually, planning your educational program and choosing a vocation are closely related. You should not do one without considering the other. But the most important factor to consider is not the education or the vocation—it is you. Therefore, we will begin with you. You should make a self-analysis to determine your educational and vocational goals.

Factors to Consider in Your Self-Analysis

Let's look at some specific aspects that are important in planning educational and vocational goals.

Your aptitudes and abilities. In Chapter 5 we said that an ability is the power to carry out some behavior. It pertains to your present state of being able to perform certain tasks. You may have the ability to chin yourself, type fifty words per minute, work problems in trigonometry, or play the piano well.

We defined aptitude as the capacity to learn a particular skill or body of knowledge. Aptitude tells us how well an individual can learn, with training and practice, some particular skill or knowledge. For example, a person who can easily distinguish different tones, recognize a simple tune from other simple tunes, and distinguish rhythm patterns has some particular abilities that give him or her an aptitude for learning musical skills.

There are several aptitudes that you should consider in planning your educational goals. An important aptitude in college is your mental aptitude, your aptitude for learning, usually called intelligence. You may have taken an intelligence test at some time as part of your school's regular testing program. Perhaps your counselor interpreted the results of the test to you. If not, you might ask

If you have a mechanical aptitude, you should take it into consideration in planning your future educational and vocational goals.

for an explanation of what the test results mean in terms of your educational goals. If you have not taken an intelligence test, you can still get some idea of your intelligence or mental aptitude by looking at your high school grades in academic subjects. Yet frequently a person's intelligence is greater than his or her school grades would seem to indicate.

Mental aptitude or intelligence is also important in choosing a vocation. It influences the type of job that an individual finds satisfying. It is related to whether the person is bored, challenged, or frustrated in performing that job.

Other aptitudes also play important parts in influencing your choice of educational goals and a vocation. Some of these aptitudes are musical, mechanical, artistic, or athletic. You need to ask yourself how you can develop all of your abilities and aptitudes to the fullest, and how you can utilize them in a future vocation.

To help you determine your aptitudes more realistically, a number of aptitude tests have been developed. Perhaps your high school counselor can give you information on these tests. You may wish to look into two free sources outside of your school. One is the *Armed Services Vocational Aptitude Battery*. To find out about this test, call or visit your neighborhood Armed Services (Army, Navy, Air Force, Marines) recruiting office. There is no obligation to join the armed services in taking this test. The second is the *General Aptitude Test Battery*, which is given by state Departments of Employment. It should be available through the local office of your state's Department of Employment.

Your physical characteristics. Are you healthy? Do you have good vision, hearing, sense of smell, reflexes, muscular coordination, and overall strength? Do you have any physical handicaps? If so, what are they and how would they affect your education or future vocation?

Specific physical characteristics are an important part of some jobs. For instance, excellent color vision is essential for airplane pilots, interior decorators, and clothing designers. Finger dexterity is important to a surgeon, watch repairer, and typist. Good general health is needed by farmers, pilots, athletes, police officers, fire fighters, astronauts, and forest rangers. Not only is physical health important, but also a particular physical appearance is necessary for some occupations. For example, some jobs have height and weight requirements. To fill other jobs, people such as models, actors, actresses, television performers, and dancers require special "good looks."

Because of their physical requirements, you would have to rule out some jobs if you have certain physical defects or weaknesses. A person with weak legs would not make a good ballet dancer. A person with hay fever or similar allergies would find farming, gardening, or working in dusty conditions extremely unpleasant. In considering your educational and vocational plans you need to take a careful look at your physical characteristics to make sure that you are physically qualified to meet your goals.

Your temperament. Your emotional temperament is another factor to examine in determining your educational and vocational goals. It can influence your success in higher education, as well as the size and type of college or university you select.

However, your temperament is apt to play a larger role in planning your vocation. For example, some jobs require persons who can remain calm, exert strong self-control, and hide their true emotions under the most trying circumstances. Police officers, nurses, doctors, social workers, morticians, clergy, and mental health workers fall into this category. For other occupations the individual must be radiant, dynamic, outgoing, friendly, and enthusiastic. These characteristics are helpful in selling, business, teaching, and for

Would you be happy at a job that involved spending a great deal of time by yourself?

television performers. In some occupations individuals must work by themselves for long periods. This is true for forest rangers and for many persons engaged in research. In other cases the individual must be able to work in an environment of constant ear-shattering noise, as found in some factories. Your basic temperament is a factor to evaluate, because it can play a major role in how successful and happy you are at a particular job.

Your social abilities. In making your educational and vocational plans you should also consider your ability to get along well with others in social situations. The type of job you choose, and the educational plan that goes with it, are often related to your social abilities. In some occupations the ability to get along well with people is an important part of the job. This applies to salespeople,

417

teachers, social workers, lawyers, doctors, and service workers. On the other hand, social ability is less important for people such as truckdrivers, researchers, farmers, railroad engineers, and artists, whose occupations do not involve constant contact with people. You should seriously consider your social abilities and choose an educational plan and vocation that fits your specific social abilities.

Your interests. Your particular interests are of great importance in determining your educational and vocational goals. Since people spend a large amount of their time at their job, they should have a job that they find interesting and enjoyable.

How do you discover your interests? One way is to examine carefully the hobbies, extracurricular school activities, school courses, and leisure-time activities that you enjoy. For instance, what type of reading do you like best? Another way to discover your general interests is to take interest inventories.

Which subjects in school do you find most interesting? What vocations are related to them?

Check with your school counselor to find out about specific inventories, such as the *Strong Vocational Interest Blank.*

After you've found out what you are interested in, you should compare your interests with your abilities and aptitudes. Liking a particular activity very much is not a sufficient basis for a vocation, unless you also have the capacity to do it well. A conflict between interest and ability should be carefully examined in making your educational and vocational plans.

Your high school experiences. Colleges have found that there is some relationship between how students do in high school and how they will do in college. Therefore, you might ask yourself some questions about your high school experiences. How good a student are you? How hard do you have to work to get the grades you receive? How good are your reading skills? How fast do you read, and what is your comprehension? How good are your writing skills? What grades do you get on papers? Do you just dash them off, or do you carefully prepare a rough draft and then polish it for the final paper? What do you like best about high school? Is it doing research, writing papers, and studying, or is it the extracurricular activities, social events, and seeing your friends? Would you have the motivation and ability to do the more challenging academic work required in college?

Your personal goals. As you think about your educational and vocational goals, you need to consider carefully your personal goals in life. What do you want out of life more than anything else? Which personal values are most important to you? Do you value helping others, acquiring material goods, having status, being respected, having leisure time, helping to improve life in your society, or what? What specific vocations would allow you to do something constructive about your personal values? Which vocations could you possibly dedicate your life to? What are the educational requirements for these vocations? Would you want to go to college to enrich your total personality? Or to get a better job? You should realize that a college education will not automatically guarantee you a better job, though it may help to improve your chances.

If you are realistic and honest with yourself in examining these factors, you should be better able to determine which goals might bring you the greatest happiness. You should have a better idea of your own physical, mental, and social abilities and your interests. This information can help you determine which vocations might fit your unique personality. It can also help you decide how you feel about further education.

SECTION REVIEW

1. What factors should you consider in making your self-analysis?
2. How are educational and vocational goals related?
3. Why are your personal goals important in deciding on your future educational and vocational plans?

SECTION 2:
Selecting an Educational Program

Although you have probably narrowed your choices through self-analysis, selecting a school or educational program from among the many possibilities is no easy task. It involves research, study, and discussion with others. You might consider the following steps in your search for the most successful educational program for you.

Determine what you want and need from an educational program. Your first decision is whether or not you want to attend school beyond high school. If you decide that you do, your next step is to determine your reasons for wanting more education. Do you want the education primarily so you can quality for a job or vocation? Have you checked to be sure just what the educational requirements for the job really are? In terms of the total number of vocational opportunities, only a few—probably less than 20 percent—require a four-year college degree. To qualify for the rest of the vocations you may need anything from on-the-job training provided by the employer to a two-year associate degree from a community or junior college.

Perhaps you wish further education primarily to expand your potential for creativity and to enrich your unique personality. Do you want a degree for the status it gives you? What other reasons might you have for desiring more education?

Determine the most appropriate type of educational program for your needs. You might consider the following questions. Could you best meet your wants and needs through night classes in adult education, an apprenticeship program, a vocational school, business school, or a junior or community college? Would your needs best be met by attending a four-year university, state college, liberal arts college, or a specialized (art, music, mining, and so forth) college or institute?

Then there is the question of how much money you have available for schooling. Have you considered what the total cost of your complete educational program might be? Will the investment of time and money pay sufficient returns? If finances are limited, have you considered the possibility of taking night classes while you work at a regular job? What are the possibilities of obtaining some kind of scholarship or grant? What

419

If you're planning to apply to a particular college or university, you might consider attending one or two classes there. It's helpful to see how members of the faculty teach.

other factors might be involved in your completing an educational program?

Examine educational directories. There are a number of directories that list all of the colleges, universities, or special schools in the United States. They include a brief description and some statistics about each school. You might glance through these directories and write down the names of some schools that look interesting to you.

Study the bulletins of specific schools. Once you have a list of colleges or schools that might interest you, the next step is to learn more about them. Usually your school library or high school counselors have college bulletins available for your use. Most public libraries also carry material on colleges and vocational, business, and technical schools. As you study these bulletins, you should take note of the following:

The objectives and philosophy of the school. If you compare the bulletins from a number of schools you will see that their objectives and philosophies differ greatly. Generally you will find this information at the beginning of the bulletins. Notice, also, the character of the school. For example, what is stressed most in the bulletin—the academic program, the athletic activities, the social or religious aspects?

The courses. What courses are given? What majors are offered? If the school does not have the courses you want, there isn't much point in continuing to investigate it. If the school does offer the courses you want, then you need to determine how good these courses really are.

The faculty. Examine the qualifications of the faculty. How many faculty members are assigned to the department in which you will do most of your work? In general, avoid one-person departments, since you will get a very narrow view of the discipline if you take all of your courses from only one individual.

Accreditation. Is the school accredited? All good colleges are accredited by one of the regional agencies of the Association of Colleges and Secondary Schools. Vocational schools and business schools should also be accredited, certified, or recommended by some agency, usually some division of the state Department of Education. If the school doesn't have the proper credentials, then other organizations may not acknowledge the credits or diplomas it gives.

The facilities. To do a good job of education a school must have adequate facilities. Consider the physical aspects of the school—the buildings, the laboratory equipment, the library, the athletic facilities, and so forth.

The location. Students often think that the best schools are all great distances away. Actually, you may have a college that is just as good only a short distance from home. There is an advantage to attending a college far enough away so that you can't come home every weekend. Then you must make your own decisions, which helps you mature. On the other hand, you may need a college close by so that you can live at home and reduce expenses. The cost of transportation is frequently one of the most important factors in considering school location.

The size of the school. Actually, the size of the school is of little importance, unless you particularly care about size. Some students from small high schools have difficulties in adjusting to life at a large university. Some students from large high schools find it difficult to adjust to a small college. How you feel about the size of the school should be your guide in this matter.

The community. The size of the community in which the school is located may be more important than the size of the school. Again this depends on your particular outlook and values. Some city youth do not want to live in a small town. Some youth from rural areas find the idea of adjusting to city life unappealing. In other cases the reverse is true—individuals who were brought up in one type of community want the experience of living in another type. How do you feel about it?

Public or private school? There are many pros and cons about the advantages of one over the other. Public schools are usually much cheaper, since a large share of the cost is paid by the taxpayers. Some private schools are more progressive, since they are not dependent on public funds. Discuss the pros and cons with other students to help you decide which one is best for you.

From your study of the college bulletins you should be able to reduce your choice to five or six or fewer schools.

Talk to students attending these schools. Probably you know or can obtain the names of students from your school or city who are attending the colleges that interest you. Make a point to see them during a school vacation when they're at home. They may be able to enlarge your perspective and answer many of your questions. This information should help you narrow the choice even further.

Visit the campus or school. A visit to the campus will tell you many things not found in the college bulletin or described by students attending the school. There may be a big difference between the way you pictured the school from its bulletin or someone else's account and the way it appears to you when you see it for yourself. For this reason you shouldn't plan to attend a college or school of any kind without first making a personal visit. This one visit could protect you from disappointment and unhappiness, and possibly save a great deal of money.

The best time to visit the school is when classes are in session and the students are on the campus, rather than during a vacation or weekend. Although you do want to see the buildings and equipment, you also want to get the feeling of the place. To do this, you need to see how the students react to one another and to the professors. You need to see the attitudes and relationships of the professors toward the students. The most important things about a college are not its buildings or equipment but the people and their interactions with one another.

While you are visiting the school, take note of all the factors that you analyzed in the bulletin to see if they meet your expectations. When you have carefully considered all aspects of campus life, you are ready to make a decision about attending the school.

SECTION REVIEW

1. What steps can you take to find an appropriate educational program for you?
2. What can you learn about a school from examining its bulletin?
3. Which aspects of an educational program are most important to you? Why?

SECTION 3:
Selecting a Vocation

There are more than 30,000 different jobs in our society. These jobs involve a wide range of educational and personal requirements. They provide a variety of working conditions, opportunities for advancement, and financial, social, and psychological rewards. Somewhere in this great number of job opportunities you should be able to find a job that you could make into a lasting career. A CAREER *is a lifelong occupation.*

What, then, is an occupation? And what is the difference between an occupation and a vocation? *An* OCCUPATION *refers to a particular type of work that is done for a living,* such as the work of a teacher, salesperson, or mechanic. Each occupation involves certain requirements and a number of specific tasks. *A* VOCATION *is an occupation for which the person feels a calling or a sense of dedication.* An occupation becomes a vocation when the person feels that it is the best way he or she can make a contribution to the society.

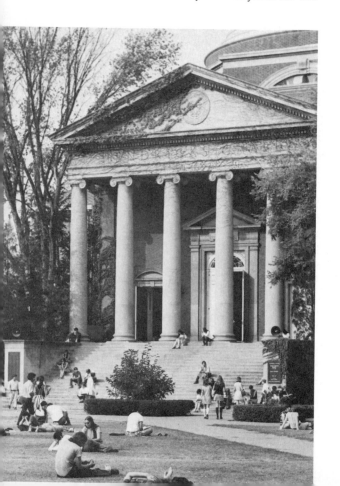

As you go about selecting a vocation, you might keep in mind several points. For one thing, it's wise not to limit yourself too much in deciding to pursue a particular occupation. Society is constantly changing, and these changes always have some effect on the work force. Jobs come and go as the society changes. A very promising job at the present time may not exist ten years from now, as new inventions take over jobs previously done by individuals. Always keep a few alternate careers in the back of your mind. Also, remember that your interests and abilities may change. If you keep yourself flexible and plan ahead, you will fare much better in the world of work in a changing society.

Sometimes young people choose occupations because they seem to offer thrills and excitement. We are often misled by the mass media in terms of the thrills of some occupations. We see the surgeon completing the life-saving operation, the lawyer arguing his or her case before the jury, or the private eye finding the clue that breaks the case. We do not see, however, the many hours of grueling work that must be done day after day to make these few spectacular moments possible. A great deal of practice and repetition is necessary to become an expert in a particular field. When people begin working, they don't start at the top. Also, many of the jobs that seem to offer thrills and excitement are unstable jobs with little future. Deep-sea divers, for example, often have difficulty in finding steady employment.

Finally, in deciding the career you will pursue, listen to parents and friends. But let the final decision be yours. For you are the one most affected by it.

How to Begin Finding a Vocation

In your search for a vocation, you might begin by asking yourself some questions. What level of occupational category can you achieve? What specific occupations fit your abilities and aptitudes? Your experiences?

423

Your interests? Your values and goals in life? What occupations could you make into vocations by dedicating your life to them? In which occupations could you be most productive?

As you go over these questions, jot down some of the occupations that you think of in connection with each question. No doubt you will come up with a long list of occupations. For there are many occupations that have similar requirements and interests.

For example, people who are interested in mechanics have a large number of occupations open to them. If they have the aptitude to prepare for a profession, they might wish to consider becoming an engineer, medical record librarian, or technical writer. In the semiprofessions they might consider the occupations of dental laboratory technician, drafter, surveyor, or teletypist. In the skilled

One way to learn more about a specific occupation that interests you is to talk to someone who holds that job.

trades they could choose to be an airplane mechanic, bookbinder, jeweler, machine tool operator, maker of mechanical instruments, optical mechanic, paperhanger, or telephone installer. In the semiskilled trades they might consider becoming an auto assembler, farm worker, production painter, service station attendant, taxi driver, or welder.

The above list is far from complete. But it should give you an idea of the extremely large number of occupations that fit any particular aptitude or interest. You should do careful research on available occupations that might fit your interests, aptitudes, and abilities. The following are some sources that you might investigate in your search.

1. *The Encyclopedia of Careers and Vocational Guidance,* Volumes I and II. Volume I, "Planning Your Career," gives valuable information on learning about yourself and your goals, where to obtain further information, using test results in vocational planning, how to find a job, and the future world of work. It also includes general information about each of the many career fields. Volume II, "Careers and Occupations," provides specific information about particular occupations. These two volumes are revised about every five years.

2. *Occupational Outlook Handbook.* Put out by the United States Bureau of Labor Statistics, this is an excellent guide to almost all occupations. It gives the nature of the work, location, training, requirements, advancement opportunities, earnings, working conditions, and where to go for more information. It is updated every two years. An important feature of this guide is that it predicts the future trends in all of the various occupations.

3. *The Explorer Program* of the Boy Scouts and Girl Scouts of America. This program allows high-school age boys and girls to explore their aptitudes and interests in occupations. They are given a chance to learn about

aspects of many different occupations. To find out about this program see your school counselor, local Scout office, or write to: Explorer Division, North Brunswick, New Jersey 08902.

4. *Your school counselor.* Don't overlook the possibilities for career information available from your school counselor. If you attend a large school, you might even have a counselor who specializes in careers. Your school may even have a "career center" for student use. Your counselors are there to help you.

5. *Libraries.* You can find a lot of career information in your school or public library. Some libraries have special sections that contain college catalogs and bulletins, occupational guides, and many books on specific jobs. Also, the *Reader's Guide to Periodical Literature* can be useful for finding current magazine articles on various occupations. If you don't find what you want, be sure to ask the librarian for help.

6. *Your local state employment office.* Your state employment office can give you information on the kinds of jobs available in the community. It can also give you some tests to determine which kinds of jobs might best fit your abilities, aptitudes, and interests.

7. *Career fairs.* Many communities sponsor career fairs, in which persons from many different vocations provide programs on various aspects of their careers. These fairs may be sponsored by your local school, your school system, the Chamber of Commerce, or a combination of many community agencies working together. To find out about them, consult with your school counselor and watch your school and community newspapers. You and your classmates may even want to help organize one.

From these sources of information you should be able to draw up a list of possible occupations related to your interests and aptitudes. Then you can go through the list and mark off those that are either below or above

When you consider the nature of the work, think about the type of tasks you would be doing.

your ability. At this point your list should be narrowed down to about a dozen or so occupations. The next step is to analyze each of these as a possible vocation.

Analyzing Possible Vocations

As you continue your research of possible vocations, there are some factors that you should consider. You need to examine the type of work involved in a particular occupation, the requirements, the working conditions, the opportunities for advancement, and the rewards. There are many questions that you can ask yourself to relate these factors to your list of occupations. Your answers should help you select an occupation that will be satisfying and suitable for you.

The nature of the work. Generally speaking, there are three basic kinds of jobs: (1) Jobs in which you work primarily with people. These would include most of the professions, as well as the work done by salespeople, personal service workers, protective service workers, and so on. (2) Jobs in which you work mostly with data. These include the work of file clerks, statisticians, mathematicians, auditors, bookkeepers, and accountants. (3) Jobs in which you work mainly with things. These include the work done by craftspeople (artists, electricians, mechanics, carpenters, TV repairers, plumbers), machine operators, and unskilled employees. Decide on the kind of basic work you would prefer to do. Then investigate various occupations in these areas.

For each of the possible occupations on your list you should analyze the exact nature of the work you would do. Would you operate a machine, attend meetings, make decisions, write reports, give speeches, drive a vehicle, paint, conduct experiments, talk on the telephone? Most occupations involve several kinds of tasks. Consider what these various tasks would be. Would there be sufficient variation of tasks to keep you from becoming bored with the occupation? Would you be in charge of the tasks or would you be supervised by someone else? If possible, visit a place where people in an occupation in which you are interested are employed. Then you can see for yourself what the nature of the work really is. Finally, ask yourself this question: Would you be happy and satisfied doing those specific tasks?

The requirements for the occupation. The questions to answer in this area include: Do you have what it takes to be successful (not necessarily the best) in this occupation? Do you have the ability to complete the education required? Do you have the aptitudes needed? Is the occupation close enough to your interests for you to be happy doing this kind of work?

If you choose an occupation requiring more talent and ability than you have, you will be frustrated. You won't be able to achieve the competence you desire. On the other hand, if you have more ability than the occupation requires, you will also be frustrated. You will probably feel that you are not making any use of some of your talents and abilities.

The working conditions. Consider the physical conditions under which you would be working. Would you be outdoors or indoors? Does a particular occupation involve working in a heated or air-conditioned office? Would the physical environment be extremely hot, cold, noisy, dirty, or hazardous? How do these conditions relate to your own physical well-being? Do you have any physical defects or weaknesses that would rule out certain occupations?

Analyze, also, the psychological environment in which you would work. Does the job involve working alone a great deal of the time? Or would you work with a small or large group? Would you be closely supervised or "on your own"? Are there any aspects of the physical conditions that would upset you emotionally or psychologically? Consider each of these factors in terms of your own personality.

Another aspect is the location of the occupation. Does the job mean that you would be living in a small town, a large city, the mountains, at the seashore, or on the plains? You can't be an oceanographer in Kansas or a forest ranger in New York City. Also, how much travel is involved? Would you live at home or travel all over the country, staying in motels and hotels? Would you travel locally in the course of the occupation? Or would you do your work at a specific place? How do the location and travel requirements fit your personal preferences?

Consider, too, the hours you would work. Would you work regular hours each day, such as eight or nine to five, or would your

These are just a few of the many possible vocations available in our society. They include working as an architect, a mail carrier, a sound engineer, and a florist.

hours vary from day to day or week to week? How well can you adjust to irregular hours? Would you be working on a year-around basis or would the work be seasonal?

These are some of the questions you need to ask about a possible occupation for you. The important thing is not how most people regard the working conditions but how you feel about working under these conditions. Would you be able to adjust easily to the specific working conditions or would they continually irritate or annoy you?

The opportunities for promotion and advancement. The psychological well-being of an individual is closely related to his or her feelings of achievement and self-esteem. Many people have a sense of achievement and feel competent in their occupations only when they receive some promotion or advancement periodically. When they do not progress forward through advancements in their job, they may feel that they are actually slipping backward. Many persons experience these frustrations because they have selected occupations that offer very little opportunity for promotion and advancement. How important is promotion or advancement to you? What are the opportunities for promotion and advancement in the occupations that you are considering? What do you have to do to receive them?

You also need to take into account the nature of the occupation itself. Is it an occupation with a future? Or, with our rapidly changing technology, will it soon become obsolete? No one can predict accurately all the changes that will take place in occupations during your lifetime. But relatively accurate predictions can be made for up to a ten-year period. The United States Department of Labor makes intensive studies to determine what the trends will be in occupations over a period of ten years. These trends are reported in the Labor Department's *Job Guide for Young Workers* and *Occupational Outlook Handbook*. Use these sources to determine

what the future might hold for occupations that you are interested in.

One important factor in obtaining a job and receiving promotions or advancement is the person's attitude toward the occupation. Some people work only to make a living and put in as little effort as possible on the job. They are often the first to be dismissed when the staff is cut. Other people view their work as a source of satisfaction and fulfillment. They are usually willing to put extra time and effort into the job.

The rewards of the occupation. There are several different kinds of rewards that you might receive from an occupation. First, there are financial rewards. These might be in the form of cash (salary or wages), fringe benefits (health insurance, sick leave, social security, paid vacations), or as payment in kind (room and board, merchandise, stock). Then there are psychological and sociological rewards. One such reward is the amount of self-esteem it gives to the individual. To determine this you might consider such questions as: Can you pursue this occupation with integrity and dignity? Will it permit you to utilize the productive powers that you have? Does it conflict in any way with your values and norms? How will the occupation affect your status? Will you be proud to be a member of this occupational group?

These are some of the factors to analyze as you attempt to determine the vocations that would be best for you. The research that you do now will be extremely helpful when you go about making your final choice. Many workers today are unhappy with their jobs and wish that they were in some other occupation. A few of these people are emotionally maladjusted and would be unhappy in any occupation. Many, however, are really in the wrong occupation. Once a person gets seniority on a job or has family responsibilities, it becomes rather difficult (though certainly never impossible) to change occupations. For this reason it is extremely important that you make the best choices. Instead of drifting into a particular occupation, it is to your advantage to plan ahead carefully for the future you want.

SECTION REVIEW

1. What aspects of your personality are important in choosing a vocation?
2. What factors should you consider in analyzing particular occupations that interest you?
3. Why is it important to make a wise career choice?

KEY TERMS

Explain and give an example of each term.

career   vocation
occupation

PROJECTS AND ACTIVITIES

1. Using the telephone directory, make a list of all educational programs beyond high school that are available in your community (you may need to call some schools to clarify the kinds of programs they offer).

2. Interview college students to find out how college differs from high school.

3. Obtain copies of college bulletins from a number of schools and compare their philosophies. How do they differ?

4. Set up a sociodrama in which the participants discuss what they expect college to be like and why. Then discuss the accuracy of the presentation.

5. Write a newspaper feature article entitled "How to Choose a College."

6. Investigate any apprenticeship programs offered in your area to find out what is involved—how long they take, what the qualifications are to enter, what is taught, and what the financial arrangements are.

7. Select a vocation that interests you and work out an educational program that would provide you with the training necessary to be successful in that vocation.

8. Make a bulletin board display that illustrates the steps to follow in carefully choosing a career.

9. Decide on a particular category of job that interests you. Then research in the *Occupational Outlook Handbook* the various kinds

of occupations that pertain to that category, to get an idea of the number and variety of occupations that exist. Notice also the information provided on the nature of the work, the qualifications, earnings, working conditions, and advancement opportunities for each occupation.

10. Look through the "help wanted" listings in the classified advertising section in a local newspaper to determine the kinds of occupations that have openings in your area.

11. Conduct research on what categories of jobs seem to be in increasing demand and what categories are predicted to be in decreasing demand in future years.

12. Interview persons employed in several occupations that interest you to obtain data about all aspects of those particular occupations. If possible, observe the types of activities and kinds of working conditions involved.

13. Carry out a sociodrama that depicts persons who are unhappy with their occupations and those who are happy with their occupations. Then discuss the implications of each situation.

14. Write a brief description of what you think one day's work would be like at a particular job. Include what you would do and why you might like or not like it.

TOPICS FOR INQUIRY

1. Discuss whether you think that people can ever be completely objective in looking at themselves, others, and their environment.

2. Which do you think is best when planning for the future—to always aim high, or to set goals that are attainable? Why?

3. Some college admissions people say that the single most important indicator of how well students will do in college is how well they've done in high school. Discuss this statement and whether you agree or disagree with it.

4. Compare the advantages and disadvantages of a liberal arts education vs. vocational training. Which would you choose? Why?

5. Discuss the pros and cons of a college education in terms of its cost (don't forget the cost of lost income while attending school).

6. Debate: If a student is interested in going to college only to be able to make more money, then he or she should invest the money rather than spending it on a college education.

7. Do you think people plan for unskilled occupations (and some semiskilled occupations), or do you think they drift into them because they can't find any other occupations? Explain.

8. Discuss the relative importance of the various kinds of rewards an individual might receive from an occupation.

9. Debate: A sense of achievement and productivity is more important in a vocation than the amount of income earned.

10. What do you consider to be the most important aspect of a vocation for you? What occupations can you think of that meet this requirement?

SUGGESTIONS FOR READING

NONFICTION

BRAUDE, Lee, *Work and Workers: A Sociological Analysis.* Praeger, 1975 (and pap.). Covers the sociology of occupations, the meaning of work, the American work force, the professionalization of occupations, and the increase in leisure.

ELLIS, Albert and HARPER, Robert A., *A Guide to Rational Living.* Prentice-Hall, 1975 or Wilshire (pap.). A guide for conducting your own self-analysis through the use of case histories of others.

SIMON, Sidney B., *Meeting Yourself Halfway.* Argus Communications, 1974 (pap.). Offers thirty-one adventures in self-discovery to help the individual find out what his or values really are.

TERKEL, Studs, *Working.* Pantheon, 1974. An investigation of the many occupations of Americans through the interview method. People talk about their work and how they feel about what they do.

VALETT, Robert E., *Self-Actualization.* Argus Communications, 1974 (pap.). Helps the individual toward self-understanding and suggests how to make the most of talents, traits, interests, and goals.

APPRENTICESHIPS

KURSH, Harry, *Apprenticeships in America.* Rev. ed., Norton.

BROWNSTEIN, Samuel C. and WEINER, Mitchel, *Barron's How to Prepare for College Entrance Examinations*. Seventh ed., Barron (and pap.).

———, *You Can Win a Scholarship*. Rev. ed., Barron (and pap.).

FINE, Benjamin, *How to Be Accepted by the College of Your Choice*. Rev. ed., Hawthorn or Popular Library (pap.).

KUSSINS, Louis and KUSSINS, Steven, *How to Prepare Your College Application*. Arco (pap.).

LASS, Abraham H., *How to Prepare for College*. Pocket Books (pap.).

———, and WILSON, Eugene S., *The College Student's Handbook*. David White (and pap.). A comprehensive guide that discusses the many academic, financial, and social problems facing all college students.

SULKIN, Sidney, *Complete Planning for College*. Rev. ed., Harper & Row.

DIRECTORIES OF COLLEGES AND VOCATIONAL SCHOOLS

Barrons' College Profiles in Depth Series. Barron.

CASS, James and BIRNBAUM, Max, *Comparative Guide to American Colleges 1973–74*. Sixth ed., Harper & Row.

———, *Comparative Guide to Senior and Two-Year Community Colleges*. Harper & Row.

The College Handbook. College Entrance Examination Board (pap.).

Directory of Sources for Higher Education. Research Associates.

GLEAZER, Edmund J. Jr. (ed.), *American Junior Colleges,* Eighth ed., American Council on Education.

GRAHAM, R. William (ed.), *Barron's Guide to the Two-Year Colleges*. 2 Vols. Rev. ed., Barron.

HAWES, Gene R., *The New American Guide to Colleges*. Fourth ed., Columbia University Press.

Junior College Directory. Washington, D.C.: American Association of Junior Colleges.

LOVEJOY, Clarence E., *Lovejoy's Career and Vocational School Guide*. Simon & Schuster (and pap.).

———, *Lovejoy's College Guide*. Simon & Schuster (and pap.).

SINGLETARY, Otis A. (ed.), *American Universities and Colleges.* American Council on Education.

DIRECTORIES OF TECHNICAL AND BUSINESS SCHOOLS

Write for lists of technical and business schools to:

National Council of Technical Schools
1507 M. Street, N. W.
Washington, D.C. 20005

United Business School Association
1518 K Street, N. W.
Washington, D.C. 20005

VOCATIONAL GUIDES

The Aim High Vocational Guidance Series, published by Rosen Press.

The Careers for Tomorrow Series, published by Walck.

The Dutton Career Books, published by Dutton.

The Encyclopedia of Careers and Vocational Guidance. Vol. I, "Planning Your Career." Doubleday. This volume gives information on learning about yourself and your goals, where to obtain further information, using test results in vocational planning, how to find a job, and the future world of work. It also gives general information about each of the many career fields.

The Encyclopedia of Careers and Vocational Guidance. Vol. II, "Careers and Occupations." Doubleday. This volume gives specific information about particular occupations.

Job Guide for Young Workers. United States Department of Labor. A guide for young people seeking jobs.

Occupational Outlook Handbook. United States Department of Labor, Bureau of Labor Statistics. An excellent guide to almost all occupations. It gives the nature of the work, the location, training, requirements, opportunities for advancement, the earnings and working conditions, and where to go for more information.

SANDMAN, P. and GOLDENSON, D., *The Unabashed Career Guide.* Macmillan. A satirical discussion of some of the major occupations, showing their unglamorous side. This book should help the individual see some aspects of these occupations more realistically.

24 Developing Relationships

▶ How important is love in a relationship?

▶ What are some characteristics of successful relationships?

▶ What can you do to improve your relationships?

SECTION 1:
You and Others

Many people believe that the most important factor in having successful relationships is choosing wisely the individuals with whom they will have those "special" relationships. Actually, the selection of the individual is less important than what you bring to the relationship. The real key to successful relationships is to be found in you and your own personality.

Your Personality and Relationships

Sometimes people find it difficult to establish satisfactory relationships with others because they aren't satisfied with themselves. They may slip into the escape mechanism of NOMADISM. This *means that they keep moving from job to job, from neighborhood to neighborhood, and from person to person in their relationships.* If you asked them why they made the change, they would probably reply that they couldn't get along with the people at that job, didn't like the neighborhood, and so on. But what they are really trying to do is run away from themselves.

What happens if you aren't satisfied with yourself and you want to change yourself? You *can* change your attitudes, thoughts, and behavior. But first you must accept yourself as you are. You may look at yourself objectively and realize that you're selfish, you use other people, or you are an expert at exploiting people for your own benefit. You don't like what you see. But unless you accept yourself as you are, you can't change and become something different. You don't have to like yourself at this point. You only have to accept yourself as being this way. Then you can ask yourself what you really want to be. And you can develop a program to change yourself.

During this process of making some changes, you should never overlook your strong points. Everyone has a great number of good characteristics. If you concentrate on the positive aspects of your personality as you work to eliminate the negative aspects, you will grow as a unique human being. As you come to like yourself more and more, you'll find that it is easier to like others. You will also find that it's easier for others to like you.

What Is a Successful Relationship?

What might be considered a successful relationship is a personal thing. It depends on what an individual wants from a relationship. We might say that a successful relationship is based on love, dignity, respect, cooperation, humility, and consideration for the other person. Such a relationship involves a high level of personal satisfaction. It helps make each person's life more abundant, meaningful, and happy. How would you describe a relationship that is successful and meaningful to you?

Some research indicates that the affectional relationships of childhood are a factor in developing successful relationships later on. If children have close attachments to their parents, and have a happy childhood, they are apt to become happy adults and establish close relationships.

Similarly, the amount of socialization experiences with others affects our relationships. We tend to grow as persons through the experiences we have. The more we grow, the more mature we are. The more mature we are, the more we're able to have successful relationships with others. Furthermore,

Children who have positive socialization experiences and happy social relationships are likely to grow up to be happy adults.

experience in social relationships makes us more effective in establishing relationships. We learn by doing. The best way to develop good social relationships is simply to practice. We don't learn effective social relationships by withdrawing from people.

A Self-Inventory of Your Social Relationships

To help you grow in your relationships with others, try to look at yourself and your relationships objectively and realistically. You might consider the following questions. Do you really like yourself? Are you really happy to be you? Are you generally friendly, open, honest, and natural in relating to others? If not, are you trying to hide something?

When problems develop in a relationship, do you first ask yourself, "What am I doing wrong in this relationship?" Do you blame it on the other person? If your relationships break up, who is apt to bring about the break-up—you or the other person?

How do you usually see others—do you see mainly their good points or their faults? Do you give to others or primarily take from others? Are you able to apologize when you've hurt someone? Can you forgive others when they hurt you? Do you have a sense of humor that enables you to laugh at yourself?

How well do you personally fit the characteristics you desire in your friends? Do you treat your friends the same way you want them to treat you? Do you accept others as they are, or do you tend to judge others on the basis of your standards?

Are you able to see yourself as you really are and accept yourself as being that way, even though you don't really like being that way? Or are you hiding your true self from yourself because you can't accept yourself as being that way? If you've accepted yourself realistically, are you trying to change and grow to become the you that you want to be?

Do you keep in mind the really good things about yourself? Are you attempting to like yourself more fully so that you can love others?

SECTION REVIEW

1. How does your personality affect the kinds of relationships that you have?
2. What factors do you consider necessary for a successful relationship?
3. How would you go about looking at yourself and your relationships objectively and realistically?

KEY TERMS

Define and give an example of the following term.

nomadism

SECTION 2:
Love in a Relationship

It's difficult to discuss relationships without mentioning love. Everyone talks about love. And everyone experiences love to some extent. But does everyone agree on what it is? You are probably familiar with some of the "love sayings" of cartoonist Charles M. Schulz, creator of the famous *Peanuts* comic strip. Love is walking hand in hand. Love is tickling. Love is mussing up someone's hair. Love is a valentine with lace all around the edges. Love is hating to say good-by. Love is letting someone win even though you know you could slaughter that person. Love is wondering what the person is doing right now at this very moment. Do you agree?

What Is Love?

What do *you* think love is? The following statements about love are offered to help stimulate your own ideas about love and how it might enrich your life.

Love is concern. When you love someone, you are concerned about that person. You're concerned about that person's life and well-being. You're concerned about that person's growth—physically, emotionally, mentally, and spiritually. When you love, you care. If there is no caring, there is no love.

Concern is also important in love of self. If you love yourself, you are concerned about your life, growth, and well-being. And you care about your sense of self.

Love is respect. Love without respect is empty. If you love a person, you respect that person as a unique individual human being. Respect includes trying not to exploit that person in any way. You want the person to be what he or she wants to be. You want the person to grow for his or her own sake rather than for yours.

Respect also implies acceptance of the other person as that person really is, faults and all. If you love another person, you accept the values, norms, ideas, beliefs, and aspirations of that person as an important part of the individual's personality, even though you may disagree with them. You don't try to force that person to change his or her values, norms, ideas, beliefs, or aspirations just because you want theirs to agree with yours. Respect means, further, that you don't try to make the person do anything that is contrary to his or her values and norms.

Love is humility. To be humble means that you aren't conceited or self-centered. It means that you don't think of yourself more highly than you should.

Humility also means that you accept yourself as you are. Only by being humble can you see yourself realistically and objectively, because your ego isn't threatened. If you are self-centered, you interpret everything in terms of what it does to your ego. Some people are afraid to laugh at themselves because they're afraid they will puncture their own blown-up importance. They have a great time at parties pulling chairs out from under people who are about to sit down. They laugh heartily as the person lies on the floor in embarrassment or pain. If someone pulls a chair from underneath them, however, they get angry. Their ego has been bruised. But a humble person isn't threatened by such things. Being humble means that your self-acceptance, self-esteem, and self-love are not dependent on others.

Love is understanding. To love another person, you must have an understanding of that person. This means going beneath the surface of the loved one and not stopping at appearances. You must discover the true meaning of the actions, moods, and expressions of someone you love.

Understanding, like respect, involves acceptance. You may have heard this verse: "Accept me as I am—only then will we discover each other." Unless you accept the other person on his or her own terms, you can't really understand or know that person.

Love is giving. If you really love another person, you will give your love to that person without placing conditions on it. If you say, "I'll love you if you'll go with me to the party," you are saying, "I don't really love you." Conditional love doesn't work very

well. One person generally feels exploited. If you really love someone, you will give unconditionally and regardless of how much the person gives back in return. Genuine love involves a lot of giving.

Love is more than a feeling. Romanticism puts great emphasis on that special feeling which we call love. When we are "in love" we feel "butterflies in the stomach" or that we're "floating on cloud nine." We all know that feelings are fickle, that they change rapidly as the situation changes. If you identify love with a feeling, you will possibly become a fickle lover.

Nevertheless, feelings are important to love. Love can't grow between two people unless they have some feelings of attraction for each other. It's just that feelings alone are a shaky foundation for love.

Love is commitment. Have you ever stopped to think how tremendously important the words "I love you" really are? If they are sincere, the words "I love you" are a commitment made to the person to whom they are addressed. Your love is your response to the needs of that person. You want to help the one you love to grow and develop and enjoy life to the fullest. To say "I love you" is a commitment that involves a great responsibility.

You can't enter into this commitment with many people. You don't have enough emotional capacity to commit yourself to such a deeply personal and loving relationship with many people. Therefore you must choose carefully the person or persons to whom you will make this commitment.

You should be careful not to make a commitment that you are unable to honor. How would you like to have someone make the "I love you" commitment to you and then later take it back, saying, "I didn't really mean it"? This is certainly one of the worst of all ego hurts we can receive in our human relationships. You may not have any control over who makes the commitment to you.

You do have control over your own commitment to others. What do the words "I love you" really mean to you? What do you want them to mean to the person to whom you say them?

Love is action. The old statement "Actions speak louder than words" is very applicable to love. Suppose someone said "I love you" to you, but showed no concern for your well-being or did nothing for you. Would you believe the person meant those three words? Loving someone means being in a constant state of concern for the well-being of that person, and showing it. Love is action. If there is no active concern, there is no love.

Love is forgiveness. Probably the most remembered expression from the novel and movie *Love Story* is "Love means never having to say you're sorry." Nothing could be further from the truth. Genuine love involves always being ready to say "I'm sorry—forgive me." If you have a meaningful relationship with another person, sooner or later you are going to say or do something which hurts that person. You will in some way wound that person's ego. The natural response of the other person is to fight back. The result is a physical, mental, or emotional battle. Communication breaks down. And no relationship can last without effective communication.

One way to restore communication is to say "I'm sorry—forgive me." The sooner it is said the better, because the longer you wait, the harder it is to say. The sooner you say it, the sooner effective communication can resume. The relationship and both individuals will grow as a result.

Love is communion. Real love between two people involves a level of communication that we might call communion. COMMUNION *is the sharing of your feelings and emotions with another human being.* As you express your true feelings and emotions, you are exposing your inner self and sharing it with the other person.

When communication breaks down in a relationship, it is usually due to emotional problems. An individual's feelings of love and self-worth are threatened. The result is anger. When we are angry, we say and do things that we don't really mean. We are attempting to protect our egos. Nothing else is important. We argue about everything except the real issue. We often blame the other person for making us angry. Yet it isn't really the other person's fault. Other people can't cause or be responsible for our emotions. They can only stimulate in us the emotions that are already there.

What can you do if the person you love gets angry at you without just cause? One possibility is to accept the person's anger and encourage the person to share his or her feelings with you. You can try to make the person feel less threatened and more secure. You can help the person restore his or her sense of self-worth. This then opens the door to real communion—the sharing of feelings and emotions.

Two people can have a very wonderful loving relationship, even though they disagree on a great number of things, as long as they can have a communion of their emotions. When we accept the other people's emotions, we help them understand themselves. As a result, they grow. If, on the other hand, we are judgmental rather than accepting, we close the door to both communication and communion. If two people are completely accepting and honest with each other, they help each other grow as individuals. And the relationship of love grows as well.

Love is a personal orientation. Love is a personal orientation or attitude that determines how individuals relate to themselves, to others, and to their world. Love is much more than just a way of feeling and acting toward a very special person. It is an attitude that affects all of life. Love of self and others,

441

An important part of a relationship is the ability to listen to what the other person is saying. To be able to listen and to respond is a sign of caring.

and a love for life itself, can make the difference between life lived to the fullest and mere existence.

Although love is a personal attitude, all love has essential elements in common. These elements are present whether the love is directed toward a "special" person of the opposite sex, parents, brothers or sisters, close personal friends, or to human beings in general. In all these cases love involves care, concern, respect, humility, understanding, giving, responsibility, commitment, action, forgiveness, and communication.

How do you feel about love? With which of the statements about love given here do you agree? Disagree? Why? What other elements are involved in loving someone?

SECTION REVIEW

1. Briefly summarize the statements made in this section about what love is.

2. Which of these statements do you think are most important in developing a loving relationship? Least important?
3. How would *you* define love?

KEY TERMS

Explain this word in terms of social relationships.

communion

SECTION 3:
Establishing Satisfying Male-Female Relationships

No doubt your relationships with others are very important to you. You've probably

442

thought a good deal about your relationships with members of the opposite sex, in particular. How do you establish such relationships? How can you improve them?

Some Guidelines

Often much of our personal satisfaction in life comes from our relationships with that "special" person of the opposite sex. Perhaps the following suggestions can help improve your relationships and make them more meaningful for you.

Keep the lines of communication open. As we've said, communication is necessary for a long-term relationship. But communication alone will not insure a satisfactory relationship. The communication must be open and honest. Also, emotions and feelings should be shared with the other person. In other words, communion must be present if the love relationship is to endure. Each person needs to accept the emotions and feelings of the other so that each may continue to grow.

If you keep the lines of communication open, you can resolve any differences as they come along. Differences that are left to take care of themselves will tend to grow and become more damaging to the relationship. By communicating and dealing with any differences when they develop, you can keep the relationship dynamic and satisfying.

Work hard to carry out the roles you have determined for yourselves. The roles that society sets for males and females are not nearly as important as the roles you set for yourselves. You should discuss carefully the roles you feel each should play in the relationship. Then work hard to carry them out. It is a good idea to keep the roles flexible, though. If the two of you alternate roles occasionally, you will understand the other person better.

An important part of your role is to show the other person that you are proud of him or her. At the same time you should work hard to make the other person proud of you. Genuine compliments are always pleasant to receive and help us increase our sense of self-worth. Compliments cannot be made too often if they are deserved and given sincerely.

Base your relationship on trust. If a relationship isn't based on trust, it does not have a very firm foundation. To have a relationship based on trust does not mean that you have a lot of rules—lots of do's and don'ts—by which you relate to each other. It means, rather, an open trust, in which each trusts the other. Basically it means a foundation

Sharing some of the household responsibilities equally can help the two people feel equal.

upon which communication and communion may take place in the relationship. Trust works both ways. You must trust your partner. But you must also be worthy of your partner's trust in return.

Base your relationship on equality. We know very well that males and females are not the same. There are distinct differences between the sexes. But this doesn't mean that they aren't equal. Equality means that each partner has the right to be his or her own person, a unique human personality. If each of you recognizes the other as an equal, you can help each other grow as individuals.

Be aware that you will meet many situations beyond your control. We never know what the future holds. But we can expect a certain amount of tragedy and hardship. You will be required to meet and adjust to many hardships. They may strengthen or weaken your relationship, depending on how you deal with them. If you face them realistically and objectively, you may find that they will strengthen your relationship.

Realize that conflicts are normal in any close relationship. The couple who say: "We love each other so much that we could never have any conflicts" are only fooling themselves. No two people can have a close relationship without having conflicts arise. Love doesn't keep conflicts from developing. It does help the couple face the conflicts realistically and work them out to the satisfaction of both.

Realize each individual's need to grow. In our society we have tended to overemphasize togetherness. The typical comment of the couple in love is: "We love each other so much that we never want to be apart." The fact is, however, that we need to be by ourselves at times to find out who we are, so we can grow as individuals. We need to pursue our own individual hobbies and interests. Being apart gives us separate experiences to talk about and share with each other.

One of the things that a couple must decide is how to spend their leisure time. How much of the leisure activities should be done together and how much should be done separately?

Only by being apart can we fully appreciate being together.

Also, each of us needs many relationships with a variety of people, if we are to grow as individuals. Our outside contacts help that "special" relationship to grow. Sometimes, however, outside relationships arouse the jealousy of one member. We may think that such jealousy is an indication of another's love for us. Actually it is not an indication of love but selfish possession, in which one person doesn't want to share his or her "property" with anyone else. If you really love the other person, you want to share that person's personality with others. You want the person to have the opportunity to grow and thereby improve the relationship you have with each other.

These, then, are some of the factors involved in establishing a satisfying relationship with that "special" person. An objective consideration of all these factors could help you have a very successful and rewarding relationship.

SECTION REVIEW

1. What are some guidelines that can be helpful in establishing a meaningful relationship?
2. Which guidelines do you think are most important? Least important?
3. Can you think of some guidelines not mentioned here that might help improve relationships?

445

1. Watch a number of installments of some serialized television programs, and take note of the problems in the relationships shown. How realistically do you feel the problems are presented? How would you have handled the problems?

2. Do research to attempt to determine how the changing values of the society affect male-female relationships.

3. Write a short story or drama that shows what you consider to be an ideal relationship between a man and a woman.

4. If possible, visit an organization or agency that scientifically matches people who are interested in marrying. Find out what guidelines they use in matching potential husbands and wives.

5. Do a sociodrama of a happily married couple. Afterward, discuss some of the factors that were suggested as being responsible for the successful marriage.

6. Observe a number of cases in a divorce court. What are the conflicts that seemingly led to the divorce proceedings? Do you think the conflicts presented in the court are necessarily the real reasons for the breakup of the marriage? Explain.

7. Interview a minister, priest, or rabbi (or preferably all three) about their views on successful relationships.

8. Read a romantic novel or poem about love, and compare the author's concept of love with your own.

9. Create a collage, bulletin board, or poster that illustrates your ideas of what love is.

10. Do a survey of teen-agers and adults to determine what the word "love" means to them. Try to determine if the meaning of love changes with time, age, and experience.

11. Do research on the problems of developing relationships.

TOPICS FOR INQUIRY

1. Debate: You must accept yourself as you really are before you can change yourself.

2. Do you agree with the statement that the way to establish satisfying relationships with others is to first establish a satisfying relationship with yourself? Why or why not?

3. Discuss: No one person can be everything to another person.

4. What are your ideas of a successful relationship?

5. Discuss the "Love is" statements in the chapter. Which do you agree with? Disagree with? Why? What other statements could you add?

6. Do you think the guidelines in the chapter for establishing satisfying male-female relationships are reasonable and practical? Explain. Which guidelines do you disagree with? Why? Which guidelines do you think are most important? Why? What other guidelines would you add?

7. Debate: No relationship should be considered satisfactory unless it allows each individual to grow as a unique human being.

8. Suggest several possible conflicts that you think would be most damaging to a relationship. How can such conflicts be avoided or resolved?

SUGGESTIONS FOR READING

FORD, Edward E., *Why Marriage? A Reality Therapist Looks at Married Life.* Argus Communications, 1974 (and pap.). Covers every aspect of preparing for marriage.

FRANKL, Viktor E., *Man's Search for Meaning.* Beacon, 1963 or Pocket Books (pap.). A psychiatrist tells about his experiences in a Nazi prison camp and how he developed his theories on the meaning of life.

FROMM, Erich, *The Art of Loving: An Inquiry into the Nature of Love.* Harper & Row, 1974 or Bantam (pap.). A discussion of the theory and art of love as applied to human relationships. Stresses how individuals can find happiness and meaning for their lives through an attitude of love.

LORAND, Rhoda L., *Love, Sex, and the Teen-ager.* Macmillan, 1965. A psychotherapist discusses the anxieties of teen-agers and offers specific suggestions for improving personality and social relationships.

MCCARY, James L. *Freedom and Growth in Marriage.* Hamilton, 1975 (and pap.). The author views marriage within the larger framework of human relationships and stresses the need for individuality.

MAY, Rollo, *Love and Will.* Norton, 1969 or Dell (pap.). Dr. May, a well-known psychotherapist, author, and developer of existential psychology, analyzes the quest of individuals to find themselves in today's changing technological society.

————, *Man's Search for Himself.* Norton, 1953 or Dell (pap.). A discussion of some of the difficulties and processes involved in self-discovery and self-understanding.

NEWMAN, Mildred and BERKOWITZ, Bernard, *How to Be Your Own Best Friend.* Ballantine, 1974 (pap.). A popular book on discovering and liking yourself.

O'NEILL, Nena and O'NEILL, George, *Open Marriage.* Avon, 1975 (pap.). A description of ways in which the husband and wife can help each other grow as unique individuals and have a fulfilling relationship.

POWELL, John, *The Secret of Staying in Love.* Argus Communications, 1974 (pap.). A discussion of love and the secret of good human relationships.

SAKOL, Jeanne, *What About Teen-age Marriage?* Messner, 1961. A book that discusses teen-age marriage in all of its many aspects— emotional, sexual, spiritual, and financial.

SHEDD, Charlie W., *Letters to Karen: On Keeping Love in Marriage.* Avon, 1974 (pap.). Written with delightful intimacy and good humor, this book deals with all aspects of marriage from the viewpoint of the wife.

————, *Letters to Philip: On How to Treat a Woman.* Doubleday, 1968 or Pyramid (pap.). A humorous and commonsense look at the male role in marriage.

Highlight

How do people interact in relationships?

The following photographs all show human relationships—the subject of study for sociologists. A sociologist's main concern, as you know, is to determine the causes and consequences of human relationships. By investigating social situations, the sociologist can increase our understanding of human behavior. If you were a sociologist, you would be studying the interactions of people, such as those shown below and on the following pages.

As you examine these pictures, you might select one of them. You might consider how a sociologist would go about studying the interaction that is presented in the picture. What questions might a sociologist ask? What techniques might be used to find answers? Would you be interested in becoming a sociologist and doing such research on human behavior?

Glossary

ability: the power to carry out some behavior act.

accommodation: a social process that attempts to bring a state of equilibrium between cooperation and conflict. It is achieved through a conscious effort by the conflicting parties to reach an agreement that will bring equilibrium.

acculturation: the intermixture of the shared, learned behaviors (or cultures) of two previously distinct groups.

achieved status: status earned by an individual through competition with others.

actuarial work: work that involves making statistical calculations, such as calculating life expectancy rates or insurance premiums.

adolescence: a term given to youth ranging from about twelve years of age into the twenties; the period between the onset of puberty and the attainment of full maturity.

advertising: a type of propaganda that has as its goal the motivation of people to purchase a particular product.

age categories: stages of social development that are defined mainly by cultural conditions, such as adolescence, middle age, and old age.

aggravated assault: an attack by one person on another for the purpose of inflicting bodily harm.

amalgamation: acceptable intermarriage between two previously distinct groups.

analysis: a process by which data are separated into parts and examined to determine the relationships of the various parts.

annulment: a court decision that declares a marriage null and void because of some legal reason, such as coercion, underage, or bigamy.

anomie: a state or condition of normlessness, in which there are no set rules of behavior or the rules are not clear.

anomie theory: a theory developed by Robert Merton that describes five ways in which people relate to the widely held goals in the society and to the socially approved means of achieving these goals.

aptitude: the capacity of an individual to learn a specific skill or to acquire a particular body of knowledge.

arbitration: a device used to bring about a compromise in which the conflicting parties agree to accept the decision of a neutral party, such as a judge, who settles the dispute.

arson: willful or malicious burning, or attempts at such burning.

ascribed status: status assigned to the individual by the society on the basis of some fixed category (such as race or sex), without regard for the individual's abilities or performances.

assimilation: a process by which two previously distinct groups blend into one unified group, or by which groups take in and absorb new members.

associations: special-purpose organizations that are composed of many smaller groups that do not all interact with one another at any one time nor are they together physically. Some examples are labor unions, political parties, corporations, and fraternal lodges.

audience: a transitory group subjected to a common stimulus, such as a film or a lecture.

barter system: a system of exchange in which goods are traded for other goods.

beliefs: all matters that a person accepts as true or actual, including attitudes, values, and knowledge.

bilateral: a method of determining kinship in which the descent is traced on both the father's and mother's sides.

birth rate: the number of births per 1,000 members of the population during a year.

boom: a craze that is related to a "get rich quick" scheme.

burglary: an attempt at or unlawful entry of a structure to commit a felony or theft.

capital: wealth that is used to finance the production and distribution of goods and services.

capitalism: a politico-economic system that is characterized by extensive private ownership and management of economic resources.

career: a lifelong occupation.

career mobility: a type of social mobility brought about by individuals changing their occupations or jobs.

case study method: an intensive study of a person, group, organization, or institution, using all available sources of obtaining data.

caste system: a social class structure in which individuals must remain in the social class of their birth.

casual crowd: a crowd that has no real structure and a very low amount and intensity of interaction.

cause-and-effect relationship: a relationship in which one variable is caused by another variable.

church: a number of people organized for religious purposes, with a hierarchy of officials and a set of doctrines that provide some unity of belief and practice.

civil law: the type of law that protects individuals against unreasonable conditions or acts by other citizens or by their government.

clergy: persons who have special training in religion and theology and who have been ordained or licensed to carry out the work of the church.

coercion: a situation in which the stronger party brings about accommodation by force or restraint.

collective behavior: in sociology, a term that refers to the study of relatively unstructured situations such as crowds, riots, fads, fashions, and social movements.

common law: an unwritten law built over the centuries on local custom and precedent and elaborated by decisions of judges in the courts.

communication: the transmission of ideas, information, and emotions by the use of symbols, such as words, pictures, and gestures.

communications revolution: the name given to the tremendous increase in communication techniques and media in recent years.

communion: in relationships, the sharing of feelings and emotions with another person.

communism: a politico-economic system in

which there is no private property beyond strictly private and personal possessions. All other property is owned collectively by the people through the state.

community: a number of people who live in a certain geographic area and have a social structure that provides for their physical and social needs.

competition: a social process in which two or more groups or individuals oppose one another to achieve a goal that only one can attain.

compromise: an accommodation reached because each side agrees to give up some of its demands for the sake of resolving the conflict.

conflict: a social process in which individuals or groups deliberately attempt to coerce, oppose, harm, or resist the will of another individual, group, or groups.

congeniality group: a group of individuals who get together because they like one another's company and enjoy doing many things together.

constitutional law: a formalized norm that appears in the constitution of a state.

consumer: a person in the society who purchases and uses the goods and services produced.

content analysis: a research technique that involves determining how many times a given word, attitude, or value appears in a given context (usually in the mass media).

continuum: a straight line with opposites at each end. A continuum can be used to show the degree to which something possesses a particular characteristic. For instance, if black were at one end and white the other, any place on the line would represent some degree of gray, ranging from very light to very dark.

contract law: the type of law that protects the right of an individual or group to make contractual agreements with other individuals or groups.

controlled observation: a research technique in which scientists set up and control a situation in which they can observe the phenomena that take place.

cooperation: a social process in which two or more groups or persons work together to achieve a goal from which all will benefit.

craze: the spread of some relatively superficial and external pattern of behavior that is very emotional in nature, such as flagpole sitting or goldfish swallowing.

crime: any act prohibited by law and punishable by the state. *Part I crimes* are the crimes of criminal homicide, forcible rape, robbery, aggravated assault, burglary, larceny, and auto theft. *Part II crimes* are crimes in the United States other than those just mentioned.

crime rate: the number of Part I crimes per 100,000 members of the population.

crimes against the person: crimes that involve physical contact with another person, such as rape, murder, and robbery.

crimes against property: crimes that do not involve physical contact with another individual but involve the property of another, such as burglary, larceny, or vandalism.

crimes against public safety and morals: crimes that involve public rules of right conduct, such as gambling, prostitution, and drunkenness.

criminal homicide: all willful killing. Also called murder and nonnegligent manslaughter.

criminal law: the type of law that protects the rights of members of the society by insuring the stability of the government or state.

crowd: a number of individuals who are together physically, who happen to be at the same place at the same time, but have a minimal amount of interaction.

cult: a small local religious group characterized by one doctrine that predominates, an emotional attachment to the leaders, and displays of great devotion on the part of the followers.

cultural alternatives: the many choices open to the individual for meeting the required cultural universals of the society.

cultural base: the total number of culture traits that a society has at a particular time.

cultural change: the process by which new patterns of shared, learned behavior are developed to meet the needs of the people not provided by the traditional patterns.

cultural lag: a situation in which some aspects of a society change less rapidly, or lag behind, other aspects of that society.

cultural relativity: the belief that any one of a large number of possible cultural practices may satisfy the needs of a particular society. One cultural practice may be best for one society but not for another.

cultural specialties: learned behavior shared by the members of a particular social category but not by the majority of the members of the society.

cultural universals: learned behaviors that are widely accepted and required by a particular society.

cultural values: shared assumptions (largely unconscious) of what is right, good, or important.

culture: the way of life of a people. The shared, learned behavior of the members of a society.

culture complex: a cluster of interrelated culture traits.

culture conflict theory: a theory of crime causation advocated by Thorsten Sellen that explains crime in terms of the conflicts that arise between different groups in the society who have differing norms of behavior. For example, if individuals follow the norms of a subculture, they could be breaking the laws of the culture.

culture pattern: a combination of a number of culture traits and complexes into an interrelated whole, such as an educational pattern.

culture of poverty: the concept that the people who live in poverty have a culture all their own that they pass on to their children, thus continuing it.

culture trait: an individual tool, act, or belief related to a particular situation or need.

death rate: the number of deaths from all causes during one year per 1,000 persons alive at the middle of the year. Sometimes called mortality rate.

defendant: the person or party required to answer the plaintiff and defend itself in a lawsuit.

deferred gratification: the putting off of an immediate satisfaction in favor of some long range goal and future reward.

denomination: an association of people adhering to a particular creed within a larger church, such as the Baptist Church and the Lutheran Church within the Protestant church.

dependent variable: the change that results from varying the independent variable.

desertion: in marriage, a situation in which one spouse abandons the other.

deviance: the situation that exists when some persons fail to obey the norms of their group or society.

deviant label: the designation given to people who are perceived to have broken the norms, whether or not they actually have broken the norms. According to sociologist Howard S. Becker, this deviant label affects people's interactions with others, forcing them to associate with other deviants and perhaps leading them to become more deviant in their behavior.

differential association theory: a theory of crime causation advocated by Edwin Sutherland which states that individuals learn patterns of criminal behavior through their associations with persons who break the laws.

differential fertility: the fact that the fertility rate varies according to many different factors, such as place of residence, color, social class level, and income.

differentiation: the process by which people are described in terms of certain personal characteristics and then classified into specific social categories on the basis of these characteristics.

diffusion: the process by which culture traits spread from one society to other societies.

discovery: the finding of some element or principle not previously known.

discrimination: overt behavior toward another person that is different from the individual's usual behavior toward others.

distribution system: the organization of persons and machines for the purpose of distributing goods or services to the consumer. A distribution system has three elements: the product or service; capital to provide buildings, machines, a labor force, etc.; and labor to carry out the distribution.

divorce: the legal dissolution of an officially recognized marriage.

Durkheim, Emile (1858–1917): a Frenchman who was the first sociologist to test a major sociological theory with carefully collected statistical data. His book *Le Suicide,* published in 1897, is still regarded as an important study on suicide.

duty: the obligation of other individuals to allow a person to act.

dyad: a two-person group.

dynamic society: a society in which change is taking place quite rapidly.

ecology: the study of the relationships between organisms and their environments; the study of structure and function in ecosystems.

economic institution: the system of norms, values, and roles through which the patterned and orderly distribution of the limited resources is achieved in a society.

ecosystem: a unit of biological organization consisting of all the populations of plants, animals, and human beings, interacting with one another in a physical environment.

educational institution: the social institution that has as its primary function the socialization of the new members of the society.

embezzlement: the misappropriation or misapplication of money or property entrusted to an individual's care, custody, or control.

emigration: the movement of people out of a society.

emotional contagion: the rapid spreading of a strong emotion, such as fear, among persons until almost all the individuals present are displaying the same emotion and participating in the same type of behavior.

endogamy: a marriage restriction that a person marry someone within the tribe, race, social class, religion, etc.

environment: the totality of situations and stimuli, both natural and social, that affect an individual.

equalitarian: a type of family organization in which the authority is shared by the husband and wife.

esteem: an evaluation of role behavior (how the individual carries out his or her role).

ethnocentrism: the belief that one's own group, race, or nation is the best.

evangelist: a traveling preacher or revivalist.

exogamy: a marriage restriction that requires a person to marry someone outside his or her immediate family, clan, village, or tribe.

experiment: an arranged situation in which the variables may be controlled or manipulated.

expulsion: the removal of minority persons from the society by the dominant members.

extended family: a type of family organization in which several generations of blood relatives live together.

extermination: the attempt of the dominant members of the society to solve the minority problem by the annihilation of the minorities.

fad: the spread of some relatively superficial and external pattern of behavior, such as hula hoops or bumper stickers.

family: the social institution whose basic function is the regulation of the replacement of the members of a society through sexual reproduction.

family allotment plan: a type of welfare plan in which all children receive allotments from the government sufficient to provide them with the basic necessities of life.

fascism: a politico-economic system based on the concept of "state absolutism"—the idea that the state has meaning and interests which transcend the welfare of its citizens.

fashion: the relatively short-term, socially approved, continuous variations in specific aspects of the culture, such as in dress, art, or furniture design.

felony: a major crime that is punishable by imprisonment for longer than one year.

fertility: the actual reproduction that occurs in a population.

fetishism: the belief that some object, either animate or inanimate, is possessed by indwelling spirits.

folkways: the etiquette and customs of a people that are not of critical importance to the society; the less important norms of the society.

forcible rape: the sexual violation of a female by force and against her will.

foreign born: a classification of the United States Census Bureau that includes all persons born outside of the United States or its possessions who do not have one parent who was born in the United States.

foreign white stock: a classification of the United States Census Bureau that comprises children of foreign-born parents.

formal group: a recurrent group that has an officially constituted structure or formal organization, such as officers and bylaws.

formal group goal: a goal that is clearly stated and understood by all members of the group. It may be found in the constitution or bylaws of the group.

formal religious structure: a secondary group, organization, or association related to the beliefs and practices of religion.

formal sanction: a reward or punishment used to enforce the laws or rules of some organization, institution or state. Formal sanctions are carried out by some regulatory body.

function: what something does. Scientists are concerned with what a structure, or part of a structure, does.

generalization: a statement about the relationship between the events or situations under study, based on the data collected in the study.

"generalized others": anonymous persons or roles to which the child learns to relate in an abstract way, such as bus drivers or store clerks.

group: two or more individuals who are interacting with one another and are together physically.

group dynamics: a technique for studying groups developed by Kurt Lewin that is concerned with the meaning the group has for its members and how participation in the group changes a person's behavior.

group goal: an object, situation, or satisfaction that the group wishes to achieve.

group marriage: a form of marriage in which there is more than one partner of each sex.

group mobility: the movement of a whole group, class, or caste in relation to the entire social class structure.

group norms: the rules of behavior that govern the actions of individual members in the group.

group sanction: a reward or punishment used by the group to enforce the norms and establish social control in the group.

guaranteed income plan: a type of welfare plan that provides a basic minimal income for every person. Individuals wanting more than this minimal amount can work for additional income. When their income reaches a certain level, they no longer receive the payments.

habit: a specific way of acting, feeling, or behaving that individuals have acquired through learning to the extent that they do it without thinking.

heredity: the transmission of genetic characteristics from parents to their children.

historical analysis: a research technique in which the scientist attempts to determine what has taken place in the past from records and remains.

horizontal mobility: a type of social mobility in which the individual moves from one position in a social class level to another position in that same social class level.

human ecology: the area of sociology that investigates and analyzes the causes and consequences of the spatial distribution of human populations.

human relationships: the ways in which people relate to one another as members of groups.

hypothesis: a tentative assumption or an untested generalization.

immigration: the movement of people into a society.

independent variable: the factor under study in a research situation.

indictment: a statement charging a person or corporation with an offense.

infant mortality rate: the number of infants who die before their first birthday per every 1,000 live births.

informal group: a group that does not have an officially constituted structure or formal organization. It has no charter, bylaws, or officers.

informal group goal: a goal that is not officially stated by the group and not consciously recognized by the group members.

informal religious structure: the type of religious structure found in some early societies in which the natural and supernatural are fused together and all phenomena are explained in terms of a god or gods.

informal sanction: a reward or punishment used to enforce the folkways and mores of the group or society. Informal sanctions are carried out by public opinion.

in-group relationship: a human relationship in which the individual feels a sense of loyalty, solidarity, friendliness, and identification, such as "my" team.

institutionalized inequality: the extent to which we have institutionalized certain patterns of inequality that then contribute to the continuation of poverty, such as the stratification system, the tax structure, and government subsidy programs.

integration: the process by which the dominant and minority categories function in the society as equals.

interaction: the behavior of one individual causing another individual or individuals to act, or two or more persons mutually influencing one another. *Physical interaction* is interaction between individuals that involves physical activity, such as fighting. *Symbolic interaction* is interaction between individuals that involves the use of symbols, such as talking.

interaction process analysis: a technique for studying groups developed by Robert F. Bales that is primarily concerned with the types and methods of interpersonal behavior rather than the contents or results of group action.

interests: those things that an individual finds enjoyment in knowing, feeling, or doing.

intergenerational mobility: a type of social mobility that occurs when a child later achieves a status different from that of his or her parents. The child's status may be either higher or lower than the parents' status.

internalization: the situation in which individuals obey the norms of the society because they have come to realize that the norms ought to be obeyed, and have adopted the habit of obeying them without even thinking about them.

interview: a situation in which the interviewer asks the questions from his or her schedule (list of questions) and records the answers given by the person being polled.

invasion: an ecological process in which persons of one social category move into an area occupied by another social category, such as Mexican Americans moving into an Italian American neighborhood.

invention: the combination of known elements or principles into some new form.

investigation: a careful and thorough study carried out by the use of the scientific method.

job: a specific piece of work with a definite extent and character.

labor: the people in a production system who convert raw materials into finished products.

laity: the people of a religious faith who are not specially trained in religion or theology.

larceny: the taking or stealing of property or articles without the use of force, violence, or fraud.

laws: norms that are set up and enforced by the state.

life chances: the probability that people will have certain experiences because of their placement in the social class structure.

life expectancy: the average number of years a person can expect to live.

"looking-glass self": the theory of Charles Horton Cooley which emphasizes that children develop an image of themselves only by finding out what other people think of them — by using other persons as a mirror to discover what they are like.

magic: pertains to any supernatural art or sorcery. It is often a part of primitive religions.

mass communication: the simultaneous exposure of a large number of people to stimuli transmitted by impersonal means from an organized source.

mass media: channels of communication to which many people are exposed, such as newspapers, magazines, radio, television, books, movies, and billboards.

matriarchal: a type of family organization in which the mother has the authority.

matrilineal: a method of determining kinship in which the descent is traced through the mother's line.

matrilocal: a type of family residence in which the husband moves in with or near the wife's family.

mediation: a device used to bring about a

compromise in which the conflicting parties allow a third party to act as adviser and counselor in helping them reach an agreement.

minister: a person who is authorized to preach the gospel and administer the sacraments or ordinances of the church.

minority: a category of people who are discriminated against or made a subclass in the social structure because they are believed to be inherently different from the dominant members of the society. A *racial minority* is a category of persons who have a physical appearance different from that of the dominant members of the society. An *ethnic minority* is a category of persons who have a culture or subculture which differs from that of the dominant members of the society.

misdemeanor: a crime that is punishable by imprisonment for less than one year.

missionary: a person who takes his or her particular faith to nonbelievers, whether in the local community or on the other side of the world.

mob: a crowd (and a transitory group) that is characterized by highly emotional and usually aggressive behavior and by much interaction.

mobility ethic: the belief that the individual not only has the right to succeed but has the duty to succeed as well.

monetary system: a system in which some form of money is used as a means of exchange.

monogamy: the marriage of one man to one woman.

mores: rules of behavior that are very important to the society and whose violation would endanger the stability of the society.

multiple causation: the concept that no single cause brings about a particular social problem, but rather a combination of causes.

mystic: an individual who believes that he or she has direct communication with the supernatural through dreams, visions, or other subjective experiences.

natural observation: a research technique in which scientists observe from a distance so that they will not cause any change in the natural phenomena taking place.

negative sanction: a sanction that punishes the individual for behavior that is not approved by the society or group.

neolocal: a type of family residence in which the married couple move away from both sets of parents and establish a completely new household.

net immigration: the total number of immigrants minus the total number of emigrants.

nomadism: an escape mechanism in which the individual attempts to get away physically from a frustrating situation. The person may move from job to job, neighborhood to neighborhood, or partner to partner.

norms: the group-shared rules of behavior; the expected ways of behaving.

nuclear family: a type of family organization in which family membership consists only of the married couple and their dependent children.

objective approach: a method of studying social stratification in which the sociologist uses such criteria as income, occupation, education completed, and housing.

occupation: a particular type of work that is done for a living.

open-class system: a social class structure in which individuals may move from one social class level to another.

organized crime: a term referring to the large organizations or syndicates that pursue crime as big business.

orgy: a situation in which the customary taboos and restraints are temporarily relaxed and the group members engage in an indulgence of appetite, such as a drinking orgy.

out-group relationship: a human relationship in which the individual feels a sense of disinterest, scorn, avoidance, distrust, competition, fear, or, in some cases, hatred.

panic: a situation in which persons, in the face of danger, are retreating in a disorderly fashion from the threatening situation.

participant observation: a research technique in which the observer is involved in the interaction under study.

patriarchal: a type of family organization in which the father has the authority.

patrilineal: a method of determining kinship in which the descent is traced through the father's line.

patrilocal: a type of family residence in which sons and their wives and children move in with or near the sons' parents.

pattern: the repetition of behavior that makes prediction possible.

peer group: a group of individuals who are equals. Usually they are equals because they are approximately the same age.

personality: the basic organization of the individual. It determines the uniqueness of people's interactions with themselves, with others, and with the nonhuman aspects of their environment.

physical sanction: a sanction that involves the physical well-being of the individual, that brings physical pleasure or pain.

plaintiff: the complaining party, the person who begins a lawsuit.

plea bargaining: an arrangement in the court system whereby the defendant agrees to plead guilty to a lesser charge and the prosecutor agrees to drop the original, more serious, charge.

political institution: a system of norms, values, and roles that define and locate the ultimate authority in a society and the agencies through which that authority is established.

pollution: the addition of any substance or form of energy to the environment at a rate faster than the environment can deal with it.

polyandry: the form of marriage in which a woman is permitted to have more than one husband at a time.

polygamy: marriage to more than one partner at one time.

polygyny: the form of marriage in which a man is permitted to have more than one wife at a time.

population: the total number of people living within a particular area.

population base: the total number of persons in a society at a particular time.

population density: the number of persons per square mile of land area.

population increase: the percentage increase in total population over a specific period of time, such as a year.

positive sanction: a sanction that rewards individuals for their behavior.

poverty: a situation in which persons live below the minimum level of living that the society regards as decent and reasonable.

prejudice: an attitude, a rigid emotional predisposition to respond similarly toward all members of a particular group or social category.

prestige: an evaluation of status.

priest: an individual who is authorized to perform the sacred rites of a religion and to serve as mediator between the people and the gods or god.

primary function: the intended or anticipated function.

primary group relationship: a human relationship in which individuals are important for their entire personality, the relationship is intimate and face-to-face, communication is deep and intensive, and personal satisfactions are of primary significance.

private school: a school that is not supported by tax money but rather by tuition fees, donations and contributions, or church funds.

problem: a perplexing question for which an answer is sought.

process: the specific way in which change takes place.

production system: the organization of persons and machines for the purpose of creating goods for the society. A production system involves natural resources, a labor force, and capital.

prohibitive law: a formal regulation that states what an individual or group cannot do, such as laws concerning murder, theft, and vandalism.

propaganda: the presentation of ideas in a biased manner for the purpose of influencing group attitudes, opinions, or behavior.

psychological approach: an approach used in propaganda that is based on the belief that people are influenced by subconscious and unconscious motivations.

psychological sanction: a reward or punishment related to the feelings and emotions of the individual, such as an award or rejection.

public opinion: the pattern of combined judgments of a public on a particular issue of importance to them.

public relations: a form of propaganda in which the emphasis is on promoting the public image of the client.

public school: a school that is supported by tax money and is open to any resident of the school district.

questionnaire: a list of questions that is filled in by the person being polled.

rabbi: an authoritative teacher of Jewish law or an appointed spiritual head of a Jewish community.

racism: the belief in the superiority of a group of people on the basis of race.

raw materials: the natural resources in a production system that are used to produce goods.

recurrent group: a rather permanent group in which the individuals interact with one another many times over a long period of time.

reference group: any group with whom the individual identifies and whose attitudes and values he or she tends to adopt, such as a school club, a congeniality group, or a gang.

regulatory law: a law that regulates the behavior of the persons of the society in order to allow the citizens to go about their activities in an effective and orderly way, such as a traffic law.

relative deprivation: the determining of the poverty level by the minimum level of living that the society regards as decent and reasonable—meaning that the level is relative to a particular society and will vary from one society to another.

religion: a system of beliefs and practices by which people recognize the apparent existence of one or more supernatural beings and attempt to either control these beings or live in conformity with them.

religious institution: the social institution that has as its basic function the providing of a sense of purpose for the people of the society.

religious leader: a philosopher or founder who originates a new religion, such as Gautama Buddha or Jesus Christ.

reputational approach: a method of studying social stratification in which the sociologist has the people of the community classify one another into social class levels, rating each individual on the basis of his or her reputation in the community.

research design: a set of directions for conducting research.

right: an opportunity or privilege for an individual to act, either verbally or physically.

riot: a situation in which a number of mobs are engaged in randomly destructive behavior.

robbery: taking something of value from a person by force or threat of force.

role: the behavior expected of a person because of the person's position in the social structure or group.

role allocation: the division of labor that takes place in a group as different members begin to accept and carry out specific responsibilities.

role behavior: the actual behavior of individuals in carrying out their role.

role conflict: a situation in which individuals find that some of the roles they play conflict with one another.

rumor: a story or information passed from person to person without confirmed evidence to support it.

rural community: people who live on farms or in small towns and villages having populations of less than 2,500.

rural-urban continuum: a straight line upon which we can place a community to show the degree to which it possesses certain characteristics that are rural or urban in nature. The rural characteristics are put at one end of the line and the urban characteristics at the other.

sacred: those things that are set apart from the other elements of the culture and that are, in a way, forbidden.

sample: in research, a portion of the total population that is selected in a way that all members of the population have an equal chance of being represented.

sanction: a reward or punishment used by the society or group to enforce the norms and bring about social control. Sanctions are either positive or negative, physical or psychological, and formal or informal.

scapegoat: a person, group, or object that is assigned the blame for the mistakes of others.

schedule: a list of questions that the sociologist asks a person being polled in an interview situation.

scientific method: an empirical, objective, and logical method of collecting data and arriving at conclusions.

secondary function: a function that is unintended or unanticipated.

secondary group relationship: a human relationship in which individuals are important solely for the function they perform and only a part of their personality is reacted to.

sect: a small body of persons who separate from a larger church or denomination.

segregation: the spatial separation of one category of persons from the other members of the society.

self-fulfilling prophecy: the theory that when individuals belong to a category of people who are stereotyped in some way, they tend to act in the way they are expected to act, thus fulfilling the prophecy.

separation: a situation in which the husband and wife are legally married but are not living together by common consent.

service system: the organization of persons and objects for the purpose of providing special services to the members of the society, such as medical services, legal services, and repair services.

sex ratio: the proportion of men to women in the population, stated as the number of males per 100 females.

sexism: the belief that the members of one sex are superior to the members of the other sex.

"significant others": persons who have a special importance to the child, such as parents, siblings, and close friends.

social category: two or more persons who have something in common and are aware of what they have in common but are not in interaction with one another, such as women or farmers.

social change: a change in the structure of the social relationships among the people of a society.

social class structure: a hierarchy of social classes that results from the social processes of differentiation and stratification.

social control: the obedience to the norms of the group or society by almost all the people, whether by internalization or by the use of sanctions.

social definition: the way a particular society defines persons who belong to a social category.

social institution: an enduring cultural structure through which certain fundamental needs of the society are met and social control is established.

social mobility: the movement of individuals and groups within the social class structure.

social movement: an organized attempt over a period of time to bring about some change in the society, such as the civil rights movement.

social problem: a condition involving human relationships that is considered undesirable by a large number of people.

social self: the way that individuals see themselves as a result of how other persons relate to them.

social stratification: the layering of social categories into higher and lower positions of prestige or respect.

social work: the task of applying the knowledge of social phenomena to the improvement of people's social situation.

socialism: a politico-economic system in which the major economic enterprises, including industries and public utilities, are both owned and regulated by the government.

socialization: the process of cultural molding by which the individual learns the basic skills, values, beliefs, and behavior patterns of the society.

society: a number of persons living within a certain geographic area who share a common culture and have a feeling of solidarity that binds them together into a social unit.

sociocultural approach: an approach used in propaganda in which an attempt is made to define or redefine the norms that are guidelines for people's behavior.

sociogram: a diagram showing the relationship among people in a group.

sociologist: a person who is versed in the subject matter of sociology and who is devoted to research and investigation in the field of sociology.

sociology: the science that deals with the investigation and analysis of human relationships, their causes and consequences.

sociometry: a technique for studying groups developed by J. L. Moreno that examines the patterns of interaction in an informal group structure and the position of each individual in relation to the others.

special education: educational programs offered by special schools for exceptional children, such as children who have speech defects or are mentally retarded, emotionally disturbed, or unusually gifted.

stable society: a society in which change is taking place quite slowly.

statistical analysis: a research technique that makes precise use of mathematical data, permitting scientists to describe empirical data and make generalizations about a population of which they have observed only a part.

statistical category: two or more persons who have something in common but are not particularly conscious of what they have in common and are not in interaction, such as all eighteen-year-olds.

status: the individual's position in the social structure of the group or society.

status insecurity: a condition that often accompanies upward social mobility in which the individuals are unsure of what constitutes appropriate behavior in their new class.

statutory law: a regulation that has been enacted by a legislative body.

stereotyping: a process by which we tend to treat all members of a particular social category as being alike.

structure: the way something is organized and the relationship of the various parts to one another.

structured behavior: group behavior that is controlled by some type of group structure, such as common values, group norms, and specific role relationships.

subculture: the way of life of a number of people in a society who have enough specialties not shared by the society as a whole to make them recognizably different and distinct.

subjective approach: a method of studying social stratification in which the sociologist asks the people where they place themselves in the social class structure.

suburb: a community related to, but beyond the limits of, the core, or central, city.

suburbanization: the movement of people from the core city to the surrounding suburbs.

succession: an ecological process in which a new group succeeds, or takes over the neighborhood from, a previous group.

survey method: a way of obtaining data from many people about their attitudes, opinions, values, or behavior, usually involving the use of the schedule or the questionnaire.

sweeping generalities: statements that are very general rather than specific, often involving the use of such words as "most," "the majority," or "always."

system of exchange: a system by which individuals exchange goods and services. It may be a simple barter system or a complex system involving money, checking accounts, and forms of credit.

technique: a method or manner by which research is conducted.

temperament: the fundamental emotional disposition of an individual.

theory: a combination of generalizations to explain some phenomena.

toleration: a form of accommodation without formal agreement in which the disagreeing parties avoid conflict by developing an attitude of "live and let live."

tool: in research, an instrument, apparatus, arrangement, or situation used by scientists to help in the collection of data.

trained incapacity: the fact that the culture of poverty produces an incapacity to break out of poverty by making it difficult for poor people to learn the language and habits necessary for success in the society.

transaction: a stimulus from one person and a response from one or more other individuals.

Transactional Analysis: a theory that explains socialization in terms of transactions, which lead people to adopt one of four life positions.

transitory group: a temporary group that meets only once for a relatively short time.

triad: a group consisting of three or more persons.

truce: an accommodation in which the conflicting parties agree to stop the conflict for a period of time so that negotiations may take place.

universal social processes: the five types of social interaction that are found in all societies and therefore called universal—cooperation, competition, conflict, accommodation, and assimilation.

unstructured behavior: group behavior that takes place in social situations when common values, group norms, and specific role relationships are not present.

urban community: people who live in an area with a population of 2,500 or more.

urbanization: the movement of people from the farms to the cities.

vagrancy: a situation in which a person is begging or loitering and has no apparent means of support.

vandalism: the willful or malicious destruction, injury, disfigurement, or defacement of property.

variable: a situation, factor, or event that can change or vary.

vertical mobility: a type of social mobility in which the individual moves from one social class level to another—either a higher or a lower level.

vested interest: the concern that an individual or individuals have for maintaining the status quo because it favors them in some way.

vocation: an occupation for which the individual feels a calling or sense of dedication.

weasel words: words that are used to avoid making a direct statement. The result is a statement that is misleading but not factually wrong.

Weber, Max (1864–1920): a German sociologist who wrote thirteen full-length works on many areas of sociology, including his well-known *The Protestant Ethic and the Spirit of Capitalism.*

welfare system: a complicated arrangement for allocating funds to those persons who have no legitimate way of providing for their own needs.

Index

Page numbers in *italics* that have *c, h, n,* or *p* written next to them refer to charts and tables (*c*), highlights (*h*), footnotes (*n*), or pictures (*p*). Page numbers in **boldface** show that the word's meaning is given on that page.

B

Bales, Robert F., 110–11
Barter system, 288
Becker, Howard S., 70, 73–74
Behavior: collective, **183**; criminal, theories of, 369–71; culture and (*see also* "Cultural"; Culture), 29; pattern, **6**; role (*see also* Roles), 55–56. *See also* Structured behavior; Unstructured behavior.
Behavioral sciences, 3–4
Beliefs, 30, **87,** socialization and, **88**
Bigness, value stress on, 54
Bilateral descent, 239
Birth rate, **166,** 167, 349; economy and, 169; population growth and, 166; school needs and, *h267*; social mobility and, 136; status and, 132
Blacks, 152; acculturation, 116, 157; activists, 159; aggression, 159; black power movement, 329; civil disorders and riots, 190, 327, 371; civil rights, 319–20, 327, 329–30; consciousness and self-identity, 320–21, 326–27, *p327*; culture, 157; discrimination, 326; economic competition and conflict, 331–32; exploitation, economic, 331–32; integration, 156; population in U.S., *c148*; poverty, 385; protest, organized, 157; "racial" characteristics, 148; as scapegoats, 332; segregation, 155, 156; separatism and nationalism, 157, 326
"Body Ritual Among the Nacirema" (Miner), *h233n.*
Blackstone, William, 374
Books and pamphlets, 93, 202, 255
Booms, 194
Boy Scouts, 92, 424–25
Brown v. Board of Education of Topeka, Kansas, 155, 320

Bureau of Labor Statistics, 424

C

Cady v. Dombrowsky, 374
Campfire Girls, 92
Capital, 286
Capitalism, 294–96; Protestant Ethic and, 277–79, *p278, p279*
Career mobility, 134–38, *p135, p138. See also* Employment; Occupations.
Carmichael, Stokely, 326
Carnegie, Andrew, *p278*
Case study method, 9
Caste system, 123
Categories: age, 399–403; invasion, **177**; minorities, 147–50, *c148*; scientific, 4; social, 102; statistical, 102; stereotyping, **151**–52
Cause-and-effect relationships, 16
Census Bureau, 149, 175, 385
Charisma, 43
Chavez, Cesar, 328
Chicano movement, 328
Chinese: population in U.S., *c148*; "voluntary" segregation, 157, 177, *p177*
Chromosomes, *p84*
Churches, 271–72; denominations, **272**; sects, **272.** *See also* Religion.
Civil law, *h381*
Civil rights and liberties, 319; Affirmative Action, 329–30; American Indians, 324; "backlash," 327; blacks, 319–20, 327, 329–30; criminal justice system and, 374; cultural factors and, 333–34; cultural rights and, 324–25; ecological crisis and, 351; economic competition and conflict and, 331–32; ethnic minorities (*see also* names), 319–24, 326–38; exploitation, eco-

nomic, 321, 331–32; frustration-aggression theory of prejudice and, 332–33; Hispanic Americans, *p321,* 321–22, 328–30; integration, **156;** law and, *h381;* legislation and court rulings, 155, 320; movements, 43, 210, 320–21, 326–29; protests, organized, 157, *p158;* as social problem, 319–34; white ethnics, 324, 330–31; women, 322–23, 328–30. *See also* Discrimination; Segregation; specific subjects.
Class structures: American, 127–39; caste system, **123;** differentiation and, 123; esteem, **124;** lower classes, 131; Marxist view of, 127; middle classes, 130–31; open-class system, **123;** prestige, **123, 124;** rigid, 123; role, **123;** role behavior, 124; role conflict, 123–24; social mobility, **134**–39; status, 123; upper classes, 129–30; "Yankee City" study, 127–31, *c128. See also* Classes; Stratification; specific classes.
Classes: attitudes and behavior, *p132,* 132–33, *p133;* class consciousness, 127, 172; criminal justice system, attitudes toward, 373–74; cultural specialties, 33; distribution, 127, *c128;* endogamy, **237;** fertility differential, 170; institutionalized inequality, **386**–87; labeling likelihood and, 76; life chances, **131**–32; placement criteria, 127–31; as reference groups, **93;** resistance to change, 46; status and, 121–22, 127–33; structures (*see also* Class structures), 123–26; as subcultures, 133; urban areas, 173–74. *See also* Stratification; specific classes.

Clubs: as formal groups, 104; socialization and, 92, 93

Coercion, 113–14

Collective behavior, 183; communication and, 201. *See also* Structured behavior; Unstructured behavior.

Colleges, *c255;* accreditation, 424; deciding to go to, 418, 419; desegregation, 320; financing, 260, 261; marriage market, 259; number and enrollment, 259, 260; private, 262; selecting, 419–22, *p420;* student riots, *371;* types of, 254

Colonialism, minorities and, 152–53

Commoner, Barry, 340

Comfort, value stress on, 55

Communes, *p72, 237*

Communication, 201; group, 109; in love relationship, 440–41; in male-female relationships, 443; mass (*see also* Mass communications), 201; opinion leaders, 207

Communion, 440–41

Communism, *p295, 295–96*

Communities, 171; retirement, 409; rural, **171–72,** *p172;* school control, 262; suburban, **175,** *p175;* urban, **171,** *p173. See also* Rural communities; Urban communities.

Competition, *p112, 112;* conflict compared to, 112–13; cooperation and, 113

Compromise, 114, *p114;* arbitration, **114;** mediation, **114**

Conflict, 111; accommodation, **113–15;** arbitration, **114;** coercion, **113–14;** competition and, **112–13;** compromise, **114,** *p114;* corporate, 111–12; culture, and criminal behavior, 369–70; culture, and poverty, 390–91; in male-female relationship, 444;

mediation, **114;** occupational labeling and, 405; personal, 111, 112; role, 123–24; in socialization, 93; tolerance, **114–15;** truce, **114**

Conformity, 71, *c71;* labeling effect on, 76; sanctions and, 58–62

Congeniality groups, 104, *c106*

Congress of Racial Equality (CORE), 157

Consensus, 109, 112

Consultants, sociologists as, 18

Consumers, ecological, 340, *c341;* economic, 288; socialization and, 255

Content analysis, 11

Contract law, *h381*

Cooley, Charles Horton, 88, *p89*

Cooperation, 113; accommodation, **113–15;** and competition, 113

Courts, 372–74. *See also* Criminal justice system.

Crazes, 192–94, *p193*

Crime, 360; arrests, 367, *p367, c368;* causes of, 369–71; classification, 360–62, *p361;* corporate, 363; criminal justice system and, 371–75; deviance and, 73; felonies, **362;** governmental or political, *363;* juvenile delinquency, 168, *p364,* 364–65; misdemeanors, **362;** organized, 362; patterns in U.S., 366–69, *c368;* population density and, 168; property recovery, 369; rate, **367,** 369, 374; rural, 366, 369; sociologial view of, 359–60; statistics, limitations of, 365–66; unreported, 365; urban, 168, 366, 369. *See also* Criminals.

Criminal justice system, 371; civil rights and, 374; class, and attitudes toward, 373–74; court system, 372–73; indictment, **372;** laws and (*see*

also Laws), *h380–81;* philosophies, *p373, 374;* plaintiff, **372;** plea bargaining, **373;** police, 371–72, *p372;* prisons, *p370,* 374–75, *p375*

Criminals: age, and arrest rate, 369; anomie theory of behavior, 370; civil rights, 374; classification of, 362–65; culture conflict theory of behavior, 369–70; differential association theory of behavior, 369, *p370;* habitual or situational, 364; imprisonment, *p370,* 374–75, *p375;* labeling and, 73, 74–76, *p75;* professional, 364; rehabilitation, 375, *p375;* sex, and arrests, 369; "white-collar," 363. *See also* Crime.

Crowds, 183, 185–88, **189;** audience, 189–90; casual, 189; mobs, **190;** orgy, **190–91;** panic, 183, 186–88, **191;** riot, **190**

Cults, 272. *See also* Religion.

Cultural alternatives, 33

Cultural base, 41

Cultural change, 40–41; cultural base, **41;** cultural lag, **46;** diffusion of cultural traits, **42;** discovery and invention and, 41–42; ethnocentrism opposed to, 46, *p47;* fear of new or unknown and, 45–46; habit opposed to, 45; interests and, *p45,* 46; laws and, 43; mass media and, 203; natural disasters and, 43–44; problems created by, 46–47; religion and, 46, 277–79; resistance to, 44–47, 277–79; social change and, 41; social movements, **42–43,** *p43,* 194; wars and, 44

Cultural environment, 339–40

Cultural lag, 46

Cultural relativity, 308

Cultural specialties, 33

Cultural universals, 32–33

226; service systems, 286–87; as social institution, 222, 223, *c223*; socialist, 296; socialization and, 255; structures, formal, 285–88

Ecosystem, 339; air pollution, 343–44, *p344*; balancing, 340; consumers, 340, *c341*; crisis, ecological, 343–54; decomposers, 340, *c341*; economy and, 352–54; energy flow, 340, *c341*; interdependence, 340–42; international relations and trade, 353–54; land use, 351–52, *p352*; "laws" of ecology, 340–43; natural resources, 346–48, *p348*; noise pollution, 346; personal freedom and, 351; pollution, 194, **340,** 342–46; population growth and, 348–51; producers, 340, *c341*; reservoirs, *c341*; solid wastes and, *p342,* 345–46; values and, 340; water pollution, 345, *p345, p347*

Education: ages, 254, *c255*; control, 262; cultural alternatives, 33; culture conflict, 390; degrees, academic, 254, *c255*; in early societies, 253–54; elementary, 254, *c255,* 255–56, *p256,* 259–60, *c261*; expenditure per pupil, 261; fertility differential and, 170; financing, 260–62, *c261*; formal structures, 253–54; functions, 255–59; growth, 259–60; higher, 254, *c255*; income and, *c257*; informal structures, 253; and labor market, 257; mass media, 203; in Middle Ages, 254; patterns and processes, in U.S., 259–63; police, 371–72, *p372*; of poor, 385, 389, 390; private schools, 262, *p263*; professional schools, 254, *c255*; protected by society, 227–28; public, 254; by residence, *c176*; roles in, 225, 226; rural, 259; segregation/desegregation, 155, 262, 320; sex discrimination, 254; social activities and, 258; social change, 258; social contacts and, *p258,* 259; as social institution, 220, 221, 223, *c223,* 225; social institutions, other, affected by, *h267*; social mobility and, 137, 257; socialization, 92, 253–56, *p256*; special 262–63; status and, 131; technical schools, 254, *c255*; U.S. structure, 254, *c255*; value stress on, 54; vocational schools, 254, *c255. See also* Colleges; Educational planning; Schools; Secondary schools.

Educational planning: aptitudes and abilities and, 415–16, *p416*; high school experiences and, 418; interests and, 418, *p418*; personal goals and, 418–19; physical characteristics and, 416–17; program selection, 419–22; school selection, 419–22; self-analysis and, 415–19; social abilities and, 417–18; temperament and, 417

Efficiency, value stress on, *p54*

Egotistic suicide, *h26*

Emigration, 166

Emotions: appeal to, 16, *p17,* 208; communication, **201;** communion, **440**–41; contagion, emotional, **187**–89, *p188*; family and, *p90,* 240; psychological sanctions, 60, *c60*; socialization and, *p90,* 90–91; temperament, **85**–86. *See also* Love.

Employment: Affirmative Action and, *p329,* 329–30; career mobility, **134,** *p135,* 135–38, *p138*; categories of, by sex, and social mobility, *h145*; competition, and prejudice, 331; discrimination, 150, 320, 322, 331; ecological crisis and, 352–53; in recession, 387; secondary group relationship, 105, *c106*; socialization and, 92; unemployment, 385, *c388*; welfare programs and, 392–93; women, 247, *p247*; youth, urban minority, as social problems, *h316. See also* Labor; Occupational analysis in vocational planning; Occupations; Vocational planning.

Encyclopedia of Careers and Vocational Guidance, 424

Endogamy, 237

Environment, 85, 339; biological, 339; cultural, 339–40; and cultural variation, 36–37; home, 390; human ecology and, 339–40; personality and, 85; physical, 339; and social problems, 309. *See also* Ecosystems.

Environmental Protection Agency, 344

Equal Rights Amendment, 328

Equalitarian family, 239

Escobedo v. Illinois, 374

Esteem, 124

Ethnic minorities, 148–49, *c150. See also* Minorities; names.

Ethnocentrism, 32; and cultural change, 46, *p47*; ingroup, 106, in religion, 276

Evaluation: of data, 13; of statements, 13–16

Exchange systems, 288, *p289*

Exogamy, 237

Explorer Program, of Boy Scouts and Girl Scouts, 424–25

Expulsion, as minority policy, **154–55,** 156, *c156,* 157

Extended family, 237, 238

473

Extermination, as minority policy, **154,** 156, *c156*

F

Fads, 183–84, **192,** *p193;* booms, **194;** crazes, **192–94,** *p193;* mass media and, 203

Family: American patterns and processes, 241–47; attitudes and behavior and status, 132; authority, 238–39; broken, *c242,* 243–44, 390; companionship, affection, and intimacy, 240; as economic unit, 241; education as social institution and, *h267;* equalitarian, **239;** extended, **237,** 238; functions, 239–41, *p240;* home environment, 390; income, by residence, 176; intergenerational mobility, **135,** *p135;* kinship, 239; labor, division of, 241; marriage forms (*see also* Marriage), 235–37; matriarchal, **238;** nuclear, **237–** 38; organization, 237–38, *p238;* patriarchal, **238;** primary group relationship, 104–05, *c106;* property transmission function, 241; protected by society, 227; reproduction function, 221, 239; residence, 238; roles, 225, 226, 405; sex norms and, 240; size, 132, 136, *c176,* 246, *p246,* 385; social control, 240–41; social institution, 221, 223, *c223;* social structure, 237–39; as socialization agent, 91, 93, 239, 253, 254; status ascription, 239–40; welfare programs and (*see also* Poverty), *c176,* 393

Family allotment plan, 393

Farmers: census statistics, *c176;* institutionalized in-

equality, 387; pollution problems, 343, 344, 350

Fascism, 296

Fashions, 183–84, **191–92**

Federal Bureau of Investigation, 360–62, 366

Fertility, 169; differential, 170; rate, by residence, *c176*

Fetishism, 271

Films. *See* Movies.

Folkways, 56, *p57, p61,* 62; laws compared to, 57

Food: prices, *p304, p306;* production, fertilizer and, 349–50, *p350;* sea life, water pollution and, 345; stamp program, *p393;* supply, 349–50

Foreign white stock, 149, *c150.* *See also* Immigrants.

Formal groups, 104

Formal sanctions, 61

4H Clubs, 92

Freedom, personal, and ecological crisis, 351

Frustration-aggression theory of prejudice, 332–33

Function, 6

Furman v. Georgia, 374

G

Gang, 187

General Aptitude Test Battery, 416

Generalities, evaluating, 13–14

Generalization, 5, *h24;* in Durkheim's study of suicide, *h26;* evaluation guideline, 14–15; hypothesis and, 4–5

"Generalized others," 88–89

Generation gap, 404. *See also* Age.

Genetic characteristics, 84, *p84*

Geography, cultural variation and, 36

Ghettos, 155

Girl Scouts, 424–25

Goals, individual: educational (*see also* Educational planning, individual), 415–19; self-analysis, and, 415–19; vocational (*see also* Vocational planning), 415–19

Government: agent of society, 291; capitalism, 294–96; characteristics, 291–92; communism, *p295,* 295–96; conflict settlement, 293; crimes, 363; culture conflict, poverty and, 390–91; economy relationship, 294–96; education financing, 260–62, *c261;* and education, interdependence of, *h267;* fascism, 296; force monopoly, 291; functions, 292–93; institutionalized inequality and, 387; laws and norms, 292–93; protective function, 293; roles in, 225, 226; sanctions, 292–93, *p293;* services, 293; as social institution, 222, 223, *c223,* 225, *p228,* 228–29; socialism, 296; sovereignty, 292; territorial jurisdiction, 291; universality, 291–92; welfare system, 387, 392–93

Group marriage, 237

Groups, 101; accommodation, **113–15,** *p114;* acculturation, **115;** activities, deviance and, 77; amalgamation, **115;** arbitration, **114;** assimilation, *p115,* **115–16;** associations compared to, 102–03; behavior (*see also* Collective behavior, Structured behavior, Unstructured behavior, subjects; categories compared to), 102; coercion, **113–14;** communication, 109; competition, *p112,* **112–13;** compromise, **114,** *p114;* conflict, **111–12,** 113; congeniality, 104, *c106;* consensus, 109, 112; continuum of relationships, 104–06, *c106;* coopera-

rate, **166,** 349; class distribution, 127, *c128;* control, 348, 351; death rate, **166;** density, **167–**68, *p168,* 172, 173, 348; ecosystem and, 346–51; emigration, **166;** explosion, 166, 348; farm, 176, *c176;* fertility differential, 169–70; food supply, 349–50; foreign white stock in U.S., 149, *c150;* human ecology, 170–77; immigrant, *c148,* 149, *c150,* 166; immigration, **166;** increase, **165–**66; invasion, **177;** life expectancy, **166,** 167; minorities, in U.S., *c148,* 149, *c150;* movement, 166, 176–77; natural resources and, 346–48; net immigration, **166;** poor (*see also* Poverty), *c176,* 385; reproduction and replacement, 220–21, *c223;* rural, 171–72, *c174,* 176; school-age, and economy, *h267;* segregation, **177,** *p177;* sex distribution, 166–67; social problems and, 168; suburbanization, **177;** succession, **177;** urban, 171, 173, *c174,* 176–77; urbanization, **176–77**

Positive sanctions, 58–59, *c60*

Postman, Leo, 195

Post-secondary schools: deciding to attend, 418, 419; selecting, 419–22, *p420;* types of, 254

Poverty: categories of poor, *p391,* 391–92; causes, *p386,* culture of, 389–93; culture conflict, 390–91; deprivation, relative, **384,** *p384;* distribution of families, by residence, *c176;* education and, 385, 389, 390; family size, 385; home environment, 390; inflation and, 387; institutionalized inequality, **386–**87; minorities, 385, 389; population, 385; population den-

sity and, 168; recession and, 387; relative concept of, 383–85; structure of, 383–87; trained incapacity, 389–90; unemployment and, 385, *c388;* welfare and assistance programs, 387, 392–93, *p393*

Prejudice, 151; culture factors in, 333–34; discrimination and, 152; economic competition and conflict and, 331–32; frustration-aggression theory, 332–33; personality of prejudiced, 332–33; racism, **333,** *p333;* scapegoating, 332, *p332;* self-fulfilling prophecy and, **333–**34; sexism, **333,** *p333;* stereotyping, **333**

Prestige, 123; esteem compared to, 124

Primary group relationship, 104–05, *c106*

Prisons, *p375;* functions, 374; reform proposals, 374–75

Private property, transmission of, 241

Problem, in research, **24**

Problems, social. *See* Social problems.

Process, 6. *See also* Social processes.

Producers, ecological, 340, *c341*

Professions, *See* Employment; Occupations.

Propaganda, 208; advertising and, 208–10, *p211,* 212–13, *p213;* aims, 209; emotional appeal, 16, 208; evaluation of, 208; mass media and, 208–09; professions, 209; psychological approach, 209–10; public relations, 210–12, *p211;* social control, 208; sociocultural approach, 210

Protest, organized, 157, *p158*

Protestant Ethic and the Spirit of Capitalism (Weber), 277–78

Psychological sanction, 60, *c60*

Psychology, 3–4

Public opinion, 206; mass media and, *p206,* 206–08, *p207*

Public relations, 210–12, *p211*

Puerto Ricans, 322, 328, 331–32

Punishment, 59–61, *c60*

Purpose, sense of, society and, 221–22, *c223*

Q

Questionnaire, 9

R

Races: acculturation, 116; characteristics, 148; classification, 148; corporate conflict, 111; endogamy, **237;** ethnocentrism, **32;** fertility differential, 170; intermarriage, 116; labeling likelihood and, 76; riots, 190, 327; social concept, 148; subcultures, 34

Racism, 326, 327, **333,** *p333. See also* Blacks; Civil rights and liberties; Prejudice.

Radio, 93, 202, 255

Rationalization complex of minorities, 157

Rebellion, deviance and, *c71,* 72, 73

Recession, 387

Recurrent groups, 104, *p108;* communication, 109; conflict, 111, 112; consensus, 109, 112; formal, **104;** function, 109; goals, formal and informal, 107; informal, **104;** norms, 109; patterns of behavior, 109; processes, 109; role behavior, 108–09; roles, 107–08; sanctions, 109; structure, 109

Recycling of wastes, 345–46

Reference groups, 93

Relationships: cultural, and

meaning, *h97–98;* in-group, **106,** 112; interaction in (*see also* Interaction), *h449–51;* love, 437–42; male-female, 442–45; nomadism, **435;** out-group, **106;** personality and, 435–36; primary group, **104–05,** *c106;* secondary group, **105–06,** *c106;* self-inventory, 437; social, and meaning, *h97–98;* successful, 436–37

Relative deprivation, *p384,* **384–85**

Religion, 269; churches, **271–**72; clergy, 272; conflicts, 274; cults, **272;** and cultural change, 46, 277–79; cultural specialties, 33; culture and, 29, 275–79; denominations, **272;** diversity, 275–76; education as social institution and, *h267;* endogamy, **237;** ethnocentrism, 276; evangelist, 273, *p273;* fertility differential and, 170; fetishism, **271;** formal structures, **271–**72; functions, 273–74; informal structures, 271, *p271;* laity, 272; magic and, *p276,* 277; meaning of, 276; minister, 272; minorities, 149, *c150;* missionary, 273; mystic, 273; norms and, 274; organization, 270–71; priest, 272; protected by society, 228; Protestant Ethic and capitalism, 277–78; rabbi, 272; reliance on, 276; religious leader, 273; roles, 225, 226, 272–73, *p273;* sacredness concept, 277; sects, **272;** secularization, 277; social control, 274; as social institution, 222, 223, *c223;* and socialization, 92; sociological approach, 269–70, *p270;* suicide rate and, *h25, h26;* values and, 274, 275

Reputational approach to stratification study, 126

Research: design, **25;** design in Durkheim's study of suicide, *h25;* Durkheim's study of suicide as example of, *h24–26;* and graduate study, 254; methodology and techniques, 4–5, 8–12, *h24–26;* of unstructured behavior, *h198–99. See also* Science; Sociology.

Researchers, sociologists as, 18

Residence: matrilocal, **238;** neolocal, **238;** patrilocal, **238;** population statistics by, *c176;* as status characteristic, 127, 129–31. *See also* Neighborhood; Rural communities and areas; Urban communities and areas.

Retirement communities, 408–09

Retreatism, deviance and, *c71,* 71–73, *p72*

Rights, and roles, 108

Riots, 183, **190;** police and, 371; race, 190, 327

Ritualism, deviance and, 71, *c71,* 72

Ritualization and social institutions, *h232–33*

Roles, 55–56, **126;** allocation, in groups, 107; behavior, 108–09, 124; behavior, structured and unstructured, and, 184, *p184,* 185, *p185,* 186, *c187,* 189; conflicts, 123–24, 226; deviance and, 75–76, 77; duties of, 108; esteem, **124;** labeling effect on, 75–76; in male-female relationships, 443; of married women, 246–47, *p247;* reciprocal, 108; religious, 225, 226, 272–73, *p273;* rights of, 108; social institutions and, 225–26; status and, 126

Rossi, Peter, *h145n.*

Rumors, 184, **194–95**

Rural communities and areas, 171–72, *p172;* characteristics,

172–73; crime, 366, 369; ecological crisis and, 343, 344, 351–52; education, 259; family, economic function of (*see also* Family), 241; farm population (*see also* Farmers; Labor, farm), 176, *c176;* fertility differential, 170; rural-urban continuum, *c174;* suburbs compared to, 175, *c176;* suicide rate, *h26;* urbanization and, 176

S

Salk, Jonas, *p124*

Samples, 9; generalization from inadequate, 15–16; selection, 9, *h24*

Sanctions, 58, 61–62; formal, **61;** government, 292–93, *p293;* group, 109; informal, **61;** negative, **59,** 60; physical, **60;** positive, **58–59,** 60; psychological, **60;** rural communities, 173, *c174;* urban communities, *c174,* 175; value and norm interrelationships with, 62

Scapegoating, 332, *p332*

Schedule, of questions, **9**

Schools: aptitude tests, 416; as associations, 220; attendance laws, 254, 257; decentralization (community control), 262; deviance effects, 76, 78; financing, 260–62, *c261;* intelligence tests, 416; interdependence with social institutions, *h267;* labeling of students, 404; labor market and, 257; number and enrollment, 259–60; occupation of children and youth, 256; private, 262, *p263;* public, early, 254; segregation/desegregation, 155, 262, 320; socialization agents, 92, 254, 255–56, *p256;* specialized,

sex differences, 322–23; social institutions and, 221, c223, 255; Transactional Analysis (TA) of, 89–91, p90; transactions, 89; unconscious or unintended, 91, 92

Social mobility, 134; birth rate differential, 136; career, **134;** downward, 134, 136–37; education and, 136, 257; ethic, **135–36;** group, **135;** horizontal, **134;** immigration and, 136, p137; intergenerational, **135,** p135; marriage and, 137–38; measurement of, h143–45; mobility, spatial, 134; occupational status and, h143–45; open-class systems, 123; sex, occupational status and, h145; status insecurity and upward mobility, 138–39; technological innovation and, 136; upward, 134–39, p137, p138, h143–45; in U.S., 135–39, p137, p138; vertical, **134**

Social movements, 42–43, p43, **194;** charismatic leaders, 43; unstructured behavior, 183, 194

Social norms, 55–57. *See also* Norms.

Social organization, deviance effects, 76–78, p77

Social problems, 303; agreement lack on what are problems, 305–06; attitudes toward, 306; "bad" people as cause of, 307; biological factors, 309; crime, 359–75; criteria of, 303–05, p304; cultural relativity concept, 308; environment, physical and cultural and, 309; fallacies, 305–07; mass media and, 205–06; multiple causation concept, 309–10, p310; normality of, 307; poverty, 383–93; psychological factors,

309–10; and social change, 308; social factors and, 310; and social institutions, 308; sociologists' perspective, 308–10, h316–17; sociologist's role in solving, 310–11; solvability, 306, p306; study, p310, 311–12; time as solution to, 310; urban, 168, violence, p309

Social processes, 109; accommodation, **113–16;** competition, p112, **112–13;** conflict, **111**–13; cooperation, **113;** differentiation, **122;** socialization, 88; stratification, **121;** universal, 111–16. *See also* specific processes.

Social relationships. *See* Relationships.

Social sciences, 3–4

Social self, 88; "generalized others," 88–89; "looking-glass self," 88; "significant others," 88; Transactional Analysis (TA) theory, 89–91, p90. *See also* Self.

Social stratification. *See* Stratification.

Social structure: American, 127–33; family, 235–39; group, 109. *See also* Classes; Class structures; Social institutions.

Social values. *See* Values.

Social work, sociology compared to, 18–19

Society, 30; age categories and, 399–403; culture and (*see also* "Cultural," Culture), 30, h97–98; deviance effects, 76–78, p77; fundamental needs of, 220–24, c223; government as agent of whole, 291; meaning and, h97–98; order and security and, 222, c223; political institution of, **290–93;** population replacement and, 220–21, c223; production and distribution of

goods and services, 222, c223; protection of social institutions, 227–29, p228; sense of purpose and, 221–22, c223; socialization, 221, 223, c223

Sociogram, 110, c110

Sociologists, 3; actuarians, 18; administrators, 18; consultants, 18; objectivity of, h316–17; researchers, 18; and social problem solving, 310–11, h316–17; social workers, 18–19; teachers, 17–18; writers and editors, 18

Sociology, 3; evaluation of data, guidelines for, 13–16; human relationships study, **7–8;** investigation and analysis, **5–7;** life goals and, 415; methodology and techniques (*see also* Scientific method), 4–5, 8–12, h24–26; prediction from data, 4, 6; as science, 3–5; social work compared to, 18–19; tool, 8–**9**

Sociometry, 109–10

Southern Christian Leadership Conference (SCLC), 157, 326

Sovereignty, 292

Spanish-speaking, *See* Hispanic Americans; specific groups

Spatial mobility (movement). *See* Mobility, spatial (physical).

Statements, evaluation guidelines for, 13–16

Statistical analysis, 12

Statistical categories, 102

Status, 121, 123; achieved, **122;** ascribed, **121**–22, 239–40; and attitudes and behavior, p132, 132–33, p133; cultural specialties, 33; dwelling area (neighborhood), 127, 129–31; and education, 131;

family ascribed, 239–40; and family characteristics, 132; and group membership and activities, 131; housing, 127, 129–31, *p130;* income source, 127, 129–31; "Index of Status Characteristics," 127–31; insecurity and upward mobility, 138–39; and kinship relationships, 132; and life chances, **131**–32; and life expectancy, 131; and life style, *p132,* 133, *p133;* marital, and suicide rate, *h25, h26;* mass media and, 205; and mental health, 131; minority acceptance of, 157; and mobility, spatial, 131; occupational, and social mobility, *h143–45;* occupations and, 127–37; and politics, 132–33; prestige and, **123,** 124; role, **123;** and values and norms, 133; women, *h145,* 240

Stereotyping, 151–52, **333;** self-fulfilling prophecy, 152, **333**–34

Stratification, 121; differentiation, *p172,* **122**–23; economy and, 289; esteem, **124;** institutionalized inequality, **386**–87; objective approach, 125; prestige, **123,** 124; reputational approach, 126; role, **123;** role behavior, 124; role conflict, 123–24; status, 121–22, 123; study approaches, *p125,* 125–26; subjective approach, *p125,* 125–26. *See also* Classes; Class structure; specific classes.

Strong Vocational Interest Blank, 418

Structure, 5–6. *See also* Class structure; Social Structure.

Structured behavior, 184, *p184;* characteristics, 184–85; emotional contagion, 187; unstructured-structured continuum, 184–87, *c187*

Student Non-Violent Coordinating Committee, 157

Students for a Democratic Society (SDS), 72

Study of Man, The (Linton), *h67n.*

Subcultures, 33–34; fashion and, 191; social class as, 133; youth, 34, 401

Subjective approach to stratification study, *p125,* 125–26

Suburbanization, 177

Suburbs, 175, *p175;* characteristics, 175, *c176;* noise pollution, 346; rural communities and areas compared to, 175, *c176*

Succession, 177

Suicide: altruistic, *h26;* anomic, *h26;* and deviance, *p74;* egotistic, *h26;* study of by Durkheim, *h24–26*

Superstition, *p276, 277*

Survey method, 9

Sutherland, Edwin, 369

Symbolic interaction, 101

T

Taboo, incest, 237

Tastes, status and, 133

Taxes: institutionalized inequality and, 387; school financing, 260–61

Teacher Corps, 261

Technique, research, **9**

Technology: cultural change and, 41–42; cultural variation and, 37–39; *p38;* ecological crisis and, 343–48; politico-economic relationships and, 294; social mobility and, 136; value stress on, 55

Teen-agers. *See* Youth.

Television: advertising, 209–10, 212; as mass media, 202–08, *p207;* socialization, 93, 255

Temperament, 85–86; individual goals and, 417

Theory, scientific, **5**

Time: use of, 390, *p390;* value stress on, 55

Toleration, 114–15

Tool, sociological, 8–9

Trade, natural resources and, *p353,* 353–54

Trained incapacity, 389–90

Transaction, 89

Transactional Analysis (TA), 89–91, *p90*

Transitory groups, *p103,* 103–04; conflict, 111–12

Transportation: ecological crisis and, 343–44; institutionalized inequality, and, 387

Triads, 104, *p105*

Truce, 114

Trust: deviance and, 77; in male-female relationships, 443–44

U

Unemployment, 385, *c388;* of youth, urban minority, as social problem, *h316. See also* Employment.

Universities, *c255. See also* Colleges.

Unstructured behavior, 183–**84,** *h198–99;* audiences, 189–90; booms, **194;** characteristics, 185–87; crazes, 192–94, *p194;* crowds, 183, 185–88, **189**–91; emotional contagion, 187–89; fads, 183–84, **192**–94, *p194;* fashions, 183–84, **191**–92; mobs, **190;** orgy, **191**–92; panics, 183, 186, 187–88, **191;** religious, 183; research of, *h198–99;* riots, 183, **190;** social change, 183; social movement, 183, **194;** structured - unstructured continuum, 184–87, *c187*

Upper classes: attitudes and behavior, 132–33, *p133*; institutionalized inequality, 387; life chances, **131–32**; population distribution, *c128*; status characteristics, 129–30, *p130*; status insecurity, 138–89

Urban communities and areas, **171**, *p173*; air pollution, 343–45; characteristics, 173–75, *c176*; crime, 168, 366, 369; family, economic function of (*see also* Family), 241; fertility differential, 170; ghettos, 155; groups in, *c174*, 174–75; housing, 174, *c174*; immigrants, 177; invasion, **177**; land use, ecological crisis and, 351–52; neighborhoods, 177, *p177*; police, 371–72; pollution and, 343–46; population, 171, 173, *c174*, 176–77; rural-urban continuum, *c174*; segregation, **177**, *c177*; size, 173, *c174*; social problems, 168; suburbanization and, **177**; suburbs compared to, 175, *c176*; succession, **177**; suicide rate, *h26*; transportation, 387; unemployment of minority youth, as social problem, *h316*; waste disposal, 345–46; water supply, pollution and, 345; welfare programs, 392

Urbanization, 176–77

V

Values: basic, **39**; behavior, structured - unstructured, and, 184, *p184*, 185, *p185*, *c187*, 189; cultural, **53–54**; ecosystem and, 340; freedom from, and social problem solving, *h316–17*; norm and

sanction interrelationship with, 62; religion and, 274, 275, 277–79; responses to, 70–73, *c71*; schools and, 92; social institutions and, 224; social problems and, 303–04; socialization and, **88–93**; status and, 133

Variables, **10**; dependent, **10**; independent, **10**

Vested interest, and social change, *p45*, 46

Vietnamese, *p115, p149*

Violence, as social problem, *p309*

Vocational planning: analysis of occupations, 425–29; apprenticeships, 254; aptitudes and abilities and, 415–16, *p416*; educational program, 254, 419–22; information sources, *p424*, 424–25; interests and, 418, *p418*; personal goals and, 418–19; physical characteristics and, 416–17; selecting a vocation, 422–29; self-analysis, 415–19; social abilities and, *p417*, 417–18; temperament and, 417. *See also* Occupations.

W

Warner, W. Loyd, 127–31

Wars: and cultural change, 44; cultural variation, 34–35; minorities and, 153; rumors in, 195

WASP's, 323–24, 330

Wastes, pollution and, *p342*, 345–46

Water pollution, 345, *p345*, *p347*. *See also* Ecosystem.

Way of life: *See* Life style.

Weasel words, 13

Weatherman faction of Students for a Democratic Society (SDS), 72

Weber, Max, 277–78, *h316*, *h317*

Welfare, and religious organizations, 274

Welfare system, 392; dependency and, 392; families receiving public assistance, by residence, *c176*; family allotment plans, 393; foodstamp program, *p393*; guaranteed income proposals, 392–93; institutionalized inequality, 387; recipients, 392

Wesley, John and Charles, 183

White ethnics, 323–24, *p330*, 330–31

Women: Affirmative Action and, 329–30; civil rights, 322–23, 328–30; discrimination, 150, 322; in labor force, *h145*, 246, *p247*; liberation movement, 42, *p43*, 194, 247, 322, 328–29; marriage and social mobility, 137–38; married, role of, 246–47, *p247*; occupational categories, changes in, *h145*; socialization, and behavior, differences, 322–23; status, 240

Wonder, Stevie, *p138*

Y

"Yankee City" study, 127–31, *c128*

Youth: adolescence, 399–401; alcohol consumption, 408; drug use, 407–08; hippies, 72, *p151*, 206, 237; labeling and, 404–05; police and, 371; population and economy, 169, *p169*; problems of, 404–05; rebellion, 72; subcultures, 34, 401; unemployment of urban minority, as social problem, *h316*; voting, *p405*; young adulthood, 401

PICTURE CREDITS

Key: (*t*) top; (*b*) bottom; (*l*) left; (*r*) right.

Cover: Harbrace
Unit Openers: John Caldwell
Charts: Graphic Presentation Services

Pages ii, (*l*) Al Kaplan—DPI; (*r*) De Wys; iii, (*l*) De Wys, (*r*) Harbrace; 2, Charles Gatewood; 5, Daniel Brody—Stock, Boston; 6, De Wys; 8, Elihu Blotnick—BBM Assoc.; 10, Ken Heyman; 11–14, Gordon H. Lord, Bill Rafferty—Monkmeyer; 15, 17, Heinrich Hoffmann from The Lundoff Collection; 28, (*t*) Harbrace, (*bl*) Mimi Forsyth—Monkmeyer, (*br*) Harbrace; 31, (*t*) Peter Dublin—De Wys; (*b*) William Mares—Monkmeyer; 35, (*l*) Jeanne Thwaite—BBM Assoc., (*r*) Dick Smith—Frederic Lewis; 37, George R. Olson; 38, Jacques Jangoux; 40, cartoon by Henry R. Martin, reprinted from *The Saturday Review*, November 1, 1975; 43, Jean-Claude Lejeune—Stock, Boston; 45, Leonard Lee Rue III—Monkmeyer; 47, Clinton S. Bond—BBM Assoc.; 52, Bob Fitch—Black Star; 54, Sven Simon—Katherine Young; 57, Peter Mackay—Monkmeyer; 59, Vivienne—DPI; 61, Bruce Anspack—EPA; 68, Arthur Tress; 72, Orville Schell—Jeroboam, Inc.; 74, UPI; 75, Cary Wolinsky—Stock, Boston; 77, Clinton S. Bond—BBM Assoc.; 82, Karen Collidge; 84, T. T. Puck; 86, Frank Siteman—Stock, Boston; 89, Marion Faller—Monkmeyer; 90, (*l*) Chester Higgins—Rapho/Photo Researchers, (*r*) Freda Leinwand—Monkmeyer; 92, Phiz Mezey—DPI; 100, John Lennard; 103, Grete Mannheim—DPI; 105, Harbrace; 108, Marbeth—Photo Trends; 112, Cary Herz—Nancy Palmer; 114–15, UPI; 120, Harbrace; 122, Bill Anderson—Monkmeyer; 124, The National Foundation; 125, United Nations; 130, Hank Stebbins; 132, Libby Silverstein; 133, Horst Schaffer—Photo Trends; 135, Grant Heilman; 137, Culver; 138, NEWSWEEK—Lester Sloan; 146, Tim Carlson—Stock, Boston; 149, (*l*) UPI, (*r*) Michael Gamer—Photo Researchers; 153, Michal Heron—Woodfin Camp Assoc.; 155, UPI, 158, (*t*) John Gray—Nancy Palmer; (*b*) Daniel S. Brody—Stock, Boston; 164, Richard L. Stack—Black Star; 167–68, Elizabeth

Crews, David Glaubinger—Jeroboam; 169, Harbrace; 171, (*1*) Jeffrey Blankfort—BBM Assoc., (*r*) Everett Johnson—De Wys; 172, Donald Dietz—Stock, Boston; 173, Henry Monroe—DPI; 175, Mimi Forsyth—Monkmeyer; 177, De Wys; 182, Helmut Gritscher—DPI; 184, Herbert—Frederic Lewis; 185, Ken Heyman; 188, Toby Massey—Photo Trends; 190, Fred Mayer—Woodfin Camp Assoc.; 192, EPA; 193, (*tl*) UPI, (*tr*) Culver, (*br*) UPI; 200, Charles Gatewood; 202, Harbrace; 205, Andrew Sacks—EPA; 206, Steve Rose—Nancy Palmer; 207, Harbrace; 209, (*t*) Henry Monroe—DPI, (*b*) Syd Greenberg—DPI; 211, Aluminum Company of America; 213, Courtesy, American Tourister, Inc.; 218, UPI; 220, Harbrace; 221, Ken Heyman; 225, (*l*) Harbrace Archives, (*r*) General Electric Co.; 227–28; Rhoda Galyn, Michelle Vignes—Photo Researchers; 234, Edward Howard, Jr.—EPA; 236, Courtesy, Union Pacific Railroad; 238, George Gardner; 239, Rothco; 240, Fujihira—Monkmeyer; 245, (*tl*) Mimi Forsyth—Monkmeyer, (*tr*) Peter Dublin—De Wys, (*bl*) Mimi Forsyth—Monkmeyer, (*br*) David Fiedler—Photo Trends; 246, Harbrace; 247, Jim Cartier—Photo Researchers; 252, Paolo Koch—Rapho/Photo Researchers; 256, Russell Abraham—Jeroboam, Inc.; 258, Hugh Rogers—Monkmeyer; 260, Marion Bernstein—EPA; 263, Marion Faller—Monkmeyer; 268, New York Times—Tyrone Dukes; 270, De Wys; 271, The Bettmann Archive; 273, Bruce Roberts—Rapho/Photo Researchers; 275, Michael Abramson—Black Star; 276, (*l*) K. R. Greene—Photo Researchers, (*r*) Harbrace; 278, Culver; 279, Ron Engh—Photo Researchers; 284, PROPIX—Monkmeyer; 286–87, Eastern Photo, Alon Reininger—De Wys; 289, Harbrace; 290, Richard L. Stack—Black Star; 293, Charles Gatewood; 295, Martine Franck—Woodfin Camp Assoc.; 302, Charles Gatewood; 304, Harry Wilks—Stock, Boston; 306, Dieter Grabitzky—Monkmeyer; 309, Wide World; 310, J. Berndt—Stock, Boston; 312, David Strickler—Monkmeyer; 318, Marion Bernstein; 320, Owen Franken—Stock, Boston; 321, Sybil Shelton—Monkmeyer; 322, (*l*) De Wys, (*r*) Erika

Stone—Peter Arnold; 323–25, Paul Conklin, Michal Heron—Monkmeyer; 327, Marion Bernstein; 328, Michal Heron—Monkmeyer; 329, Michael Hayman—Photo Researchers; 330, Michael Abramson—Photo Trends; 332, Culver; 333–38, Charles Gatewood; 341, Howard S. Friedman; 342, Andrew Sacks—EPA; 344, (*l*) Lizabeth Corlett—DPI, (*r*) Arthur Tress—Woodfin Camp Assoc.; 345, Daniel S. Brody—EPA; 347, Dave Repp—National Audubon/Photo Researchers; 348, Ellis Herwig—Stock, Boston; 349, Der Stern—Black Star; 350–52, Michel Renaudeau, Svat Macha—De Wys; 353, Leslie Salt Co.; 358, Charles Gatewood; 361–64, Mimi Forsyth, Michal Heron—Monkmeyer; 367, Ken Heyman; 370, Danny Lyon—Magnum; 372, De Wys; 373, Ellis Herwig—Stock, Boston; 375, David Strickler—Monkmeyer; 382, Charles Harbutt—Magnum; 384, Paul Conklin—Monkmeyer; 386, Michael Abramson—Black Star; 390, Harbrace; 391, Charles Harbutt—Magnum; 393, Doug Wilson—Black Star; 398, Les Mahon—Monkmeyer; 400, James Carroll—EPA; 402, Marion Bernstein; 403, David Strickler—Monkmeyer; 405, Owen Franken—Stock, Boston; 406, (*t*) Bruce Roberts—Rapho/Photo Researchers, (*b*) Erika Stone—Peter Arnold; 408, The Advertising Council; 409, David Strickler—Monkmeyer; 414, Harbrace; 416, Andrew Sacks—EPA; 417, Ralph Crane—Black Star; 418–22, Bill Anderson, Hugh Rogers—Monkmeyer; 423–24, Harbrace; 425, Werner Wolf—Black Star; 427, (*tl*) Alva Ramphal—EPA, (*tr*) St. Louis Post/Dispatch—Black Star, (*bl*) Freda Leinwand—Monkmeyer, (*br*) Peter Southwick—Stock, Boston; 434, Guy Gillette—Photo Researchers; 435, Bob Mann—BBM Assoc.; 438, Dan O'Neill—EPA; 439, Feily—Monkmeyer; 441, Harvey Stein; 442, Mini Forsyth—Monkmeyer; 443, Erika Stone—Peter Arnold; 444, De Wys; 445, Marion Bernstein; 449, (*l*) Bullaty Lomeo—Photo Researchers, (*r*) Ginger Chih—Peter Arnold; 450, (*t*) Rocky Weldon—De Wys, (*bl*) Photo Trends, (*br*) Marion Faller—Monkmeyer; 451, (*tl,r*) Hugh Rogers—Monkmeyer, (*b*) Sam Falk—Monkmeyer.